Political Humor in a Changing Media Landscape

D0878658

Lexington Studies in Political Communication

Series Editor: Robert E. Denton, Jr., Virginia Tech University

This series encourages focused work examining the role and function of communication in the realm of politics including campaigns and elections, media, and political institutions.

Recent Titles in This Series

Political Humor in a Changing Media Landscape: A New Generation of Research
Edited by Jody C Baumgartner and Amy B. Becker

The Influence of Polls on Television News Coverage of Presidential Campaigns
By Vincent M. Fitzgerald

Political Conversion: Personal Transformation as Strategic Public Communication
By Don Waisanen

The 2016 American Presidential Campaign and the News: Implications for the American Republic and Democracy
Edited by Jim A. Kuypers

A Rhetoric of Divisive Partisanship: The 2016 American Presidential Campaign Discourse of Bernie Sanders and Donald Trump
By Colleen Elizabeth Kelley

Studies of Communication in the 2016 Presidential Campaign
Edited by Robert E. Denton, Jr.

The Monstrous Discourse in the Donald Trump Campaign: Implications for National Discourse
By Debbie Jay Williams and Kalyn L. Prince

The Political Blame Game in American Democracy
Edited by Larry Powell and Mark Hickson

Political Campaign Communication: Theory, Method, and Practice.
Edited by Robert E. Denton Jr.

Political Humor in a Changing Media Landscape

A New Generation of Research

Edited by
Jody C Baumgartner and Amy B. Becker

LEXINGTON BOOKS
Lanham • Boulder • New York • London

Published by Lexington Books
An imprint of The Rowman & Littlefield Publishing Group, Inc.
4501 Forbes Boulevard, Suite 200, Lanham, Maryland 20706
www.rowman.com

Unit A, Whitacre Mews, 26-34 Stannary Street, London SE11 4AB

Copyright © 2018 The Rowman & Littlefield Publishing Group, Inc.

All rights reserved. No part of this book may be reproduced in any form or by any
electronic or mechanical means, including information storage and retrieval systems,
without written permission from the publisher, except by a reviewer who may quote
passages in a review.

British Library Cataloguing in Publication Information Available

The hardback edition of this book was previously catalogued by the Library of Congress
as follows:

Library of Congress Cataloging-in-Publication Data Is Available

ISBN 978-1-4985-6508-0 (cloth: alk. paper)
ISBN 978-1-4985-6510-3 (pbk : alk. paper)
ISBN 978-1-4985-6509-7 (electronic)

♾™ The paper used in this publication meets the minimum requirements of American
National Standard for Information Sciences—Permanence of Paper for Printed Library
Materials, ANSI/NISO Z39.48-1992.

Printed in the United States of America

Contents

List of Figures

List of Tables

Introduction

Still Good for a Laugh? Political Humor in a Changing Media Landscape

Jody C Baumgartner and Amy B. Becker

In the run-up to the 2016 general election, we both spoke with Voice of America radio about the place of humor in American politics. Interspersed between clips from *The Late Show with Stephen Colbert* and the presidential debates was the somewhat contradictory commentary of this volume's coeditors. While Amy spoke about the potential of political comedy to engage voters and make them feel more efficacious about their own ability to participate in politics, Jody speculated about eroding public trust and the cynicism that can result from prolonged exposure to such critical, satirical content. In many ways, Amy saw the glass as half full, while Jody saw the glass as half empty. Despite our varying viewpoints and perspectives, the interview helped to spark a conversation between the two of us and brought a communication scholar and a political scientist together as colleagues.

A little more than a decade ago Baumgartner and Morris' *Laughing Matters: Humor and American Politics in the Media Age* was published. At the time, political humor on late-night TV was beginning to attract a great deal of attention from political observers. David Letterman was regularly claiming during presidential election campaigns that "the road to the White House ran through" him and Jon Stewart was being celebrated as a twenty-first century Mark Twain. *Laughing Matters* was an attempt to gather the nascent and disparate scholarship focused on this subgenre into one volume. In retrospect we believe it made some minor contribution to the field by formally giving it an identity, so to speak, in addition to providing researchers working in the new field an opportunity to showcase their work.

The conversation led us both to conclude that it was time for a new edition of *Laughing Matters*. Since its publication, numerous journal articles, book chapters, and some books have been published which deal with the subject of

1

political humor. The field has come of age. *Political Humor in a Changing Media Landscape: A New Generation of Research* is, in a very real sense, a sequel to *Laughing Matters*. It is our attempt to summarize the results of the first generation of political humor scholarship and add to it by present-ing lines of research that are both new and emerging. In addition, *Political Humor in a Changing Media Landscape* looks forward to where we believe the field should be going next.

In the book we feature the work of both well-established senior scholars and newer, more junior researchers. Importantly, while the volume certainly focuses heavily on the US media and political environment, we also include a range of international perspectives, bringing in fresh research that focuses on comparative contexts in Europe (e.g., The Netherlands, Italy, the United Kingdom, Austria, and Germany) and the Middle East, or more specifi-cally, Israel. While we believe that *Political Humor in a Changing Media Landscape* represents the latest thinking and work on the impact of political humor, we recognize that the political humor landscape is rapidly changing and that we may find the need for version 3.0 of this volume to emerge in five years' time, rather than let a decade elapse again between volumes.

Ultimately, though, the present volume points to five current trends in political humor research that are important for consideration right now and will also be instrumental in guiding future research efforts. Included are chapters dealing with various aspects of appreciation for political humor, the shifting landscape of late-night political humor as well as more normative examinations of comics as activists or advocates.

THE CHANGING POLITICAL HUMOR LANDSCAPE

In addition to the fact that political humor scholarship has moved the field forward in the past decade, much has changed in the world of politics and political humor. The year 2008, for example, saw the election of the first Afri-can American president. The 2016 presidential election pitted the first major party female presidential candidate against the first reality TV star turned presidential candidate.

The landscape of late-night political comedy has changed as well. The first, and perhaps most obvious change concerns the lineup of late-night hosts and offerings. From the mid-1990s through 2015, late-night talk shows were domi-nated by Jay Leno and David Letterman. While Jon Stewart began his tenure at *Comedy Central* earlier, he truly became part of the late-night conversation sub-sequent to the 2000 election. At 12:35 a.m., Conan O'Brien, Craig Ferguson, and Jimmy Fallon had enjoyed respectable followings for several years. Finally, in 2006, Stephen Colbert added his voice to the chorus of late-night hosts.

By September 2015, the late-night lineup had almost completely changed. At 11:35 p.m., Letterman was replaced by Colbert on CBS, and on NBC, Leno was replaced by Fallon. On ABC, Jimmy Kimmel had moved from midnight to the 11:35 p.m. time slot in 2013. At 12:35 a.m., Ferguson was replaced by James Corden on CBS, while *Saturday Night Live* alum Seth Meyers replaced Fallon on NBC. On Comedy Central, Trevor Noah took over *The Daily Show* from Jon Stewart, while *The Colbert Report* was replaced with *The Nightly Show with Larry Wilmore*. Although Wilmore's show was canceled after twenty months, Comedy Central continued to experiment with late-night political humor programming.

Conan O'Brien, after a brief run with NBC's *Tonight Show*, had been on TBS at 11:00 p.m. since 2010, while *TBS* added *Daily Show* veteran Samantha Bee to their lineup, Wednesdays at 10:30 p.m. with *Full Frontal*. John Oliver, yet another former cast member of *The Daily Show*, joined Bill Maher with a weekly program on cable's HBO. Finally, NBC's *Saturday Night Live* continued to be popular, enjoying a renewed relevance in 2008 with Tina Fey's Sarah Palin impressions and Alec Baldwin's portrayal of Donald Trump in 2016.

In sum, by 2015, there were twelve late-night choices, of which seven aired four or five nights per week. All of these shows aired some amount of political humor.

Another change that has occurred in the late-night television universe is that by 2015, all of the programs had their own YouTube channel, some of which were (are) very highly ranked in terms of subscriptions. Jimmy Fallon's *Tonight Show*, for example, ranks in the top 100 of most subscribed channels on YouTube. Given changes in how people view televised content in the past decade (e.g., the increased use of digital video recorders and the number of people cancelling their cable television subscriptions), this is significant. People can now watch late-night television, without watching late-night television, so to speak. Moreover, when thinking about the reach of these programs and any effects viewing them may have on political knowledge, opinion, or engagement, this YouTube multiplying effect must now be considered. The potential audience of any particular program, or individual clips, is much greater than traditional television ratings data might suggest.[1]

Finally, there has been a fundamental shift in the expectations placed on late-night talk show hosts. Gone are the days when late-night programming was simply comedy and light banter between host and guests. It is increasingly the case that hosts are expected to be politically relevant. Johnny Carson hosted the *Tonight Show* for three decades, and viewers would have been very hard pressed to guess his political views.[2] In this modern era, political views of most late-night talk show hosts are known—and known to be left of center. Moreover, they are expected to approach their shows from a more blatant and obvious political perspective, not unlike political advocacy. Gone, it seems, are the days of simply tuning in to late-night talk shows for simple entertainment.

This then is the foundation for our volume, the place from which we start. The modern political humor environment is characterized by new hosts, new offerings, newer mechanisms for content delivery and a new, more political climate.[3] Scholarship has started to reflect and explore these changes, and our hope with this book is to gather what we know about these changes into one volume.

PLAN OF THE BOOK

The book is divided into five sections, each of which corresponds to what we have identified as important areas of political humor research that are either emerging or ongoing.

Section I, "Comedy, Advocacy, Journalism, or Something Else Entirely? It's Not Just Entertainment Anymore," focuses on the content of political comedy and satire. In chapter 1, "The Rise of Advocacy Satire," Don Waisanen analyzes changes that have occurred in contemporary political humor since Jon Stewart left *The Daily Show*. His central argument is that changes in the political humor landscape can best be described in terms of the "dawn of advocacy satire," where political humor evolved to be a much more biting, pointed, and immediate form of advocacy. In chapter 2, "Journalist or Jokester?," Julia Fox examines the idea that some of the newer late-night television programming like *Last Week Tonight with John Oliver* combines satire with "real" journalistic content to form a potentially new hybrid form of public discourse, satiric journalism. Chapter 3, "Partisan Trends in Late Night Humor," by Robert Lichter and Stephen Farnsworth, uses data from the Center for Media and Public Affairs at George Mason University to show that Republican presidential candidates are joke targets more frequently than their Democratic counterparts.

In Section II, "Impacting Citizenship: The Effects of Exposure to Political Comedy on Democratic Engagement," our attention turns to the various effects humor viewership has on individuals. The section starts with Jody Baumgartner's "The Limits of Attitude Change" (chapter 4), which explores the idea that when humor targets well-known public figures its persuasive power dwindles to insignificance. Chapter 5, "Interviews and Viewing Motivations," by Amy Becker, explores the differential impact of exposure to cable news versus political satire interviews on viewers' reported elaborative processing. The chapter shows that viewers who think they learn from comedy programming and prefer entertaining as opposed to serious news are more likely to engage in elaborative processing given exposure to a political satire rather than a cable news interview. Josh Compton's review essay, "Inoculation against/with Political Humor" (chapter 6), suggests that scholars pay greater attention to what makes attitudes, beliefs, and behaviors more resistant to change, suggesting that inoculation theory provides a fertile theoretical space for just that.

Section III, "Humor Appreciation: Audience Responses to Political Comedy," explores how audiences seem to respond to various types of political humor. In chapter 7, "The Political Ethology of Debate Humor and Audience Laughter," Patrick Stewart and his colleagues examine audience laughter in response to Donald Trump and Hillary Clintons' humor during their general election debates. Their examination formally explores the idea that humor might be used by candidates to connect with their audience. Chapter 8, "The Joke Is On You," breaks with the practice of emphasizing the productive and progressive ways that satire can encourage an active and engaged citizenry. In her contribution, Sophia McClennen examines how satire's out-groups can lash back when they feel like they are the butt of the joke. In chapter 9, "What Is Funny to Whom?," Christiane Grill proposes a theoretical framework for humor appreciation. Results suggest that the well-established disposition theory of humor, information appreciation, and ego as well as issue involvement, significantly predict perceived humor.

In Section IV, "It's Gone Global: International Perspectives on Political Comedy," the book turns its attention to humor and humor research outside of the American context. In chapter 10, "Political Entertainment in Comparative Perspective," Michael Xenos, Patricia Moy, Gianpetro Mazzoleni, and Julian Meuller-Herbst look at the extent to which variations in media systems and political contexts may affect the applicability of the "gateway effect" of political entertainment viewing on political knowledge. Their findings highlight a variety of similarities and differences in the way the gateway effect plays out in different country settings, in which not only the features of political entertainment but also the contexts in which it appears, are subject to systematic variations. Using the Netherlands as a context for inquiry, Mark Boukes explores "The Causes and Consequences of Affinity for Political Humor" in chapter 11. More specifically, the chapter looks at how demographic variables might predict an individual's affinity for political humor, and the impact that affinity for political humor has on the processing and appreciation, as well as the perceived influence of satire. The section concludes with Edo Steinberg's "Freedom of the Press in Israeli and American Satire" (chapter 12), which examines the ways Israeli and American satire address the issue of freedom of the press as a national core value. Steinberg uses content analysis to measure the frequency of the defense of freedom of the press and criticism of the media in Israeli shows, *Eretz Nehederet* and *Gav Ha'Uma* and American shows, *The Late Show with Stephen Colbert, Late Night with Seth Meyers,* and *Saturday Night Live.*

In Section V, "Prospects for a New Generation of Laughter: The Evolution of Political Comedy," we turn our attention to how consumers and politicians have responded to changes in the political humor landscape. In chapter 13, "A New Generation of Satire Consumers?," Stephanie Edgerly examines the prevalence of exposure to news satire across a range of media devices and compared to other forms of news, and the socialization factors that predict news satire use among today's adolescents. Michael Parkin's "The Context for Comedy" (chapter 14) looks at why presidential candidates have flocked to comedy television over the past few decades, arguing that contextual factors like timing, momentum, and legitimacy have made it easier for certain candidates to embrace comedy while making it difficult for others to avoid it. In chapter 15, "The Ides of September," Jonathan Morris provides an in-depth exploration of the shift toward partisan political humor on late-night television and its implications.

The book's concluding chapter, "Looking Ahead to the Future," by Amy Becker and Jody Baumgartner, explores where political humor and political humor research will, and in the case of the latter, should be headed, in the future. The chapter also looks at the experience of teaching about political humor and comedy in the Trump era. In this concluding piece, we also make the case that in an increasingly fragmented media environment, understanding how and why a polarized electorate consumes political humor and the effects it may have on both individuals and society as a whole matters.

NOTES

1. Jody C Baumgartner, "Late Night Talk Moves Online: Political Humor, You-Tube, and the 2016 Presidential Election," in *The Internet and the 2016 Presidential Campaign*, eds. Jody C Baumgartner and Terri Towner (Lanham, MD: Lexington Books, 2017), 245–63; Amy B. Becker, "Live from New York, It's Trump on Twitter! The Effect of Engaging with *Saturday Night Live* on Perceptions of Authenticity and the Saliency of Trait Ratings," *International Journal of Communication* 12 (2018): 1736-1757.

2. S. Robert Lichter, Jody C Baumgartner, and Jonathan S. Morris, *Politics Is a Joke!: How TV Comedians Are Remaking Political Life* (Boulder, CO: Westview Press, 2014).

3. Amy B. Becker and Leticia Bode, "Satire as a Source for Learning? The Differential Impact of News versus Satire Exposure on Net Neutrality Knowledge Gain," *Information, Communication & Society* 21, no. 4 (2018): 612–25.

REFERENCES

Baumgartner, Jody C. "Late Night Talk Moves Online: Political Humor, YouTube, and the 2016 Presidential Election." In *The Internet and the 2016 Presidential Campaign*, edited by Jody C Baumgartner and Terri Towner, 245–63. Lanham, MD: Lexington Books, 2017.

Becker, Amy B. "Live from New York, It's Trump on Twitter! The Effect of Engaging with *Saturday Night Live* on Perceptions of Authenticity and the Saliency of Trait Ratings." *International Journal of Communication* 12 (2018): 1736-1757.

Becker, Amy B., and Leticia Bode. "Satire as a Source for Learning? The Differential Impact of News Versus Satire Exposure on Net Neutrality Knowledge Gain." *Information, Communication & Society* 21, no. 4 (2018): 612–25.

Lichter, S. Robert, Jody C Baumgartner, and Jonathan S. Morris. *Politics Is a Joke!: How TV Comedians Are Remaking Political Life*. Boulder, CO: Westview Press, 2014.

Section I

COMEDY, ADVOCACY, JOURNALISM, OR SOMETHING ELSE ENTIRELY?

It's Not Just Entertainment Anymore

Chapter 1

The Rise of Advocacy Satire

Don J. Waisanen

Several decades ago, if I'd told you that a public figure had bought up to $15 million in medical debt and paid it off for 9,000 people, you'd have guessed that the source of this deed could be traced to a wealthy business-person, a major philanthropist, or some kind of nonprofit or charity dedicated to helping the disadvantaged. The idea that a comedian would have been responsible for this act—as a routine feature of their television programming, no less—would have been difficult to believe. But that's exactly what John Oliver, the cheeky host of HBO's *Last Week Tonight*, did to spotlight how easy it is to start up a debt collection company that targets low-income communities. Oliver's act moved beyond the distanced irony that has constituted much political comedy programming,[1] instead intervening directly into public affairs and "making $15 million the biggest TV show giveaway in history (adding a 'BLEEP you, Oprah!' after beating her TV giveaway record)."[2]

Although he appears to be leading the way in these efforts, Oliver's perfor-mance isn't an isolated incident. In recent years, above and beyond their roles as commentators, political comedians of all kinds have emerged as activists, pushing beyond the boundaries of their television studios and other, typical spheres of influence to engage in the public arena. Given these developments, I argue that a qualitative shift has been occurring in contemporary political humor toward greater uses of "advocacy satire."[3] I define advocacy satire as the use of political humor to take action on behalf of disadvantaged individu-als or groups, lending force to their voices by making a direct intervention into public affairs. At a minimum, advocacy satire can mean using a humor-ous platform to speak on behalf of disadvantaged individuals or groups. Yet what's particularly distinctive about the concept is how comedians are now engaging in actions in the public interest—the kinds of actions that were formerly the exclusive preserve of lobbyists, movement leaders, investigative journalists, and others.

In doing so, comedians have updated satire for the twenty-first century by engaging in a biting and immediate form of advocacy that invites citizens to get more involved in politics. From Jon Oliver's clear uses of long-form investigative journalism wrapped in comedic garb, to Bassem Youssef's *The Daily Show* (*TDS*) imitations that put both his show and his life at risk in Egypt, much current political humor is rising to a level of political advocacy seldom seen in previous years. This chapter will provide some background for the rise of advocacy satire, highlight several factors that have likely contributed to its use, and reflect on the future challenges and opportunities for this form of activism in public affairs.

ADVOCACY SATIRE'S EMERGENCE

The exponential increase in political comedy programming is a relatively recent historical phenomenon, a rise that has been covered by many scholars.[4] Given the number of late-night shows and other platforms for political humor (e.g., online sites such as *Funny or Die*), this trend shows no signs of abating. What's new is the development of action-oriented advocacy within these structures. Working hand in hand with advocacy, "satire" is used deliberately here as the use of humor to target and lambaste the substance of some entity.[5] Overall, I find that four factors have set the stage for the development of advocacy satire in contemporary political humor: (1) new forms of media advocacy, (2) the comic precursors to this type of activism, (3) international political humor shows that have been influenced by the general advance of satire in public affairs, and (4) the neoliberal accelerations that all political comedians now must contend with at a structural level. To understand how advocacy satire has evolved, it's first useful to attend to how advocacy itself has developed in the modern world, especially in its relationship with a changing media environment.

New Media Advocacy

Advocates "adopt a stance, advance a cause, and attempt to produce a result [on] behalf of an interest of a person, group or cause."[6] G. Thomas Goodnight finds that advocacy's historical roots tie back to the classical world, with the relationships between dueling adversaries, pleaders, and judges in a court of law as one example of the form that has carried through to the present.[7] During the enlightenment and modernity, advocacy became much more of a social phenomenon, and in a globalized world, it has become a rapid, complex, hybridized, swirling assemblage of technologies, symbolic forms (i.e., images, texts, etc.), and representations that defy traditional standards of reasoning or logic.[8] As Manuel Castells notes, a shift from media systems structured around one-way broadcast messages to a "global web of horizontal communication networks that include the multimodal exchange of interactive messages from many to many both synchronous and asynchronous" and defined by "mass self-communication"[9] now constitutes the horizon of our media, politics, and public cultures.

The shift from comedian as commentator to comedian as advocate runs parallel to these developments. Late-night shows now get as much traction from having particular segments uploaded to YouTube and shared across collapsing media boundaries as they do via their television broadcasts. Although many political humorists rely on the tried and true convention of performing long-form comedic monologues at the camera in each of their shows, there's been an environmental pressure to get beyond this format and engage in two-way interactions with viewers and diverse publics at a greater level.

Many comedians have subsequently shifted to political humor 2.0, as seen in the calls to action through the "Green Screen Challenge" on *The Colbert Report* (*TCR*) during its tenure on *Comedy Central*.[10] Consistent with expectations for mass self-communication, comedians have become a locus around which people and causes can be centered amid the swirl of information in an attention economy.[11] From this perspective, the move from comedic commentary to actual political advocacy has been forwarded as much by contextual changes as desires to reach more audiences and make a greater impact in public affairs.

Comedians like John Oliver have made advocacy satire a staple feature of their programming, but this blend of comedy and activism didn't emerge in a vacuum. Turning some attention to what came before in the landscape of political comedy programming can also help us understand more about the rise of this kind of rhetoric.

Comic Precursors

Surveying political humor in the last several decades, it's clear that advocacy satire has come about in fits and starts leading to our current moment. Where comedians such as Jon Stewart and Stephen Colbert could previously be counted on to berate the media, government administrations, and more, they only had limited moments of actual public "advocacy" on their shows. For example, Jon Stewart's advocacy on behalf of 9/11 first responders or Stephen Colbert's political intervention of starting a Super PAC to draw attention to campaign finance issues were ultimately fleeting moments given most of their programming. The goal here is less to document everything that's been done along these lines than to highlight some key moments in the emergence of this type of persuasive humor.

Stewart's case is illustrative. The former host of *TDS* reached a moment in his career when an issue of personal and geographical concern became too important not to do something about. Rather than stare at the camera and make jokes about the lack of Congressional action in getting 9/11 first responders funding for the healthcare they needed, Stewart decided to devote an entire show to having a dialogue with a group of four such men about their health problems and the need for policy action. In fact, one of the most noticeable features of this show was the absence of humor and laughing.[12] To meet the political exigency Stewart and his team felt a pull to use their powers for good, becoming public advocates by using *TDS*'s platform to foster change. That the satire and advocacy were separated so starkly on the show, however, shows that the potential relationship between these two realms had not been worked out in practice.

More so, that journalists and others saw the moment as distinctive speaks to how the segment broke from routine. Once the bill had passed in Congress, Bill Carter and Brian Stelter noted how "there have been other instances when an advocate on a television show turned around public policy almost immediately by concerted focus on an issue—but not recently, and in much different circumstances."[13] The bill's passage led public figures such as then New York City Mayor Michael Bloomberg to remark further that, "Success always has a thousand fathers. . . . But Jon [Stewart] shining such a big, bright spotlight on Washington's potentially tragic failure to put aside differences and get this done for America was, without a doubt, one of the biggest factors that led to the final agreement."[14]

Although Stewart had ventured outside the boundaries of his show before—such as during his 2004 appearance on the CNN show *Crossfire*[15]— something new and different was happening within the show's contours. In the former *Crossfire* appearance, Stewart appealed to the need for a general civil discourse in the media. But in the 9/11 responder segment, the advocacy was on behalf of a time-sensitive, specific political issue: the kind that lobbyists undertake to get representatives to take immediate actions on their respective causes.

Stephen Colbert also tested the boundaries of advocacy satire in his previous *Comedy Central* show. Much scholarly work has analyzed how Colbert's formation of a Super PAC taught citizens about campaign finance laws, promoting a counterfactual vision of the ways that these laws could operate in a democratic society.[16] Colbert and Stewart's Washington, DC event, *The Rally to Restore Sanity and/or Fear,* similarly broke beyond the boundaries of both comedians' shows to advocate for reasonability and less political polarization throughout the land.[17]

Yet the emergence of advocacy satire on *TCR* was most epitomized in Colbert's visit to the US Congress to advocate on behalf of migrant farm-workers in 2010. Desiring to help the United Farm Workers (UFW) push "for a bill that would give undocumented farm workers currently in the United States the right to earn legal status," Colbert "told members of a House Judiciary subcommittee that he hoped to bring attention to the workers' hardships," and joked that, "I certainly hope that my star power can bump this hearing all the way up to C-SPAN 1."[18]

Although the visit earned him mixed reactions from Congressional members (Colbert went into Congress in his conservative blowhard character, only dropping the veneer at a few points to make some serious points), he earned much praise from the UFW and supporters for bringing attention to an issue that they had struggled to advance. Writing about Colbert's intervention, Sarah Bishop argues:

> While Colbert may venture into territories where no comic has gone before, his persona is so predictable that even in unfamiliar contexts the audience knows exactly what to expect. Because he offers this assurance in any circumstance, Colbert is able to surpass the typical territorial boundaries of comedy. Colbert has run for President, stuffed his mouth impossibly full of Cheez-Its, created a Super PAC that raises over a million dollars, interrogated world leaders about the validity of war, . . . and none of it appeared to be outside of his purview. He is, in effect, the master of all of these ceremonies, managing to infiltrate each with the kind of good-natured optimism his audience both expects and respects.[19]

In essence, Colbert's interactions with audiences and ability to cross and adapt across boundaries made advocacy satire a natural next step in the evolution of his comedy and programming. When Colbert transitioned from cable to his mainstream late-night show on *CBS*, he largely abandoned the former character that had provided him with an ability to flex easily across a variety of political spaces. This relates to a problem that comedians have faced since ancient times, namely, how to use humor persuasively between the poles of free expression and structural expectation.[20]

As time has gone on, however, and particularly with the advent of the Trump administration, Colbert's *CBS* show has arguably become more political and satirical. As he experiments with the boundaries of what is permissible on the mainstream network, the comedian may perform more advocacy satire in the future. New media advocacy and comic precursors have certainly played a part in the rise of advocacy satire, but a third development also provides insight into how and why this type of activism is being advanced by political humorists.

International Political Humor

There have always been satirical political shows in international contexts—for example, the British television show *Spitting Image*, which used puppets to mock political leaders in the 1980s and 1990s.[21] But the move to advocacy satire appears to be a newer development across the globe. The internet and other spaces with a global reach have made the ability to imitate what's happening in other countries both more accessible and less costly.[22] As the stakes for comedy shows to make actual political interventions have been raised, in international contexts comedians have both recursively mimicked and invented new models for political engagement, normalizing advocacy satire as a technique across borders. Although there are many examples that could be cited in support of this idea, I see two as key in illustrating the emergence of this critical practice.

Probably more than anyone else, former heart surgeon turned political comedian Bassem Youssef crossed the lines between satire and advocacy by starting a political humor show during the Egyptian revolution in 2011. In the midst of life and death circumstances, Bassem was inspired by shows such as *TDS*, but took the format to a new level by putting political humor in the service of changing a decades-long regime. In effect, "from a laundry room in his apartment he started a political satire show that captured the passion of the 2011 uprising and turned him into one of the most influential voices in the Middle East," yet once the new government was in place, the military takeover of President Abdel Fattah Sisi and continual threats to Youssef's life forced the comedian to leave the country.[23]

Youssef's *The Show* went viral on YouTube, becoming the country's most viewed program and reaching about 40 percent of Egyptians, but "in 2013, after mocking Morsi—he made fun of his hat—the comedian was arrested for insulting Islam and the president. He was released, but when Sisi and the army came to power . . . there was even less tolerance for dissident humor."[24] While political jokes have long played a role in overthrowing regimes, gradually chipping away at the façade of societal power structures in an everyday, subversive manner,[25] Youssef's situation and actions stand out as distinctive for how much he was seen as a leader in his efforts. In recent histories, champions for the people have come in the form of figures such as Gandhi, Nelson Mandela, and Martin Luther King, Jr. Among the many other leaders and movements that formed to topple Mubarek's regime, that a comedian was called to speak on behalf of Egypt's citizens is no small thing. Overall, the claim that "comedy is the soft spot of all dictatorships"[26] has taken on greater meaning with such international examples. At the same time, Youssef's show certainly highlights the limits of advocacy satire—despite making a contribution to the politics of the moment, humor ultimately had to retreat in the face of violence.

Where Youseff has been referred to as "Egypt's Jon Stewart," in a different context, "Mexico's Jon Stewart," Chumel Torres, has also forwarded advocacy satire as a legitimate tool for political humorists, especially through the massive following the comedian originally gained on YouTube that attacked "Mexican politicians and pro-government media."[27] Television stations in Mexico are well known for being channels through which the rich and powerful disseminate their messages. So Torres's use of an online platform to bring his pointed satirical show *The Pulse of the Republic* to citizens earned him much credibility among Mexicans.[28] Torres now has his own show on HBO Latino (*Chumel con Chumel Torres*) and has been riding high on the format that his tweets and YouTube videos first begun. Like Youssef, Torres jumped from a completely different career (as a mechanical engineer) into political comedy, given his developing interest and following.

Using a team of comedy writers, researchers, and journalists, Torres's show bears many of the marks of his US predecessors such as Stewart and Oliver. But the comedian also shows more restraint on some issues (e.g., drug cartels) and has exhibited decidedly conservative stances on other issues,[29] which may explain why he's yet to engage in the bolder uses of advocacy satire outside of his show that many other political comedians have demonstrated. Torres has been clear that his comedy programming is framed from an advocacy viewpoint, however:

> If you talk about corruption, we may not say the same name, but we have the same situations and that doesn't change, not only in Latin America, I'm talking globally. And if it matters to you because it affects your children, or your health care system or your education or your retirement, at least you want somebody to say something, even if it's a clown on a television, you want him to say [something], to tell it like it is.[30]

Implicitly, Torres's presence in Mexican and now larger Latin American media has also advocated on behalf of less censorship and expanded media options in the region. He has further contributed to the public discourse on a range of pressing political topics, such as sexual harassment in the workplace.[31]

As these international examples highlight, expectations for advocacy satire as a regular part of political communication hasn't been confined to insular locales, but has been flowing across borders as a legitimate form of marketing social change. As new media have opened opportunities for advocacy with audiences across regions, in particular, comedians have been both building an expectation for this form of activism and, as might be reasonably surmised, increasingly expected to engage in this kind of work to stay relevant in the overall political economy of media.

Neoliberal Accelerations

For the foregoing reasons, and especially since advocacy satire emerged prior to the 2016 US presidential election, we shouldn't see the actions of comedians in the civic realm as an effect of what's happened recently in US politics. Still, the Trump presidency, the rightward turns in many international elections, and developments such as Brexit have likely played a role in accelerating advocacy satire in our contemporary political climate. If anything, at least in the US context, given the break from the normality of political discourse (and that's surely a point that both supporters and detractors of Trump can agree on), the administration has offered more of a foil for political comedy than has been the case for some time.

There's also a larger way of looking at what advocacy satire responds to in this climate of government deregulation, tax breaks, and other forms of corporate appeasement: an accelerating neoliberalism. In the United States, for example, despite the changes from Democrat to Republican regimes and back, a consistent thread for the past several decades has been a move toward increasingly neoliberal policies and practices across society.[32] Neoliberalism is "a philosophy viewing market exchange as a guide for all human action."[33] Neoliberalism hides "the means for redressing inequality and mobilizing diversity by weakening relations among people and devaluing coordinated design," since "public engagement draws on the promise of a public good, which neoliberalism disavows through its strict reliance on a narrow individualism."[34] Although there's much to debate about the term and its nuances, it can still provide an instructive perspective on how Trumpism and its offshoots have generally put neoliberalism on the fast track, subsequently providing humorists with clearer targets and raising the stakes for humor that works on behalf of public rather than private interests.

A CNN report recently urged viewers, for instance, to "Look at an episode of 'The Late Show' or 'Jimmy Kimmel Live' from before the election, and then look at a recent episode. The shows are more pointed now. Some of them could be called 'activist comedy.' At least a couple of the hosts are openly campaigning for Trump's downfall."[35] Ironically, Trump has also legitimized satire as a political weapon by bringing attention to how unfunny he finds Alec Baldwin's impersonation of him on *Saturday Night Live* (*SNL*). In making *SNL* a topic worthy for the president of the United States to talk about on a recurrent basis, Trump has framed political comedy as a central rather than peripheral forum for partisan, activist battles. Who is winning (and how much comedy can win) that battle is yet to be determined, though, as Amy Becker found in an experimental study that "viewing Trump's Twitter response accusing *SNL* of media bias inoculates viewers against Baldwin's anti-Trump satire that is present in the original skit."[36]

At the same time, while advocacy satire can make small but important interventions into public affairs, it can additionally highlight how comedians are trying to find a way to have an impact in their own very neoliberal circumstances. While seldom pointed out, most comedy production is after all connected directly to advertising and corporate revenue streams. Larry Wilmore's post-*TCR The Nightly Show* got pulled from the airwaves as a "business decision," first and foremost.[37] On the other hand, although Trevor Noah had a tough start on *TDS* after Jon Stewart left, he has retained his position due to the show's ratings having soared over time.[38] Being on cable has provided Noah with a certain amount of freedom to find his voice in the crowded late-night landscape, but in both Wilmore and Noah's cases, what's clear is that *Comedy Central*'s central concern has been the bottom line.

One of the reasons John Oliver seems to be leading the way with advocacy satire is likely due to the advantage he has of working on HBO, a network less tied to advertising revenues and more free to experiment and engage in a variety of rhetorical practices.[39] Oliver aired a long segment urging his audiences to support net neutrality and asked viewers to go to the Federal Communications Commission site to signal their support for net neutrality, which led to so many people visiting the site that it became temporarily disabled.[40] With less neoliberal pressures directing the show (i.e., ties to particular advertisers), we've seen much bolder advocacy and active viewer responses on behalf of public interest issues on Oliver's show than many others.

Compare this to Colbert's *The Late Show* on CBS, where the host has ramped up his political critiques over time but, at least thus far, has not exhibited the same kind of public advocacy stunts that characterized Colbert's previous show. Having been trained in creative processes and divergent thinking, comedians will likely continue to figure out how to operate in an environment of accelerating neoliberalism. New ways of forwarding advocacy satire might be found, in the same way that Oliver's show took the benchmark features of *TDS* and *TCR* and adapted them to have more of a focus on public activism and long-form investigative journalism. From all appearances, though, the structural connections between politics and business will continue to play a part in influencing the extent to which the direct interventions of advocacy satire can be enacted.

WHAT NOW?

This chapter has explored the emergence of a remarkable form of comic activism in public affairs: advocacy satire. What developed on a sporadic basis has become a regular feature of comic programming, especially in John Oliver's work. Among other potential factors giving rise to advocacy satire, four key developments have forwarded a qualitative shift toward its use, including (1) new media advocacy, (2) comic precursors, (3) international political humor, and (4) neoliberal accelerations. Taking action on behalf of disadvantaged individuals or groups and lending force to their voices by making a direct intervention into public affairs, advocacy satire moves comedians beyond simply making commentary at a distance. In essence, for many of our political humorists, advocacy satire has provided a way of more closely aligning comedy and civic engagement.

Where the path leads from here is unknown. Whether comedians will use more or less advocacy satire in the future may depend on a variety of factors. But from the foregoing analysis, a few concluding comments about the future of this practice are deserved. For one, more research examining how broad or narrow advocacy satire can or should be in its applications to a variety of political exigencies would be useful. Remembering that Jon Stewart had a difficult time performing humor on his show dedicated to advocating on behalf of 9/11 first responders shows that the laughs may, at times, get in the way of serious policy advocacy.[41] Then again, that John Oliver has joined advocacy and satire with, from many indications, a great deal of success, suggests that there are times and places where these concepts can be fused well for political purpose and impact.

Just as *TDS* has inspired the rise of many new forms of political comedy across different contexts, we should also examine how a variety of political humorists, in turn, adapt and evolve advocacy satire. Both Bassem Yousseff and Chumel Torres have taken the form as far as they can in their own countries, but in the swirl of new media advocacy, the crossings between advocacy and satire appear to be heading in an even more porous direction.

Take Samantha Bee's discovery that a job candidate for her show, *Full Frontal*, turned out to be a sting by a Project Veritas reporter, which turned into an unexpected comedic segment. In this instance, Bee moved beyond planned and strategic comedy, demonstrating how her show is playing such a part in politics that a counter-activist showed up at her very studio to create advocacy satire on the spot. Leading toward this discovery, Bee asked the candidate why he wanted to work for her, and his dumb response, "I just really love girl things and doing feminism,"[42] further underscores the feminist theme that lies at the heart of much of Bee's advocacy. Satire and politics have generally had a masculine bent in the United States,[43] so given the additional coverage that such events tend to generate across media outlets, advocacy satire stands to be adapted and evolved, raising the status and stakes for this work.

Finally, understanding advocacy satire and its potential conditions can lead us to new questions about similar concepts that focus whether or not political humor helps or hinders democracy and citizenship. Defining "advocacy" in relation to its classic and contemporary understandings is critical, since it's a term that's often stretched far beyond its elastic. Getting more precise about the generic patterns and expectations of modern political comedy should help us see more about where these kinds of phenomena have come from and where they're going.

For example, after Colbert's Comedy Central show ran its course, as mentioned, the network put in place *The Nightly Show* with Larry Wilmore.[44] Although Wilmore engaged in a great deal of advocacy satire in his segments on, for example, the water crisis in Flint, Michigan,[45] much of the show also used a quasi-roundtable comic "dialogue" and "deliberation" format, which begs questions about different genres of humor and their political effects.[46] In general, we need to know more about how communication forms that are often in direct tension, such as advocacy and deliberation,[47] play out in late-night shows and their offshoots. Parsing the thresholds of these concepts, or even seeing how one genre of political humor blends into another, could help us further understand these pressures and how they ultimately advance or detract from political persuasion.

Regardless of how comedians will use strategy in the future, it looks like advocacy satire is here to stay. John Oliver once mentioned that "democracy is like a tambourine—not everyone can be trusted with it."[48] As long as our humorists are seen as trustworthy players among the cacophony of voices in public affairs, both their satire and their advocacy should be seen as significant interventions on behalf of democracy and the building of better worlds.

NOTES

1. See, for example, Richard Van Heertum, "Irony and the News: Speaking Cool to American Youth," in *The Stewart/Colbert Effect: Essays on the Real Impacts of Fake News*, ed. Amarnath Amarasingam (Jefferson, NC: McFarland, 2011), 117–35.

2. Leslie Salzillo, "John Oliver Buys Up $15 Million in Medical Debt, then Pays off the Debt for 9,000 People in Hardship," *Daily Kos*, June 6, 2016, www.dailykos.com/stories/2016/6/6/1535091/-John-Oliver-buys-up-15-million-in-medical-debt-then-pays-off-the-debt-for-9–000-people-in-hardship.

3. I first came across this term in an article covering Jon Stewart's advocacy on behalf of 9/11 first responders. Bill Carter and Brian Stelter, "In 'Daily Show' Role on 9/11 Bill, Echoes of Murrow," *The New York Times*, December 26, 2010, par. 10, www.nytimes.com/2010/12/27/business/media/27stewart.html. Other scholars such as Joseph Faina have also used this emerging term to describe the parallels between advocacy journalism and comedians' contributions to public culture. Joseph Faina, "Ballin' It Up: Ironic Intellectualism of Stewart Colbert and 'Advocacy Satire,'" *Dr. Joe*, January 7, 2011, https://faination.wordpress.com/2011/01/07/ballin-it-up-ironic-intellectualism-of-stewart-colbert-and-advocacy-satire/; Joseph Faina, "Public

Journalism is a Joke: The Case for Jon Stewart and Stephen Colbert," *Journalism* 14 (2013): 541–55.

4. See, for example, Jeffrey P. Jones, *Entertaining Politics: Satiric Television and Political Engagement* (New York: Rowman & Littlefield, 2010).

5. This is differentiated from comedic types such as irony and parody that are more about internal, subtextual undertow or external, formal replication as a means of humor production. For an extended discussion of these differences, see Don J. Waisanen, "Crafting Hyperreal Spaces for Comic Insights: The Onion News Network's Ironic Iconicity," *Communication Quarterly* 59 (2011): 508–28; Linda Hutcheon, *A Theory of Parody* (Champaign: University of Illinois Press, 1985); Jon Vorhaus, *The Comic Toolbox* (Los Angeles: Silman-James Press, 1994).

6. Elias Cohen, "Advocacy and Advocates: Definitions and Ethical Dimensions," *Generations* 28 (2004): 9.

7. G. Thomas Goodnight, "The Duties of Advocacy: Argumentation under Conditions of Disparity, Asymmetry, and Difference," in *Pondering on the Problems of Argumentation*, eds. Frans H. van Eemeren and Bart Garssen (The Netherlands: Springer, 2009), 269–86.

8. Ibid. See also Bruce A. Williams and Michael X. Delli Carpini, *After Broadcast News: Media Regimes, Democracy, and the New Information Environment* (New York: Cambridge University Press, 2011); Michael Crozier, "Recursive Governance: Contemporary Political Communication and Public Policy," *Political Communication* 24 (2007): 1–18.

9. Manuel Castells, "Communication, Power and Counter-Power in the Network Society," *International Journal of Communication* 1 (2007): 247–48.

10. M. J. Stephey, "Colbert's Green-Screen Challenge," *Time*, November 3, 2008, http://content.time.com/time/specials/packages/article/0,28804,1855948_1864122_1864113,00.html.

11. For more on the "attention economy," see Marty Kaplan, "What Is Entertainment, Anyway? Welcome to the Attention Economy," *The Norman Lear Center*, n.d., https://learcenter.org/video/entertainment-anyway-welcome-attention-economy/; advocacy satire also fits within a media ecology and era defined by "celebrity advocacy." See G. Thomas Goodnight, "The Passion of the Christ Meets Fahrenheit 9/11: A Study in Celebrity Advocacy," *American Behavioral Scientist* 49 (2005): 410–35.

12. "9/11 First Responders React to the Senate Filibuster," *The Daily Show*, December 16, 2010, www.cc.com/video-clips/nuwe6u/the-daily-show-with-jon-stewart-9–11-first-responders-react-to-the-senate-filibuster.

13. Carter and Stelter, "In 'Daily Show,'" par. 11.

14. Ibid., par. 9.

15. See Paul Begala, "The Day Jon Stewart Blew Up My Show," *CNN*, February 12, 2015, www.cnn.com/2015/02/12/opinion/begala-stewart-blew-up-crossfire/index.html.

16. Don Waisanen, "The Comic Counterfactual: Laughter, Affect, and Civic Alternatives," *Quarterly Journal of Speech* (2017): 1–23; Bruce W. Hardy, Jeffrey A. Gottfried, Kenneth M. Winneg, and Kathleen Hall Jamieson, "Stephen Colbert's Civics lesson: How Colbert Super PAC Taught Viewers about Campaign Finance,"

Mass Communication and Society 17 (2014): 329–53; Matthew R. Meier, "I Am Super PAC and So Can You! Stephen Colbert and the Citizen-Fool," *Western Journal of Communication* 81 (2017): 262–79.

17. Art Herbig and Aaron Hess, "Convergent Critical Rhetoric at the 'Rally to Restore Sanity': Exploring the Intersection of Rhetoric, Ethnography, and Documentary Production," *Communication Studies* 63 (2012): 269–89.

18. Alan Silverleib, "Colbert Storms Capitol Hill for Migrant Workers," *CNN*, September 24, 2010, www.cnn.com/2010/POLITICS/09/24/colbert.house.immigration/index.html.

19. Sarah Bishop, "'I'm Only Going to Do It If I Can Do It in Character': Unpacking Comedy and Advocacy in Stephen Colbert's 2010 Congressional Testimony," *The Journal of Popular Culture* 48 (2015): 555.

20. Don J. Waisanen, "A Funny Thing Happened on the Way to Decorum: Quintilian's Reflections on Rhetorical Humor," *Advances in the History of Rhetoric* 18 (2015): 29–52.

21. Adam Boult, "Spitting Image to Make a Comeback with New Series," *The Telegraph*, April 24, 2017, www.telegraph.co.uk/tv/2017/04/24/spitting-image-make-comeback-new-hbo-series/.

22. Don J. Waisanen, "(Trans)national Advocacy in the Ousting of Milošević: The Otpor Movement's Glocal Recursions," *Communication Studies* 64 (2013): 158–77.

23. Jeffrey Fleishman, "'Egypt's Jon Stewart' Is Living in Exile and Trying to Make His Satire Work in America," *Los Angeles Times*, June 29, 2017, http://beta.latimes.com/entertainment/movies/la-ca-bassem-youssef-exile-20170613-story.html, par. 2–3.

24. Ibid., par. 10, 7.

25. See Kerry K. Riley, *Everyday Subversion* (East Lansing: Michigan State University Press, 2008); Amber Day, *Satire and Dissent* (Bloomington: Indiana University Press, 2011).

26. This quote is from the movie *Red Chapel*, as cited in Nick Schager, "Red Chapel," *Slant Magazine*, March 12, 2010, www.slantmagazine.com/film/review/the-red-chapel.

27. Fleishman, "Egypt's"; "Meet Mexico's Jon Stewart: Chumel Torres," *YouTube*, February 29, 2016, www.youtube.com/watch?v=BlfwMimo63A, par. 1.

28. Jo Tuckman, "El Pulso de la Republica: meet Chumel Torres, Mexico's answer to Jon Stewart," *The Guardian*, August 28, 2015, www.theguardian.com/world/2015/aug/28/el-pulso-de-la-republica-chumel-torres-mexico-youtube-show.

29. Tuckman, "El Pulso," par. 15.

30. Teresa Mioli, "Chumel Torres Brings the Intersection of Comedy and Journalism to Latin America and Delivers News with Humor and Intelligence," *Knight Center for Journalism in the Americas*, March 17, 2017, https://knightcenter.utexas.edu/blog/00–18115-chumel-torres-brings-intersection-comedy-and-journalism-latin-america-and-delivers-new, par. 25.

31. "Tania Reza and How Mexico Began Talking about an On-Air 'Groping,'" *BBC*, November 1, 2015, www.bbc.com/news/blogs-trending-34679077.

32. David Harvey, *A Brief History of Neoliberalism* (New York: Oxford University Press, 2007).

33. Jodi Dean, *Democracy and Other Neoliberal Fantasies: Communicative Capitalism and Left Politics* (Durham, NC: Duke University Press, 2009), 51.

34. Robert Asen, "Neoliberalism, the Public Sphere, and a Public Good," *Quarterly Journal of Speech* (2017): 1–21.

35. Brian Stelter, "Has President Trump Changed Late Night TV Permanently?" *CNN*, November 20, 2017, http://money.cnn.com/2017/11/20/media/late-night-tv-president-trump/.

36. Amy B. Becker, "Trump Trumps Baldwin? How Trump's Tweets Transform SNL into Trump's Strategic Advantage," *Journal of Political Marketing* (2017): 1.

37. Cynthia Littleton, "Larry Wilmore's 'Nightly Show' Cancelled at Comedy Central," *Variety*, August 16, 2016, http://variety.com/2016/tv/news/larry-wilmore-nightly-show-canceled-comedy-central-1201837298/, par. 7.

38. Lucas Shaw, "'The Daily Show' Host Trevor Noah Lands New Deal after Ratings Success," *Bloomberg*, September 14, 2017, www.bloomberg.com/news/articles/2017–09–14/-daily-show-host-noah-lands-new-deal-as-trump-bits-lift-ratings.

39. Don J. Waisanen, "The Political Economy of Late-Night Comedy," in *Political Comedy Encounters Neoliberalism*, ed. Julie Webber (Lanham, MD: Lexington Books, forthcoming).

40. Deen Freelon, Amy B. Becker, Bob Lannon, and Andrew Pendleton, "Narrowing the Gap: Gender and Mobilization in Net Neutrality Advocacy," *International Journal of Communication* 10 (2016): 5910.

41. For a similar point about the tensions between the "comic" and "counterfactual" parts of the "comic counterfactual" construct, see Waisanen, "The Comic."

42. Lee Moran, "Samantha Bee Expertly Trolls That Failed Sting on the Washington Post," *Huffington Post*, November 29, 2017, www.huffingtonpost.com/entry/samantha-bee-project-veritas-trolls-undercover-sting_us_5a1e6847e4b0dc52b02a4a28.

43. Jessica M. Peterson, "Funny in a Man's World: Women Comedians' Use of Political Satire at the White House Correspondents' Dinner" (Master's thesis, University of South Dakota, 2017), vii.

44. Eric Deggans, "Why Didn't 'Nightly Show' Connect with More Viewers? Larry Wilmore's Not Sure," *NPR*, August 16, 2016, www.npr.org/2016/08/16/490174005/comedy-central-cancels-nightly-show-with-larry-wilmore.

45. "The Larry People vs. Flint – Checking in on Michigan's Water Crisis," *Comedy Central*, August 9, 2016, www.cc.com/video-clips/u71f1w/the-nightly-show-with-larry-wilmore-the-larry-people-vs--flint---checking-in-on-michigan-s-water-crisis.

46. I should note that Bill Maher's long-standing discussion format has fared well on his *HBO* show *Real Time with Bill Maher* (and its prior incarnation on a mainstream network, *Politically Incorrect*), so there's further comparisons to be drawn between these shows. For another call to define political comedy's terms more precisely, see Lance R. Holbert, Jay Hmielowski, Parul Jain, Julie Lather, and Alyssa Morey, "Adding Nuance to the Study of Political Humor Effects: Experimental Research on Juvenalian Satire versus Horatian Satire," *American Behavioral Scientist* 55 (2011): 187–211.

47. See Don J. Waisanen, "Toward Robust Public Engagement: The Value of Deliberative Discourse for Civil Communication," *Rhetoric & Public Affairs* 17 (2014): 287–322.

48. Daniel Kurtzman, "John Oliver Quotes," *ThoughtCo.*, August 11, 2017, www.thoughtco.com/john-oliver-quotes-2734481, par. 19.

REFERENCES

"9/11 First Responders React to the Senate Filibuster." *The Daily Show*, December 16, 2010. www.cc.com/video-clips/nuwe6u/the-daily-show-with-jon-stewart-9-11-first-responders-react-to-the-senate-filibuster.

Asen, Robert. "Neoliberalism, the Public Sphere, and a Public Good." *Quarterly Journal of Speech* (2017): 1–21.

Becker, Amy B. "Trump Trumps Baldwin? How Trump's Tweets Transform SNL into Trump's Strategic Advantage." *Journal of Political Marketing* (2017): 1–19. doi: 10.1080/15377857.2017.1411860

Begala, Paul. "The Day Jon Stewart Blew Up My Show." *CNN*, February 12, 2015. www.cnn.com/2015/02/12/opinion/begala-stewart-blew-up-crossfire/index.html.

Bishop, Sarah. "'I'm Only Going to Do It If I Can Do It in Character': Unpacking Comedy and Advocacy in Stephen Colbert's 2010 Congressional Testimony." *The Journal of Popular Culture* 48 (2015): 548–57.

Boult, Adam. "Spitting Image to Make a Comeback with New Series." *The Telegraph*, April 24, 2017. www.telegraph.co.uk/tv/2017/04/24/spitting-image-make-comeback-new-hbo-series/.

Carter, Bill, and Brian Stelter. "In 'Daily Show' Role on 9/11 Bill, Echoes of Murrow." *The New York Times*, December 26, 2010. www.nytimes.com/2010/12/27/business/media/27stewart.html.

Castells, Manuel. "Communication, Power and Counter-Power in the Network Society." *International Journal of Communication* 1 (2007): 247–48.

Cohen, Elias. "Advocacy and Advocates: Definitions and Ethical Dimensions." *Generations* 28 (2004): 9–16.

Crozier, Michael. "Recursive Governance: Contemporary Political Communication and Public Policy." *Political Communication* 24 (2007): 1–18.

Day, Amber. *Satire and Dissent*. Bloomington: Indiana University Press, 2011.

Dean, Jodi. *Democracy and Other Neoliberal Fantasies: Communicative Capitalism and Left Politics*. Durham, NC: Duke University Press, 2009.

Deggans, Eric. "Why Didn't 'Nightly Show' Connect with More Viewers? Larry Wilmore's Not Sure." *NPR*, August 16, 2016. www.npr.org/2016/08/16/490174005/comedy-central-cancels-nightly-show-with-larry-wilmore.

Faina, Joseph. "Ballin' It Up: Ironic Intellectualism of Stewart Colbert and 'Advocacy Satire.'" *Dr. Joe*, January 7, 2011. https://faination.wordpress.com/2011/01/07/ballin-it-up-ironic-intellectualism-of-stewart-colbert-and-advocacy-satire/.

———. "Public Journalism Is a Joke: The Case for Jon Stewart and Stephen Colbert." *Journalism* 14 (2013): 541–55.

Fleishman. "Egypt's"; "Meet Mexico's Jon Stewart: Chumel Torres." *YouTube*, February 29, 2016. www.youtube.com/watch?v=BlfwMimo63A.

Fleishman, Jeffrey. "'Egypt's Jon Stewart' Is Living in Exile and Trying to Make His Satire Work in America." *Los Angeles Times*, June 29, 2017. http://beta.latimes.com/entertainment/movies/la-ca-bassem-youssef-exile-20170613-story.html.

Freelon, Deen, Amy B. Becker, Bob Lannon, and Andrew Pendleton. "Narrowing the Gap: Gender and Mobilization in Net Neutrality Advocacy." *International Journal of Communication* 10 (2016): 5908–30.

Goodnight, G. Thomas. "The Passion of the Christ Meets Fahrenheit 9/11: A Study in Celebrity Advocacy." *American Behavioral Scientist* 49 (2005): 410–35.

———. "The Duties of Advocacy: Argumentation under Conditions of Disparity, Asymmetry, and Difference." In *Pondering on the Problems of Argumentation*, edited by Frans H. van Eemeren and Bart Garssen. Dordrecht: Springer, 2009.

Hardy, Bruce W., Jeffrey A. Gottfried, Kenneth M. Winneg, and Kathleen Hall Jamieson. "Stephen Colbert's Civics Lesson: How Colbert Super PAC Taught Viewers about Campaign Finance." *Mass Communication and Society* 17 (2014): 329–53.

Harvey, David. *A Brief History of Neoliberalism*. New York: Oxford University Press, 2007.

Herbig, Art, and Aaron Hess. "Convergent Critical Rhetoric at the 'Rally to Restore Sanity': Exploring the Intersection of Rhetoric, Ethnography, and Documentary Production." *Communication Studies* 63 (2012): 269–89.

Holbert, Lance R., Jay Hmielowski, Parul Jain, Julie Lather, and Alyssa Morey. "Adding Nuance to the Study of Political Humor Effects: Experimental Research on Juvenalian Satire versus Horatian Satire." *American Behavioral Scientist* 55 (2011): 187–211.

Hutcheon, Linda. *A Theory of Parody*. Champaign: University of Illinois Press, 1985.

Jones, Jeffrey P. *Entertaining Politics: Satiric Television and Political Engagement*. New York: Rowman & Littlefield, 2010.

Kaplan, Marty. "What Is Entertainment, Anyway? Welcome to the Attention Economy." *The Norman Lear Center*, n.d. https://learcenter.org/video/entertainment-anyway-welcome-attention-economy/.

Kurtzman, Daniel. "John Oliver Quotes." *ThoughtCo.*, August 11, 2017. www.thoughtco.com/john-oliver-quotes-2734481, par. 19.

Littleton, Cynthia. "Larry Wilmore's 'Nightly Show' Cancelled at Comedy Central." *Variety*, August 16, 2016. http://variety.com/2016/tv/news/larry-wilmore-nightly-show-canceled-comedy-central-1201837298/.

Meier, Matthew R. "I Am Super PAC and So Can You! Stephen Colbert and the Citizen-Fool." *Western Journal of Communication* 81 (2017): 262–79.

Mioli, Teresa. "Chumel Torres Brings the Intersection of Comedy and Journalism to Latin America and Delivers News with Humor and Intelligence." *Knight Center for Journalism in the Americas*, March 17, 2017. https://knightcenter.utexas.edu/blog/00-18115-chumel-torres-brings-intersection-comedy-and-journalism-latin-america-and-delivers-new.

Moran, Lee. "Samantha Bee Expertly Trolls That Failed Sting on the Washington Post." *Huffington Post*, November 29, 2017. www.huffingtonpost.

com/entry/samantha-bee-project-veritas-trolls-undercover-sting_us_5a1e6847
e4b0dc52b02a4a28.

Peterson, Jessica M. "Funny in a Man's World: Women Comedians' Use of Political Satire at the White House Correspondents' Dinner." Master's thesis, University of South Dakota, 2017.

Riley, Kerry K. *Everyday Subversion.* East Lansing: Michigan State University Press, 2008.

Salzillo, Leslie. "John Oliver Buys up $15 Million in Medical Debt, then Pays off the Debt for 9,000 People in Hardship." *Daily Kos,* June 6, 2016. www.dailykos.com/stories/2016/6/6/1535091/-John-Oliver-buys-up-15-million-in-medical-debt-then-pays-off-the-debt-for-9-000-people-in-hardship.

Schager, Nick. "Red Chapel." *Slant Magazine,* March 12, 2010. www.slantmagazine.com/film/review/the-red-chapel.

Shaw, Lucas. "'The Daily Show' Host Trevor Noah Lands New Deal after Ratings Success." *Bloomberg,* September 14, 2017. www.bloomberg.com/news/articles/2017-09-14/-daily-show-host-noah-lands-new-deal-as-trump-bits-lift-ratings.

Silverleib, Alan. "Colbert Storms Capitol Hill for Migrant Workers." *CNN,* September 24, 2010. www.cnn.com/2010/POLITICS/09/24/colbert.house.immigration/index.html.

Stelter, Brian. "Has President Trump Changed Late Night TV Permanently?" *CNN,* November 20, 2017. http://money.cnn.com/2017/11/20/media/late-night-tv-president-trump/.

Stephey, M. J. "Colbert's Green-Screen Challenge." *Time,* November 3, 2008. http://content.time.com/time/specials/packages/article/0,28804,1855948_1864122_1864113,00.html.

"Tania Reza and How Mexico Began Talking about an On-Air 'Groping." *BBC,* November 1, 2015. www.bbc.com/news/blogs-trending-34679077.

Tuckman, Jo. "El Pulso de la Republica: Meet Chumel Torres, Mexico's Answer to Jon Stewart." *The Guardian,* August 28, 2015. www.theguardian.com/world/2015/aug/28/el-pulso-de-la-republica-chumel-torres-mexico-youtube-show.

Vorhaus, Jon. *The Comic Toolbox.* Los Angeles: Silman-James Press, 1994.

Waisanen, Don J. "Crafting Hyperreal Spaces for Comic Insights: The Onion News Network's Ironic Iconicity." *Communication Quarterly* 59 (2011): 508–28.

———. "(Trans)national Advocacy in the Ousting of Milošević: The Otpor Movement's Glocal Recursions." *Communication Studies* 64 (2013): 158–77.

———. "Toward Robust Public Engagement: The Value of Deliberative Discourse for Civil Communication." *Rhetoric & Public Affairs* 17 (2014): 287–322.

———. "A Funny Thing Happened on the Way to Decorum: Quintilian's Reflections on Rhetorical Humor." *Advances in the History of Rhetoric* 18 (2015): 29–52.

———. "The Comic Counterfactual: Laughter, Affect, and Civic Alternatives." *Quarterly Journal of Speech* (2017): 1–23.

———. "The Political Economy of Late-Night Comedy." In *Political Comedy Encounters Neoliberalism,* edited by Julie Webber. Lanham, MD: Lexington Books, forthcoming.

Williams, Bruce A., and Michael X. Delli Carpini. *After Broadcast News: Media Regimes, Democracy, and the New Information Environment.* New York: Cambridge University Press, 2011.

Chapter 2

Journalist or Jokester?

An Analysis of Last Week Tonight with John Oliver

Julia R. Fox

While the resemblance of comedic news to traditional news has been more production style than content, some of the newer comedic news programs' similarity to serious news programs goes beyond appearances. This study examines the content of *Last Week Tonight with John Oliver*, perhaps the first comedic news program to combine satire with "real" journalistic content, not just format, as a potentially new hybrid form of public discourse, *satiric journalism.*

IS COMEDIC NEWS REAL NEWS?

Some of the early studies of comedic news declared it to be a new form of critical journalism while other research referred to comedic news programs as "fake" news shows—often comparing them to "real" news programs.[1] But it is important to distinguish the political humor in comedic news programs as something other than "fake" news, particularly given the rise of actual fake news in this most recent presidential election cycle. Calling it "fake" news is an oversimplification of the genre that merely defines these shows by what they are not—traditional journalism.

A more fruitful direction would be to consider not whether one is fake and the other real—or whether one, as an authentic fake, is more real than the actual[2]—but rather that comedic (not fake) news programs are uniquely situated to offer two types of real public discourse—journalism and political satire—in the same show.

Simply resembling a traditional newscast with theme music, an anchor at a desk, and the use of news footage and reporter field packages does not make comedic news journalism—real or fake. But while the resemblance of comedic news shows to traditional news has been more in format and production features than in content, in examining both the formal structural features as well as the content of *The Daily Show with Jon Stewart* in his close read, Baym suggested the show be considered a new form of critical journalism and/or an experiment in political journalism.[3] Tally argued that *The Daily Show* and *The Colbert Report* often did a better job at journalism than journalists, particularly in terms of more and better social critique.[4] And two studies published in 2007—one quantitative and one qualitative—found the content of *The Daily Show with Jon Stewart* to be as substantive as traditional television news sources.[5] Although Fox and colleagues did find *The Daily Show* to be just as substantive as the networks' nightly newscasts in its political coverage, that study also found *The Daily Show*'s content to be considerably more humorous than substantive, in keeping with Stewart's insistence that he was a comedian, not a journalist.[6] Similarly, the following year The Pew Research Center found almost half of *The Daily Show*'s content to be about politics, although it was often more humorous than serious in tone.[7]

But this does not preclude comedic news as a genre from resembling real journalism as much as comedy programming. For one comedic news program in particular, *Last Week Tonight with John Oliver*, the similarity to serious news programs goes well beyond appearances; the show includes in-depth reporting on an important issue in each episode (e.g., net neutrality, corporate consolidation, vaccines, public defender case backlogs, etc.) and won a Peabody Award in 2014, the year it premiered, "for bringing satire and journalism even closer together."[8] *Last Week Tonight with John Oliver* may be a new hybrid form of satiric journalism, offering a more balanced combination of satire and serious journalism. In a *Rolling Stone* magazine cover story interview, Oliver said his intention is to blend both journalism and comedy within the show's stories, noting, "I like the balance between seriousness and stupidity. I think I would get depressed if I was gonna start doing just one of them," adding "the harder, the drier the story is, the more we try and balance that with the stupidest thing you can imagine, either with part of that story or in the show in general."[9]

As an initial investigation into the journalistic and satiric content of the show, this study compares the presentation of facts versus jokes on *Last Week Tonight with John Oliver*, to see if a systematic examination of the content reflects the recognition the show has received for balancing real journalism with satiric humor. Comparing the balance of facts and jokes in the show's main stories is a first step in considering whether that content may represent a new hybrid type of public discourse—satiric journalism.

FACTS VERSUS JOKES

One of the most important functions of journalism is to provide facts to citizens, particularly those that politicians and government officials hide, distort, or deny.[10] The *Rolling Stone* cover story called *Last Week Tonight with John Oliver* the "most thoroughly fact-checked comedy show in the history of television."[11]

Facts are verifiable propositions, empirically determinable answers to questions.[12] The answers to the first four W's of journalism—who, what, when, and where—are considered fixed, factual elements of journalism in the form of names, numbers, locations, and dates.[13] The underlying assumption of journalism is that empirical inquiry about external reality is possible, based on a belief in objective truth.[14] In this study, a fact is defined as information that is said and/or shown that is verifiable, particularly when used as evidence in a report.

Unlike facts, which are considered to have intrinsic characteristics about an external reality, psychological theories of humor suggest that jokes have no intrinsic humorous characteristics, but rather that the humor in a joke depends on the context and its ability to provoke a sense of humor in the mind of the receiver while cognitively processing the joke.[15] Jokes in one language may get lost in translation, they can be culturally dependent, and their ability to evoke amusement or laughter may depend on the joke recipient's prior knowledge.[16] Hurley and colleagues argue that we "get" jokes in the mental spaces created in our working memory through spreading activation of semantically related concepts; they propose a just-in-time spreading activation (JITSA) model to explain how the cognitive processing of jokes results in amusement or laughter when we have activated the necessary concepts in our working memory in time to process the misfit of humorous stimuli within that mental space.[17] According to Hurley and colleagues, comedians rely on "the assumption that any more or less unified population, any gathered audience, as a result of having had similar experiences in the world, will share enough beliefs (and covert structures of association between them) to generate much the same processes of JITSA when targeted with well-aimed set ups."[18] Similarly, Gruner defined the communicative functions of wit and humor in mass communication as the effects on audiences intended by the humorist.[19]

In laying out their empirical theory of humor and the brain, Hurley and colleagues argue that, if they are right, studying humorous texts and artifacts is "systematically forlorn" as "funny things can be identified only by their similar effects on properly tuned normal human cognitive and emotional systems."[20] Thus coding transcripts of comedic news shows could prove problematic. However, in addition to evoking laughter in the audience at home, comedic news programs also have in-studio audiences laughing in real time as the jokes are delivered; those studio audience responses can serve as cues as to when to code a joke. In this study, a joke is defined as something that is said and/or shown to evoke amusement or laughter.

The primary research question in this study concerns the overall balance of facts and jokes presented in *Last Week Tonight with John Oliver*, focusing specifically on the main story in the episode.

RQ1: Will there be a difference in the number of facts and jokes presented in the main stories? If so, will the stories have more facts than jokes or more jokes than facts?

DISCURSIVE AUTHORITY OF
COMEDIC NEWS ANCHORS

In addition to how many facts are presented, it is important to examine how those facts are presented. Baym noted that news, politics, and entertainment—once discreet forms of discourse—have become inseparable, a phenomenon he referred to as discursive integration.[21] McKain considered that the performance of a comedic news anchor, in mimicking real TV news anchors, might in itself lend some discursive authority to the show host; in "sitting behind a desk, running news clips, constructing a narrative of the day's events, and asking anchorman-type questions," McKain argued, the comedic news anchor "is co-opting the performative and formal qualities or 'strategies' of the conventional broadcast, all the things that convince an audience that News is News."[22] And, as Carlson and Peifer noted, in moving from humorous to serious, comedic news can assume the discursive authority of journalism.[23] Similarly, McKain suggested that legitimacy for comedic news shows "spills over from an authorization to be funny to an authority predicated on knowledge."[24] To extend this to the show host, the more facts that are presented by the host the greater his/her discursive authority should be in delivering serious information, as opposed to having serious information presented primarily in other ways, such as sound bites from other sources or on-screen graphics, with the host mostly following up those facts with zingers and punch lines. Therefore, this study examines whether the facts in the main stories on *Last Week Tonight with John Oliver* are presented primarily by Oliver himself or through other means.

RQ2: Will most of the facts in the main stories be presented by John Oliver himself, or through other sources?

METHOD

The sample in this study is a saturation sample of all thirty episodes from 2017, the most recent full season of the show. The episode dates are February 12, 19, and 26; March 5, 12, and 19; April 2, 9, 16, and 23; May 7, 14, and 21; June 4, 11, 18, and 25; July 2 and 30; August 6, 13, 20; September 10 and 24; October 1, 8, 15, and 29; and November 5 and 12.

The unit of analysis is the main story. The main story usually follows and often precedes an "And Now" segment in the show. It is mostly introduced with the phrase "Our main story tonight," but may also be introduced with other phrases such as "Tonight, I would like to talk to you about . . ." or "Tonight we need to talk about . . ." and it is the longest story in the show. Coders were instructed to identify the main story in each episode and code facts and jokes in each, as detailed below.

Coders were instructed to count how many factual statements were presented in the story by John Oliver, in sound bites, and in visual graphics. Coders were also instructed to count how many jokes were presented during the story.

Concept Operationalizations

Fact

A fact is defined as information that is said (can be a phrase, sentence, or sentences) and/or shown that is verifiable, particularly when used as evidence in a report. Indicators of facts are found in both the audio and video portions of the story and include precise numbers (e.g., dollar amounts, percentages), dates, job titles or role definitions, lists (count each list as one fact, rather than coding each item in the list separately), identification of specific group or groups impacted or projected to be impacted (can be groups of people—e.g., income groups: specific racial, religious, gender, etc. demographic groups; geographic groups, etc.—or agencies/organizations—e.g., governmental agencies, NGOs, etc.). Coders were instructed not to code descriptive phrases (e.g., this proposal serves as a blue print) as facts.

Joke

A joke is defined as something that is said (can be a phrase, sentence, or sentences) and/or shown to evoke amusement or laughter. Indicators of jokes are found in both the audio and video portions of the story. Indicators used for this study were based on Fox and colleague's coding of humorous content in *The Daily Show with Jon Stewart*.[25]

Audio

Funny music; statement of silly, untrue fact; making fun of the way someone looks; silly voice; sarcastic or mocking tone of voice; sudden change in pitch or volume; sound of laughing or chuckling.

Video

Silly faces; raised eyebrows; skewed, wide open, or pinched mouth; mocking faces; silly gestures; obviously altered images; smiling.

Some jokes may have double punch lines, with the second being delivered after laughter from the first has died down.[26] Coders were instructed to code those as separate jokes.

Intercoder Reliability

After reviewing the conceptual and operational definitions of facts and jokes and discussing the coder instructions, three study coders each coded three episodes from 2017 (10% of the sample) from April 2, October 8, and October 15, to establish intercoder reliability.

Pearson's correlation coefficient (r) is used to measure the degree to which coders vary together when coding interval or ratio-level data.[27] As with previous content analyses examining the content of broadcast and comedic news programs, this study uses Pearson correlation coefficients from distances correlations, which measure similarities (or dissimilarities) between pairs of cases based on selected variables of interest; for intercoder reliability, pairs of coders can be compared for similarities in their coding of the study categories.[28] In this study, distances correlations compared pairs of coders on the study variables of factual statements presented by John Oliver, factual statements presented in sound bites, factual statements presented in visual graphics, total facts coded (combining the previous three categories), and jokes for each of the dates coded.

As Fox and colleagues noted, the Pearson correlation from this measure is parsimonious in rendering one statistic to indicate how similar two coders are on all the study variables, while at the same time providing useful information regarding where reliability problems might be occurring among individual coders, unlike other measures of reliability that render only one statistic for the entire group of coders.[29] Pearson correlation coefficients from the distances correlations indicated that the data coders in this study had high intercoder reliability, as all but one coefficient was .90 or higher (lowest Pearson correlation coefficient r = .88). Previous research has accepted Pearson's correlation coefficients of .84 or higher as indicators of good intercoder reliability.[30]

Because the distance correlation statistics renders one statistic for all study variables, reliability analyses were also conducted using the general linear model and independent samples t-tests among pairs of coders. These additional indications of the reliability of the coding scheme ensured that there were no statistically significant effects of assignment to a particular coder on any of the individual study variables. No significant differences between coders were found.

RESULTS

RQ1 asked if there would be a difference in the number of facts and jokes presented in the main stories and, if so, would the stories have more facts than jokes or more jokes than facts.

While some shows had more facts than jokes and some more jokes than facts, a paired samples t-test found, on average, there was no statistically significant difference in the average number of facts and jokes presented per episode in the main stories during the 2017 season, as can be seen in Table 2.1.

RQ2 asked whether most of the facts in the main stories would be presented by John Oliver himself or through other sources. To answer this research question, facts presented in sound bites and in graphics were combined into one category and compared to facts presented by John Oliver. As can be seen in Table 2.2, there were significantly more facts in the main stories presented by John Oliver than through other sources.

Table 2.1   Balance of Facts and Jokes in the Main Stories on *Last Week Tonight with John Oliver*

	Total Facts		Jokes		Significance Test		
	M	SD	M	SD	t	d	p (two-tailed)
2017 Episodes	47.57	11.26	46.13	13.01	0.60	29	0.55

Table 2.2   Facts Presented by John Oliver versus Other Sources in the Main Stories on *Last Week Tonight*

	John Oliver		Other Source		Significance Test		
	M	SD	M	SD	t	d	p (two-tailed)
2017 Episodes	34.70	9.13	12.87	6.00	11.30	29	.001

DISCUSSION

Unlike previous studies that found comedic news shows to be more humorous than substantive, this study found evidence of real journalistic content in a "fake" news format given the even balance of facts and jokes in the main stories from the 2017 episodes of *Last Week Tonight with John Oliver*. This study also found that nearly three times as many facts in the main stories were presented by Oliver, rather than other sources. Oliver is not relying on traditional news sources for factual clips about topical stories. Rather, he is the discursive authority in the main stories on his show.

McKain noted that nightly comedic news shows, such as *The Daily Show*, in parodying the news media, address material that has already been vetted by the news media gatekeepers; the logistics of recording a nightly show necessitate their dependence on information that has already passed through the news media gates.[31] Similarly, McChesney, though suggesting that "fake" (comedic) news gets closer to the truth than mainstream journalism, also argued that nightly comedic shows like *The Daily Show* and *The Colbert Report* were not real news as they did not break stories or have their own investigative teams.[32] In contrast, *Last Week Tonight with John Oliver* does not rely on news indexing to frame the problem and does not have the logistical limitations of nightly comedic news programs. Because his show is weekly, not nightly, Oliver has time to explore in-depth important issues that nightly comedic news shows do not. Whereas *The Daily Show*'s yesterday tonight approach legitimizes news gatekeeping, even as it criticizes it, Oliver's *Last Week Tonight* has the time to generate and investigate its own stories, thus passing McChesney's bar for real news that nightly comedic news shows fail to clear.

But while *Last Week Tonight with John Oliver* may pass a "real news" bar, it is clearly different than traditional "objective" journalism and, with its main stories, it may actually do a better job than nightly "real" news shows in reporting complex social, economic, scientific, and policy issues. The twenty-four-hour news cycle, with its deadline demands of daily reporting, coupled with the limited budgets and resources of even major network news operations, makes reporters more reliant on the practice of reporting what other sources say and makes it difficult for reporters to provide analysis and context.[33] In contrast, *Last Week Tonight with John Oliver* more closely resembles investigative journalism, which also deviates from the routines of daily news writing and reporting in taking considerably more time and leg work in providing extensive analysis into issues.[34] Investigative journalism, like satire, points out social problems, exposes wrongdoings, and often takes a side or an advocacy position in speaking truth to power with facts.[35] In general, investigative reporting does not strive for the same even-handed, balanced presentation of two sides of seemingly equal weight; rather, it takes a stand after gathering the evidence and determining which side is favored by the weight.[36] Oliver does likewise, blending humor in with the factual evidence, as opposed to objective reporting's neutral but often artificial balance of facts as if there are two and only two equally valid sides to a story.

However similar to investigative journalism *Last Week Tonight with John Oliver* may be, it is clearly more than just journalism. As Oliver was careful to point out in the *Rolling Stone* magazine cover story interview, his intentions for the show are not solely journalistic. "I certainly get really allergic to the sentiment that what we do is purely journalism, because I'm being defensive of people who actually are journalists. So, we did a whole twenty-minute piece this year about journalism. We need actual journalists doing their jobs so that we can take what journalism does and frame it."[37] And the frame Oliver uses for that is satire, which speaks truth to power with humor.[38] Satire ridicules misdoings even as it is also humorous. While funny, satire is clearly critical, often with a sarcastic or demeaning tone in pointing out uncomfortable truths and holding accountable individuals, groups, and institutions in power.[39]

Being funny, Oliver's style of satiric journalism may do a better job than serious journalism in drawing attention to important problems. As Romano noted, "The social-responsibility theory that the press should act as a watchdog on government fuels both incisive and boring political coverage."[40] Satiric journalism could be uniquely poised to function as a watchdog by being both incisive and funny, thus not losing the attention of viewers uninterested in important but potentially boring topics such as agribusiness, corporate consolidation, and public defender caseloads, all of which have been covered as the main story on *Last Week Tonight with John Oliver*.

The question of whether increased attention to comedic political coverage will help viewers learn information is a bit more complicated. An earlier review of wit and humor in mass communication found little evidence from empirical studies that humor enhances learning of information compared to serious presentations.[41] A more recent review of specifically comedic news programming found mixed support for comedic news presentations bolstering learning, while an even more recent study specifically comparing learning from *Last Week Tonight with John Oliver* to ABC News found both to be equally good sources for knowledge gain about net neutrality.[42] These studies all compared presentations that were humorous to presentations that were serious; but to understand when and how comedic news might be as good or even better a source for knowledge gain than traditional news requires looking at the pattern of fact and joke presentation within comedic news to consider how that pattern might enhance or inhibit learning of facts, particularly in the rapid-fire presentation that is Oliver's signature style. As he described it in the *Rolling Stone* interview, "It's so densely written so that we want to have a joke on every single fact or clip or anything, that you're kind of diving for the finish line."[43]

Future studies could examine how often factual information precedes and follows jokes and/or laughter on the show and how that barrage of facts and jokes impacts learning the factual information. Lang's Dynamic Human-Centered Communication Systems Theory (DHCCST) suggests a number of things to consider in examining how Oliver's style of presenting facts and jokes impacts learning of information that has not been incorporated into previous studies. In the dynamic system state space of an audience member interacting with the main story on *Last Week Tonight with John Oliver*, there are both order parameters to consider that reduce the range of responses in the perceptual, motivational, cognitive, and behavioral systems based on the content and structure of the message (and the medium) as well as control parameters, such as motivational activation and cognitive load, that determine which qualitatively different states will arise.[44] And because the communication space is dynamic, the space needs to be examined over time.

For example, the sound of studio audience laughter is likely to evoke an orienting response (OR) in the viewer; this automatic attentional response brings with it an automatic allocation of cognitive processing resources that can help encode what follows the OR-eliciting stimulus.[45] Further, jokes should activate the appetitive motivational system, and cognitive resource allocation increases as appetitive motivational system activation increases.[46] So in the main story on *Last Week Tonight with John Oliver*, following the presentation of a joke with a fact may result in proactive enhancement for learning that fact. However, following that fact with another joke may result in retroactive inhibition of learning the fact as the joke, a motivationally relevant stimuli, would draw cognitive processing resources to encoding it and away from storing the fact that had previously been encoded.[47] If the viewer uses most or all of his/her available cognitive resources to encode the joke—which Hurley and colleagues suggest takes up considerable mental space in order to "get" it just-in-time—then there may be insufficient resources available to also properly store the fact that had just been encoded prior to the presentation of the joke.[48] In addition, the switching back and forth between jokes and facts, which in news often points out negative aspects of the main story topics, will continuously increase and decrease activation in the viewer's appetitive and aversive motivational systems, both of which impact cognitive resource allocation and thus encoding and storage of information.[49] Rather than looking for global effects, DHCCST suggests Oliver's presentation of facts and jokes in his main stories presents an ideal study for time series analysis of the space in which facts come both before and after jokes, often in rapid succession.

Clearly, there is much more that can be explored in examining this particular style of comedic news. In the meantime, this preliminary investigation of the presentation of facts and jokes in the main stories on *Last Week Tonight with John Oliver* suggests the show's blend of journalism and satire is more balanced than its predecessors. Both satire and journalism aim to speak truth to power. Despite this similar function, they have generally been considered to be very different types of public discourse. That distinction becomes blurred when satire takes the form of comedic news, particularly with this recent incarnation of the genre that provides an evenly balanced mix of facts and jokes, with most of the facts being presented by the comedic host himself.

NOTES

1. Amarnath Amarasingam, ed., *The Stewart/Colbert Effect: Essays on the Real Impacts of Fake News* (Jefferson, NC: McFarland, 2011), 3; Geoffrey Baym, "The Daily Show: Discursive Integration and the Reinvention of Political Journalism," *Political Communication* 22 (2005): 261; Jeffrey P. Jones, "'Fake' News versus 'Real' News as Sources of Political Information: The Daily Show and Postmodern Political Reality," in *Politicotainment: Television's Take on the Real*, ed. Kristina Riegert (New York: Peter Lang, 2007), 129.

2. Robert T. Tally, "I Am the Mainstream Media (and So Can You!)," in *The Stewart/Colbert Effect: Essays on the Real Impacts of Fake News*, ed. Amarnath Amarasingam (Jefferson, NC: McFarland, 2011), 162.

3. Baym, "The Daily Show," 261.

4. Tally, "I Am," 151.

5. Julia R. Fox, Glory Koloen, and Volkan Sahin, "No Joke: A Comparison of Substance in *The Daily Show* with Jon Stewart and Broadcast Network Television Coverage of the 2004 Presidential Election Campaign," *Journal of Broadcasting & Electronic Media* 51, no. 2 (2007): 213; Jones, "Fake News," 129.

6. Fox, Koloen, and Sahin, "No Joke," 220.

7. "Journalism, Satire, or Just Laughs? *The Daily Show with Jon Stewart* Examined," Pew Research Center, May 8, 2008, http://www.journalism.org/2008/05/08/journalism-satire-or-just-laughs-the-daily-show-with-jon-stewart-examined/.

8. "Last Week Tonight with John Oliver (HBO)," Peabody Awards, accessed February 10, 2018, http://www.peabodyawards.com/award-profile/last-week-tonight-with-john-oliver.

9. Brian Hiatt, "John Oliver: Can the Sharpest Voice on TV Win the War on Trump?" *Rolling Stone*, February 23–March 9, 2017, 56.

10. Kirsten A. Johnson, "Gatekeeping in the Digital Age: A New Model for a Post-Objective World," in *News with a View: Essays on the Eclipse of Objectivity in Modern Journalism*, eds. Burton St. John III and Kirsten A. Johnson (Jefferson, NC: McFarland, 2012), 232; Jeffrey Scheuer, *The Big Picture: Why Democracies Need Journalistic Excellence* (New York: Routledge, 2008), 68.

11. Hiatt, "John Oliver," 34.

12. Herbert J. Gans, *Deciding What's News: A Study of CBS Evening News, NBC Nightly News, Newsweek and Time* (New York: Vintage Books, 1980), 306; Scheuer, "The Big Picture," 78.

13. Scheuer, "The Big Picture," 70.

14. Gans, "Deciding What's News," 306; Steven Maras, *Objectivity in Journalism* (Cambridge: Polity Press, 2013), 82; Scheuer, "The Big Picture," 65.

15. Matthew M. Hurley, Daniel C. Dennett, and Reginald B. Adams, Jr., *Inside Jokes: Using Humor to Reverse-Engineer the Mind* (Cambridge, MA: The MIT Press, 2011), 17.

16. Hurley, Dennett, and Adams, "Inside Jokes," 31.

17. Hurley, Dennett, and Adams, "Inside Jokes," 101.

18. Hurley, Dennett, and Adams, "Inside Jokes," 216.

19. Charles R. Gruner, "Wit and Humor in Mass Communication," in *Humor and Laughter: Theory, Research, and Applications*, eds. Antony J. Chapman and Hugh C. Foot (London: John Wiley & Sons, 1976), 287.

20. Hurley, Dennett, and Adams, "Inside Jokes," 301.

21. Baym, "The Daily Show," 262.

22. Aaron McKain, "Not Necessarily Not the News: Gatekeeping, Remediation, and *The Daily Show*," *The Journal of American Culture* 28, no. 4 (2005): 425.

23. Matt Carlson and Jason Peifer, "The Impudence of Being Earnest: Jon Stewart and the Boundaries of Discursive Responsibility," *Journal of Communication* 63, no. 2 (2013): 339.

24. McKain, "Not Necessarily," 427.

25. Fox, Koloen, and Sahin, "No Joke," 218–19.

26. Hurley, Dennett, and Adams, "Inside Jokes," 272.

27. Stephen Lacy, Daniel Riffe, and Quint Randle, "Sample Size in Multi-Year Content Analyses of Monthly Consumer Magazines," *Journalism and Mass Communication Quarterly* 75, no. 2 (Summer 1998): 410; Daniel Riffe, Stephen Lacy, and Fred Fico, *Analyzing Media Messages: Using Quantitative Content Analysis in Research* (Mahwah, NJ: Lawrence Erlbaum Associates, Inc., 1998).

28. Julia R. Fox, James R. Angelini, and Christopher Goble, "Hype versus Substance in Network Television Coverage of Presidential Election Campaigns," *Journalism and Mass Communication Quarterly* 82, no. 1 (Spring 2005): 102; Fox, Koloen, and Sahin, "No Joke," 219–20; Julia R. Fox and Byungho Park, "The 'I' of Embedded Reporting: An Analysis of CNN Coverage of the 'Shock and Awe' Campaign," *Journal of Broadcasting & Electronic Media* 50, no. 1 (2006): 44.

29. Fox, Angelini, and Goble, "Hype versus Substance," 102; Fox, Koloen, and Sahin, "No Joke," 220.

30. Lacy, Riffe, and Randle, "Sample Size," 417.

31. McKain, "Not Necessarily," 418.

32. Robert W. McChesney, "Foreword," in *The Stewart/Colbert Effect: Essays on the Real Impacts of Fake News*, ed. Amarnath Amarasingam (Jefferson, NC: McFarland, 2011), 2.

33. Daniel C. Hallin, "Cartography, Community, and the Cold War," in *Reading the News*, eds. Robert Karl Manoff and Michael Schudson (New York: Pantheon,

1987), 131; Michael Schudson, "Deadlines, Datelines, and History," in *Reading the News*, eds. Robert Karl Manoff and Michael Schudson (New York: Pantheon, 1987), 80; Leon V. Sigal, "Sources Make the News," in *Reading the News*, eds. Robert Karl Manoff and Michael Schudson (New York: Pantheon, 1987), 16.

34. James Aucoin, "Investigative Reporting," in *History of the Mass Media in the United States*, ed. Margaret A. Blanchard (Chicago: Fitzroy Dearborn Publishers, 1998), 282; Gerry Lanosga, "A New Model of Objectivity: Investigative Reporting in the Twentieth Century," in *News with a View: Essays on the Eclipse of Objectivity in Modern Journalism*, ed. Burton St. John III and Kirsten A. Johnson (Jefferson, NC: McFarland, 2012), 53.

35. Aucoin, "Investigative Reporting," 281–282; Edwin Diamond, *Good News, Bad News* (Cambridge, MA: The MIT Press, 1980) 234, 239; Lanosga, "A New Model," 48, 52.

36. Lanosga, "A New Model," 52.

37. Hiatt, "John Oliver," 56.

38. Julia R. Fox, "Wise Fools: Jon Stewart and Stephen Colbert as Modern-Day Jesters in the American Court," in *The Stewart/Colbert Effect: Essays on the Real Impacts of Fake News*, ed. Amarnath Amarasingam (Jefferson, NC: McFarland, 2011), 136.

39. Asa Berger, *An Anatomy of Humor* (New Brunswick, NJ: Transaction Publishers, 1993), 49; Murray S. Davis, *What's So Funny? The Comic Conception of Culture and Society* (Chicago: The University of Chicago Press, 1993), 157; Gruner, "Wit and Humor," 288; Charles R. Gruner, *Understanding Laughter: The Workings of Wit & Humor* (Chicago: Nelson-Hall, 1978), 125; Gilbert Highet, *The Anatomy of Satire* (Princeton, NJ: Princeton University Press, 1962), 233; Rod A. Martin, *The Psychology of Humor: An Integrative Approach* (Burlington, MA: Elsevier Academic Press, 2007), 13.

40. Carlin Romano, "The Grisly Truth About Bare Facts," in *Reading the News*, eds. Robert Karl Manoff and Michael Schudson (New York: Pantheon, 1987), 74.

41. Gruner, "Wit and Humor," 289.

42. Amy B. Becker and Leticia Bode, "Satire as a Source for Learning? The Differential Impact of News versus Satire Exposure on Net Neutrality Knowledge Gain," *Information, Communication & Society* 21, no. 4 (2018): 612; Julia R. Fox and Edo Steinberg, "Comedic News," in *Oxford Bibliographies in Communication*, ed. Patricia Moy (New York: Oxford University Press, 2017).

43. Hiatt, "John Oliver," 56.

44. Annie Lang, "Dynamic Human-Centered Communication Systems Theory," *The Information Society* 30 (2014): 67.

45. Lang, "Dynamic Human-Centered," 67, 68; Annie Lang, "Using the Limited Capacity Model of Motivated Mediated Message Processing to Design Effective Cancer Communication Messages," *Journal of Communication* 56 supplement (2006): S59.

46. Lang, "Dynamic Human-Centered," 68; Lang, "Using the Limited," S62.

47. Lang, "Using the Limited," S61.

48. Hurley, Dennett, and Adams, "Inside Jokes," 119, 120.

49. Lang, "Dynamic Human-Centered," 68; Lang, "Using the Limited," S61, S62.

REFERENCES

Amarasingam, Amarnath, ed. *The Stewart/Colbert Effect: Essays on the Real Impacts of Fake News*. Jefferson, NC: McFarland, 2011.

Aucoin, James. "Investigative Reporting." In *History of the Mass Media in the United States*, edited by Margaret A. Blanchard, 281–82. Chicago: Fitzroy Dearborn Publishers, 1998.

Baym, Geoffrey. "The Daily Show: Discursive Integration and the Reinvention of Political Journalism." *Political Communication* 22 (2005): 259–76.

Becker, Amy B., and Leticia Bode. "Satire as a Source for Learning? The Differential Impact of News versus Satire Exposure on Net Neutrality Knowledge Gain." *Information, Communication & Society* 21, no. 4 (2018): 612–25. doi:10.1080/1369118X.2017.1301517.

Berger, Asa. *An Anatomy of Humor*. New Brunswick, NJ: Transaction Publishers, 1993.

Carlson, Matt, and Jason Peifer. "The Impudence of Being Earnest: Jon Stewart and the Boundaries of Discursive Responsibility." *Journal of Communication* 63, no. 2 (2013): 333–50.

Davis, Murray S. *What's So Funny? The Comic Conception of Culture and Society*. Chicago: The University of Chicago Press, 1993.

Diamond, Edwin. *Good News, Bad News*. Cambridge, MA: The MIT Press, 1980.

Fox, Julia R. "Wise Fools: Jon Stewart and Stephen Colbert as Modern-Day Jesters in the American Court." In *The Stewart/Colbert Effect: Essays on the Real Impacts of Fake News*, edited by Amarnath Amarasingam, 136–48. Jefferson, NC: McFarland, 2011.

Fox, Julia R., James R. Angelini, and Christopher Goble. "Hype versus Substance in Network Television Coverage of Presidential Election Campaigns." *Journalism and Mass Communication Quarterly* 82, no. 1 (2005): 97–109.

Fox, Julia R., Glory Koloen, and Volkan Sahin. "No Joke: A Comparison of Substance in *The Daily Show with Jon Stewart* and Broadcast Network Television Coverage of the 2004 Presidential Election Campaign." *Journal of Broadcasting & Electronic Media* 51, no. 2 (2007): 213–27.

Fox, Julia R., and Byungho Park. "The 'I' of Embedded Reporting: An Analysis of CNN Coverage of the 'Shock and Awe' Campaign." *Journal of Broadcasting & Electronic Media* 50, no. 1 (2006): 36–51.

Fox, Julia R., and Edo Steinberg. "Comedic News." In *Oxford Bibliographies in Communication*, edited by Patricia Moy. New York: Oxford University Press, 2017.

Gans, Herbert. *Deciding What's News: A Study of CBS Evening News, NBC Nightly News, Newsweek and Time*. New York: Vintage Books, 1980.

Gruner, Charles R. "Wit and Humor in Mass Communication." In *Humour and Laughter: Theory, Research, and Applications*, edited by Antony J. Chapman and Hugh C. Foot, 287–311. London: John Wiley & Sons, 1976.

Gruner, Charles R. *Understanding Laughter: The Workings of Wit & Humor*. Chicago: Nelson-Hall, 1978.

Hallin, Daniel C. "Cartography, Community, and the Cold War." In *Reading the News*, edited by Robert Karl Manoff and Michael Schudson, 109–45. New York: Pantheon, 1987.

Hiatt, Brian. "John Oliver: Can the Sharpest Voice on TV Win the War on Trump?" *Rolling Stone*, February 23–March 9, 2017.

Highet, Gilbert. *The Anatomy of Satire*. Princeton, NJ: Princeton University Press, 1962.

Hurley, Matthew M., Daniel C. Dennett, and Reginald B. Adams, Jr. *Inside Jokes: Using Humor to Reverse-Engineer the Mind*. Cambridge, MA: The MIT Press, 2011.

Johnson, Kirsten A. "Gatekeeping in the Digital Age: A New Model for a Post-Objective World." In *News with a View: Essays on the Eclipse of Objectivity in Modern Journalism*, edited by Burton St. John III and Kirsten A. Johnson, 222–37. Jefferson, NC: McFarland, 2012.

Jones, Jeffrey P. "'Fake' News versus 'Real' News as Sources of Political Information: *The Daily Show* and Postmodern Political Reality." In *Politicotainment: Television's Take on the Real*, edited by Kristina Riegert, 129–49. New York: Peter Lang, 2007.

Lacy, Stephen, Daniel Riffe, and Quint Randle. "Sample Size in Multi-Year Content Analyses of Monthly Consumer Magazines." *Journalism and Mass Communication Quarterly* 75, no. 2 (Summer 1998): 408–17.

Lang, Annie. "Using the Limited Capacity Model of Motivated Mediated Message Processing to Design Effective Cancer Communication Messages." *Journal of Communication* 56 supplement (2006): S57–S80.

Lang, Annie. "Dynamic Human-Centered Communication Systems Theory." *The Information Society* 30 (2014): 60–70.

Lanosga, Gerry. "A New Model of Objectivity: Investigative Reporting in the Twentieth Century." In *News with a View: Essays on the Eclipse of Objectivity in Modern Journalism*, edited by Burton St. John III and Kirsten A. Johnson, 42–57. Jefferson, NC: McFarland, 2012.

Maras, Steven. *Objectivity in Journalism*. Cambridge: Polity Press, 2013.

Martin, Rod A. *The Psychology of Humor: An Integrative Approach*. Burlington, MA: Elsevier Academic Press, 2007.

McChesney, Robert W. "Foreword." In *The Stewart/Colbert Effect: Essays on the Real Impacts of Fake News*, edited by Amarnath Amarasingam, 1–2. Jefferson, NC: McFarland, 2011.

McKain, Aaron. "Not Necessarily Not the News: Gatekeeping, Remediation, and *The Daily Show*." *The Journal of American Culture* 28, no. 4 (2005): 415–30.

Peabody Awards. "Last Week Tonight with John Oliver (HBO)." Accessed February 10, 2018. http://www.peabodyawards.com/award-profile/last-week-tonight-with-john-oliver.

Pew Research Center. "Journalism, Satire, or Just Laughs? *The Daily Show with Jon Stewart* Examined." May 8, 2008. http://www.journalism.org/2008/05/08/journalism-satire-or-just-laughs-the-daily-show-with-jon-stewart-examined/.

Riffe, Daniel, Stephen Lacy, and Fred Fico. *Analyzing Media Messages: Using Quantitative Content Analysis in Research*. Mahwah, NJ: Lawrence Erlbaum Associates, 1998.

Romano, Carlin. "The Grisly Truth about Bare Facts." In *Reading the News*, edited by Robert Karl Manoff and Michael Schudson, 38–78. New York: Pantheon, 1987.

Scheuer, Jeffrey. *The Big Picture: Why Democracies Need Journalistic Excellence*. New York: Routledge, 2008.

Schudson, Michael. "Deadlines, Datelines, and History." In *Reading the News*, edited by Robert Karl Manoff and Michael Schudson, 79–108. New York: Pantheon, 1987.

Sigal, Leon V. "Sources Make the News." In *Reading the News*, edited by Robert Karl Manoff and Michael Schudson, 9–37. New York: Pantheon, 1987.

Tally, Robert T. "I Am the Mainstream Media (and So Can You!)." In *The Stewart/ Colbert Effect: Essays on the Real Impacts of Fake News*, edited by Amarnath Amarasingam, 149–63. Jefferson, NC: McFarland, 2011.

Chapter 3

Partisan Trends in Late Night Humor

S. Robert Lichter and Stephen J. Farnsworth

The 2016 election drew public attention to long-standing acrimony between late-night talk show hosts and Republican politicians. Exhibit A is the extent to which Donald Trump became the go-to target for late-night talk show comedians. But the profusion of Trump jokes can be viewed in the context of what many Republicans see as a long-term tilt against them on these shows. This chapter examines the Trump factor in political humor as an exaggerated version of previous partisan trends in late-night humor. Following a qualitative historical overview of political humor on late-night talk shows, we examine the results of content analyses of jokes told during the 2016 elections. The results are compared with jokes about presidential nominees from 1992 to 2012.

THE CHANGING POLITICS OF LATE-NIGHT HUMOR

On September 19, 2017, in his opening monologue for ABC's *Jimmy Kimmel Live!*, Kimmel departed from the usual string of jokes about celebrities, current events, and public affairs to issue a point-by-point criticism of health care insurance legislation pending in Congress. He concluded by exhorting his studio and television audience to actively lobby against the legislation ("So if this bill isn't good enough for you, call your congressperson."). *Politico* later calculated that Kimmel devoted twenty-four minutes of airtime in three nights to defeating the Republican bill designed to repeal the Affordable Care Act.[1]

Heard in its entirety, Kimmel's commentary sounds considerably more like stump speeches than a laugh fest. In any event, Kimmel's engagement with health care legislation illustrates the extent to which the juncture of news and entertainment in politics can quickly expand to encompass the juncture of political advocacy and entertainment. In fact, a *Newsweek* story asserted that Kimmel "has proved to be the nation's most effective critic of the Graham-Cassidy bill that would repeal and replace the Affordable Care Act."[2]

Of course, news reports are hardly reliable accounts of media effects. But they are an indicator of agenda setting and, perhaps, priming, as Kimmel linked his own infant son's need for expensive heart surgery to such problems as coverage of preexisting conditions and lifetime caps on coverage. All this also fed into a media narrative about the politicization of late-night entertainment, in particular the frequent focus of comedians on Donald Trump and his administration. As former *The New York Times* writer and historian of late-night entertainment Bill Carter put it, "There's no example of any kind of sustained attack like this on a politician. . . . There's a horde of writers writing jokes about Donald Trump every single night."[3]

In fact, late-night hosts are now being criticized not for being too partisan but for not being partisan enough. This happened to Jimmy Fallon during the 2016 general election, after he had Trump as a guest and did a routine that culminated with him tousling Trump's hair. After a deluge of articles and social media posts that accused him of "normalizing" Trump, a contrite Fallon insisted that he had intended not to "humanize" his guest but to "minimize" him.[4]

Once again, however, these themes are based on the perceptions of journalists and pundits generalizing from particular incidents, rather than any systematic study. Moreover, it is not obvious that the animus toward Trump is in fact historically unprecedented. Previous frequent targets of late-night humor include Bill Clinton, Dan Quayle, and Sarah Palin. Nevertheless, Trump has since blasted talk show hosts with all the fervor that he applies to denouncing the news media. He has gone so far as to demand equal time to balance the comedians' "one-sided" treatment of his administration.[5]

Of course, Trump is the latest in a long line of media bashers on the right side of the political spectrum. Republicans and conservatives, for whom the "liberal news media" is a long-standing staple of their rhetorical repertoire, have long complained about its counterpart among Hollywood liberals, including the hosts of late-night talk shows.[6] But the criticisms were mostly intermittent and episodic, as the following brief historical survey of politics on late-night talk shows illustrates. (Note: this overview excludes *Saturday Night Live*, a weekly variety show built around comedy sketches that often last several minutes, hence a different genre from the nightly talk shows with their relatively brief politically oriented opening monologues that often address a number of potentially humorous topics).

HISTORICAL OVERVIEW

The genre of late-night talk became institutionalized under the direction of Johnny Carson. His *Tonight Show* on NBC dominated the ratings competition from 1962 until his retirement three decades later in 1992. Operating in an environment with little competition, Carson aimed for the great middle of the national audience, with monologues and guests that were for the most part comforting and inoffensive. As noted film director Billy Wilder put it, "He's the cream of middle-class elegance. . . . He has captivated the American bourgeoisie without ever offending the highbrows, and he has never said anything that wasn't liberal or progressive."[7]

Carson included political material in his monologues, but usually in a way that would not offend most viewers. This meant making fun of politicians who were embroiled in scandals and those who committed gaffes. His centrism and light touch with politics left it to his various competitors to tap into the underserved audience for more contentious or ideological material. These competitors included Merv Griffin and Dick Cavett, who brought in political material and controversial guests on the Vietnam War. But they were always a sidelight to Carson.

The competition to succeed Carson ended with comedian Jay Leno inheriting *The Tonight Show*. The unhappy loser was David Letterman, whose *Late Show* had long followed Carson's. He moved to CBS to directly compete with Leno, an arrangement that lasted nearly a quarter century, until Leno retired in 2014 and Letterman followed in 2015. They set the tone for late-night humor, despite competition at various times from Conan O'Brien, Arsenio Hall, Bill Maher, and others. The great exception, discussed below, was the satirical "fake news" format developed by Jon Stewart on Comedy Central.

Leno was the closest match of his generation to Carson, relying on old-fashioned zingers and one-liners that would get a laugh in Middle America but not necessarily among urban hipsters. However, it was Leno who trended toward using politics as a central topic of his routines. In 1993, when Leno and Letterman went head-to-head for the first time, Leno used nearly twice as much political material as his rival, by 1,535 to 883 jokes.[8] But his material was relatively low key, and he was rarely accused of partisanship.

Eventually, Republican politicians and conservative commentators began to adopt Leno as their favorite late-night comedian. In fact, a *Breitbart* reporter labeled him "the last fair, balanced late-night host."[9] The politics of Hollywood being what they are, Leno found it necessary to protest publicly that he was in fact a died in the wool liberal—a Michael Moore fan whose joke writers include no Republicans. Specifically, "I'm not conservative. I've never voted that way in my life."[10] However, compared to some of the current highly political late-night entrants, from Stephen Colbert and Samantha Bee to John Oliver and Bill Maher, it's easy to see why conservatives would have looked to Leno for old-fashioned, middle of the road humor.

By contrast, David Letterman was widely regarded as apolitical until late in his tenure. The transformation appears to have occurred in the wake of the tumultuous 2008 presidential election.[11] This was the campaign in which Republican nominee Sen. John McCain made the mistake of cancelling his *Late Show* appearance at the last minute. An outraged Letterman fought back through his monologues, with a profusion of ridicule that eventually brought the abashed candidate back on the show, where he delivered an abject apology, admitting to his inquisitor, "I screwed up." This incident produced Letterman's famous pronouncement, "the road to the White House runs right through me!" That observation may be hyperbole, but the exchange certainly illustrates the changing balance of power between politicians and comedians.[12]

Letterman's highly visible personal feuds with politicians may have contributed to the politicization of Letterman's monologues as his career progressed.[13] That observation is supported by Center for Media and Public Affairs (CMPA) data showing that Letterman's political joke totals jumped from 1,208 in 2007 to 3,187 in 2008 and 3,206 in 2009. By 2013, Letterman was using his "Stooge of the Night" routine to wage war against the Republican Congress for its opposition to gun control. The segments showed images of senators opposing tougher background checks in gun purchases with superimposed graphics showing how much money they had received from progun groups.

Even as Leno and Letterman were dominating late-night comedy on the broadcast network stage, the action was moving to the cable network Comedy Central. In 1999, Jon Stewart began to transform *The Daily Show* into a new format for political humor, which the host was proud to call "fake news." Put simply, Stewart brought satire to late-night talk. In addition, the show was more narrowly focused on the world of politics and public affairs than any other television talk show. The nightly skewering of politicians and the journalists who covered them found a strong audience among younger viewers, in sharp contrast to the graying audience for Leno and Letterman on NBC and CBS respectively.

The Daily Show benefited early on from some lucky timing. A continuing feature satirized the foibles of the candidates and the campaign news throughout the 2000 elections under the rubric "Indecision 2000." As it happened, the 2000 presidential election featured the greatest indecision in modern American politics, helping to build an audience for the show right up until the decision was made, not by the voters but by the Supreme Court, on December 12. Stewart also became personally involved in occasional political causes. For example, he helped push through the Senate a bill to provide health care for 9/11 early responders, by bludgeoning recalcitrant senators with a barrage of jokes (and by inviting some of the workers onto his show). More generally, Stewart was widely regarded as a valued social and political critic and even a legitimate journalist. In fact, a Pew Center poll found that the public rated him as one of the most highly respected journalists in America.[14] His work was a major factor in getting politicians and the public alike to take late-night humor as a valuable source of information about politics.

In 2005 *The Daily Show* produced a highly successful spinoff called *The Colbert Report*. Stephen Colbert, who functioned as a kind of fake news correspondent on *The Daily Show*, adopted the persona of a loud-mouthed right-wing pundit, at least partly modeled on such Fox News personalities as Bill O'Reilly and Glenn Beck. He became involved in real world national politics by attempting to run a parody presidential campaign (running as both a Democrat and a Republican) and later by forming a super-PAC, which raised over a million dollars. Some of the money was used to air spoof campaign ads. Colbert also teamed up with Stewart to stage a "Rally to Restore Sanity and/or Fear," which drew over two hundred thousand people to the National Mall in Washington, DC, for the avowed cause of mobilizing reason and moderation against partisanship and extremism. Colbert also testified before a Congressional subcommittee on the plight of migrant workers.

Meanwhile, more traditional and less visible hosts came and went, mostly without making a long-term mark politically with their monologues. They have included, among others, Arsenio Hall, forever remembered for helping revive the scandal-scarred presidential candidacy of Bill Clinton; Conan O'Brien, whose numerous late-night slots included a brief and controversial stint as Jay Leno's would-be successor on *The Tonight Show*; and Seth Meyers, best known for his association with *Saturday Night Live* before he took over *The Late Show* in 2014. One decidedly political voice belongs to Bill Maher, who proudly wears his liberalism on his sleeve. His *Politically Incorrect* talk show on ABC more than lived up to its name when, in the wake of the 9/11 attacks, he defended the terrorists against charges of cowardice. Maher argued instead that, "we have been the cowards, lobbing cruise missiles from 2,000 miles away. That's cowardly."[15] The comment cost his show acrimony and advertisers, and it was canceled at the end of the season. The next season, however, it was picked up by HBO as a weekly talk show titled, *Real Time with Bill Maher*. It has remained on HBO's evening schedule ever since, where he was joined in 2014 by "Daily Show" alumnus John Oliver, who also featured heavily political material.

Two other voices with broadcast network slots honored political material mostly in the breach, even as they became more prominent in recent years— Jimmy Kimmel and Jimmy Fallon. Until recently Kimmel has been known for his light material and focus on celebrities. Fallon was a relative latecomer to the late-night talk scene, taking over *Late Night* in 2009. Five years later, following Jay Leno's retirement, he graduated to *The Tonight Show*. If anything, Fallon's lack of interest in monologues featuring political material exceeded that of Kimmel. Fallon specialized in creating a genial milieu with devices that include music, dance, impersonations, and games.

Finally, after two decades of late-night talk show dominance by Jay Leno and David Letterman, and fifteen years after the emergence of Jon Stewart as a "fake news" host, there was a remarkable shuffling of the deck that in rapid succession produced new hosts of *The Tonight Show*, *Late Night*, and *The Daily Show*. In addition, ABC moved up the starting time of *Jimmy Kimmel Live* to allow Kimmel to compete directly with the flagship talk shows on CBS and NBC. In 2014, Leno retired and Jimmy Fallon took over *The Tonight Show*. In May 2015, Letterman retired and Stephen Colbert took over *Late Night*, while *The Colbert Report* ceased production. In August of the same year Stewart retired, and South African Trevor Noah took over *The Daily Show* a month later. So, three of the four leading talk shows had new hosts in place just in time for the 2016 presidential election to begin. It is to that event, and its role in late-night humor, that we now turn.

METHOD

In the empirical section of this chapter, we report on results drawn from a content analysis conducted by CMPA at George Mason University. This study examined 5,862 jokes aired by leading late-night comics during the 2016 presidential elections. This included 2,854 jokes aired about all presidential candidates during the preseason and primary campaign from September 1, 2015, through April 30, 2016 (by which time it had become clear which candidates were going to be the Republican and Democratic presidential nominees), as well as 3,008 jokes that focused on the two presidential nominees between September 1, 2015, and November 11, 2016, including the immediate aftermath of the general election.

The jokes were drawn from the opening monologues of Jimmy Fallon (*The Tonight Show* on NBC), Stephen Colbert (*The Late Show* on CBS), Jimmy Kimmel (*Jimmy Kimmel Live!* on ABC), and *The Daily Show*, the Comedy Central program with new host Trevor Noah. The study of the latter began on September 28, 2015, when Noah formally took over from Jon Stewart. The hosts of the shows on the three broadcast networks had the largest audiences of any late-night talk shows, while *The Daily Show* has been widely influential and especially popular with young adults. In addition, we drew on election year data from the CMPA data base, which includes jokes told by hosts on popular late-night TV shows in every election year from

1992 through 2012. This allowed comparisons of the treatment of Donald Trump and Hillary Clinton with that of other Democratic and Republican nominees across the six most recent presidential election campaigns. All coding was done by students who were trained by CMPA staff members. Coders had to attain a level of reliability of at least 80 percent agreement, and their coding continued to be spot checked throughout the analysis.

RESULTS

Donald Trump established himself as the comedians' primary target early in the campaign preseason, over a year before Election Day. Thus, the analysis of jokes involving the struggle for the party nominations covers the final four months of 2015 and the first four months of 2016, a period that included the rise and fall of several candidacies, especially in the crowded GOP field.

Throughout this eight-month period, early establishment favorites such as Jeb Bush performed poorly and became the butt of many jokes for being losers, while new faces like Ben Carson and Bernie Sanders emerged as interesting newcomers to national campaigns. But the overriding event was the emergence of Donald Trump, who was previously regarded by most journalists and politicians alike as a fringe figure not to be taken seriously. That lasted until he began to dominate the GOP debates and was rewarded with a rise in popularity with Republican party members and primary voters.

As Table 3.1 shows, Trump not only attracted more jokes (1,105) than any other candidate of either party, he was featured in nearly twice as many punch lines as Democratic favorite Hillary Clinton (314) and her main challenger Bernie Sanders (302) combined. He was also the target of more jokes than the second and third ranked Republicans combined, not to mention attracting more than six times as many jokes as the president of the United States.

Table 3.1   Top Joke Targets, September 2015 to April 2016

Candidate	Number of Jokes
Donald Trump	1105
Hillary Clinton	314
Bernie Sanders	302
Jeb Bush	250
Ben Carson	204
Ted Cruz	196
Barack Obama	171
Marco Rubio	90
Chris Christie	83
John Kasich	52

Once the field narrowed to the two party nominees, one might have expected a more equal distribution of jokes. After all, Democratic nominee Hillary Clinton offered a wealth of material from her past roles as First Lady, Senator, and Secretary of State, as well as an ongoing scandal involving her use of a private email server to conduct official business. Yet Trump proved just as dominant in the head-to-head joke race as he was in the crowded contest that preceded the party conventions. As Table 3.2 shows, he was targeted by more than three out of every four jokes (76 to 24% for Clinton) directed at the two nominees from the party convention weeks through Election Day.

Notably, this general election disparity followed the pattern that was set during the earlier phase of the campaign. To display this pattern, we divided the prenomination period into the preseason, represented by September through December 2015, and the primary and caucus contest period, from January 2016 (when campaigning started to focus heavily on the Iowa caucuses and New Hampshire primary) through April 2016 (by which time both nominating contests had for all intents and purposes been decided).

Table 3.2 also shows that Trump outpaced Clinton in the joke race by 81 to 19 percent during the preseason and 79 to 21 percent during the period of primary races. When combined with the general election findings, this demonstrates that Trump's margin over Clinton in the race for campaign laughingstock varied hardly at all throughout the entire 2016 election. When all three periods are combined, the margin is 78 percent for Trump versus 22 percent for Clinton.

To this point the data confirm Trump's widely accepted status as a figure of ridicule without peer in the 2016 elections. But how does he stack up against his predecessors on the campaign trail? To find out, we turned to CMPA's historical data, which include joke totals from major talk show monologues in presidential election years 1992, 1996, 2000, 2004, 2008, and 2012. The shows are not always the same over such a long period of time, but all six time periods include Leno and Letterman, and all but 2012 include Conan O'Brien. So there is a core of continuity behind the comparisons. A full list of shows that were coded appears in the Appendix.

Table 3.2 Jokes Directed at Trump and Clinton

Time Period	Trump	Clinton	Total Number of Jokes
Prenomination Season (9/1–1/31)	81	19	833
Nomination Season (2/1–7/17)	79	21	1066
General Election Season (7/18–11/11)	76	24	1103
Total (9/1/15–11/11/16)	78	22	3002

Table 3.3 shows the percentage of jokes made about the two major party nominees during election years from 1992 through 2016. (The 2016 data for Trump and Clinton stop shortly after Election Day, on November 11, 2016.) Trump's total of 78 percent of jokes, compared to 22 percent for Hillary Clinton, represents the most one-sided distribution of jokes between the two major party nominees in the entire quarter century. However, Trump was only 1 percent point ahead of Mitt Romney's 77 percent share, compared to Barack Obama's 23 percent, in 2008. The third greatest disparity occurred in 2004, when George W. Bush was targeted by 70 percent of all jokes compared to 30 percent for John Kerry. In descending order, the next biggest difference was the 64 percent of jokes aimed at John McCain, compared to 36 percent for Obama in 2008, followed by George W. Bush's 62 percent versus Al Gore's 38 percent in 2000, Bob Dole's 56 percent compared to Bill Clinton's 44 percent in 1996, and George H. W. Bush's 59 percent versus Clinton's 41 percent in 1992.

Thus, the tilt in jokes about Trump is not so one-sided in historical context as it is relative to other contenders in the 2016 election. The most consistent division was partisan—Republican candidates always attracted substantially more jokes than their Democratic opponents. Moreover, the gap became increasingly great over time, from less than a three-to-two margin in the earliest two elections to more than a three-to-one margin in the most recent two contests. Even Bill Clinton, whose behavior was like catnip to comedians, generated fewer jokes than his GOP opponents in both 1992 and 1996. And there is a limiting factor on Trump's contribution to the partisan trend. With the tilt already up to 77 percent toward the Republican in the previous election, there was simply not much room for an additional increase without the monologues becoming all Trump all the time (as sometimes seemed the case).

Table 3.3   Proportion of Jokes about the Two Presidential Nominees, 1992–2016

Year	Republican	Percentage of Jokes (%)	Democrat	Percentage of Jokes (%)	Total Number of Jokes
1992	Bush	59	Clinton	41	1,033
1996	Dole	56	Clinton	44	1,496
2000	Bush	62	Gore	38	1,451
2004	Bush	70	Kerry	30	1,674
2008	McCain	64	Obama	36	2,126
2012	Romney	77	Obama	23	1,462
2016	Trump	78	Clinton	22	2,329

Note: Totals for 1992–2012 are for entire calendar year in which election took place; totals for 2016 are for January 1 to November 11.

DISCUSSION AND CONCLUSION

This chapter has analyzed the treatment of Donald Trump and other presidential candidates by late-night comedians. Content analysis of jokes about Trump during the 2016 presidential election shows that he far outstripped his competition as a target of late-night jokes. However, historical data show that Trump's dominance as a joke target during the election may be at least partly explained by a long-standing partisan cast to political humor in election years.

The reasons for Trump's predominance in the joke race parallel the reasons that he attracted more news media coverage than any other presidential candidate.[16] He was a new face, at least in the context of electoral politics. But he was also known as an entertainer himself, who gained fame as longtime host of the reality show, *The Apprentice*. In addition he had an outsized personality and a colorful private life that had long provided fodder for the New York City tabloids. Finally, as his campaign progressed, he continued to confound expectations, not least by courting controversy without paying the usual price, and engaging in policies and campaign practices that went beyond the bounds of civility and fair play.

Given his domination of the late-night talk show monologues, it is easy to forget that Trump was following a path previously trodden by every other Republican presidential nominee since 1992. But the surprise election of Trump ensured that partisan politics would continue to generate news to a greater extent than usual. For example, Stephen Colbert scrambled to overcome initial low ratings on *The Late Show* until he shifted to a heavier dose of Trump bashing, after which his ratings soared.[17] And, as noted, Jimmy Kimmel found an unexpected new role for himself as a critic of Trump's policies and those of the Republican Congress. Finally, Trump himself has added criticism of the late-night hosts to his usual condemnation of journalists. For all these reasons, late-night talk shows are likely to remain a source of partisan commentary and criticism long after Trump leaves the White House.

APPENDIX

Shows included in the study:

- 2016: *Tonight Show* (NBC), *Late Show* (CBS), *Jimmy Kimmel Live!* (ABC), *Daily Show* (Comedy Central)
- 2012: *Tonight Show* (NBC), *Late Show* (CBS), *Daily Show* (Comedy Central), *Colbert Report* (Comedy Central)

- 2008: *Tonight Show* (NBC), *Late Show* (CBS), *Daily Show* (Comedy Central), *Colbert Report* (Comedy Central), *Late Night* (NBC)
- 2004: *Tonight Show* (NBC), *Late Show* (CBS), *Daily Show* (Comedy Central), *Late Night* (NBC)
- 2000: *Tonight Show* (NBC), *Late Show* (CBS), *Politically Incorrect* (ABC), *Late Night* (NBC)
- 1996: *Tonight Show* (NBC), *Late Show* (CBS), *Politically Incorrect* (ABC), *Late Night* (NBC)
- 1992: *Tonight Show* (NBC), *Late Show* (CBS), *Arsenio* (Fox)

NOTES

1. Dan Diamond, "Kimmel Tells Viewers: 'We have until Sept. 30' to Stop GOP Health Bill," *Politico*, September 21, 2017, https://www.politico.com/story/2017/09/21/jimmy-kimmel-obamacare-repeal-bill-cassidy-243002.

2. Alexander Nazaryan, "Jimmy Kimmel Is Killing the Health Care Bill, and Delighting His Viewers in the Process," *Newsweek*, September 22, 2017, http://www.newsweek.com/jimmy-kimmel-bill-cassidy-obamacare-republicans-repeal-replace-669309.

3. Quoted in Jim Rutenberg, "Colbert, Kimmel and the Politics of Late Night," *New York Times*, September 24, 2017, https://www.nytimes.com/2017/09/24/business/colbert-kimmel-and-the-politics-of-late-night.html.

4. Travis M. Andrews, "Jimmy Fallon Says People 'have a right to be mad' at His Friendly Hair-Tousling of Trump," *Washington Post*, May 18, 2017, https://www.washingtonpost.com/news/morning-mix/wp/2017/05/18/jimmy-fallon-says-people-have-a-right-to-be-mad-at-his-friendly-hair-tousling-of-trump/?utm_term=.8cf5bb9fe9bb.

5. Associated Press, "Trump Hits Back at Late Night Shows Critical of Republicans," *Boston Globe*, October 7, 2017, https://www.boston.com/news/politics/2017/10/07/trump-hits-back-at-late-night-shows-critical-of-republicans.

6. Alison Dagnes, *A Conservative Walks into a Bar: The Politics of Political Humor* (New York: Palgrave Macmillan, 2012).

7. Quoted in Kenneth Tynan, "Fifteen Years of the Salto Mortale," *The New Yorker*, February 20, 1978.

8. S. Robert Lichter, Jody C Baumgartner, and Jonathan S. Morris, *Politics Is a Joke! How TV Comedians are Remaking Political Life* (Boulder, CO: Westview Press, 2015).

9. Christian Toto, "Goodnight, Jay. Leno last Fair, Balanced Late Night Host," *Breitbart.com*, February 6, 2014, http://www.breitbart.com/big-hollywood/2014/02/06/leno-last-fair-balanced-late-night/.

10. Carl Franzen, "Which Way Does Leno Lean?" *The Atlantic*, September 27, 2009, https://www.theatlantic.com/entertainment/archive/2009/09/which-way-does-leno-lean/348011/.

11. Bill Carter, "Leno Takes a Turn towards the Political," *New York Times*, September 20, 2009, http://www.nytimes.com/2009/09/21/business/media/21letterman.html.

12. Lichter, Baumgartner, and Morris. *Politics Is a Joke!*, 199.

13. Carter, "Leno Takes a Turn towards the Political."

14. Megan Garber, "Shocker of the Day: Stewart (Still) Most Trusted Newscaster in America," *Columbia Journalism Review*, July 23, 2009, http://archives.cjr.org/the_kicker/shocker_of_the_day_stewart_sti.php.

15. Celestine Bohlen, "In New War on Terrorism, Words Are Weapons, too," *New York Times*, September 29, 2001, http://www.nytimes.com/2001/09/29/arts/think-tank-in-new-war-on-terrorism-words-are-weapons-too.html.

16. Thomas E. Patterson, "News Coverage of the 2016 General Election: How the Press Failed the Voters," Shorenstein Center on Media, Politics and Public Policy, Kennedy School of Government, Harvard University. Report dated December 7, 2016. https://shorensteincenter.org/news-coverage-2016-general-election/.

17. John Kolbin, "A Sharp Decline for Jimmy Fallon's 'Tonight Show,'" *New York Times*, November 28, 2017, https://www.nytimes.com/2017/11/28/business/media/jimmy-fallon-tonight-show-ratings-colbert-kimmel-decline.html.

REFERENCES

Andrews, Travis M. "Jimmy Fallon Says People 'have a right to be mad' at His Friendly Hair-Tousling of Trump." *Washington Post*, May 18, 2017. https://www.washingtonpost.com/news/morning-mix/wp/2017/05/18/jimmy-fallon-says-people-have-a-right-to-be-mad-at-his-friendly-hair-tousling-of-trump/?utm_term=.8cf5bb9fe9bb.

Associated Press. "Trump Hits Back at Late Night Shows Critical of Republicans." *Boston Globe*, October 7, 2017. https://www.boston.com/news/politics/2017/10/07/trump-hits-back-at-late-night-shows-critical-of-republicans.

Baumgartner, Jody, and Jonathan S. Morris. "Stoned Slackers or Super Citizens? 'Daily Show' Viewing and Political Engagement of Young Adults." In *The Stewart/Colbert Effect: Essays on the Real Impacts of Fake News*, edited by Amarnath Amarasingam. (Jefferson, NC: McFarland, 2011).

Bohlen, Celestine. "In New War on Terrorism, Words Are Weapons, too." *New York Times*, September 29, 2001. http://www.nytimes.com/2001/09/29/arts/think-tank-in-new-war-on-terrorism-words-are-weapons-too.html.

Campbell, James E. *Polarized: Making Sense of a Divided America*. Princeton, NJ: Princeton University Press, 2016.

Carter, Bill. "Leno Takes a Turn towards the Political." *New York Times*, September 20, 2009. http://www.nytimes.com/2009/09/21/business/media/21letterman.html.

Dagnes, Alison. *A Conservative Walks into a Bar: The Politics of Political Humor*. New York: Palgrave Macmillan, 2012.

Diamond, Dan. "Kimmel Tells Viewers: 'We have until Sept. 30' to Stop GOP Health Bill." *Politico*, September 21, 2017. https://www.politico.com/story/2017/09/21/jimmy-kimmel-obamacare-repeal-bill-cassidy-243002.

Farnsworth, Stephen J., S. Robert Lichter, and Deanne Canieso. "Donald Trump Will Probably be the Most Ridiculed President Ever." *Washington Post,* January 21, 2017. https://www.washingtonpost.com/news/monkey-cage/wp/2017/01/21/donald-trump-will-probably-be-the-most-ridiculed-president-ever/?utm_term=.98d31b3485e9.

Feldman, Lauren, and Dannagal G. Young. "Late-Night Comedy as a Gateway to Traditional News." *Political Communication* 25 (2005): 401–22.

Franzen, Carl. "Which Way Does Leno Lean?" *The Atlantic,* September 27, 2009. https://www.theatlantic.com/entertainment/archive/2009/09/which-way-does-leno-lean/348011/.

Garber, Megan. "Shocker of the Day: Stewart (Still) Most Trusted Newscaster in America." *Columbia Journalism Review,* July 23, 2009. http://archives.cjr.org/the_kicker/shocker_of_the_day_stewart_sti.php.

Kolbin, John. "A Sharp Decline for Jimmy Fallon's 'Tonight Show.'" *New York Times,* November 28, 2017. https://www.nytimes.com/2017/11/28/business/media/jimmy-fallon-tonight-show-ratings-colbert-kimmel-decline.html.

Lichter, S. Robert, Jody C Baumgartner, and Jonathan S. Morris. *Politics Is a Joke! How TV Comedians are Remaking Political Life.* Boulder, CO: Westview Press, 2015.

Nazaryan, Alexander. "Jimmy Kimmel Is Killing the Health Care Bill, and Delighting His Viewers in the Process." *Newsweek,* September 22, 2017. http://www.newsweek.com/jimmy-kimmel-bill-cassidy-obamacare-republicans-repeal-replace-669309.

Patterson, Thomas E. "News Coverage of the 2016 General Election: How the Press Failed the Voters." Shorenstein Center on Media, Politics and Public Policy, Kennedy School of Government, Harvard University. Report dated December 7, 2016. https://shorensteincenter.org/news-coverage-2016-general-election/.

Postman, Neil. *Amusing Ourselves to Death.* New York: Penguin, 1985.

Rutenberg, Jim. "Colbert, Kimmel and the Politics of Late Night." *New York Times,* September 24, 2017. https://www.nytimes.com/2017/09/24/business/colbert-kimmel-and-the-politics-of-late-night.html.

Stromer-Galley, Jennifer. *Presidential Campaigning in the Internet Age.* Oxford: Oxford University Press, 2014.

Toto, Christian. "Goodnight, Jay. Leno last Fair, Balanced Late Night Host." *Breitbart.com,* February 6, 2014. http://www.breitbart.com/big-hollywood/2014/02/06/leno-last-fair-balanced-late-night/.

Tynan, Kenneth. "Fifteen Years of the Salto Mortale." *The New Yorker,* February 20, 1978.

IMPACTING CITIZENSHIP

The Effects of Exposure to Political Comedy on Democratic Engagement

Chapter 4

The Limits of Attitude Change

Political Humor during the 2016 Campaign

Jody C Baumgartner

Much has been made in recent years of the role of political humor, both simple comedy and satire, in public life. Humorists such as Jon Stewart, Stephen Colbert, David Letterman, John Oliver, Samantha Bee, and more, have become household names, in large part because of their politically oriented humor. This was especially true during the 2016 presidential campaign season, when candidates Hillary Clinton and Donald Trump were excoriated nightly by an expanded late-night television cast.

The average citizen might be excused if he or she believed that the constant barrage of jokes directed at the two lowered opinions of each. In fact, a number of individual-level analyses over the years, both experimental and cross-sectional, have shown that most political humor does indeed have a deleterious effect on opinions of the target (more on this below). But is this always the case? Are there circumstances which might mitigate, or immunize the target altogether from, this effect?

This research examines this idea. Experimental analysis reveals that while a comedic video clip portraying Ben Carson lowered evaluations of him immediately prior to the Iowa caucuses in 2016, the same was not true for either Clinton or Trump. Being well-known public figures before the campaign season even began, opinions of each were relatively immune to change as the result of viewing political comedy directed at them. The chapter adds to our understanding of the effects of viewing political humor on attitudes and opinion by suggesting that there are limits to its persuasive power.

REVIEW OF THE LITERATURE

There has been a wealth of scholarship in the past two decades examining the effect that viewing (or reading) political humor may have on the political engagement and understanding of individuals. Avenues of research include humor's effect on cognition (knowledge, learning, and attentiveness to politics), participation and attitudes.[1] Much of this literature has focused on the latter, establishing fairly conclusively that political humor has the power to change attitudes, at least in certain circumstances. In most cases the attitudes in question move in a message-consistent direction.[2]

For example, one very early study found that cartoons moved respondents "like-dislike" responses in a direction consistent with its depiction.[3] Another, not focused on politics, found that other-disparaging humor lowered attitudes toward the target.[4] More recently, Young's research found that low-knowledge viewers of late-night talk shows had lower evaluations of both Al Gore and George W. Bush during the 2000 presidential campaign.[5] Experimental research focused on Bush and John Kerry in 2004 showed that viewership of *The Daily Show* (*TDS*) lowered evaluations of both candidates.[6] Another study showed that *TDS* special coverage of the 2004 Republican convention was far more critical than that of the Democratic convention, and as the result, viewers' evaluations of the Republican candidates Bush and Vice President Dick Cheney were lowered more than for Democrats Kerry and John Edwards.[7] Baumgartner's examination of the effects of animated cartoons targeting 2008 presidential nominees during the nomination season showed lowered evaluations of most.[8]

The pattern here is clear: simple other-disparaging humor seems to lower evaluations of the target of the humor. Exposure to Tina Fey's 2008 impersonations of Sarah Palin on *Saturday Night Live* (*SNL*) lowered evaluations of Palin, particularly among self-identified Republicans.[9] Viewing *TDS* clips targeting Democrats in the House of Representatives lowered opinion about both Democrats and then-Speaker Nancy Pelosi, and this effect was highest among self-identified Democrats.[10] In fact the negative, message-consistent effect of viewing political humor seems to extend beyond perceptions of individuals. Morris and Baumgartner found that *TDS* viewership also lowered opinion about the news media, a frequent target of the program.[11] Humor viewership, it seems, has a message-consistent (primarily negative) effect on perception of its target, whether the target be individual, institution, or policy.[12]

There is some evidence that the effects of viewing political humor may extend beyond the targets themselves as well. In particular, Baumgartner found that viewing candidate-centered humor lowered individuals' overall trust in government itself.[13] Complex satire, which contains both explicit and implicit messages (e.g., *The Colbert Report*), also seems to produce a message-consistent effect on attitudes, with audiences drawn to agree with the explicit message.[14] Although several studies have shown that political knowledge, sophistication, and partisanship can mediate the effects of viewing political humor on attitudes and opinions of the target,[15] viewership of other-disparaging humor has a negative effect on opinions of the target. The only exception to this rule is the case of self-deprecating humor, which serves to raise opinion of the target.[16]

This said, a number of questions remain regarding other-disparaging humor's effect on attitudes. For example, it is as yet unclear exactly why humor has a message-consistent effect on opinion of the target. Many early studies[17] on the persuasiveness of humorous messages focused on the elaboration likelihood model (ELM) of persuasion.[18] This model centers around the idea that messages are processed through either a central (i.e., cognitive) or peripheral (non-cognitive) route. Humorous messages, according to this model, have the power to change attitudes because they are not examined critically, or via the central route,[19] making it more likely receivers will agree. This line of research suggests that critical examination of humorous messages (argument scrutiny) is lowered because the receiver is not motivated to do so. Many maintain that argument scrutiny is lowered as the result of the cognitive effort expended to process the incongruity that is at the core of many jokes.[20] In other words, cognitive effort is diverted away from the argument. Others suggest that attitudes may change in a message-consistent direction as the result of greater liking of the source of the message.[21] It should also be noted that some research based on the ELM suggests that humor actually has little by way of persuasive power because viewers understand that they are hearing a joke.[22] This is known as the discounting cue theory.

Other questions regarding political humor's potential to change attitudes include whether or not the effects of humor are lasting. For example, most research which examines the effects of political humor on attitude change is experimental in nature and measures only short-term effects.[23] One study of aggregate data suggests that political humor, as well as negative news stories, affect opinion of the president on an ongoing basis, but more research is needed in order to clarify these relationships.[24]

Another question is, under what circumstances, if any, might attitudes be resistant to change after viewing political humor? There are at least two reasons to expect that humor's effects on attitudes might be limited in some cases. First, marketing research suggests that humor's effect on attitudes toward various products is stronger for low-involvement products, or those that are inexpensive or represent a low risk to the potential buyer.[25] In context of a presidential election it is not difficult to imagine that people do not view their candidates as "low-involvement" choices.

A second factor that may serve to inoculate attitudes from the persuasive power of humor is knowledge of the target. In their 2006 study of *TDS*'s effect on evaluations of the 2004 presidential candidates, Baumgartner and Morris found that viewership lowered evaluations of a collective index of Kerry and Bush, as well as of Kerry. Importantly, this was not the case for Bush evaluations.[26] Their post-*facto* reasoning for this was that Bush has been president for four years and opinion of him was fairly well-formed. This notion is consistent with market research which suggests that resistance to attitude change is dependent on various factors, including the "importance of the attitude object [and] the amount of knowledge regarding the attitude object."[27] Matthew Baum found that in 2000, those who were less well-informed about candidates Al Gore and George Bush were more susceptible to attitude change.[28]

This latter factor may be relevant in an examination of the effect humor has on presidential candidates during a nomination season, especially in 2016. Many, if not most nominees for their party's presidential nomination were not necessarily household names. In other words, many are unknown to many citizens. All other things being equal, we might therefore expect that humor targeting these lesser-known candidates had a greater effect on individuals' opinion of them. On the other hand, some few candidates were known to most people, which suggests that humor aimed at them might have less of an effect on viewers' evaluations.

Just such a situation prevailed in 2016, making the 2016 presidential nomination season an ideal test case for the idea that humor might have differential effects on evaluations of various presidential candidates based on how much is known about them. Most of the seventeen Republican and four Democratic presidential candidates were relative unknowns. There were three exceptions to this: Hillary Clinton, Jeb Bush, and Donald Trump. Both Clinton and Trump had been in the national spotlight for many years, while Bush enjoyed name recognition as the result of his last name.

To illustrate how well known both of these tiers of candidates were, Table 4.1 shows the percentage of people who selected the generic "don't know" (DK) option in favorability polls taken immediately before the 2016 Iowa caucuses. After this point most candidates become better known as the result of the intense media scrutiny of this first-in-the-nation nomination event. Data were culled from publicly available polls reposted on pollingreport.com. All used variations of the basic favorability question, "Overall, do you have a favorable or unfavorable impression of [CANDIDATE NAME]?"[29]

A variety of response choices were counted as DKs (see column three), but what all have in common is that they were not the "favorable" or "unfavorable" response. There may be a number of reasons why individuals would select one of the DK response choices. This said, it seems safe to assume

Table 4.1 Percentages Selecting "DK" Options on Favorability of Presidential Candidates

	Poll Date	"DK" Response Wording	
Carson			
ABC News/Washington Post	Jan. 6–10, 2016	"No opinion"	16%
CNN/ORC	Dec. 17–21, 2015	"Never heard of," "No opinion"	18
Quinnipiac University	Dec. 16–20, 2015	"Haven't heard enough"	24
Suffolk University/USA Today	Dec. 2–6, 2015	"Never heard of," "Undecided"	19
Mean			*19.3*
Sanders			
Suffolk University/USA Today	Dec. 2–6, 2015	"Never heard of," "Undecided"	22%
CNN/ORC	Dec. 17–21, 2015	"Never heard of," "No opinion"	17
ABC News/Washington Post	Nov. 4–8, 2015	"No opinion"	21
ABC News/Washington Post	Jan. 6–10, 2016	"No opinion"	16
Quinnipiac University	Dec. 16–20, 2015	"Haven't heard enough," "Refused"	29
Mean			*20.8*
Clinton			
Suffolk University/USA Today	Dec. 2–6, 2015	"Undecided"	7%
CNN/ORC	Dec. 17–21, 2015	"Never heard of," "No opinion"	2
Bloomberg Politics	Nov. 15–17, 2015	"Unsure"	6
ABC News/Washington Post	Nov. 4–8, 2015	"No opinion"	3
Quinnipiac University	Dec. 16–20, 2015	"Haven't heard enough," "Refused"	6
Mean			*4.3*
Trump			
Quinnipiac University	Dec. 16–20, 2015	"Haven't heard enough," "Refused"	8%
CNN/ORC	Dec. 17–21, 2015	"Never heard of," "Can't rate,"	3
ABC News/Washington Post	Nov. 4–8, 2015	"Refused"	3
Bloomberg Politics	Nov. 15–17, 2015	"No opinion"	5
Mean			*4.0*

Source: All data from PollingReport.com.

that in many (if not most) cases it was the result of the fact that people may not have heard about the candidate, or heard enough to form an opinion. And in this regard the table illustrates the differences between well-known and lesser-known candidates clearly. Both Ben Carson and Bernie Sanders' DK numbers hover in the 20 percent range. Most other candidates, both Democrat and Republican, have similar numbers. Clinton and Trump's DKs, on the other hand, are approximately 4 percent. Not even Jeb Bush had a similar level of DKs at this stage of the campaign.

The point is that there is a clear separation between top tier, well-known candidates (Clinton and Trump), and virtually all others. This difference, according to some theory, should be reflected in how individuals evaluate each as the result of viewing political comedy. Accordingly, I hypothesize the following:

H1: Viewing political comedy targeting Bernie Sanders and Ben Carson will be associated with lower evaluations of each.

H2: Viewing political comedy targeting Hillary Clinton and Donald Trump will not be associated with evaluations of each.

DATA AND METHODS

To test these propositions, I employed a post-test only experimental design.[30] One group served as the control group, and took a survey without viewing any video clips. Prior to taking the survey, the second group was asked to view a video clip from *SNL* lampooning the first Democratic debate, held on October 13, 2015, and hosted by CNN. The clip, titled "Democratic Debate Cold Open," was posted to YouTube on October 18, 2015.[31] The original clip, featuring cast members impersonating all four Democratic candidates and CNN's Anderson Cooper, ran ten minutes and twenty-three seconds. I edited the clip to shorten it and focus only on Clinton (played by Kate McKinnon), Sanders (Larry David), and Anderson Cooper (Jon Rudnitsky). This edited version was five minutes and forty-six seconds. It portrayed Clinton as a contrived personality, anxious to find a formula for winning, which included making forced pop culture references in order to reach out to younger Sanders supporters. McKinnon's Clinton was also clearly feeling somewhat entitled to the nomination and was quite frustrated by the email scandal surrounding her campaign. Sanders is portrayed as an amiable, yet somewhat confused and grumpy older man, attempting to portray his particular beliefs as obvious common sense.

A third group viewed a clip from *The Tonight Show with Jimmy Fallon* titled "Donald Trump & Ben Carson Watch Democratic Debate" before taking the survey. This clip was originally posted to the Web on September 30, 2015.[32] In this clip Jimmy Fallon plays Donald Trump while David Alan Grier portrays Ben Carson. In the clip, Trump calls Carson to chat while watching the Democratic presidential debate. The clip portrays Carson as subdued and somnolent ("I get four hours of sleep per hour") and somewhat out of touch. Trump is portrayed by Fallon in a fashion similar to the dozens of other Trump impersonations that have emerged in the past few years as a small cottage industry: blustery, not very bright, with a short attention span. The clip ran five minutes and twenty-three seconds.

Both clips were quite popular. As of December 2015, the *SNL* clip had been viewed well over seven million times on YouTube and the Fallon clip over two million times. Both clips were also available for viewing on NBC's official site, Hulu, and any number of other sites which wrote about and linked to each video.

Subjects were recruited from the undergraduate student population of East Carolina University. A total of 22,668 students were sent an email on November 30, 2015, offering them "a chance to be heard" by taking the "2016 ECU Presidential Election Survey." Follow-up emails were sent on November 30 and December 4. The survey was closed on December 15.

A total of 731 individuals responded to the survey, resulting in a meager 3.22 percent response rate. While low, this was hardly surprising given the institutional survey fatigue afflicting university students in the United States. A manipulation check asked respondents to name at least one of the individuals parodied in the clip. Incorrect responses to this question led to the elimination of sixty-three cases. Further eliminating students who were over 24 and under 18 years of age (153) left me with a final "N" of 515: 308 in the control group, 89 in the Democratic clip condition, and 118 in the Republican clip condition.

The dependent variables in this study are various measures that gauge how individuals view political candidates. Respondents were asked, "On a scale of 1 to 10, where 1 is NOT WELL AT ALL, and 10 is EXTREMELY WELL, how well do the following words or phrases describe the following candidates for president?" The four candidates in question were "Democratic candidate Bernie Sanders," "Democratic candidate Hillary Clinton," "Republican candidate Donald Trump," and "Republican candidate Ben Carson." There were a total of twelve characteristics or qualities measured: (1) "Really cares about people like me," (2) "is experienced," (3) "is trustworthy," (4) "is qualified to be president," (5) "is a strong leader," (6) "is knowledgeable about public affairs," (7) "understands the problems of people like me," (8) "is honest," (9) "has integrity," (10) "would do a good job as President," (11) "sticks to his/her core principles and beliefs," and (12) "is an inspiring leader."

The primary independent variable of interest is whether the individual viewed one of the video clips. I also controlled for how much the respondent claimed to have heard about each of the candidates by asking, "How much would you say you have heard about the following candidates for president?" (1= none at all, 2 = hardly any, 3 = some, and 4 = quite a lot). I controlled for partisan identification by asking, "Generally speaking, do you consider yourself a Republican, a Democrat, an independent, or what?" Responses choices included "strong Democrat," "Democrat," "independent," "Republican," "strong Republican," and "neither, or I don't know." Responses were recoded into two dummy variables. "Strong Democrat" and "Democrat" were coded as "1" and all other responses were "0." Similarly "strong Republican" and "Republican," were coded as "1" and all others as "0." "Independent" and "neither, or I don't know" were left as the reference category.

Respondents were also asked, "How much thought have you given to the presidential election that will take place in 2016?" (1 = none at all, 2 = hardly any, 3 = some, and 4 = quite a lot). I measured respondents' level of knowledge of public affairs by creating an index (0–4) of correct responses to the following (multiple choice) questions: "Who is the speaker of the U.S. House of Representatives?," "Which political party controls the majority in the House and Senate of the U.S. Congress?," "Who is the current Secretary of State?," and "Who is the Chief Justice of the U.S. Supreme Court?" Finally, I controlled for race (recoded as 1 = nonwhite, 0 = white), gender (1 = female, 0 = male), and age (as entered by respondent). As can be seen below in Table 4.2, there is little appreciable difference between conditions on the characteristics of the sample.

Table 4.2 Sample and Condition Characteristics

	Condition			
	Control	Democratic Clip	Republican Clip	Total Sample
Race				
White	75.7%	73.0%	75.4%	75.2%
Nonwhite	24.4	27.0	24.6	24.9
Gender				
Female	62.0	65.2	58.5	61.8
Male	38.0	34.8	41.5	38.3
Partisan ID				
Democrat	30.2	29.2	26.3	29.1
Republican	27.9	31.5	32.2	29.5
Age	20.1 (SD=1.47)	20.3 (SD=1.54)	20.36 (SD=1.77)	20.19 (SD=1.56)
Public knowledge	2.39 (SD=1.47)	2.81 (SD=1.33)	2.75 (SD=1.48)	2.54 (SD=1.46)
Though about election	3.41 (SD=.75)	3.37 (SD=.80)	3.39 (SD=.68)	3.40 (SD=.74)

FINDINGS

Table 4.3 shows partial results of regression analyses of the twelve individual candidate traits for each candidate as well of the index scores. For the sake of space, the full tables are omitted. Cell entries first report the results for the video clip condition in each case (the uppermost entry). In the case of non-significant results the entry reads "n.s." Values that are reported are regression coefficients with standard error in parentheses. The second entry in each cell is the adjusted R^2 for each analysis.

The table shows partial support for *H1* and strong support for *H2*. The first hypothesis predicted that viewing video clips targeting Carson and Sanders would be associated with lower evaluations of each. Table 4.3 shows that this was the case in seven of the twelve analyses of the Carson traits, as well as the index score. The evidence here is admittedly not overwhelming, but given that *H1* was not the primary focus of this research, and that previous studies point in the same direction, there seems to be little cause for concern.

Far more interesting—and at first surprising—are the results for Sanders. In four of the twelve analyses, viewing the clip lampooning Sanders was actually associated with higher opinions of him. These include evaluations of how trustworthy and honest respondents thought he was, whether he "has integrity," and how well he "sticks to core principles and beliefs." In hindsight it is probably the case that based on the content of the Sanders clip, *H1* was mis-specified. As noted in the literature review political humor typically has a message-consistent effect on attitudes. In the case of most political comedy and satire, the message is negative.[33]

However, the *SNL* clip did not necessarily paint Sanders in a terribly negative light. Guest host Larry David portrayed the Vermont senator as a "grumpy grandpa," not afraid to say what came to his mind. Not only did David's impersonation rival that of Tina Fey's Sarah Palin in terms of its accuracy (both physically and vocally), but it did so in a manner that positively highlighted the traits and characteristics associated with a loveable and forthright old man. In other words, the *SNL* clip portraying Sanders could probably be classified as having a positive message, and the results of the analyses would be consistent with a hypothesis which predicted a message-consistent effect.

The analyses of the effect the clips had on Trump and Clinton's evaluations are more straightforward and strongly support *H2*. In only one case, the evaluation of Trump's trustworthiness, were evaluations of either significantly associated with viewing the clip targeting each. Index scores for each were similarly unaffected. Difference of means tests also showed no significant change in scores across the two conditions (viewed the clip vs. the control condition). Opinion of each of these well-known public figures seemed to have been fairly well-set and relatively immune to change.

Jody C Baumgartner

Table 4.3 Analysis of Candidate Traits (Video Clip Condition and Adjusted R^2 Scores Only)

	Carson (n=424)	Sanders (n=395)	Clinton (n=395)	Trump (n=424)
Really cares	−.47 (.27)* (Adj. R^2=.25)	n.s. (Adj. R^2=.37)	n.s. (Adj. R^2=.30)	n.s. (Adj. R^2=.26)
Experienced	n.s. (Adj. R^2=.15)	n.s. (Adj. R^2=.30)	n.s. (Adj. R^2=21)	n.s. (Adj. R^2=.14)
Trustworthy	−.69 (.28)** (Adj. R^2=.26)	.51 (.28)* (Adj. R^2=.42)	n.s. (Adj. R^2=32)	−.44 (.26)* (Adj. R^2=.22)
Qualified to be president	n.s. (Adj. R^2=.23)	n.s. (Adj. R^2=.41)	n.s. (Adj. R^2=31)	n.s. (Adj. R^2=.21)
Strong leader	−.54 (.26)** (Adj. R^2=.26)	n.s. (Adj. R^2=.43)	n.s. (Adj. R^2=32)	n.s. (Adj. R^2=.19)
Knowledgeable public affairs	n.s. (Adj. R^2=.25)	n.s. (Adj. R^2=.33)	n.s. (Adj. R^2=25)	n.s. (Adj. R^2=.22)
Understands problems people like me	−.57 (.27)** (Adj. R^2=.28)	.72 (.30)** (Adj. R^2=.39)	n.s. (Adj. R^2=28)	n.s. (Adj. R^2=.24)
Honest	−.66 (.28)** (Adj. R^2=.27)	n.s. (Adj. R^2=.36)	n.s. (Adj. R^2=31)	n.s. (Adj. R^2=.17)
Has integrity	−.68 (.29)** (Adj. R^2=.26)	.52 (.30)* (Adj. R^2=.35)	n.s. (Adj. R^2=32)	n.s. (Adj. R^2=.23)
Would do good job as president	n.s. (Adj. R^2=.28)	n.s. (Adj. R^2=.44)	n.s. (Adj. R^2=35)	n.s. (Adj. R^2=.33)
Sticks to core principles and beliefs	n.s. (Adj. R^2=.22)	.51 (.31)* (Adj. R^2=.26)	n.s. (Adj. R^2=21)	n.s. (Adj. R^2=.12)
Inspiring leader	−.72 (.29)** (Adj. R^2=.29)	n.s. (Adj. R^2=.41)	n.s. (Adj. R^2=28)	n.s. (Adj. R^2=.29)
Index score	−5.88 (2.84)** (Adj. R^2=.30)	n.s. (Adj. R^2=.44)	n.s. (Adj. R^2=.35)	n.s. (Adj. R^2=.39)

* $p<.1$; ** $p<.05$.

Perusing the adjusted R^2 scores for the analyses suggests that on the whole the models were fairly well specified. Only five analyses, four for Trump and one for Carson, resulted in scores below .20, while five (all for Sanders) were above .40. The remainder fell between these two values. It is worth noting that a few of the other variables performed as might have been expected. Partisan identification, both Republican and Democrat, was significant and in the expected direction, in all but one of the fifty-two analyses. Having heard about the candidate was associated with positive evaluations in 67 percent of Clinton, 75 percent of Carson, and 100 percent of the Sanders analyses. Unsurprisingly, youth was associated with support for Sanders, but so was lack of public knowledge. Clinton's evaluations were positively associated with females in 67 percent of the analyses, while 83 percent of Trump's were associated with males. Race was similarly predictable in the case of Trump and Clinton. A full 100 percent of the Trump analyses were associated with whites, while 92 percent of Clinton's were associated with nonwhites. What was somewhat unexpected was the fact that in 100 percent of the Carson analyses whites were associated with positive evaluations of the candidate.

DISCUSSION

In one important and obvious respect this chapter is unusual. In particular, it is relatively rare for a research project to hypothesize and highlight null results, which is precisely what this essay has done. However, in context of previous research into the effects of political humor on attitudes, this chapter makes an important contribution. Under certain circumstances various attitudes might be immune or resistant to the persuasive power of political humor. This proved to be true in the cases of evaluations of Hillary Clinton and Donald Trump *prior* to the start of the 2016 nomination season. It was probably the case that most people, even the younger citizens who partook in the experiment, already had fairly well-formed opinions of both of these individuals. Both, after all, have been prominent in public life for decades. These findings are consistent with earlier studies by Baum, and Baumgartner and Morris, as well as other marketing research, which found that prior knowledge of the target of the humor affects susceptibility to attitude change.[34]

This chapter has also highlighted an important aspect of research into the effects of viewing political humor, namely, to carefully consider the content. While some attempt has been made to classify political humor in recent years,[35] most fall short in one respect or another with regards to their utility in predicting attitudinal effects of viewing. In the case of this research, the assumption that all political comedy and satire should be conceptualized as negative or attack humor proved to be too facile. In turn, this led to the incorrect prediction that viewing the Sanders impersonation by Larry David would lower evaluations of Sanders. In actual fact, the impersonation was fairly positive, which meant that the message-consistent effect should have been hypothesized to be positive.

This research suffers from the same problems as most experimental social science practiced by academicians in that it relies on a smaller sample of college-aged students from the same university. In other words, it was hardly a robust and diverse sample. Mitigating this, however, is the fact that younger adults were less likely to know as much or have fully formed opinions about Trump or Clinton. In this sense the test was a conservative one. Less easily ignored is the low response rate. The possibility that only the more politically interested and aware self-selected into the survey cannot be ignored. If this was the case, the hardened opinion toward Trump and Clinton are easier to understand.

Shortcomings aside, this research showed that both Trump and Clinton, well-known public figures before the start of the nomination season, were relatively immune to changes in public approval as the result of the humor directed at them. The chapter contains at least one lesson with regard to the role of political comedy or satire in public life. Those who think or hope that Trump's approval ratings (or Trump himself) may be affected by the constant barrage of jokes made at his expense may be disappointed. While there may be a correlation between public opinion, negative news, and the number of jokes told at the president's expense,[36] this research suggests the correlation may be weaker when the public holds definite opinions about the president. In short, the barrage of satire directed Trump may do little to affect the public's view of him. It is probably the case that one either loves or hates him, irrespective of what the satirists are saying.

NOTES

1. For a full review, see Jody C Baumgartner, "Political Humor and Its Effects: A Review Essay," in *Los Efectos Del Humor: Una Perspectiva TranSDisciplinar* (*The Effects of Humor: A Trans-Disciplinary Perspective*), Ediciones Universidad Cooperativa de Colombia. (forthcoming).

2. For an early study, see Charles R. Gruner, "Wit and Humor in Mass Communication," in *Humor and Laughter: Theory, Research, and Applications*, eds. Anthony J. Chapman and Hugh C. Foot (New Brunswick, NJ: Transaction Publishers), 287–311.

3. R. Asher and Sargent S. Stansfield, "Shifts in Attitude Caused by Cartoon Caricatures," *Journal of General Psychology* 25, no. 2 (1941): 451.

4. Michael Z. Hackman, "Audience Reactions to the Use of Direct and Personal Disparaging Humor in Informative Public Addresses," *Communication Research Reports* 5, no. 2 (Dec. 1988): 126.

5. Dannagal G. Young, "Late-Night Comedy in Election 2000: Its Influence on Candidate Trait Ratings and the Moderating Effects of Political Knowledge and Partisanship," *Journal of Broadcasting & Electronic Media* 48, no. 1 (March 2004): 1.

6. Jody C Baumgartner and S. Jonathan Morris, "The "Daily Show" Effect: Candidate Evaluations, Efficacy, and American Youth," *American Politics Research* 34, no. 3 (May 2006): 341.

7. Jonathan S. Morris, "*The Daily Show with Jon Stewart* and Audience Attitude Change During the 2004 Party Conventions," *Political Behavior* 31, no. 1 (March 2009): 79.

8. Jody C Baumgartner, "Polls and Elections: Editorial Cartoons 2.0: The Effects of Digital Political Satire on Presidential Candidate Evaluations." *Presidential Studies Quarterly* 38, no. 4 (Dec. 2008): 735.

9. Jody C Baumgartner, Jonathan S. Morris, and Natasha L. Walth, "The Fey Effect: Young Adults, Political Humor, and Perceptions of Sarah Palin in the 2008 Presidential Election Campaign." *Public Opinion Quarterly* 76, no. 1 (Feb. 2012): 95.

10. Michael A. Xenos, Patricia Moy, and Amy B. Becker, "Making Sense of *The Daily Show*: Understanding the Role of Partisan Heuristics in Political Comedy Effects," in *The Stewart/Colbert Effect: Essays on the Real Impacts of Fake News*, ed. Amarnath Amarasingam (Jefferson, NC: McFarland, 2011), 47–62.

11. Jonathan S. Morris and Jody C Baumgartner, "*The Daily Show* and Attitudes Toward the News Media," in *Laughing Matters: Humor and American Politics in the Media Age*, eds. Jody C. Baumgartner and Jonathan S. Morris (New York: Routledge, 2008), 315–32.

12. Paul R. Brewer and Jessica McKnight, "Climate as Comedy: The Effects of Satirical Television News on Climate Change Perceptions," *Science Communication* 37, no. 5 (Aug. 2015): 635; Thomas E. Ford and Mark A. Ferguson, "Social Consequences of Disparagement Humor: A Prejudiced Norm Theory," *Personality and Social Psychology Review* 8, no. 1, (Feb. 2004): 79; Robin L., Nabi, Emily Moyer-Gusé, and Sahara Byrne, "All Joking Aside: A Serious Investigation Into the Persuasive Effect of Funny Social Issue Messages," *Communication Monographs* 74, no. 1 (March 2007): 29; Larry Powell, "Satire and Speech Trait Evaluation," *Western Journal of Speech Communication* 41, no. 2 (Spring 1977) 117; Dannagal G. Young, "Late-Night Comedy in Election 2000: Its Influence on Candidate Trait Ratings and the Moderating Effects of Political Knowledge and Partisanship," *Journal of Broadcasting & Electronic Media* 48, no. 1 (March 2004): 1.

13. Jody C Baumgartner, "No Laughing Matter? Young Adults and the 'Spillover Effect' of Candidate-Centered Political Humor," *Humor* 26, no. 1 (Feb. 2013): 23.

14. Jody C Baumgartner and Jonathan S. Morris, "One 'Nation,' Under Stephen? The Effects of *The Colbert Report* on American Youth," *Journal of Broadcasting & Electronic Media* 52, no. 4 (Dec. 2008): 622; Jody C Baumgartner and Jonathan S. Morris, "Research Note: The 2008 Presidential Primaries and Differential Effects of 'The Daily Show' and 'The Colbert Report' on Young Adults," *Midsouth Political*

Science Review 12 (2012): 87; Neil Vidmar and Milton Rokeach, "Archie Bunker's Bigotry: A Study in Selective Perception and Exposure," *Journal of Communication* 24, no. 1 (March 1974): 36.

15. Robert F. Priest, "Election Jokes: The Effects of Reference Group Membership," *Psychological Reports* 18, no. 2 (April 1966): 600; Robert F. Priest and Joel Abrahams, "Candidate Preference and Hostile Humor in the 1968 Elections," *Psychological Reports* 26, no. 3 (June 1970): 779; Young, "Late-Night Comedy in Election 2000."

16. Jody C Baumgartner, "Humor on the Next Frontier: Youth, Online Political Humor, and the JibJab Effect," *Social Science Computer Review* 25, no. 3 (Aug. 2007.): 319; Jody C Baumgartner, Jonathan S. Morris, and Jeffrey Michael Coleman, "Did the 'Road to the White House Run Through' Letterman? Chris Christie, Letterman, and Other-disparaging versus Self-deprecating Humor," *Journal of Political Marketing* 73, no. 3 (2018): 1; Susan E. Esralew, "Beating Others to the Punch: Exploring the Influence of Self-Deprecating Humor on Source Perceptions through Expectancy Violations Theory." Electronic Thesis. Ohio State University, 2012. https://etd.ohiolink.edu/.

17. See, for example, Jim Lyttle, "The Effectiveness of Humor in Persuasion: The Case of Business Ethics Training," *The Journal of General Psychology* 128, no. 2 (2001): 206; Brian Sternthal and C. Samuel Craig, "Humor in Advertising," *Journal of Marketing* 37, no. 4 (Oct. 1973): 12; Yong Zhang, "Responses to Humorous Advertising: The Moderating Effect of Need for Cognition," *Journal of Advertising* 25, no. 1 (Spring 1996): 15; Yong Zhang, "The Effect of Humor in Advertising: An Individual-Difference Perspective," *Psychology & Marketing* 13, no. 6 (Sept. 1996): 531.

18. Richard E. Petty and John T. Cacioppo, *Communication and Persuasion: Central and Peripheral Routes to Attitude Change* (New York: Springer-Verlag, 1986).

19. John A Jones, "The Masking Effects of Humor on Audience Perception of Message Organization," *Humor* 18, no. 4 (Oct. 2005): 405.

20. Leon Festinger and Nathan Maccoby, "On Resistance to Persuasive Communications," *The Journal of Abnormal and Social Psychology* 68, no. 4, (May 1964): 359; Heather L. LaMarre and Whitney Walther, "Ability Matters: Testing the Differential Effects of Political News and Late-Night Political Comedy on Cognitive Responses and the Role of Ability in Micro-Level Opinion Formation," *International Journal of Public Opinion Research* 25, no. 3 (Sept. 2013): 303; Robert A. Osterhouse and Timothy C. Brock, "Distraction Increases Yielding to Propaganda by Inhibiting Counterarguing," *Journal of Personality and Social Psychology* 15, no. 4 (Aug. 1970): 344.

21. Robin L. Nabi, Emily Moyer-Gusé, and Sahara Byrne, "All Joking Aside: A Serious Investigation Into the Persuasive Effect of Funny Social Issue Messages," *Communication Monographs* 74, no. 1 (March 2007): 29.

22. Nabi, Moyer-Gusé, and Byrne, "All Joking Aside"; Jeremy Polk, Dannagal G. Young, and R. Lance Holbert, "Humor Complexity and Political Influence: An Elaboration Likelihood Approach to the Effects of Humor Type in The Daily Show with Jon Stewart," *Atlantic Journal of Communication* 17, no. 4 (Nov. 2009): 202;

Michael A. Xenos and Amy B. Becker, "Moments of Zen: Effects of *The Daily Show* on Information Seeking and Political Learning," *Political Communication* 26, no. 3 (July 2009): 317; Dannagal G. Young, "The Privileged Role of the Late-Night Joke: Exploring Humor's Role in Disrupting Argument Scrutiny," *Media Psychology* 11, no. 1 (March 2008): 119.

23. However, see Nabi, Moyer-Gusé, and Byrne, "All Joking Aside," which found a small "sleeper effect" of viewing political comedy after one week.

24. S. Robert Lichter, Jody C Baumgartner, and Jonathan S. Morris, *Politics Is a Joke! How TV Comedians are Remaking Political Life* (Boulder, CO: Westview Press, 2015).

25. Jim Lyttle, "The Effectiveness of Humor in Persuasion: The Case of Business Ethics Training," *The Journal of General Psychology* 128, no. 2 (2001): 206.

26. Baumgartner and Morris, "The Daily Show Effect."

27. Joan S. Spira, "Attitude Strength and Resistance to Persuasion," in *NA—Advances in Consumer Research*, volume 29, ed. Susan M. Broniarczyk and Kent Nakamoto (Valdosta, GA: Association for Consumer Research, 2002), 180–81.

28. Matthew A. Baum, "Talking the Vote: Why Presidential Candidates Hit the Talk Show Circuit," *American Journal of Political Science* 49, no. 2 (April 2005): 213.

29. This particular form of the question is from the ABC News/Washington Post Poll.

30. Donald T. Campbell and Julian C. Stanley, *Experimental and Quasi-Experimental Designs for Research* (Chicago: Rand McNally, 1963).

31. See https://www.youtube.com/watch?v=pfmwGAd1L-o.

32. Originally the clip was posted to YouTube, but is no longer available there. It can now be seen at http://www.nbcnewyork.com/entertainment/entertainment-news/Tonight-Show-Donald-Trump-Ben-Carson-Watch-Democratic-Debate-332998401.html.

33. David S. Niven, S. Robert Lichter, and Daniel Amundson, "The Political Content of Late Night Comedy," *Harvard International Journal of Press/Politics* 8, no. 3 (July 2003): 118.

34. Baumgartner and Morris, "The Daily Show Effect"; Baum, "Talking the Vote"; Spira, "Attitude Strength and Resistance to Persuasion."

35. See, for example, R. Lance Holbert, Jay Hmielowski, Parul Jain, Julie Lather, and Alyssa Morey. "Adding Nuance to the Study of Political Humor Effects: Experimental Research on Juvenalian Satire versus Horatian Satire," *American Behavioral Scientist* 55, no. 3 (Mar. 2011): 187.

36. See Lichter, Baumgartner, and Morris, *Politics Is a Joke!*

REFERENCES

Asher, R., and Sargent S. Stansfield. "Shifts in Attitude Caused by Cartoon Caricatures." *Journal of General Psychology* 25, no. 2 (1941): 451–55.

Baum, Matthew. "Talking the Vote: Why Presidential Candidates Hit the Talk Show Circuit." *American Journal of Political Science* 49, no. 2 (April 2005): 213–34.

Baumgartner, Jody C. "Political Humor and Its Effects: A Review Essay." In *Los Efectos Del Humor: Una Perspectiva TransDisciplinar* (*The Effects of Humor: A Trans-Disciplinary Perspective*), Ediciones Universidad Cooperativa de Colombia (forthcoming).

————— "Humor on the Next Frontier: Youth, Online Political Humor, and the JibJab Effect." *Social Science Computer Review* 25, no. 3 (August 2007): 319–38.

—————. "Polls and Elections: Editorial Cartoons 2.0: The Effects of Digital Political Satire on Presidential Candidate Evaluations." *Presidential Studies Quarterly* 38, no. 4 (December 2008): 735–58.

—————. "No Laughing Matter? Young Adults and the 'Spillover Effect' of Candidate-Centered Political Humor." *Humor* 26, no. 1 (February 2013): 23–43.

Baumgartner, Jody C., and Jonathan S. Morris. "The 'Daily Show' Effect: Candidate Evaluations, Efficacy, and American Youth." *American Politics Research* 34, no. 3 (May 2006): 341–67.

—————. "One 'Nation,' Under Stephen? The Effects of *The Colbert Report* on American Youth." *Journal of Broadcasting & Electronic Media* 52, no. 4 (December 2008): 622–43.

—————. "Research Note: The 2008 Presidential Primaries and Differential Effects of 'The Daily Show' and 'The Colbert Report' on Young Adults." *Midsouth Political Science Review* 12 (2012): 87–102.

Baumgartner, Jody C., Jonathan S. Morris, and Natasha L. Walth. "The Fey Effect: Young Adults, Political Humor, and Perceptions of Sarah Palin in the 2008 Presidential Election Campaign." *Public Opinion Quarterly* 76, no. 1 (February 2012): 95–104.

Baumgartner, Jody C., Jonathan S. Morris, and Jeffrey Michael Coleman. "Did the 'Road to the White House Run Through' Letterman? Chris Christie, Letterman, and Other-disparaging versus Self-deprecating Humor." *Journal of Political Marketing* 73, no. 3 (2018): 1–19.

Brewer, Paul R., and Jessica McKnight. "Climate as Comedy: The Effects of Satirical Television News on Climate Change Perceptions." *Science Communication* 37, no. 5 (August 2015): 635–57.

Campbell, Donald T., and Julian C. Stanley. *Experimental and Quasi-Experimental Designs for Research*. Chicago: Rand McNally, 1963.

Chung, Hwiman, and Xinshu Zhao. "Humour Effect on Memory and Attitude: Moderating Role of Product Involvement." *International Journal of Advertising* 22, no. 1 (February 2003): 117–44.

Esralew, Sarah. "Beating Others to the Punch: Exploring the Influence of Self-Deprecating Humor on Source Perceptions through Expectancy Violations Theory." Electronic thesis. Ohio State University, 2012. https://etd.ohiolink.edu/.

Festinger, Leon, and Nathan Maccoby. "On Resistance to Persuasive Communications." *The Journal of Abnormal and Social Psychology* 68, no. 4 (May 1964): 359–66.

Ford, Thomas E., and Mark A. Ferguson. "Social Consequences of Disparagement Humor: A Prejudiced Norm Theory." *Personality and Social Psychology Review* 8, no. 1 (February 2004): 79–94.

Gruner, Charles R. "Wit and Humor in Mass Communication." In *Humor and Laughter: Theory, Research, and Applications*, edited by Antony J. Chapman and Hugh C. Foot, 287–311. New Brunswick, NJ: Transaction Publishers, 1996.

Michael Z. Hackman. "Audience Reactions to the Use of Direct and Personal Disparaging Humor in Informative Public Addresses." *Communication Research Reports* 5, no. 2 (December 1988): 126–30.

Holbert, R. Lance, Jay Hmielowski, Parul Jain, Julie Lather, and Alyssa Morey. "Adding Nuance to the Study of Political Humor Effects: Experimental Research on Juvenalian Satire versus Horatian Satire." *American Behavioral Scientist* 55, no. 3 (March 2011): 187–211.

Jones, John A. "The Masking Effects of Humor on Audience Perception of Message Organization." *Humor* 18, no. 4 (Oct. 2005): 405–17.

LaMarre, Heather L., and Whitney Walther. "Ability Matters: Testing the Differential Effects of Political News and Late-Night Political Comedy on Cognitive Responses and the Role of Ability in Micro-Level Opinion Formation." *International Journal of Public Opinion Research* 25, no. 3 (September 2013): 303–22.

Lichter, S. Robert., Jody C Baumgartner, and Jonathan S. Morris. *Politics Is a Joke! How TV Comedians are Remaking Political Life.* Boulder, CO: Westview Press, 2015.

Lyttle, Jim. "The Effectiveness of Humor in Persuasion: The Case of Business Ethics Training." *The Journal of General Psychology* 128, no. 2 (2001): 206–16.

Morris, Jonathan S. "*The Daily Show with Jon Stewart* and Audience Attitude Change During the 2004 Party Conventions." *Political Behavior* 31, no. 1 (March 2009): 79–102.

Morris, Jonathan S., and Jody C Baumgartner, eds. "*The Daily Show* and Attitudes Toward the News Media." In *Laughing Matters: Humor and American Politics in the Media Age*, 315–32. New York: Routledge, 2008.

Nabi, Robin L., Emily Moyer-Gusé, and Sahara Byrne. "All Joking Aside: A Serious Investigation into the Persuasive Effect of Funny Social Issue Messages." *Communication Monographs* 74, no. 1 (March 2007): 29–54.

Niven, David, S. Robert Lichter, and Daniel Amundson. "The Political Content of Late Night Comedy." *Harvard International Journal of Press/Politics* 8, no. 3 (July 2003): 118–33.

Osterhouse, Robert A., and Timothy C. Brock. "Distraction Increases Yielding to Propaganda by Inhibiting Counterarguing." *Journal of Personality and Social Psychology* 15, no. 4 (August 1970): 344–58.

Petty, Richard E., and John T. Cacioppo. *Communication and Persuasion: Central and Peripheral Routes to Attitude Change.* New York: Springer-Verlag, 1986.

Polk, Jeremy, Dannagal G. Young, and R. Lance Holbert. "Humor Complexity and Political Influence: An Elaboration Likelihood Approach to the Effects of Humor Type in The Daily Show with Jon Stewart." *Atlantic Journal of Communication* 17, no. 4 (November 2009): 202–19.

Powell, Larry. "Satire and Speech Trait Evaluation." *Western Journal of Speech Communication* 41, no. 2 (Spring 1977): 117–25.

Priest, Robert F. "Election Jokes: The Effects of Reference Group Membership." *Psychological Reports* 18, no. 2 (April 1966): 600–02.

Priest, Robert F., and Joel Abrahams. "Candidate Preference and Hostile Humor in the 1968 Elections." *Psychological Reports* 26, no. 3 (June 1970): 779–83.

Spira, Joan S. "Attitude Strength and Resistance to Persuasion." In *NA—Advances in Consumer Research*, volume 29, edited by Susan M. Broniarczyk and Kent Nakamoto, 180–81. Valdosta, GA: Association for Consumer Research, 2002.

Sternthal, Brian, and C. Samuel Craig. "Humor in Advertising." *Journal of Marketing* 37, no. 4 (October 1973): 12–18.

Vidmar, Neil, and Milton Rokeach. "Archie Bunker's Bigotry: A Study in Selective Perception and Exposure." *Journal of Communication* 24, no. 1 (March 1974): 36–47.

Xenos, Michael A., and Amy B. Becker. "Moments of Zen: Effects of *The Daily Show* on Information Seeking and Political Learning." *Political Communication* 26, no. 3 (July 2009): 317–32

Xenos, Michael A., Patricia Moy, and Amy B. Becker. "Making Sense of *The Daily Show*: Understanding the Role of Partisan Heuristics in Political Comedy Effects." In *The Stewart/Colbert Effect: Essays on the Real Impacts of Fake News*, edited by Amarnath Amarasingam, 47–62. Jefferson, NC: McFarland, 2011.

Young, Dannagal G. "Late-Night Comedy in Election 2000: Its Influence on Candidate Trait Ratings and the Moderating Effects of Political Knowledge and Partisanship." *Journal of Broadcasting & Electronic Media* 48, no. 1 (March 2004): 1–22.

———. "The Privileged Role of the Late-Night Joke: Exploring Humor's Role in Disrupting Argument Scrutiny." *Media Psychology* 11, no. 1 (March 2008): 119–42.

———. "A Flip-Flopper and a Dumb Guy Walk into a Bar: Political Humor and Priming in the 2004 Campaign." *Humor* 25, no. 3 (January 2012): 215–31.

Zhang, Yong. "Responses to Humorous Advertising: The Moderating Effect of Need for Cognition." *Journal of Advertising* 25, no. 1 (Spring 1996): 15–32.

———. "The Effect of Humor in Advertising: An Individual-Difference Perspective." *Psychology & Marketing* 13, no. 6 (September 1996): 531–45.

Chapter 5

Interviews and Viewing Motivations

Exploring Connections between Political Satire, Perceived Learning, and Elaborative Processing

Amy B. Becker

Capturing the largest share of the under-thirty news audience, both *The Daily Show* (*TDS*) and *The Colbert Report* (*TCR*; up until 2014), have served as a source of entertaining, satirical news for Millennial viewers for the last few election cycles.[1] Today, in the aftermath of the 2016 election cycle, the field of political satire is now ripe with a wide range of diverse offerings including *Last Week Tonight with John Oliver* and *Full Frontal with Samantha Bee*, as well as new iterations of *The Daily Show* (now with host Trevor Noah) and a new version of CBS' *Late Show* starring an out-of-character Stephen Colbert. Research suggests that young audience members view political comedy content to satisfy a range of media needs—from the desire to be entertained, to an interest in acquiring news information that is free from bias.[2] Prior research has shown that comedy content tends to be processed peripherally; viewers focus on getting the joke rather than on working to carefully inspect the quality of the arguments being offered.[3] Despite this less effortful media behavior, we know that viewers do learn from watching political comedy content even if the knowledge acquired is an incidental by-product, or unintended consequence of exposure.[4]

Specifically, even though viewing political comedy tends to aid in the recognition rather than recall of political information, intensifies knowledge of "easier," political facts, and promotes online-based rather than memory-based information processing, the consensus is that viewers do learn about current events from satire programs.[5] While much of this learning is conditional on the motivations and ability of the viewer or on key moderating variables like political interest, viewing political comedy engenders greater

cognitive engagement and information seeking behavior, encouraging viewers to connect the dots between the comedy they view and what they already
know from traditional news sources.[6] Exposure to political satire not only
encourages knowledge gain and learning, but also encourages viewers to
participate in the political process.[7]

Of particular interest to political communication scholars are the interview
segments that conclude most satire programs. Previous research has shown
that watching a politician being interviewed on a program like *TDS* or *TCR* as
opposed to a traditional network or cable news program results in higher
recall of basic factual information, a greater likelihood of engaging in acts of
political expression, and more positive evaluations of the interviewee.[8] Politicians also appreciate the experience of the political satire interview because it
offers an opportunity to engage in a conversation that is often more substantive, light-hearted, and friendly than the equivalent opportunity on a cable or
network news program.[9] Political satire also enables politicians to connect
with an audience that is younger, liberal, more educated, and more male than
female.[10] While a handful of political communication scholars have examined
the text of these interview conversations more closely and have started to
document the behavioral effects that result from exposure to these segments,
research has yet to consider whether exposure to political comedy interviews
can encourage viewers to make connections between the satirical conversations they're viewing and what they already know from prior learning or
related news content.[11] The present study considers this question as well as
whether the connections viewers make between satire, other content, and preexisting knowledge are dependent upon prior comedy viewing motivations,
namely perceived comedy learning and an affinity for entertaining news.

READING BETWEEN THE LAUGHS: ELABORATIVE
PROCESSING AND POLITICAL SATIRE INTERVIEWS

Conceptually, "elaboration is the process of connecting new information to
other information stored in memory, including prior knowledge, personal
experience, or the connection of two new bits of information together in new
ways."[12] Elaborative processing has been shown to mediate the relationship
between news exposure and learning across a variety of mediums, particularly
for those who rely on news content as a source of information (e.g., those who
are driven by surveillance motivations) and those who show greater interest
in the topic.[13] While research on political comedy and cognitive elaboration
is less established than work connecting the cognitive mediation model with
traditional news exposure, recent studies suggest that viewers' prior orienta-
tions toward comedy shape their information processing behaviors.

For example, Feldman (2013) has shown that viewers who classify *TDS* as news or a news/entertainment hybrid are more likely to engage in effortful processing than those who label the program as entertainment.[14] In Feldman's experiment, viewers who classified *TDS* as entertainment were only more likely to engage in effortful processing if prompted at the outset by researchers to meet certain information processing goals. Work by Matthes (2013) has suggested that the need for humor (NFH) positively moderates the relationship between cognitive elaboration and knowledge acquisition given exposure to thematically related humor content, while Young (2013) has offered evidence of the connection between the need for cognition (NFC), satire exposure, and the desire to engage in integrative thinking in order to draw connections with relevant news content.[15] Finally, LaMarre and Walther suggest that the cognitive elaboration that results from humor exposure is conditional on processing ability.[16]

In line with previous research, exposure to comedy interviews should result in increased elaborative processing among those who are already positively predisposed toward entertaining news.[17] Specifically, individuals with a greater affinity for entertaining news should be more likely to engage in post-interview elaborative processing than individuals who lack an affinity for entertaining news, yet are exposed to the same comedy interview content. These high entertainment affinity individuals should be less likely to discount the message in the comedy or scrutinize the arguments being made, particularly if they like the comic source.[18] In sum, these high entertainment affinity viewers should ultimately engage more with the humor than those who lack an affinity for entertaining news.

Similarly, elaborative processing should be greater among those who perceive comedy programs as a source of information or learning or those—who perhaps even without fully realizing it—apply surveillance motivations to guide their comedy viewing behavior.[19] In effect, these individuals are relying upon or using comedy to satisfy or gratify their information gathering needs; comedy is an information-rich part of their media diet.[20] As such, the elaborative processing that results from exposure to a comedy interview should be conditional upon an individual's amount of perceived comedy learning; the more an individual believes they learn from political comedy programs at the outset, the greater the likelihood of elaborative processing behavior given exposure to a political comedy interview.[21] The hypotheses outlined below test for direct and moderating relationships between affinity for entertaining news, perceived comedy learning, comedy interview exposure, and elaborative processing:

H1: An affinity for entertaining news will be positively related to elaborative processing; those who express a greater affinity for entertaining news will be more likely to engage in elaborative processing.

H1a: An affinity for entertaining news serves as a moderator in the relationship between comedy interview exposure and elaborative processing; high affinity for entertainment individuals exposed to a comedy interview will be more likely to engage in elaborative processing, while low affinity for entertainment individuals will be less likely to engage in elaborative processing.

H2: Perceived learning from comedy programming will be positively related to elaborative processing; those who believe they learn from political comedy programming will be more likely to engage in elaborative processing.

H2a: Perceived learning from comedy content serves as a moderator in the relationship between comedy interview exposure and elaborative processing; individuals with higher levels of perceived learning exposed to a comedy interview will be more likely to engage in elaborative processing, while individuals with lower levels of perceived learning will be less likely to engage in elaborative processing.

DATA AND METHODS

A five-group experiment ($N = 222$) was conducted at a mid-Atlantic university between March 26 and April 13, 2012. The university IRB approved the experiment as exempt in January 2012. Undergraduates from communication classes were recruited via email to take part in the twenty-minute online experiment via a secure link. Students were offered course extra credit in exchange for their participation.

After completing a pretest questionnaire that measured political interest, general patterns of media consumption, affinity for entertaining news, perceived comedy learning, and other antecedent variables, participants in the experiment were then randomly assigned to view one of five video interviews featuring either former Democratic Governor of Michigan Jennifer Granholm or Republican Governor of Indiana Mitch Daniels talking about their new book with a comedy or news host (e.g., Stewart, Colbert, Keith Olbermann, or Greta van Susteren). Each interview was approximately 6–8 minutes long and featured a broad discussion of economic policy as outlined in each politician's book. The clips shared striking similarity in terms of length, visual, and graphic displays, and substance despite being from different types of programs (satire vs. cable news) and airing on different news networks with varied political leanings (e.g., MSNBC vs. FOX News). Specifically, subjects in the first condition viewed Granholm being interviewed by Stewart on *TDS* ($n = 53$) while subjects in the second condition ($n = 54$) viewed Granholm being interviewed by Keith Olbermann on MSNBC. Subjects in the third condition viewed Daniels being interviewed on *TDS* ($n = 41$) while subjects in the fourth condition ($n = 38$) viewed Daniels being interviewed by Greta van Susteren on FOX News. Subjects in the fifth condition ($n = 36$) viewed Granholm being interviewed by Colbert on *TCR*.

For analytical purposes, those exposed to the comedy interviews ($n = 130$) were compared against those who viewed a news interview ($n = 92$). After the video stimuli, a series of manipulation checks followed confirming that subjects could recall the interviewer and the interviewee, the position of the interviewee and their political party, and the television network of the original program.[22] Finally, subjects completed a posttest questionnaire that tapped key concepts like elaborative processing, political trust, political engagement, and demographics. The relevant measures used in the analyses are outlined below:

KEY MEASURES

Dependent Variable

Elaborative Processing ($M = 3.41$, $SD = 1.65$; 1 = "strongly disagree," to 7 = "strongly agree") was based on agreement with two correlated items ($r = .70$, $p < .001$): (1) "I often thought about how what I saw in the video relates to other things I know," and (2) "I often made connections between what I saw in the video and things I've learned about elsewhere."[23]

Experimental Condition

Assignment to a comedy condition ($n = 130$) was included as a variable in the analysis; those in the news conditions ($n = 92$) were treated as the default and not specified in the model.

Perceived Comedy Learning

Mirroring questions asked by the Pew Research Center, subjects were asked in the pretest questionnaire to indicate how often (1 = "never," to 4 = "regularly") they "learn something about politics and public affairs," from *TDS* or *TCR* ($M = 2.15$, $SD = 1.03$).

Affinity for Entertaining News

In the pretest questionnaire, subjects were asked to indicate their affinity for entertaining news content.[24] The responses to two items ($M = 2.82$, $SD = .36$; 1 = "does not matter," 2 = "dislike," 3 = "like") were added together to reflect a preference for entertainment-oriented news: (1) "when a news source is sometimes funny," (83% like), and (2) "when a news source makes the news enjoyable and entertaining," (86% like).

Political Interest

Political interest (M = 2.11, SD = 1.09) reflected a response to the question, "Would you say that you follow what's going on in politics and government..." (0 = "never," 1 = "hardly at all," 2 = "only now and then," 3 = "some of the time," and 4 = "most of the time").

Predispositions

Party identification or being a "Democrat," (40% of sample coded as 1; 28% of the sample was Independent/something else; 32% Republican) was used in the analysis along with political ideology (M = 3.12, SD = 2.02; 1 = "strong liberal," to 7 = "strong conservative").

Demographics

Age (M = 22.00, SD = 3.87) and gender (75% female; 25% male) were included as demographic controls.

RESULTS

Ordinary least squares (OLS) regression was used to analyze the experimental data and examine the relationships between viewing motivations (e.g., affinity for entertaining news, perceived comedy learning), comedy interview exposure, and reported elaborative processing behavior.[25] As Table 5.1 shows, an affinity for entertainment-oriented news was approaching significance (β = .11, p < .10), thus only offering tepid support for *H1*. Perceived learning from cable comedy content was a significant, positive predictor of reported elaborative processing behavior (β = .15, p < .05); *H2* was therefore supported. Exposure to a comedy interview (as opposed to a news interview) was significant in the initial model (β = .12, p < .05), yet assignment to the experimental comedy conditions was only marginally significant once the interaction terms were included (β = .12, p = 0.59). Overall, the direct effects model explained 20.3 percent of the variance in self-reported elaborative processing behavior.

   Two sets of interaction terms were created in order to test for any potential moderating relationships between comedy motivations (e.g., affinity for entertaining news, perceived comedy learning), interview exposure, and elaborative processing behavior. Specifically, the standardized values of key main effect variables (affinity for entertaining news, perceived comedy learning, assignment to a comedy condition) were multiplied to create two

Table 5.1 OLS Regression Explaining Variation in Elaborative Processing

	Model 1	Model 2
Block 1: Direct Effects		
Female	−.00	.00
Age	.24***	.23***
Democrat	.11	.10
Ideology (conservative = high)	.09	.10
Political Interest	.23***	.25***
Affinity for Entertaining News (Affinity)	.10#	.11#
Perceived Comedy Learning (Learn)	.16*	.15*
Comedy Interview Condition	.12*	.12#
Incremental R^2	20.3%	
Block 2: Interactions		
Affinity*Comedy		.14*
Learn*Comedy		.06
Incremental R^2		2.1%
Final R^2		22.4%

Note: $N = 221$. Cell entries for block 1 are final standardized regression coefficients; cell entries for block 2 are before-entry standardized regression coefficients. #$p < .10$, *$p < .05$, **$p < .01$, ***$p < .001$.

interaction terms for use in further analysis: (1) the interaction between affinity for entertaining news and viewing a comedy interview, and (2) the interaction between perceived comedy learning and viewing a comedy interview. Using standardized values helped prevent possible multicollinearity problems.[26] The interaction terms were included as the second block of the regression model and explained an additional 2.1 percent of the variance in reported elaborative processing behavior (Final $R^2 = 22.4\%$).

Only the interaction between affinity for entertaining news and comedy exposure was significant ($\beta = .14$, $p < .05$). As Figure 5.1 shows, individuals with a higher affinity for entertaining news were more likely to engage in elaborative processing behavior given exposure to a comedy interview ($M = 3.64$) as opposed to a news interview ($M = 3.17$), while those with a lower affinity for entertaining news were more likely to engage in elaborative processing behavior given exposure to a news ($M = 3.53$) rather than a comedy interview ($M = 3.14$). In effect, the self-reported elaborative processing behavior that resulted from exposure to a comedy interview was greater among those who exhibit a greater affinity or orientation toward entertaining, fun news than those who prefer more traditional formats.

A probing of the significant interaction effect using the PROCESS macro created by Hayes (2013) suggested that being exposed to a comedy interview had a conditional effect on elaborative processing for those with low-very high levels (25th percentile or above) of an affinity for entertaining news $t(222) = 1.85$, $p < .07$, yet the elaborative processing for those with very low levels of an affinity for entertaining news (10th percentile or below) was not

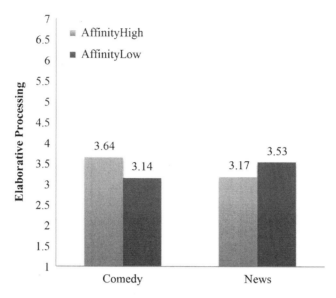

Figure 5.1 Interview Exposure, Affinity for Entertaining News, and Elaborative Processing.

conditional on exposure to a comedy versus news interview.[27] *H1a* was therefore supported; yet the data failed to indicate support for *H2a* or a conditional relationship between perceived comedy learning, interview exposure, and elaborative processing.

DISCUSSION

The study considered the impact of exposure to political satire interviews, exploring the relationships between comedy viewing motivations (e.g., affinity for entertaining news, perceived comedy learning), comedy interview exposure, and self-reported elaborative processing behavior in order to add to our understanding of the effects of tuning into these hybrid political satire conversations relative to traditional news interviews. The results suggest that motivations for attending to comedy (in this case perceived learning) are positively related to reported elaborative processing behavior; those who believe that they learn something about politics and public affairs from programs like *TDS* and *TCR* are more likely to report that they draw connections between interview content and other things they've seen before or already know. The results also indicate that those who have a higher affinity for entertaining news trend toward being more likely to engage in elaborative processing behavior. Further, the results show that an affinity for entertaining news moderates the impact of comedy interview exposure on self-reported elaborative processing behavior. Subjects with a greater affinity for entertaining news were more likely to engage in elaborative processing behavior given exposure to a comedy rather than a news interview.

Before concluding, it is valuable to point out some limitations of the current study. It is of course unfortunate that both governors did not appear on TDS and TCR. As a result, more subjects viewed interviews with Granholm, the Democrat ($n = 143$) than Daniels, the Republican ($n = 79$). Similarly, the Republican, Daniels, was only featured on the more conservative leaning network, FOX News, while Granholm, the Democrat, was only featured on the more liberal leaning network, MSNBC. Despite this imbalance, the interviews were all comparable in terms of length and substance, making them a robust set of stimuli for use in the experiment. In addition, the study relied solely on a college student subject pool. While not ideal, this is often the standard in political comedy effects research as this group does represent the core of the late-night comedy audience. While our measure of affinity for entertaining news was reliable and drawn from prior research, a newer measure like affinity for political humor (AfPH) might be more appropriate for future research efforts.[28] Further, future research might consider including an expanded measure of elaborative processing or a thought-listing exercise to tap elaboration, similar to efforts featured in work by LaMarre and Walther (2013).[29] While the items in the present measure of elaborative processing behavior were highly correlated ($r = .70$, $p < .001$), the measure still relies on subjects to self-report their perceived elaborative processing rather than engage in an activity that directly measures elaborative processing in direct response to the experimental stimuli. Finally, the present investigation ends at elaboration and does not consider the influence of elaborative processing on knowledge gain or learning as is the emphasis in Feldman's (2013) piece.[30] Future research on the impact of political satire interviews should consider the potential mediating role of elaborative processing on post-interview exposure knowledge gain and learning.

Overall, the present study enhances our understanding of the impact of political satire programming and the interview segments in particular on political learning and knowledge. The results suggest that viewers report that they connect the dots between what they see during conversations with political satire hosts and what they already know from traditional news or other sources. This is particularly true if viewers think they learn from political comedy and have a greater preference or affinity for entertaining news content. In sum, these political comedy interviews are something that politicians and media scholars alike need to take seriously, because they are impactful for viewers and encourage connections between comedy, news, and prior information and political learning.

Moreover, research has shown that political comedy content may have even started to eclipse traditional news as a source for knowledge and learning. A pair of studies examining the case of Stephen Colbert's Super PAC found that viewers learned more about the issue of campaign finance reform from Colbert himself in his role as host of *TCR* than from exposure to traditional news stories about campaign finance reform or when watching Colbert appear in character on traditional news programming to talk about the issue.[31] Moreover, recent work on the net neutrality issue has shown that comedy is as good a source of learning as traditional news.[32] Thus, as the political comedy landscape continues to evolve with Stephen Colbert's move to host CBS' *Late Show* and the emergence of new hosts like John Oliver, Trevor Noah, and Samantha Bee as formative interviewers, it will be important to continue to monitor the impact of exposure to interviews from political satire and other hybrid news programs on key democratic outcomes like elaborative processing, broader patterns of knowledge acquisition and learning, and political participation.[33]

The experiment presented here offers a useful framework for future research efforts and suggests that consistent with prior research, satire interviews are more than just funny conversations, they are indeed teaching us about politics.[34] This is especially important for the Millennial audience that prefers entertaining news to traditional formats and reports that they are both entertained and informed by political satire programming. In sum, political satire interviews may be making us smarter, helping us to connect the dots in an increasingly fragmented news media environment.

NOTES

1. Pew, "Section 4: Demographics and Political Views of News Audiences," http://www.people-press.org/2012/09/27/section-4-demographics-and-political-views-of-news-audiences/.

2. Dannagal G. Young, "Laughter, Learning, or Enlightenment? Viewing and Avoidance Motivations Behind the Daily Show and the Colbert Report," *Journal of Broadcasting & Electronic Media* 57, no. 2 (2013).

3. Robin L. Nabi, Emily Moyer-Guse, and Sahara Byrne, "All Joking Aside: A Serious Investigation into the Persuasive Effect of Funny Social Issue Messages," *Communication Monographs* 74, no. 1 (2007); Dannagal G. Young, "The Privileged Role of the Late-Night Joke: Exploring Humor's Role in Disrupting Argument Scrutiny," *Media Psychology* 11, no. 1 (2008).

4. Matthew A. Baum, *Soft News Goes to War: Public Opinion and American Foreign Policy in the New Media Age* (Princeton, NJ: Princeton University Press, 2003).

5. Young Min Baek and Magdalena E. Wojcieszak, "Don't Expect Too Much! Learning from Late-Night Comedy and Knowledge Item Difficulty," *Communication Research* 36, no. 6 (2009); Bruce A. Hollander, "Late-Night Learning: Do Entertainment Programs Increase Political Campaign Knowledge for Young Viewers?" *Journal of Broadcasting & Electronic Media* 49, no. 4 (2005); Young Mie Kim and John Vishak, "Just Laugh! You Don't Ned to Remember: The Effects of Entertainment Media on Political Information Acquisition and Information Processing in Political Judgment," *Journal of Communication* 58, no. 2 (2008); Michael A. Xenos and Amy B. Becker, "Moments of Zen: Effects of *the Daily Show* on Information Seeking and Political Learning," *Political Communication* 26, no. 3 (2009).

6. Xaoxao Cao, "Political Comedy Shows and Knowledge About Primary Campaigns: The Moderating Effects of Age and Education," *Mass Communication and Society* 11, no. 1 (2008); Lauren Feldman and Dannagal G. Young, "Late-Night Comedy as a Gateway to Traditional News: An Analysis of Time Trends in News Attention among Late-Night Comedy Viewers During the 2004 Presidential Primaries," *Political Communication* 25, no. 4 (2008); Dannagal Young, "Laughter, Learning, or Enlightenment? Viewing and Avoidance Motivations Behind the Daily Show and the Colbert Report."

7. Amy B. Becker, "What About Those Interviews? The Impact of Exposure to Political Comedy and Cable News on Factual Recall and Anticipated Political Expression," *International Journal of Public Opinion Research* 25, no. 3 (2013); Xaoxao Cao and Paul R. Brewer, "Political Comedy Shows and Public Participation in Politics," ibid. 20, no. 1 (2008); Lindsay H. Hoffman and Dannagal G. Young, "Satire, Punch Lines, and the Nightly News: Untangling Media Effects on Political Participation," *Communication Research Reports* 28, no. 2 (2011).

8. Becker, Amy B. "What About Those Interviews? The Impact of Exposure to Political Comedy and Cable News on Factual Recall and Anticipated Political Expression"; Lindsay H. Hoffman, "Breaking Boundaries | Political Interviews: Examining Perceived Media Bias and Effects across Tv Entertainment Formats," *International Journal of Communication* 7 (2013); Patricia Moy, Michael A. Xenos, and Verena K. Hess, "Priming Effects of Late-Night Comedy," *International Journal of Public Opinion Research* 18, no. 2 (2006).

9. Geoffrey Baym, "Crafting New Communicative Models in the Televisual Sphere: Political Interviews on *the Daily Show*," *The Communication Review* 10, no. 2 (2007); *From Cronkite to Colbert: The Evolution of Broadcast News* (Boulder, CO: Paradigm Publishers, 2010); "Breaking Boundaries | Political Media as Discursive Modes: A Comparative Analysis of Interviews with Ron Paul from Meet the Press, Tonight, the Daily Show, and Hannity," *International Journal of Communication* 7 (2013); Emily K. Vraga et al., "The Correspondent, the Comic, and the Combatant: The Consequences of Host Style in Political Talk Shows," *Journalism & Mass Communication Quarterly* 89, no. 1 (2012).

10. Jeffrey A. Gottfried, Katerina Eva Matsa, and Michael Barthel, "As Jon Stewart Steps Down, 5 Facts About the Daily Show," http://www.pewresearch.org/fact-tank/2015/08/06/5-facts-daily-show/.

11. Geoffrey Baum, "Crafting New Communicative Models in the Televisual Sphere: Political Interviews on *the Daily Show*"; Amy B. Becker, "What About Those Interviews? The Impact of Exposure to Political Comedy and Cable News on Factual Recall and Anticipated Political Expression"; Lindsay H. Hoffman, "Breaking Boundaries | Political Interviews: Examining Perceived Media Bias and Effects across TV Entertainment Formats."

12. William P. Eveland Jr., "The Cognitive Mediation Model of Learning from the News: Evidence from Nonelection, Off-Year Election, and Presidential Election Contexts," *Communication Research* 28, no. 5 (2001): 573.

13. William P. Eveland Jr., "News Information Processing as Mediatior of the Relationship between Motivations and Political Knowledge," *Journalism & Mass Communication Quarterly* 79, no. 1 (2002); "The Effect of Political Discussion in Producing Informed Citizens: The Roles of Information, Motivation, and Elaboration," *Political Communication* 21, no. 2 (2004); William P. Eveland Jr., Dhavan V. Shah, and Nojin Kwak, "Assessing Causality in the Cognitive Mediation Model: A Panel Study of Motivations, Information Processing, and Learning During Campaign 2000," *Communication Research* 30, no. 4 (2003).

14. Lauren Feldman, "Learning About Politics from *the Daily Show*: The Role of Viewer Orientation and Processing Motivations," *Mass Communication and Society* 16, no. 4 (2013).

15. Jorg Matthes, "Elaboration or Distraction? Knowledge Acquisition Fom Thematically Related and Unrelated Humor in Political Speeches," *International Journal of Public Opinion Research* 25, no. 3 (2013); Dannagal G. Young, "Laughter, Learning, or Enlightenment? Viewing and Avoidance Motivations Behind the Daily Show and the Colbert Report."

16. Heather L. LaMarre and Whitney Walther, "Ability Matters: Testing the Differential Effects of Political News and Late-Night Political Comedy on Cognitive Responses and the Role of Ability in Micro-Level Opinion Formation," *International Journal of Public Opinion Research* 25, no. 3 (2013).

17. Jorg Matthes, "Elaboration or Distraction? Knowledge Acquisition Fom Thematically Related and Unrelated Humor in Political Speeches," ibid.

18. Nabi, Moyer-Guse, and Byrne; Young, "The Privileged Role of the Late-Night Joke: Exploring Humor's Role in Disrupting Argument Scrutiny."

19. Feldman, "Learning About Politics from *The Daily Show*: The Role of Viewer Orientation and Processing Motivations"; Young, "Laughter, Learning, or Enlightenment? Viewing and Avoidance Motivations Behind the Daily Show and the Colbert Report."

20. Jay G. Blumler and Elihu Katz, *The Uses of Mass Communications: Current Perspectives on Gratifications Research* (Beverly Hills, CA: Sage Publications, 1974); Elihu Katz, Jay G. Blumler, and Michael Gurevitch, "Uses and Gratifications Research," *Public Opinion Quarterly* 37, no. 4 (1973).

21. Feldman, "Learning About Politics from *the Daily Show*: The Role of Viewer Orientation and Processing Motivations."

22. The manipulation checks confirmed that the majority of subjects were able to identify the politician being interviewed in the segment. There was variation in recall

depending upon condition type, with recall for comedy conditions being higher than news (e.g., 72% of those viewing *TCR* correctly identified Granholm, compared to 56% for *MSNBC*; 88% correctly identified Daniels on *TDS*, compared to 76% correct identification for *FOX News*).

23. William P. Eveland Jr., "Information-Processing Strategies in Mass Communication Research," in *The Evolution of Key Mass Communication Concepts: Honoring Jack Mcleod*, ed. Sharon Dunwoody and Lee Becker (New York: Hampton Press, 2005).

24. Kevin Coe et al., "Hostile News: Partisan Use and Perceptions of Cable News Programming," *Journal of Communication* 58, no. 2 (2008).

25. An ANOVA [$F(4, 217) = 2.10$, $p = 0.82$] confirmed that elaborative processing did not vary significantly across condition. The means for elaborative processing by condition were: (1) Granholm *TDS*: $M = 3.15$, $SD = 1.51$; (2) Granholm *MSNBC* $M = 3.43$, $SD = 1.70$, (3) Daniels *TDS* $M = 3.70$, $SD = 1.58$, (4) Daniels *FOX* $M = 2.98$, $SD = 1.65$; (5) Granholm *TCR* $M = 3.89$, $SD = 1.72$.

26. Jacob Cohen et al., *Applied Multiple Regression/Correlation Analysis for the Behavioral Sciences*, 3rd ed (Mahwah, NJ: Lawrence Erlbaum Associates, 2003).

27. Andrew F. Hayes, *Introduction to Mediation, Moderation, and Conditional Process Analysis: A Regression-Based Approach* (New York: The Guilford Press, 2013).

28. Coe et al., "Hostile News: Partisan Use and Perceptions of Cable News Programming"; R. Lance Holbert et al., "Affinity for Political Humor: An Assessment of Internal Factor Structure, Reliability, and Validity," *Humor* 26, no. 4 (2013).

29. LaMarre and Walther, "Ability Matters: Testing the Differential Effects of Political News and Late-Night Political Comedy on Cognitive Responses and the Role of Ability in Micro-Level Opinion Formation."

30. Feldman, "Learning About Politics from *the Daily Show*: The Role of Viewer Orientation and Processing Motivations."

31. Bruce W. Hardy et al., "Stephen Colbert's Civics Lesson: How Colbert Super Pac Taught Viewers About Campaign Finance," ibid. 17, no. 3 (2014); Heather L. LaMarre, "When Parody and Reality Collide: Examining the Effects of Colbert's Super Pac Satire on Issue Knowledge and Policy Engagement across Media Formats," *International Journal of Communication* 7, no. 20 (2013).

32. Amy B. Becker and Leticia Bode, "Satire as a Source for Learning? The Differential Impact of News Versus Satire Exposure on Net Neutrality Knowledge Gain," *Information, Communication & Society* 21, no. 4 (2018).

33. Forrest Wickman, "John Oliver Talked to Edward Snowden About How the Government Is Spying on Your Dick Pics." http://www.slate.com/blogs/browbeat/2015/04/06/john_oliver_talks_to_edward_snowden_about_your_dick_pics_for_last_week_tonight.html.

34. Amy B. Becker and Andrew B. Goldberg, "Entertainment, Intelligent, or Hybrid Programming? An Automated Content Analysis of Twelve Years of Political Satire Interviews," *Atlantic Journal of Communication* 25, no. 2 (2017).

REFERENCES

Baek, Young Min, and Magdalena E. Wojcieszak. "Don't Expect Too Much! Learning from Late-Night Comedy and Knowledge Item Difficulty." *Communication Research* 36, no. 6 (2009): 783–809.

Baum, Matthew A. *Soft News Goes to War: Public Opinion and American Foreign Policy in the New Media Age.* Princeton, NJ: Princeton University Press, 2003.

Baym, Geoffrey. "Breaking Boundaries | Political Media as Discursive Modes: A Comparative Analysis of Interviews with Ron Paul from Meet the Press, Tonight, the Daily Show, and Hannity." *International Journal of Communication* 7 (2013): http://ijoc.org/ojs/index.php/ijoc/article/view/1942/864.

———. "Crafting New Communicative Models in the Televisual Sphere: Political Interviews on *The Daily Show.*" *The Communication Review* 10, no. 2 (2007): 93–115. doi:10.1080/10714420701350379.

———. *From Cronkite to Colbert: The Evolution of Broadcast News.* Boulder, CO: Paradigm Publishers, 2010.

Becker, Amy B. "What About Those Interviews? The Impact of Exposure to Political Comedy and Cable News on Factual Recall and Anticipated Political Expression." *International Journal of Public Opinion Research* 25, no. 3 (June 19, 2013): 344–56. doi:10.1093/ijpor/edt014.

Becker, Amy B., and Leticia Bode. "Satire as a Source for Learning? The Differential Impact of News Versus Satire Exposure on Net Neutrality Knowledge Gain." *Information, Communication & Society* 21, no. 4 (2018): 1–14. doi:10.1080/1369 118X.2017.1301517.

Becker, A. B., and A. B. Goldberg. "Entertainment, Intelligent, or Hybrid Programming? An Automated Content Analysis of Twelve Years of Political Satire Interviews." *Atlantic Journal of Communication* 25, no. 2 (2017): 127–37. doi:10.1080 /15456870.2017.1293670.

Blumler, Jay G., and Elihu Katz. *The Uses of Mass Communications: Current Perspectives on Gratifications Research.* Beverly Hills, CA: Sage Publications, 1974.

Cao, Xiaoxao. "Political Comedy Shows and Knowledge About Primary Campaigns: The Moderating Effects of Age and Education." *Mass Communication and Society* 11, no. 1 (2008): 43–61. doi:10.1080/15205430701585028.

Cao, Xiaoxao, and Paul R. Brewer. "Political Comedy Shows and Public Participation in Politics." *International Journal of Public Opinion Research* 20, no. 1 (2008): 90–99.

Coe, Kevin, David Tewksbury, Bradley J. Bond, Kristin L. Drogos, Robert W. Porter, Ashley Yahn, and Yuanyuan Zhang. "Hostile News: Partisan Use and Perceptions of Cable News Programming." *Journal of Communication* 58, no. 2 (2008): 201–19.

Cohen, Jacob, Patricia Cohen, Stephen G. West, and Leona S. Aiken. *Applied Multiple Regression/Correlation Analysis for the Behavioral Sciences.* 3rd edition. Mahwah, NJ: Lawrence Erlbaum Associates, 2003.

Eveland Jr., William P. "The Cognitive Mediation Model of Learning from the News: Evidence from Nonelection, Off-Year Election, and Presidential Election Contexts." *Communication Research* 28, no. 5 (2001): 571–601. doi:10.1177/009365001028005001.

————. "The Effect of Political Discussion in Producing Informed Citizens: The Roles of Information, Motivation, and Elaboration." *Political Communication* 21, no. 2 (2004): 177–93. doi:10.1080/10584600490443877.

————. "Information-Processing Strategies in Mass Communication Research." In *The Evolution of Key Mass Communication Concepts: Honoring Jack Mcleod*, edited by Sharon Dunwoody and Lee Becker, 217–48. New York: Hampton Press, 2005.

————. "News Information Processing as Mediatior of the Relationship between Motivations and Political Knowledge." *Journalism & Mass Communication Quarterly* 79, no. 1 (2002): 26–40.

Eveland Jr., W. P., Dhavan V. Shah, and Nojin Kwak. "Assessing Causality in the Cognitive Mediation Model: A Panel Study of Motivations, Information Processing, and Learning During Campaign 2000." *Communication Research* 30, no. 4 (2003): 359–86. doi:10.1177/0093650203253369.

Feldman, Lauren. "Learning About Politics from *the Daily Show*: The Role of Viewer Orientation and Processing Motivations." *Mass Communication and Society* 16, no. 4 (2013): 586–607. doi:10.1080/15205436.2012.735742.

Feldman, Lauren, and Dannagal G. Young. "Late-Night Comedy as a Gateway to Traditional News: An Analysis of Time Trends in News Attention among Late-Night Comedy Viewers During the 2004 Presidential Primaries." *Political Communication* 25, no. 4 (2008): 401–22. doi:10.1080/10584600802427013.

Gottfried, Jeffrey A., Katerina Eva Matsa, and Michael Barthel. "As Jon Stewart Steps Down, 5 Facts About the Daily Show." http://www.pewresearch.org/fact-tank/2015/08/06/5-facts-daily-show/.

Hardy, Bruce W., Jeffrey A. Gottfried, Kenneth M. Winneg, and Kathleen Hall Jamieson. "Stephen Colbert's Civics Lesson: How Colbert Super Pac Taught Viewers About Campaign Finance." *Mass Communication and Society* 17, no. 3 (2014): 329–53. doi:10.1080/15205436.2014.891138.

Hayes, Andrew F. *Introduction to Mediation, Moderation, and Conditional Process Analysis: A Regression-Based Approach*. New York: The Guilford Press, 2013.

Hoffman, Lindsay H. "Breaking Boundaries | Political Interviews: Examining Perceived Media Bias and Effects across TV Entertainment Formats." *International Journal of Communication* 7 (2013): http://ijoc.org/ojs/index.php/ijoc/article/view/1942/864.

Hoffman, Lindsay H., and Dannagal G. Young. "Satire, Punch Lines, and the Nightly News: Untangling Media Effects on Political Participation." *Communication Research Reports* 28, no. 2 (2011): 159–68. doi:10.1080/08824096.2011.565278.

Holbert, Lance R., Jayeon Lee, Sarah Esralew, Whitney O. Walther, Jay D. Hmielowski, and Kristen D. Landreville. "Affinity for Political Humor: An Assessment of Internal Factor Structure, Reliability, and Validity." *Humor* 26, no. 4 (2013): 551–72. doi:10.1515/humor-2013-0034.

Hollander, Bruce A. "Late-Night Learning: Do Entertainment Programs Increase Political Campaign Knowledge for Young Viewers?" *Journal of Broadcasting & Electronic Media* 49, no. 4 (December 2005): 402–15. doi:10.1207/s15506878jobem4904_3.

Katz, Elihu, Jay G. Blumler, and Michael Gurevitch. "Uses and Gratifications Research." *Public Opinion Quarterly* 37, no. 4 (1973): 509–23.

Kim, Young Mie, and John Vishak. "Just Laugh! You Don't Ned to Remember: The Effects of Entertainment Media on Political Information Acquisition and Information Processing in Political Judgment." *Journal of Communication* 58, no. 2 (2008): 338–60. doi:10.1111/j.1460-2466.2008.00388.x.

LaMarre, Heather L. "When Parody and Reality Collide: Examining the Effects of Colbert's Super Pac Satire on Issue Knowledge and Policy Engagement across Media Formats." *International Journal of Communication* 7, no. 20 (2013): 394–413. http://ijoc.org/index.php/ijoc/article/view/1939.

LaMarre, Heather L., and Whitney Walther. "Ability Matters: Testing the Differential Effects of Political News and Late-Night Political Comedy on Cognitive Responses and the Role of Ability in Micro-Level Opinion Formation." *International Journal of Public Opinion Research* 25, no. 3 (September 1, 2013): 303–22. doi:10.1093/ijpor/edt008.

Matthes, Jorg. "Elaboration or Distraction? Knowledge Acquisition Fom Thematically Related and Unrelated Humor in Political Speeches." *International Journal of Public Opinion Research* 25, no. 3 (April 6, 2013): 291–302. doi:10.1093/ijpor/edt005.

Moy, Patricia, Michael A. Xenos, and Verena K. Hess. "Priming Effects of Late-Night Comedy." *International Journal of Public Opinion Research* 18, no. 2 (June 1, 2006): 198–210. doi:10.1093/ijpor/edh092.

Nabi, Robin L., Emily Moyer-Gusé, and Sahara Byrne. "All Joking Aside: A Serious Investigation into the Persuasive Effect of Funny Social Issue Messages." *Communication Monographs* 74, no. 1 (2007): 29–54. doi:10.1080/03637750701196896.

Pew. "Section 4: Demographics and Political Views of News Audiences." http://www.people-press.org/2012/09/27/section-4-demographics-and-political-views-of-news-audiences/.

Vraga, Emily K., Stephanie Edgerly, Leticia Bode, Jasun D. Carr, Mitchell Bard, Courtney N. Johnson, Young Mie Kim, and Dhavan V. Shah. "The Correspondent, the Comic, and the Combatant: The Consequences of Host Style in Political Talk Shows." *Journalism & Mass Communication Quarterly* 89, no. 1 (2012): 5–22. doi:10.1177/1077699011428575.

Wickman, Forrest. "John Oliver Talked to Edward Snowden About How the Government Is Spying on Your Dick Pics." http://www.slate.com/blogs/browbeat/2015/04/06/john_oliver_talks_to_edward_snowden_about_your_dick_pics_for_last_week_tonight.html.

Xenos, Michael A., and Amy B. Becker. "Moments of Zen: Effects of *the Daily Show* on Information Seeking and Political Learning." *Political Communication* 26, no. 3 (2009): 317–32. doi:10.1080/10584600903053569.

Young, Dannagal G. "Laughter, Learning, or Enlightenment? Viewing and Avoidance Motivations Behind the Daily Show and the Colbert Report." *Journal of Broadcasting & Electronic Media* 57, no. 2 (2013): 153–69. doi:10.1080/08838151.2013.787080.

———. "The Privileged Role of the Late-Night Joke: Exploring Humor's Role in Disrupting Argument Scrutiny." *Media Psychology* 11, no. 1 (2008): 119–42. doi:10.1080/15213260701837073.

Chapter 6

Inoculation against/with Political Humor

Josh Compton

A dozen plus years ago, I researched inoculation theory and political humor.[1] Although some of my predictions were supported, I could not have been more wrong about one of the core predictions of my study: that a politician could inoculate against late-night television political humor ridicule. Inoculation, the classic theory of resistance to influence,[2] had a proven track record of conferring resistance to future persuasive attacks. But in my study, not only did these inoculation efforts fail—the inoculation treatments actually boomeranged, with inoculation attempts hurting candidates instead of helping them.[3] One of the main takeaways, then, was that candidates would have been better off saying nothing at all than trying to preempt late-night television ridicule.

Conventional wisdom at that time was that late-night comedy ridicule probably hurt candidates. Late-night television political joke content, after all, was mostly negative toward politicians,[4] and inoculation had successfully protected attitudes in general,[5] and attitudes toward politicians in particular,[6] in a number of previous studies. Efforts to fend off such content, then, should have helped, at least some. But the story of political humor and inoculation was not that simple.

Now, many years later, we have a much better idea of the effects of political comedy in general[7] and late-night television political comedy in particular[8]; unique effects of different programs (e.g., *Saturday Night Live*,[9] *The Colbert Report*,[10] *The Daily Show*[11]); through different mediums (e.g., online user-generated satire,[12] YouTube[13]); and when covering different issues (e.g., climate change,[14] campaign finance,[15] immigration policy[16]) and in different segments (e.g., candidate interviews,[17] skits[18]). We also have a much better understanding of inoculation theory,[19] including a better understanding of threat (or perceived vulnerability to an impending attack[20]) and how threat motivates resistance to influence,[21] including reconceptualizations of threat.[22]

And still, even with these advances in political humor and inoculation research, we have limited understanding of political humor and inoculation, together. That is not to say, of course, that scholars working outside of inoculation theory research have not addressed related issues. Consider, for example, Stewart's observation that in making his now famous debate remark about his "opponent's youth and inexperience," Ronald Reagan "not only inoculated himself from future age-related concerns by highlighting his cleverness and ability to connect with the audience, but also appeared to put Senator Mondale and the moderator off stride."[23] Nabi, Moyer-Gusé, and Byrne note that humor's "power could be harnessed to raise awareness, disseminate information, and encourage positive attitudes and behavior while simultaneously minimizing conflict, anger, and resistance."[24] Specific inoculation theory analysis of political humor, however, is much more limited, and that is unfortunate. Inoculation—a theory with roots in psychology and relevance to politics—could help address something Becker has identified as a problem in political entertainment scholarship—that it "fails to speak fully across the psychology versus political science divide."[25] Inoculation work could contribute to a growing trend in political communication toward more nuance with political comedy/satire theorizing[26] and meet the call for political communication effects research "to account for the full spectrum of persuasion-based processes,"[27] including, I argue here, *resistance*.

This chapter advances two key approaches to inoculation and political humor research and theorizing: attempts by campaigns to inoculate against political humor, and whether political humor itself inoculates against other, more conventional political attacks. With the latter, my assumption is not that political humorists are intentionally inoculating, but instead, that inherent features of political humor trigger, under certain circumstances, inoculation processes. Such unintended effects of inoculation warrant a closer look. As Holbert, Garrett, and Gleason have observed, "The primary intention of entertainment media may be to entertain . . . but these nonnews outlets can still generate a host of unintended political outcomes."[28] Might one of these unintended outcomes be resistance to future persuasion? I think it is likely.

INOCULATION THEORY

Inoculation theory offers both a messaging/campaign strategy and a theoretical explanation for resistance to influence, building from a medical analogy.[29] Bodies become inoculated against future viral threats via pre-exposure to weakened versions of the virus; attitudes (or beliefs, or values) become inoculated against future persuasive threats via pre-exposure to weakened versions of the persuasion. Decades of scholarship, including lab and field experiments as well as sophisticated theorizing, have support inoculation's efficacy in conferring resistance to influence,[30] which has been supported by a meta-analysis.[31]

One of the most studied contexts for inoculation theory scholarship is politics.[32] Much of this research looks at attempts to confer resistance to influence against traditional political attacks, like direct mail[33] or attacks made in debates.[34] Much less attention has been paid to issues of inoculation resistance and political humor, although a few studies have looked specifically at such connections. Lim and Ki found some success in inoculating against parody videos on YouTube.[35] Warner, Hawthorne, and Hawthorne confirmed that a *Colbert Report* interview segment reduced persuasive effects of a subsequent Super PAC attack ad.[36] And as mentioned in the introduction to this chapter, my study looked at attempts to inoculate against late-night television political comedy and whether late-night television political comedy inoculates against more traditional political attacks.[37] Still there remain many under- or unexplored connections between inoculation theory and political humor.

Of the many connections that can be made between inoculation theory and political research are fundamental components in the model, like initial belief, involvement levels, threat, and counterarguing. Initial belief is important because inoculation is almost always conceptualized as a preemptive strategy—a means of protecting an existing attitude or belief before it is attacked. Consequently, one of inoculation's features is that it accounts for initial attitudes—prior to inoculation treatments.[38] With political humor research, Becker has called for incorporation of "prior disposition" in political humor research,[39] and indeed, political humor scholars are finding important effects of initial attitude and political humor. One relevant finding from the work of Boukes, Boomgaarden, Moorman, and de Vreese is that when the "right" position is in place, viewers are more likely to find political satire funnier—and funniness elicits more counterarguing.[40] Bowyer, Kahne, and Middaugh's study found that many young adults did not seem to understand the arguments of satiric YouTube videos—but they did understand more if they were already predisposed to agree with the message,[41] and initial attitude is usually considered a requisite for inoculation theory's efficacy, too. Inoculation-informed research seems a good way to consider initial positions, pre-humor, since initial positions are a fundamental part of the assumptions of inoculation theory.

Another feature of conventional inoculation research is that it often includes considerations of involvement levels.[42] The idea is that people need to care enough—but not too much—about the issue for inoculation to optimally occur.[43] Political humor scholars have theorized, too, that involvement levels can help to explain when satire "misfires."[44] Each area of research—inoculation and political humor—can help to inform the other.

Threat is another component of inoculation—usually conceptualized as a recognized vulnerability to future persuasion.[45] Threat is considered to be the motivational force behind inoculation's resistance processes, something supported by a recent investigation by Banas and Richards.[46] In terms of political humor research, work with the discounting hypothesis[47] raises some interesting connections here: Under some conditions, political humor might be simply dismissed as unimportant, or discounted as merely a joke. Such an effect seems to run counter to the idea of the motivational features of inoculation's conceptualization of threat, which might explain some of the challenges of merging political humor and inoculation theory.

Finally, the counterarguing process of inoculation seems particularly pertinent to the work of political humor scholars. Inoculation treatments encourage more counterarguing about the issue, both internal and external, subvocal and vocal.[48] Inoculated individuals think and talk more about the issue. This counterarguing can persist for at least over a month.[49] Political humor scholars, too, have studied counterarguing. For example, Boukes, Boomgaarden, Moorman, and de Vreese's work supports a conceptual model of satire effects that shows how the processes of funniness and absorption can pull in opposite directions: funniness enhancing counterarguing, and absorption diminishing counterarguing.[50]

At a fundamental level, then, inoculation theory and political humor have interesting connections, with both areas exploring issues of initial position, involvement, threat, and counterarguing. The next section takes a look at how these relationships might play out in a specific application of inoculation: attempts to inoculate *against* political humor.

INOCULATING AGAINST POLITICAL HUMOR

As previously mentioned, much of the existing work with inoculation and political humor has looked at efforts to inoculate against political humor, with Lim and Ki's study finding some success,[51] while my study did not.[52] Now that we know much more about political humor and inoculation theory, we should return to the idea that political humor can be inoculated against. Extant research reveals some interesting possibilities.

Becker and Waisanen found that viewers are less likely to elaborate on humorous political messages, and that people simply dismiss political jokes, like those made during the White House Correspondence Dinner,[53] and other research suggests that individuals often dismiss other types of humor, including horatian satire.[54] But could an inoculation message counter this tendency to dismiss by either elevating the seriousness of the humor, or decreasing the perceived humor? What if an inoculation message were designed to protect against dismissing political satire as "just a joke?" Boukes and colleagues argue, based on the result of their empirical support for a conceptual model that included both funniness and absorption, that the most effective political satire might occur when satirists do "not provide too many discounting cues but make clear that although they bring their message in the form of a joke, they are serious about the content."[55] Such advice could appear in an inoculation message such as

Counterargument: It is tempting to dismiss this as just a joke.
Refutation: That would be a mistake; the accusations are serious.

Or, perhaps an inoculation message could prepare people to recognize persuasive intent in political humor. Lim and Golan's work suggests that awareness of persuasive intent leads to more attempts to counter the message,[56] and Holbert and colleagues indicate that young voters discern persuasive intent from political satire, for instance.[57] And an even more nuanced inoculation approach might be to target specific types of humor. For example, some research suggests that viewers do not counterargue as well against irony as they do sarcasm;[58] by providing sample counterarguments, practice, and/or motivation, could inoculation boost this deficit? Inoculation messages designed to target the very features of political humor that make it so persuasive could help to blunt the impact of persuasive attacks in the form of political jokes—something that might be of interest to campaigns, in practice, and would most certainly be of interest to inoculation and political humor scholars, in theory and research.

To this point, this chapter has treated political humor mostly as an attack message—something to be potentially inoculated *against*. In the next section, I look at how political humor might be functioning as an inoculation message—something to potentially inoculate *with*.

INOCULATING WITH POLITICAL HUMOR

Another way of thinking about inoculation and political humor is whether humor functions as an inoculation treatment—including monologue jokes, political parody skits, and candidate appearances on late-night television programs. One of my studies found some support for inoculation effects of political humor, including candidate appearances on late-night television talk shows.[59] The idea was that political humor contains the requisites for inoculation-conferred resistance—including the presence of counterarguments and refutations (i.e., weakened counterarguments), whether appearing in the setup to a joke or in the back-and-forth during a candidate interview, that introduces weakened counter-positions and generates threat. Inoculation effects do not require an intent to inoculate, but instead, the meeting of the theory's conditions.

We now know a great deal more about candidate appearances and potential effects. Viewers remember more political details after seeing an interview with a politician on a late-night television comedy program compared to a cable news program—and after watching interviews on *The Daily Show*, viewers reported higher intentions to engage in political behaviors, like taking part in a demonstration or signing a petition.[60] Other work suggests that political knowledge impacts how trust in candidates is affected by appearances on entertainment talk shows; viewers with high political knowledge find the politicians less trustworthy, and those with low political knowledge find politicians more trustworthy.[61] Other forms of political humor might also have inoculation effects. Landreville and LaMarre's work with political comedy and intertextuality shows that viewing a comedic film can change how one processes the news—boosting their elaboration of the news article.[62]

One of the strongest arguments for how political humor might be an effective means of inoculation relates to word-of-mouth communication (WOMC), or in the context of inoculation research, postinoculation talk (PIT). Inoculation scholars have recently revealed that inoculation treatments motivate WOMC/PIT. This effect was theorized by Compton and Pfau[63] and supported in subsequent empirical investigations.[64] This line of inoculation research matches up nicely with some recent advancements in WOMC and political humor. Lee found that watching late-night comedy led to more intrapersonal talk—and that the effect was limited on intentions to engage with non-likeminded others.[65] In another study, Lee found that exposure to online user-generated satire led to more negative views of the ridiculed politician, but after discussion, also led to negative views toward the electoral system.[66] Lee and Jang discovered that the motivation to talk post-political satire viewing, is mostly affective in general, with negative emotions (anger and worry) connected to more talk.[67] Nabi, Moyer-Gusé, and Byrne found that people were more likely to discuss humorous messages compared to serious ones.[68] Landreville and LaMarre's work with political comedy and intertextuality raises some complementary issues regarding postinoculation talk. Based on extant work, they expected to find that watching a political comedy film would increase intent to talk about related issues in a news story, but results did not support their prediction. Political comedy boosted subjects' thinking about the news article—but did not make them want to talk about it with others.[69] Landreville, Holbert, and LaMarre found that watching late-night comedy predicted debate viewing and then, more political talk, especially with younger viewers. (Their work failed to find a direct relationship between late-night comedy viewing and political talk, though.[70])

A good deal of research, then, suggests that political humor and inoculation messages boost talk (but see Landreville and LaMarre's study for an instance when it did not).[71] Any of these findings could make for an interesting premise for an inoculation theory-informed study of political humor, but consider, in particular, Lee and Jang's work. Lee and Jang found that worry and anger motivates post-satire talk.[72] Worry was one of the theorized motivators for postinoculation talk in Compton and Pfau's initial theorizing,[73] and anger and its relationship to inoculation is also receiving attention.[74]

Such research would not need to be limited to the individual level, either. In addition to the behaviors of talk, both inoculation and political humor have been found to promote political behaviors, or at least, introduce effects that are conducive to future political behavior. Pfau and colleagues' research, for example, shows positive relationships between inoculation treatments and political participation.[75] In political humor work, Lee and Kwak have revealed how political satire motivates political participation by provoking negative emotions which can, unlike cynicism, motivate political participation,[76] and Landreville, Holbert, and LaMarre's analysis shows that late-night comedy viewing predicts debate viewing[77]—another important political behavior.

But just as there are features of political humor that might make it difficult to inoculate against, there are also features that might make it difficult to inoculate with. People seem to think more about political humor than they do non-humorous content—but not about the political content of the political humor.[78] Furthermore, some research suggests that viewers do not always "get" satire,[79] although most do seem to "get" the joke.[80] The relationship between understanding ("getting" the point) and inoculation needs more exploration, and political humor seems like a particularly good area in which to do such research.

Inoculating against and with political humor are two areas that seem quite promising for future research, with potential implications for campaign strategy and political behaviors, attitudes, and knowledge. But that is not all. The work of inoculation theory and political humor, together, can reflect the increasing nuance of the work in inoculation theory and political humor, separately. I introduce some of these possibilities next.

FUTURE DIRECTIONS

The research examined in this chapter suggests promising potential for future investigations of political humor and inoculation theory, to further discover what it means to inoculate both *against* and *with* political humor. Two particularly promising directions would seem to be (1) features of political humor that make it particularly difficult to inoculate *against*; and (2) features of political humor that make it particularly effective to inoculate *with*.

Attempts to inoculate *against* political humor have had inconsistent success in empirical investigations[81]—either because humor has features that make it immune from inoculation, or messaging strategies have used ineffective approaches—or both, or something else. I have proposed in this chapter that the concept of threat (recognized vulnerability) might be a key factor: if an attack message isn't recognized as an attack, resistance strategies are unlikely to be triggered.[82] It is also worth further exploring other features of political humor that might make it particularly challenging to inoculate against, including humor's effects on affect (and affect's subsequent effects on message processing during resistance strategies[83]) and issues of source credibility, which is receiving increased attention in inoculation scholarship.[84]

Inoculating *with* humor should be further explored in both (1) how humor could be strategically, intentionally used to confer resistance to influence; and (2) how humor could have unintentional inoculation effects. In either instance, scholars should continue to look beyond conventional media effects when studying political humor. Finding that humor has immediate effects on an attitude or belief is useful, but so is testing that attitude or belief later, after it has been challenged, to see if it withstood the attack. Inoculation provides a useful framework for doing such work.

In addition to these general areas of future work—inoculating *against* and inoculating *with*—future work should also further explore some of the more specific variables that might affect inoculation-conferred resistance. For example, scholars have called for increased attention to the medium of inoculation messaging, especially in political inoculation research,[85] and I have argued before that different segments of late-night television programs likely have different effects.[86] Combining inoculation work with political humor, scholars could help to further investigate some of these shared questions. LaMarre, for example, found that viewers experienced different effects when watching Colbert on his own comedy show, *The Colbert Report*, than when watching Colbert as a guest on a political talk show (*Morning Joe*).[87] Might we find different effects with both inoculating against and with political humor, based on the message format?

We can further add nuance by looking at segment features. Consider, for example, how some hosts end a joke with a more serious, sincere statement about the issue, something Nabi, Moyer-Gusé, and Byrne describe as "reestablish[ing] serious intent."[88] Might we find that these techniques function in similar ways to epilogues after some entertainment-education narratives—final statements that explicitly summarize/emphasize the key intended takeaway from the narrative, for example, that drunk driving is deadly? Moyer-Gusé, Jain, and Chung found that such epilogues can be quite effective—strengthening attitudes toward the intended advocacy (in their study, drunk driving).[89] Innocenti and Miller point out that this type of humor message feature can circumvent discounting.[90] When such messages are included, do they make the messages more difficult to inoculate against? On the other hand, would such a message make the political humor more effective as a means of inoculation?

Do different types of humor have different effects in terms of inoculating against or with political humor? Holbert and colleagues have explored different types of satire and subsequent persuasive effects, and as they note, "It it important that any effects-based research on political satire clearly identify the type of political satire being focused on in the research effort."[91] Similarly, others have looked at different effects of irony and sarcasm.[92] After discovering that different types of satire motivate different types of argument processing, LaMarre and colleagues concluded that "harsh juvenalian satire has the potential to be extremely powerful, since the audience appears to be *robbed* of its ability to scrutinize the underlying arguments presented."[93] More broadly, and drawing on the work of Young's resource allocation hypothesis,[94] they warn:

> If . . . certain forms of satire reduce the public's motivation or ability to think about the issues, assess the strength of relevant arguments, and attend to the political issues being presented, then we are entering a world where opinion, sarcasm, innuendo, parody, and satire may have more influence on our democracy than facts and relevant truths. This is where humor can become serious business.[95]

Could inoculation messages be designed to thwart such potential effects of these forms of satire? Or, if research finds that certain types of satire are creating resistant cyncism (i.e., inoculating against perceived efficacy, or hope), what options do we have for encouraging political efficacy?

Finally, it is worth exploring whether inoculating against political humor might have an iatrogenic effect, or a side effect of sorts caused by the treatment itself—making the humor less funny. If success in inoculation hinges on making a joke come across as an attack, would the joke be considered more of a conventional argument and less as a joke, and if so, what would be the implications for humor and/or inoculation effects?

CONCLUSION

When I first set out to study inoculation and political humor, I was mostly thinking about purposeful, strategic efforts on the part of politicians to protect against humorous jabs.[96] I am not so sure now that this is the most fertile area for research in this area, though. Some of the more interesting findings, as I have tried to introduce here, might come from unintended inoculation effects—resulting from the presence of inoculation features in political humor (e.g., the setup of a joke, the back-and-forth during candidate interviews). Either way, I am convinced that work in inoculation and political humor would be mutually beneficial—developing theory and informing practice—as we try to better understand inoculating *against* and *with* political humor.

NOTES

1. Josh Compton, "Late Night Political Comedy, Candidate Image, and Inoculation: A Unique Test of Inoculation Theory" (PhD diss., University of Oklahoma, 2004).

2. William J. McGuire, "Inducing Resistance to Persuasion: Some Contemporary Approaches," in *Advances in Experimental Social Psychology*, ed. Leonard Berkowitz (New York: Academic Press, 1964).

3. Compton, "Late Night Political Comedy, Candidate Image, and Inoculation: A Unique Test of Inoculation Theory."

4. David Niven, S. Robert Lichter, and Daniel Amundson, "The Political Content of Late Night Comedy," *Harvard International Journal of Press/Politics* 8, no. 3 (2003).

5. McGuire, "Inducing Resistance to Persuasion: Some Contemporary Approaches."

6. Josh Compton and Bobi Ivanov, "Vaccinating Voters: Surveying Political Campaign Inoculation Scholarship," in *Communication Yearbook* 37, ed. Elisia L. Cohen (New York: Routledge, 2013), 250–83.

7. Josh Compton, "More than Laughing? Survey of Political Humor Effects Research," in *Laughing Matters: Humor and American Politics in the Media Age*, eds. Jody Baumgartner and Jonathan S. Morris (New York: Routledge, 2008).

8. Josh Compton, "Surveying Scholarship on *The Daily Show* and *The Colbert Report*," in *The Stewart/Colbert Effect: Essays on the Real Impacts of Fake News*, ed. Amarnath Amarasingam (Jefferson, NC: McFarland, 2011).

9. Outi J. Hakola, "Political Impersonations on *Saturday Night Live* during the 2016 US Presidential Election," *European Journal of American Studies* 12, no. 12–2 (2017).

10. Benjamin R. Warner, Hayley Jeanne Hawthorne, and Joshua Hawthorne, "A Dual-Processing Approach to the Effects of Viewing Political Comedy," *Humor* 28, no. 4 (2015).

11. Amy B. Becker, "What about Those Interviews? The Impact of Exposure to Political Comedy and Cable News on Factual Recall and Anticipated Political Expression," *International Journal of Public Opinion Research* 25, no. 3 (2013).

12. Francis L. F. Lee, "The Impact of Online User-Generated Satire on Young People's Political Attitudes: Testing the Moderating Role of Knowledge and Discussion," *Telematics and Informatics* 31, no. 3 (2014).

13. Benjamin T. Bowyer, Joseph E. Kahne, and Ellen Middaugh, "Youth Comprehension of Political Messages in YouTube Videos." *New Media & Society* 19, no. 4 (2017).

14. Paul R. Brewer and Jessica McKnight, "Climate as Comedy: The Effects of Satirical Television News on Climate Change Perceptions," *Science Communication* 37, no. 5 (2015).

15. Heather LaMarre, "When Parody and Reality Collide: Examining the Effects of Colbert's Super PAC Satire on Issue Knowledge and Policy Engagement across Media Formats," *International Journal of Communication* 7 (2013).

16. Bowyer, Kahne, and Middaugh, "Youth Comprehension of Political Messages in YouTube Videos."

17. Warner, Hawthorne, and Hawthorne, "A Dual-Processing Approach to the Effects of Viewing Political Comedy."

18. Rebecca Higgie, "Public Engagement, Propaganda, or Both? Attitudes toward Politicians on Political Satire and Comedy Programs," *International Journal of Communication* 11 (2017).

19. Josh Compton, "Inoculation Theory," in *The Sage Handbook of Persuasion*, eds. James P. Dillard and Lijiang Shen (Thousand Oaks, CA: Sage, 2013).

20. Josh Compton, "Threat Explication: What We Know and Don't Yet Know about a Key Component of Inoculation Theory," *STAM Journal* 39 (2009): 1–18.

21. Josh Compton and Bobi Ivanov, "Untangling Threat during Inoculation-Conferred Resistance to Influence," *Communication Reports* 25, no. 1 (2012).

22. John A. Banas and Adam S. Richards, "Apprehension or Motivation to Defend Attitudes? Exploring the Underlying Threat Mechanism in Inoculation-Induced Resistance to Persuasion," *Communication Monographs* 84, no. 2 (2017).

23. Patrick A. Stewart, "Presidential Laugh Lines: Candidate Display Behavior and Audience Laughter in the 2008 Primary Debates," *Politics and the Life Sciences* 29, no. 2 (2010): 56.

24. Robin L. Nabi, Emily Moyer-Gusé, and Sahara Byrne, "All Joking Aside: A Serious Investigation into the Persuasive Effect of Funny Social Issue Messages," *Communication Monographs* 74, no. 1 (2007): 51.

25. Amy B. Becker, "Humiliate my Enemies or Mock my Friends? Applying Disposition Theory of Humor to the Study of Political Parody Appreciation and Attitudes toward Candidates," *Human Communication Research* 40, no. 2 (2014): 138.

26. Hardy et al., "Stephen Colbert's Civics Lesson: How Colbert Super PAC Taught Viewers about Campaign Finance," *Mass Communication and Society* 17, no. 3 (2014).

27. R. Lance Holbert, R. Kelly Garrett, and Laurel S. Gleason, "A New Era of Minimal Effects? A Response to Bennett and Iyengar," *Journal of Communication* 60, no. 1 (2010): 17.

28. Ibid., 19.

29. McGuire, "Inducing Resistance to Persuasion: Some Contemporary Approaches."

30. Compton, "Inoculation Theory."

31. Banas and Rains, "A Meta-Analysis of Research on Inoculation Theory."

32. Compton and Ivanov, "Vaccinating Voters: Surveying Political Campaign Inoculation Scholarship."

33. Michael Pfau et al., "Efficacy of Inoculation Strategies in Promoting Resistance to Political Attack Messages: Application to Direct Mail," *Communications Monographs* 57, no. 1 (1990).

34. Chasu An and Michael Pfau. "The Efficacy of Inoculation in Televised Political Debates," *Journal of Communication* 54, no. 3 (2004).

35. Joon Soo Lim and Eyun-Jung Ki, "Resistance to Ethically Suspicious Parody Video on YouTube: A Test of Inoculation Theory," *Journalism & Mass Communication Quarterly* 84, no. 4 (2007).

36. Warner, Hawthorne, and Hawthorne, "A Dual-Processing Approach to the Effects of Viewing Political Comedy."

37. Compton, "Late Night Political Comedy, Candidate Image, and Inoculation: A Unique Test of Inoculation Theory."

38. Compton, "Inoculation Theory."

39. Becker, "Humiliate my Enemies or Mock my Friends? Applying Disposition Theory of Humor to the Study of Political Parody Appreciation and Attitudes toward Candidates."

40. Mark Boukes et al., "At Odds: Laughing and Thinking? The Appreciation, Processing, and Persuasiveness of Political Satire," *Journal of Communication* 65, no. 5 (2015).

41. Bowyer, Kahne, and Middaugh, "Youth Comprehension of Political Messages in YouTube Videos."

42. Josh Compton and Michael Pfau, "Use of Inoculation to Foster Resistance to Credit Card Marketing Targeting College Students," *Journal of Applied Communication Research* 32, no. 4 (2004).

43. Michael Pfau et al., "Enriching the Inoculation Construct The Role of Critical Components in the Process of Resistance," *Human Communication Research* 24, no. 2 (1997).

44. Boukes et al., "At Odds: Laughing and Thinking? The Appreciation, Processing, and Persuasiveness of Political Satire," 740.

45. McGuire, "Inducing Resistance to Persuasion: Some Contemporary Approaches," 201.

46. Banas and Richards, "Apprehension or Motivation to Defend Attitudes? Exploring the Underlying Threat Mechanism in Inoculation-Induced Resistance to Persuasion."

47. Nabi, Moyer-Gusé, and Byrne, "All Joking Aside: A Serious Investigation into the Persuasive Effect of Funny Social Issue Messages."

48. Compton, "Inoculation Theory," 222.

49. Michael Pfau, et al., "The Conundrum of the Timing of Counterarguing Effects in Resistance: Strategies to Boost the Persistence of Counterarguing Output," *Communication Quarterly* 54, no. 2 (2006).

50. Boukes et al., "At Odds: Laughing and Thinking? The Appreciation, Processing, and Persuasiveness of Political Satire."

51. Lim and Ki, "Resistance to Ethically Suspicious Parody Video on YouTube: A Test of Inoculation Theory."

52. Compton, "Late Night Political Comedy, Candidate Image, and Inoculation: A Unique Test of Inoculation Theory."

53. Amy B. Becker and Don J. Waisanen, "Laughing or Learning with the Chief Executive? The Impact of Exposure to Presidents' Jokes on Message Elaboration," *Humor* 30, no. 1 (2017).

54. Heather L. LaMarre et al., "Humor Works in Funny Ways: Examining Satirical Tone as a Key Determinant in Political Humor Message Processing," *Mass Communication and Society* 17, no. 3 (2014).

55. Boukes et al., "At Odds: Laughing and Thinking? The Appreciation, Processing, and Persuasiveness of Political Satire," 739.

56. Joon Soo Lim and Guy J. Golan, "Social Media Activism in Response to the Influence of Political Parody Videos on YouTube," *Communication Research* 38, no. 5 (2011).

57. R. Lance Holbert et al., "Young Voter Perceptions of Political Satire as Persuasion: A Focus on Perceived Influence, Persuasive Intent, and Message Strength," *Journal of Broadcasting & Electronic Media* 57, no. 2 (2013).

58. Jeremy Polk, Dannagal G. Young, and R. Lance Holbert, "Humor Complexity and Political Influence: An Elaboration Likelihood Approach to the Effects of Humor Type in *The Daily Show* with Jon Stewart," *Atlantic Journal of Communication* 17, no. 4 (2009).

59. Compton, "Late Night Political Comedy, Candidate Image, and Inoculation: A Unique Test of Inoculation Theory."

60. Becker, "What about Those Interviews? The Impact of Exposure to Political Comedy and Cable News on Factual Recall and Anticipated Political Expression."

61. Mark Boukes and Hajo G. Boomgaarden, "Politician Seeking Voter: How Interviews on Entertainment Talk Shows Affect Trust in Politicians," *International Journal of Communication* 10 (2016).

62. Kristen D. Landreville and Heather L. LaMarre, "Examining the Intertextuality of Fictional Political Comedy and Real-World Political News," *Media Psychology* 16, no. 3 (2013).

63. Josh Compton and Michael Pfau, "Spreading Inoculation: Inoculation, Resistance to Influence, and Word-of-Mouth Communication," *Communication Theory* 19, no. 1 (2009).

64. Ivanov et al., "Effects of Postinoculation Talk on Resistance to Influence," *Journal of Communication* 62, no. 4 (2012).

65. Hoon Lee, "Communication Mediation Model of Late-Night Comedy: The Mediating Role of Structural Features of Interpersonal Talk between Comedy Viewing and Political Participation," *Mass Communication and Society* 15, no. 5 (2012).

66. Lee, "The Impact of Online User-Generated Satire on Young People's Political Attitudes."

67. Hoon Lee and S. Mo Jang, "Talking about What Provokes Us: Political Satire, Emotions, and Interpersonal Talk," *American Politics Research* 45, no. 1 (2017).

68. Nabi, Moyer-Gusé, and Byrne, "All Joking Aside: A Serious Investigation into the Persuasive Effect of Funny Social Issue Messages."

69. Landreville and LaMarre, "Examining the Intertextuality of Fictional Political Comedy and Real-World Political News."

70. Kristen D. Landreville, R. Lance Holbert, and Heather L. LaMarre, "The Influence of Late-Night TV Comedy Viewing on Political Talk: A Moderated-Mediation Model," *The International Journal of Press/Politics* 15, no. 4 (2010).

71. Landreville and LaMarre, "Examining the Intertextuality of Fictional Political Comedy and Real-World Political News."

72. Lee and Jang, "Talking About What Provokes Us: Political Satire, Emotions, and Interpersonal Talk."

73. Compton and Pfau, "Spreading Inoculation: Inoculation, Resistance to Influence, and Word-of-Mouth Communication."

74. Miller et al., "Boosting the Potency of Resistance: Combining the Motivational Forces of Inoculation and Psychological Reactance," *Human Communication Research* 39, no. 1 (2013).

75. Michael Pfau et al., "The Effects of Party- and PAC-Sponsored Issue Advertising and the Potential of Inoculation to Combat its Impact on the Democratic Process," *American Behavioral Scientist* 44, no. 12 (2001).

76. Hoon Lee and Nojin Kwak, "The Affect Effect of Political Satire: Sarcastic Humor, Negative Emotions, and Political Participation," *Mass Communication and Society* 17, no. 3 (2014).

77. Landreville, Holbert, and LaMarre, "The Influence of Late-Night TV Comedy Viewing on Political Talk: A Moderated-Mediation Model."

78. Heather L. LaMarre and Whitney Walther, "Ability Matters: Testing the Differential Effects of Political News and Late-Night Political Comedy on Cognitive Responses and the Role of Ability in Micro-Level Opinion Formation," *International Journal of Public Opinion Research* 25, no. 3 (2013).

79. Heather L. LaMarre, Kristen D. Landreville, and Michael A. Beam, "The Irony of Satire: Political Ideology and the Motivation to See What You Want to See in *The Colbert Report*," *The International Journal of Press/Politics* 14, no. 2 (2009).

80. Shaheed Nick Mohammed, "'It-Getting' in the Colbert Nation Online Forum," *Mass Communication and Society* 17, no. 2 (2014).

81. Compton, "Late Night Political Comedy, Candidate Image, and Inoculation: A Unique Test of Inoculation Theory"; Lim and Ki, "Resistance to Ethically Suspicious Parody Video on YouTube: A Test of Inoculation Theory."

82. Compton, "Late Night Political Comedy, Candidate Image, and Inoculation: A Unique Test of Inoculation Theory."

83. Josh Compton and Michael Pfau, "Inoculation Theory of Resistance to Influence at Maturity: Recent Progress in Theory Development and Application and Suggestions for Future Research," *Annals of the International Communication Association* 29, no. 1 (2005).

84. Compton, "Inoculation Theory."

85. Compton and Ivanov, "Vaccinating Voters: Surveying Political Campaign Inoculation Scholarship."

86. Compton, "Surveying Scholarship on *The Daily Show* and *The Colbert Report*."

87. LaMarre, "When Parody and Reality Collide: Examining the Effects of Colbert's Super PAC Satire on Issue Knowledge and Policy Engagement across Media Formats."

88. Nabi, Moyer-Gusé, and Byrne, "All Joking Aside: A Serious Investigation into the Persuasive Effect of Funny Social Issue Messages," 51.

89. Emily Moyer-Gusé, Parul Jain, and Adrienne H. Chung, "Reinforcement or Reactance? Examining the Effect of an Explicit Persuasive Appeal Following an Entertainment-Education Narrative," *Journal of Communication* 62, no. 6 (2012).

90. Beth Innocenti and Elizabeth Miller, "The Persuasive Force of Political Humor," *Journal of Communication* 66, no. 3 (2016).

91. R. Lance Holbert et al., "Young Voter Perceptions of Political Satire as Persuasion: A Focus on Perceived Influence, Persuasive Intent, and Message Strength," 183.

92. Polk, Young, and Holbert, "Humor Complexity and Political Influence: An Elaboration Likelihood Approach to the Effects of Humor Type in *The Daily Show* with Jon Stewart."

93. Heather L. LaMarre et al., "Humor Works in Funny Ways: Examining Satirical Tone as a Key Determinant in Political Humor Message Processing," 421–422.

94. Dannagal Goldthwaite Young, "The Privileged Role of the Late-Night Joke: Exploring Humor's Role in Disrupting Argument Scrutiny," *Media Psychology* 11, no. 1 (2008).

95. Heather L. LaMarre et al., "Humor Works in Funny Ways: Examining Satirical Tone as a Key Determinant in Political Humor Message Processing," 422.

96. Compton, "Late Night Political Comedy, Candidate Image, and Inoculation: A Unique Test of Inoculation Theory."

REFERENCES

An, Chasu, and Michael Pfau. "The Efficacy of Inoculation in Televised Political Debates." *Journal of Communication* 54, no. 3 (2004): 421–36.

Banas, John A., and Stephen A. Rains. "A Meta-Analysis of Research on Inoculation Theory." *Communication Monographs* 77, no. 3 (2010): 281–311.

Banas, John A., and Adam S. Richards. "Apprehension or Motivation to Defend Attitudes? Exploring the Underlying Threat Mechanism in Inoculation-Induced Resistance to Persuasion." *Communication Monographs* 84, no. 2 (2017): 164–78.

Becker, Amy B. "What about Those Interviews? The Impact of Exposure to Political Comedy and Cable News on Factual Recall and Anticipated Political Expression." *International Journal of Public Opinion Research* 25, no. 3 (2013): 344–56.

———. "Humiliate my Enemies or Mock my Friends? Applying Disposition Theory of Humor to the Study of Political Parody Appreciation and Attitudes toward Candidates." *Human Communication Research* 40, no. 2 (2014): 137–60.

Becker, Amy B., and Don J. Waisanen. "Laughing or Learning with the Chief Executive? The Impact of Exposure to Presidents' Jokes on Message Elaboration." *Humor* 30, no. 1 (2017): 23–41.

Boukes, Mark, and Hajo G. Boomgaarden. "Politician Seeking Voter: How Interviews on Entertainment Talk Shows Affect Trust in Politicians." *International Journal of Communication* 10 (2016): 1145–66.

Boukes, Mark, Hajo G. Boomgaarden, Marjolein Moorman, and Claes H. de Vreese. "At Odds: Laughing and Thinking? The Appreciation, Processing, and Persuasiveness of Political Satire." *Journal of Communication* 65, no. 5 (2015): 721–44.

Bowyer, Benjamin T., Joseph E. Kahne, and Ellen Middaugh. "Youth Comprehension of Political Messages in YouTube Videos." *New Media & Society* 19, no. 4 (2017): 522–41.

Brewer, Paul R., and Jessica McKnight. "Climate as Comedy: The Effects of Satirical Television News on Climate Change Perceptions." *Science Communication* 37, no. 5 (2015): 635–57.

Compton, Josh. "Late Night Political Comedy, Candidate Image, and Inoculation: A Unique Test of Inoculation Theory." PhD diss., University of Oklahoma, 2004.

———. "More than Laughing? Survey of Political Humor Effects Research." In *Laughing Matters: Humor and American Politics in the Media Age*, edited by Jody Baumgartner and Jonathan S. Morris, 39–66. New York: Routledge, 2008.

———. "Threat Explication: What We Know and Don't Yet Know about a Key Component of Inoculation Theory." *STAM Journal* 39 (2009): 1–18.

———. "Surveying Scholarship on *The Daily Show* and *The Colbert Report*." In *The Stewart/Colbert Effect: Essays on the Real Impacts of Fake News*, edited by Amarnath Amarasingam, 9–23. Jefferson, NC: McFarland, 2011.

———. "Inoculation Theory." In *The Sage Handbook of Persuasion*, edited by James P. Dillard and Lijiang Shen, 220–36. Thousand Oaks, CA: Sage, 2013.

———. "Inoculating against a Losing Season: Can Inoculation-Informed Public Relations Strategies Protect Fan Loyalty?" *International Journal of Sport Communication* 9, no. 1 (2016): 1–12.

Compton, Josh, and Bobi Ivanov. "Untangling Threat during Inoculation-Conferred Resistance to Influence." *Communication Reports* 25, no. 1 (2012): 1–13.

———. "Vaccinating Voters: Surveying Political Campaign Inoculation Scholarship." In *Communication Yearbook* 37, edited by Elisia L. Cohen, 250–83. New York: Routledge, 2013.

Compton, Josh, and Michael Pfau. "Use of Inoculation to Foster Resistance to Credit Card Marketing Targeting College Students." *Journal of Applied Communication Research* 32, no. 4 (2004): 343–64.

———. "Spreading Inoculation: Inoculation, Resistance to Influence, and Word-of-Mouth Communication," *Communication Theory* 19, no. 1 (2009): 9–28.

Hakola, Outi J. "Political Impersonations on *Saturday Night Live* during the 2016 US Presidential Election." *European Journal of American Studies* 12, no. 12–2 (2017): 1–20.

Hardy, Bruce W., Jeffrey A. Gottfried, Kenneth M. Winneg, and Kathleen Hall Jamieson. "Stephen Colbert's Civics Lesson: How Colbert Super PAC Taught Viewers about Campaign Finance." *Mass Communication and Society* 17, no. 3 (2014): 329–53.

Higgie, Rebecca. "Public Engagement, Propaganda, or Both? Attitudes toward Politicians on Political Satire and Comedy Programs." *International Journal of Communication* 11 (2017): 930–48.

Holbert, R. Lance, R. Kelly Garrett, and Laurel S. Gleason. "A New Era of Minimal Effects? A Response to Bennett and Iyengar." *Journal of Communication* 60, no. 1 (2010): 15–34.

Holbert, R. Lance, John M. Tchernev, Whitney O. Walther, Sarah E. Esralew, and Kathryn Benski. "Young Voter Perceptions of Political Satire as Persuasion: A Focus on Perceived Influence, Persuasive Intent, and Message Strength." *Journal of Broadcasting & Electronic Media* 57, no. 2 (2013): 170–86.

Innocenti, Beth, and Elizabeth Miller. "The Persuasive Force of Political Humor." *Journal of Communication* 66, no. 3 (2016): 366–85.

Ivanov, Bobi, Claude H. Miller, Josh Compton, Joshua M. Averbeck, Kylie J. Harrison, Jeanetta D. Sims, Kimberly A. Parker, and James L. Parker. "Effects of Postinoculation Talk on Resistance to Influence." *Journal of Communication* 62, no. 4 (2012): 701–18.

LaMarre, Heather. "When Parody and Reality Collide: Examining the Effects of Colbert's Super PAC Satire on Issue Knowledge and Policy Engagement across Media Formats." *International Journal of Communication* 7 (2013): 393–413.

LaMarre, Heather L., Kristen D. Landreville, and Michael A. Beam. "The Irony of Satire: Political Ideology and the Motivation to See What You Want to See in *The Colbert Report*." *The International Journal of Press/Politics* 14, no. 2 (2009): 212–31.

LaMarre, Heather L., Kristen D. Landreville, Dannagal Young, and Nathan Gilkerson. "Humor Works in Funny Ways: Examining Satirical Tone as a Key Determinant in Political Humor Message Processing." *Mass Communication and Society* 17, no. 3 (2014): 400–23.

LaMarre, Heather L., and Whitney Walther. "Ability Matters: Testing the Differential Effects of Political News and Late-Night Political Comedy on Cognitive Responses and the Role of Ability in Micro-Level Opinion Formation." *International Journal of Public Opinion Research* 25, no. 3 (2013): 303–22.

Landreville, Kristen D., R. Lance Holbert, and Heather L. LaMarre. "The Influence of Late-Night TV Comedy Viewing on Political Talk: A Moderated-Mediation Model." *The International Journal of Press/Politics* 15, no. 4 (2010): 482–98.

Landreville, Kristen D., and Heather L. LaMarre. "Examining the Intertextuality of Fictional Political Comedy and Real-World Political News." *Media Psychology* 16, no. 3 (2013): 347–69.

Lee, Francis L. F. "The Impact of Online User-Generated Satire on Young People's Political Attitudes: Testing the Moderating Role of Knowledge and Discussion." *Telematics and Informatics* 31, no. 3 (2014): 397–409.

Lee, Hoon. "Communication Mediation Model of Late-Night Comedy: The Mediating Role of Structural Features of Interpersonal Talk between Comedy Viewing and Political Participation." *Mass Communication and Society* 15, no. 5 (2012): 647–71.

Lee, Hoon, and Nojin Kwak. "The Affect Effect of Political Satire: Sarcastic Humor, Negative Emotions, and Political Participation." *Mass Communication and Society* 17, no. 3 (2014): 307–28.

Lee, Hoon, and S. Mo Jang. "Talking About What Provokes Us: Political Satire, Emotions, and Interpersonal Talk." *American Politics Research* 45, no. 1 (2017): 128–54.

Lim, Joon Soo, and Guy J. Golan. "Social Media Activism in Response to the Influence of Political Parody Videos on YouTube." *Communication Research* 38, no. 5 (2011): 710–27.

Lim, Joon Soo, and Eyun-Jung Ki. "Resistance to Ethically Suspicious Parody Video on YouTube: A Test of Inoculation Theory." *Journalism & Mass Communication Quarterly* 84, no. 4 (2007): 713–28.

McGuire, William J. "Inducing Resistance to Persuasion: Some Contemporary Approaches." In *Advances in Experimental Social Psychology*, edited by Leonard Berkowitz, 191–229. New York: Academic Press, 1964.

Miller, Claude H., Bobi Ivanov, Jeanetta Sims, Josh Compton, Kylie J. Harrison, Kimberly A. Parker, James L. Parker, and Joshua M. Averbeck. "Boosting the Potency of Resistance: Combining the Motivational Forces of Inoculation and Psychological Reactance." *Human Communication Research* 39, no. 1 (2013): 127–55.

Mohammed, Shaheed Nick. "'It-Getting' in the Colbert Nation Online Forum." *Mass Communication and Society* 17, no. 2 (2014): 173–94.

Moyer-Gusé, Emily, Parul Jain, and Adrienne H. Chung. "Reinforcement or Reactance? Examining the Effect of an Explicit Persuasive Appeal Following an Entertainment-Education Narrative." *Journal of Communication* 62, no. 6 (2012): 1010–27.

Nabi, Robin L., Emily Moyer-Gusé, and Sahara Byrne. "All Joking Aside: A Serious Investigation into the Persuasive Effect of Funny Social Issue Messages." *Communication Monographs* 74, no. 1 (2007): 29–54.

Niven, David, S. Robert Lichter, and Daniel Amundson. "The Political Content of Late Night Comedy." *Harvard International Journal of Press/Politics* 8, no. 3 (2003): 118–33.

Pfau, Michael, Josh Compton, Kimberly A. Parker, Chasu An, Elaine M. Wittenberg, Monica Ferguson, Heather Horton, and Yuri Malyshev. "The Conundrum of the Timing of Counterarguing Effects in Resistance: Strategies to Boost the Persistence of Counterarguing Output." *Communication Quarterly* 54, no. 2 (2006): 143–56.

Pfau, Michael, Henry C. Kenski, Michael Nitz, and John Sorenson. "Efficacy of Inoculation Strategies in Promoting Resistance to Political Attack Messages: Application to Direct Mail." *Communications Monographs* 57, no. 1 (1990): 25–43.

Pfau, Michael, David Park, R. Lance Holbert, and Jaeho Cho. "The Effects of Party- and PAC-Sponsored Issue Advertising and the Potential of Inoculation to Combat its Impact on the Democratic Process." *American Behavioral Scientist* 44, no. 12 (2001): 2379–97.

Pfau, Michael, Kyle James Tusing, Ascan F. Koerner, Waipeng Lee, Linda C. Godbold, Linda J. Penaloza, Violet Shu-Huei Yang, and Yah-Huei Hong. "Enriching the Inoculation Construct the Role of Critical Components in the Process of Resistance." *Human Communication Research* 24, no. 2 (1997): 187–215.

Polk, Jeremy, Dannagal G. Young, and R. Lance Holbert. "Humor Complexity and Political Influence: An Elaboration Likelihood Approach to the Effects of Humor Type in *The Daily Show* with Jon Stewart." *Atlantic Journal of Communication* 17, no. 4 (2009): 202–19.

Stewart, Patrick A. "Presidential Laugh Lines: Candidate Display Behavior and Audience Laughter in the 2008 Primary Debates." *Politics and the Life Sciences* 29, no. 2 (2010): 55–72.

Warner, Benjamin R., Hayley Jeanne Hawthorne, and Joshua Hawthorne. "A Dual-processing Approach to the Effects of Viewing Political Comedy." *Humor* 28, no. 4 (2015): 541–58.

Young, Dannagal Goldthwaite. "The Privileged Role of the Late-Night Joke: Exploring Humor's Role in Disrupting Argument Scrutiny." *Media Psychology* 11, no. 1 (2008): 119–42.

HUMOR APPRECIATION

*Audience Responses to
Political Comedy*

Chapter 7

The Political Ethology of Debate Humor and Audience Laughter

Understanding Donald Trump, Hillary Clinton, and Their Audiences

Patrick A. Stewart, Reagan G. Dye, and Austin D. Eubanks

From the very start of the 2016 presidential campaign until three weeks before Election Day, the presidential debates provided insight into not only the candidates themselves, but also their connection with audiences. While candidates possessing a wide range of intellect and charisma have long attracted public attention due to the importance of the office, the 2016 presidential debates were undoubtedly unique. Whereas Hillary Clinton was a historical first woman major party nominee, the general public also was exposed to the first reality TV star candidate and enduringly controversial public figure, Donald Trump.

Low expectations regarding Donald Trump's general election debate performance came not only from him surprisingly being in a position normally achieved by only the most judiciously-vetted and campaign-tested political party selections, but by a nomination route that rarely saw him challenged on policy specifics. These low expectations were accentuated by high hopes for Hillary Clinton, a veteran of over thirty-five debates during the 2008 and 2016 presidential primaries. Despite Clinton's experience and well-known work ethic, remarks in advance of the debate noted that Trump had the "ability to read a room, to sense when he is losing an audience, and to try the theme or tone that will win them back."[1] In essence, while Hillary Clinton was expected to win on the basis her substance and practice, Trump's style was foreseen as being key for any success he might have.

Thus, while the script had been written for the pundits and media experts, what remained was for the studio audience and millions of viewers watching at home to judge the candidates based upon their mostly unmediated performance. For those watching at home, the candidates' ability to evoke observable audience response from those present at the event potentially played a key role in evaluation and ultimately, electoral choice. Just as studio audience laughter (and laugh tracks) indicate a successful punch line in scripted television, audience laughter signals not just successful humor, but also a connection between the audience members and the candidate. In turn, observable audience response likely indicates a candidate's electoral prospects[2] by also likely affecting the feelings of those sharing in this contagious utterance.[3]

At the same time, the humor used to elicit audience laughter provides useful insights regarding the candidates, their social intelligence and leadership traits, as well as the electoral strategy they are following. To better understand the role of candidate humor that elicits audience laughter during debates, this chapter focuses on the humor used by the Republican and Democratic Parties' presidential nominees, Donald Trump and Hillary Clinton, respectively. Our starting point sees a basic pattern in humor with laughter serving as the successful finale to a joke or witty remark, allowing us to work backward to the humorous comment.[4] We use an evolutionary-based rationale that understands audience laughter, along with other observable audience responses such as applause, cheering and booing, as indicating group attitudes and feelings toward leaders and their statements. The humor used and what this tells us about the leaders and their social intelligence, leadership traits, and strategy are next considered before we analyze Trump and Clinton during their three 2016 general election debates. Here we consider the humorous utterances that elicited audience laugher and what they reveal concerning Trump and Clinton's social intelligence, leadership traits, and strategy during the 2016 presidential general election debates, before drawing conclusions.

OBSERVABLE AUDIENCE RESPONSE GIVES FOLLOWERS VOICE

Most political events are notable for the persuasive power of the politicians involved; however, what is perhaps more important, yet underappreciated, is the role played by followers through their observable audience response to the politicians. Here, members of the audience acting in concert with each other at these varied events make their support or disapproval known through their applause, cheering, booing, laughter, chanting, and mixtures of these.[5]

While the electoral ballot, public opinion polls, campaign donations, and the range of other political processes provide politicians and political parties insight,[6] observable audience response provides contemporaneous feedback registering not only follower approval or opposition, but also intensity and the mixture of feelings. This information, however, is affected by audience numbers and composition, venue and organizational purpose, and perhaps most importantly, the reliability of such observable audience response in reflecting individual and group attitudes and future behaviors.

While audience behavior in response to politicians certainly matters for political and electoral success, the physical venue and purpose of different types of political events function to influence expectations regarding candidates and audience behavior.[7] The variety of political event types provide a diversity of political goals, such as (1) "whipping up" support for the candidates among followers and potential followers,[8] (2) unifying potentially disparate factions within political parties and governing entities to allow for successful electoral and political activities under a united banner[9] and/or as studied here, (3) pitting potential leaders head-to-head in contention for political support through debates.[10]

Political debates, like all other political forums, possess specific expectations concerning the types of acceptable behavior by the candidates and those regarding politeness of response by audience members.[11] However, presidential debates represent notably different affairs depending on whether they occur during a presidential primary or the general election.[12] During primary debates, with attendees sharing the social identity of their respective political party, the events tend to be loud and boisterous with the full range of observable audience responses, although they tend to be mostly supportive of candidates for nomination.[13] On the other hand, general election debates tend to be relatively constrained affairs with applause, cheering, booing, and (most definitely) chanting typically not apparent during the debate proper. When observable audience response does occur, it is likely to be laughter, which is difficult to control. In other words, it is easier to not applaud, cheer, or boo a candidate than it is to stifle a laugh.

AUDIENCE LAUGHTER IS A RELIABLE SIGNAL

As a result, laughter may be seen as reflecting the individual audience member's immediate, likely uncontrolled, and often shared emotional response to the candidate. Laughter is a reliable indicator of emotion by first allowing easy and accurate recognition of the emotional state and resultant behavioral intent, albeit one varying in loudness, length, and tone.[14] Laughter's qualities provide physical and social information about the laughing individual(s), influencing perceptions regarding how affiliative and approachable they might be.[15] Secondly, laughter is a reliable indicator by being costly to produce.[16] Here, laughter effectively communicates underlying physiological states, that in turn, potentiate specific behavior; even with faked laughter, physiological change can and does occur.[17] Further, laughter serves cohesion between individuals by decreasing negative affect, increasing positive affect and even pain tolerance while in turn increasing social cooperation and group identity.[18]

Laughter's vocalizations have long been studied regarding its contagiousness that bonds individuals together into groups.[19] These socially contagious group vocalizations tend to, in the words of Hatfield and colleagues, lead to "the tendency to automatically mimic and synchronize facial expressions, vocalizations, postures, and movements with those of another person's and, consequently, to converge emotionally."[20] Therefore, laughter is a very social activity that leads to coordinated behavior—and potentially, feelings and actions of connectedness.

FOLLOWERS LEAD THROUGH LAUGHTER

Thus, laughter may be seen as providing information concerning the connection between the speaker and the audience. Furthermore, laughter solidifies bonds by uniting group members through the shared and contagious experience.[21] This experience is accentuated by audience size with larger audiences exhibiting greater laughter.[22] This shared experience might also serve to coordinate group response by showing shared consent with and respect for the speaker.[23] Even if laughter does not reflect an individual's emotional state, it does serve to signal affiliative intent to unfamiliar persons.[24]

Laughter serves a dual social role. It not only connects group members together through its contagiousness, it can also do so at the expense of others. Laughter serves as a socially acceptable weapon of intimidation by designating its target as having low status relative to the laughing group. In other words, laughter likely performs as symbolic attacks on an individual or group for breaking with the norms of the group laughing at the target[25] in a manner that is similar to the synchronized "mobbing" of birds and mammals to drive intruders away.[26] Furthermore, laughter perceived as coming from members of a shared social group is more contagious and rated more positively by respondents than the same laughter seen as coming from an out-group, specifically a political party.[27] Thus humor allows its practitioners to attack opponents and create socially acceptable hostility toward them and/ or the positions they hold; this enmity is then acknowledged and supported through audience laughter.[28]

HUMOR REVEALS LEADER SOCIAL INTELLIGENCE, TRAITS, AND STRATEGY

Humor in conjunction with the laughter that results, communicates characteristics of social situations. Specifically, humor and laughter represent a dialogue between two or more individuals and provide insight into their levels of status and prestige, as well as the information and values they share while also reflecting the emotional context of a situation.[29] As a result, the use of different types of humor may be seen as influenced by a complex intermixture of physiology, psychology, status, and prestige signals interacting with the environmental context. Thus both the creation of and response to humor may be seen as accurately indicating an individual's social intelligence and personality traits.

WIT AND JOKES REVEAL SOCIAL INTELLIGENCE

Long and Graesser's system for categorizing and defining humor that occurs in conversational interactions is a useful tool for analyzing political humor[30] by differentiating between spontaneous wit and premeditated jokes. In particular, candidates using premeditated jokes or "on the fly" wit to induce audience laughter reveal their cleverness through their ability to identify a social situation where humor would be appropriate, and the humor that aptly elicits laughter. According to this system, jokes differ from wit in their ability to be written in advance and ability to fit into different social contexts. In contrast, wit is considered to be more spontaneous and cannot be repeated out-of-context and have the same humorous effect.

Wit includes at least three different approaches to induce humor. Self-deprecation, where humorous remarks target oneself as the object of the humorous comment, will be discussed in detail below due to its political importance. A second approach to humor encompasses incongruous comments including such relatively benign comments as overstatement and understatements that change meaning through different emphases, the transformation of well-known sayings, popular adages, or clichés into novel and humorous statements, and puns, which evoke a second meaning through linguistic play, usually based on a homophone. Finally, there is more aggressive humor through irony, in which the literal meaning is opposite to the meaning intended by the speaker, satire in which social institutions or social policy is made fun of, and sarcasm, whereas aggressive humor targets individuals.[31]

Debates thus include instances whereas the humor used is not necessarily context-free wit, but involves a level of premeditation by and on behalf of the candidate. Here, preplanned "wit" may be employed to deliver a humorous comment that can be plugged into particular topic areas, especially as candidates are not aware of the questions to be asked, and only the topics. Therefore, the candidate can be prepared with humorous content, but must wait for certain boundary conditions to occur in order to insert his or her comment at the appropriate moment. Consequently, the implementation of these preplanned witty remarks can successfully appear to be off-the-cuff jokes, despite the premeditated calculation behind them.

SELF- AND OTHER-DEPRECATORY HUMOR
INDICATES LEADERSHIP TRAITS

Two types of humor, self- and other-deprecatory, predominate in politics.[32] Self-deprecatory humor refers to comments used in an affiliative manner that invites the audience to share in the laughter at their self-targeted flaws. In turn, this type of humor establishes a more equal relationship of identification with the speaker,[33] by highlighting, in a socially preemptive manner, the candidate's personal flaws.[34] It does so by first signaling that the speaker recognizes her/his flaws and is willing to fully disclose them; at the same time it also signals a level of social intelligence by their eliciting of laughter.[35] Self-deprecatory humor may also signal the high quality of the person making the humorous comment by their engaging in "costly social signaling." In other words, individuals making the self-deprecatory comments present themselves as having so much social status that they can afford to, in essence, make themselves more equal with their audience by sacrificing prestige. Based upon the need for candidates to connect with potential followers by making themselves more relatable and likable, it can be expected that self-deprecatory humor will be a common tool during elections.

Other-deprecatory humor, on the other hand, creates a wedge between the speaker, together with the audience, and the target[36] through sarcasm, teasing, ridicule, derision, and disparagement.[37] Here laughter functions as sublimated, yet socially acceptable, aggression signaling joint hostility toward transgressor of group values as indicated through the humorous comment.[38] This humor enhances ties between the speaker and the audience at the expense of the target, with shared laughter denoting mutual trust, and superiority for the speaker.[39] Through the resultant laughter, this humor indicates an informal ostracism via group "moralistic aggression."[40]

The major form of other-deprecatory humor used in politics is ridicule; typically individual candidates are targeted with the focus on some attribute of their behavior, appearance, or persona. Ridicule enforces conformity and enhances the fear of failure by the target and even outside observers. Here, audiences tend to conform to group behavior expectations[41] with ridicule and implicit ostracism enforcing group norms.[42]

In debates, humor is often used to not only attack one's opponent, but also keep them on the defensive. Thus, while self-deprecatory humor does occur, other-deprecatory humor may be considered more useful when confronting the opposition.

HUMOR IS USED STRATEGICALLY

In addition to asserting dominance over others and/or enhancing status by either exhibiting social intelligence or conspicuously consuming prestige, humor can also be used to avoid directly addressing problematic issues that arise during the debates. Humor does so by making violations appear more benign[43] thus avoiding further scrutiny.[44] For instance, concerns over incumbent president Ronald Reagan's declining mental acuity highlighted during his poor first 1984 debate performance against challenger Walter Mondale were thrust aside and virtually forgotten when he remarked "I will not make age an issue of this campaign. I am not going to exploit, for political purposes, my opponent's youth and inexperience."[45] Thus while humor may be used to effectively blunt or sidestep valid concerns, for discerning observers laughter might serve as a reliable and valid indicator of sociopolitical or personal conflict. Indeed, humor that attacks a social and/or political system (e.g., satire), as opposed to other politicians or the political parties (e.g., sarcasm), and arouses robust audience laughter may be seen as indicative of legitimacy issues within a political system.[46]

While, presidential debates have historically resembled side-by-side press conferences with candidates rarely directly confronting each other and instead contend over policies, the 2016 presidential debates between Trump and Clinton were riddled with interruptions, impoliteness, and a general departure from standard debate decorum. With the 2016 presidential election characterized by a polarized electorate and with polarizing candidates sharing the stage, we found that substantive topics were rarely addressed, and the target was often too obvious to miss by focusing on the opposition candidate. Thus, the patterns that emerge over time regarding the targets and topics typically addressed by politicians, such as the economy, terrorism, healthcare, environmental issues, and national defense,[47] may not have seen the light of day due to the nature of the candidates and their strategies to hide their own or highlight their oppositions' weaknesses.

OVERVIEW OF THE 2016 GENERAL
ELECTION PRESIDENTIAL DEBATES

As has been the case since the 1992 presidential election, a three-debate approach with two podium-based events book-ending a town-hall meeting took place during the 2016 general election. The three ninety-minute debates between Democratic Party nominee Hillary Clinton and Republican Party nominee Donald Trump occurred over the course of one month with the first debate held at Hofstra University in New York on Monday, September 26, and moderated by NBC News's Lester Holt. The second debate, hosted by St. Louis, Missouri's Washington University occurred on Sunday, October 9, and was moderated by CNN's Anderson Cooper and ABC's Martha Raddatz. The third and final debate, hosted by University of Nevada, Las Vegas, took place on Wednesday, October 19, and was moderated by FOX News's Chris Wallace.

Viewership across all three debates was historically high. An estimated eighty-four million voters watched the first debate on television, making it the most watched debate in US history. Despite viewership being less than the first debate, the second debate saw an impressive 66.5 million viewers. The third and final debate had an increase in viewership from the second debate with 71.6 million viewers watching the broadcast.

With the 2016 presidential debate, norms of respectfulness and politeness, while being nodded at in the introductory statements by both candidates, soon were cast aside. Consideration of both speaking time and speaking turns by the candidates is revealing. Content analysis of the first debate indicated nearly five minutes more speaking time for Trump at forty-seven minutes compared to Clinton's forty-two minutes. This was likely due to Trump's many interruptions as he attempted to dominate speaking time, leading him to have nearly twice as many speaking turns ($n = 80$) as Clinton ($n = 43$). While the second debate found each candidate speaking for approximately forty minutes, Trump's propensity for interruptions saw him having nearly twice as many speaking turns ($n = 52$) as Clinton ($n = 28$). Finally, while during the third debate, Clinton spoke for nearly seven minutes more than Trump did, Trump again seized far more speaking turns ($n = 82$) than did Clinton ($n = 49$).

This lack of candidate politeness was apparently contagious with audience members engaging in thirty-one observable audience responses to candidate statements or retorts during the first debate. A great majority of these were laughter, with roughly two-thirds involving laughter alone ($n = 21$) or in combination with applause-cheering ($n = 8$) or booing ($n = 2$). Of these, eighteen observable audience responses were to Trump and thirteen in response to Clinton, with the largest difference between Clinton and Trump regarding audience laughter, as Trump elicited five more observable audience responses than did Clinton.

With only nine observable audience responses, the second debate proved to be a much more placid event. Besides Clinton's receiving applause-cheering from the audience twice, all other audience responses were to Trump including three laughter, one booing, one applause-cheering, and two combinations of laughter followed by applause.

Though the third debate had more audience response events than the second ($n = 11$), with Clinton and Trump each receiving applause-cheering from the audience once, there was a stark contrast between the two. Here Trump elicited audience laughter six times in comparison with Clinton's only attaining audience laughter twice and combined laughter and booing once.

Differences in the frequency of observable audience responses throughout the debates may be a function of the topics discussed, or more importantly, the ability for the moderator to control the audience and dictate standards for turn-taking between the two candidates. Another notable aspect of these debates is the lack of playful humor and the prominence of attack humor. Self-deprecatory humor was nonexistent, despite it being typically observed in presidential debates.[48] This pattern may be a function of the partisan divide[49] as seen with the divisive nature of the 2016 presidential campaign as a whole and exemplified by the humor strategies of Trump and Clinton during each of the 2016 presidential debates.

DONALD TRUMP

Donald Trump employed mostly hostile jokes and wit throughout the 2016 presidential debates with laughter being elicited in twenty-nine of thirty-two observable audience responses. In particular, wit accounted for approximately nearly three-quarters (72%, $n = 21$) of his humor, with eight jokes accounting for the remainder. Trump's wit was largely sarcastic and hostile (62%; $n = 18$), with only two ironic and one clever reply. Likewise, his jokes (including "preplanned" wit) were largely hostile (21%; $n = 6$), with one ironic and one philosophical response.

Trump initiated hostile humor within the first few minutes (8:13 p.m.; all times denoted are in Central Standard Time) of his first televised debate with Clinton. Whereas this was the pair's first face-to-face interaction as candidates, Trump set the tone from the beginning through early interruptions, as a cascade of four occurred shortly after the candidates were introduced (8:22–8:24 p.m.), and consequently directly after Clinton's first direct (and unprovoked) hostile comment toward Trump. Acerbic humor toward Clinton included sarcastic and exaggerated comments such as "No wonder you've been fighting ISIS your entire adult life" (8:25 p.m.), and "You decided to stay home and that's OK" (8:58 p.m.). The humorous attack "Nobody feels sorry for [Rosie O'Donnell]" (9:36 p.m.) was met with a mixture of laughter and boos from the bipartisan audience likely due to this comment either being perceived as an unfair attack of someone not present, or as a humorous jab at a controversial public figure unpopular among Republicans. The frequency of hostile humor toward such political figures as Clinton and President Barack Obama as well as daytime celebrity O'Donnell departed from traditional debate decorum. Trump was able to maintain a hostile tone, keeping Clinton on the defensive throughout the debate. Perhaps most important was his ability to likely divert attention from his lack of policy knowledge.

Trump can be perceived as dictating the tone of the second debate through his ability to initiate attacks through hostile humor. Clinton's lack of rejoinders, humorous or otherwise, may have either served to maintain her dignity by her being above the fray, or alternately made her look weak. Lines such as "because you would be in jail" (8:24 p.m.) and "no, I'm a gentleman Hillary. Go ahead" (8:29 p.m.) elicited a combination of applause and laughter from the audience, yet no response from Clinton. Indeed, most all of the humor that prompted laughter from the audience during the second debate may be considered "preplanned" and hostile humor. While one instance of booing occurred when Trump interrupted Clinton, suggesting part of the audience took offense, evidence suggests preparation on the part of Trump and his campaign advisers to focus on his strength as a Trump's dominant insurgent candidate.

The third and final debate saw Trump reverting back to spontaneous wit rather than preplanned jokes. For example, his clever reply with a simple (and sarcastic) "thank you" (8:28 p.m.) to a clarification interjection by moderator Chris Wallace implied Trump's annoyance with Clinton's characterization of him. Employment of irony, albeit unintentional, with the statement "Nobody has more respect for women than I do. Nobody" (8:56 p.m.), arguably gave the audience an opportunity to laugh *at* Trump's choice of words (in light of the leaked "Access Hollywood" tapes with Trump making disparaging remarks regarding women), rather than laugh *with* him.

While the proliferation of audience laughter in response to Trump, yet not Clinton, does not necessarily imply success it does suggest that Trump masterfully "worked" the audience. In contrast to notably humorous and likable politicians such as former president Reagan,[50] Trump's use of humor was attack-oriented and served chiefly to disparage his opposition. Therefore, laughter likely does not reliably indicate audience approval so much as signify shock and disbelief regarding a presidential candidate willingly disclaiming the norms of presidential debate civility.

HILLARY CLINTON

As noted, Clinton did not successfully employ humor as often as her opponent. Of Clinton's fifteen observable audience responses during the three general election debates, only thirteen derived from what may be identified as humor. Of these, wit accounted for nine (70%) and jokes four (30%). Notably, all of her humor was hostile. While it may be concluded that Clinton's overall strategy was successful due to a lack of failed humor, as indicated by booing, she lagged behind Trump in observable audience responses generally and more specifically to humorous comments. Notably, in the second debate, Clinton only prompted two observable audience responses of applause-cheering unrelated to humor. This overall strategy cohered with the traditional "polite" method for conducting presidential debates[51] and can largely be attributed to Clinton's experience as a politician rather than as a public entertainment figure. Likewise, Clinton did not violate norms of discourse through interruption allowing her to appear more "presidential"; however, her politeness provided Trump the opportunity to dominate the debates by maneuvering audience response to his advantage.

The first presidential debate is often seen as setting the tone for the remaining three debates. With Trump's early assertion of dominance through three interruptions (8:19, 8:22, and 8:24 p.m.), Clinton arguably matched her opponents' aggression with the polite, yet subtly sarcastic statement: "Donald, it's good to be with you" (8:07 p.m.). Trump's similarly polite yet condescending rejoinder: "Now in all fairness to Secretary Clinton—yes is that OK? Good. I want you to be very happy" (8:13 p.m.), while not apparently hostile in the written transcript, in the context of the debate, the apparent sarcasm sets a combative tone that predominated throughout all three debates.

There is a clear pattern of Clinton and Trump trading hostile humor throughout the first debate. On one occasion, it appears that Trump matches Clinton's hostility with interruption: "You live in your own reality" (8:21 p.m.), shortly followed by Trump's interruption, "That's about all you've . . ." (8:22 p.m.). Clinton's hostile attack on Trump, "[He] has called women pigs, slobs, and dogs" (9:34 p.m.), led to booing which could be interpreted as affiliative toward her (Bull and Miskins, 2015) by those critical of Trump's alleged behavior toward women, or may have been seen as registering disagreement in response to the attack by Trump supporters.

With only two observable audience responses during the second debate, both involving applause-cheering of Clinton's comments, humor did not apparently play a strategic role. Arguably, the town-hall style format of this debate may have influenced Clinton's approach. By politely addressing audience member questions, Clinton appeared more level-headed and civil than did Trump, underscoring her front-runner status.

The third and final debate saw Clinton use a similar approach to the first debate in response to Trump's attacks. There was only one hostile Clinton response, "Well that's because he would rather have a puppet as President of the United States" (8:31 p.m.), shortly after a jab from Trump, "That was a great pivot off the fact that she wants open borders" (8:29 p.m.). Clinton's "puppet" comment was met with laugher and boos from the audience, perhaps indicating a mixed response of approval and disapproval that was arguably based on the mixed partisan audience's candidates preferences. However, as noted, Clinton lagged well behind Trump in eliciting observable audience response.

CONCLUSION

The 2016 presidential election will likely be remembered for partisan divisiveness and candidate rancor. The three general election debates between Donald Trump and Hillary Clinton reflected the country's division through the audiences' laughter, applause, cheering, and booing and the comments that elicited them. Although the candidates, as well as the moderators in charge of the debates, may be seen as to blame for audience impoliteness, ultimately, they only served as catalysts for observable audience reactions expressing political discord.

The humor used during the presidential general election debates suggest these events validate a keen mind that not only can respond quickly with spontaneous wit, but also employ preplanned jokes at the appropriate moment. These latter forms of humor, while on the boundary between jokes and wit, provide the opportunity for humor that is encrypted to be appealing to a specific audience; in other words, these jokes are funnier for those "in the know."[52] Thus, while Trump's references to World War II and the Korean War General Douglas MacArthur in the first debate and to President Abraham Lincoln in the second debate may have been seen as non sequitur, they may have had particular appeal to those who favor authoritarian hands-off military policy and revel in the Republican Party hosting the "Great Emancipator."

Unlike presidential debates in recent years, where both candidates used self-deprecatory humor at some point to make themselves "likable enough" to win over voters,[53] the apparent focus of the humor used by both candidates was overwhelmingly that of ridicule to diminish the stature of the opposition. Although some of the humor referenced policy,[54] this was mostly in passing with the great majority of comments leading to observable audience response[55] focusing on the opposition and their shortcomings. In other words, the humor used most often and most successfully by Donald Trump (and to a lesser degree and extent of success, Hillary Clinton), was ridicule engendering the contagious "mobbing" of audience laughter.[56] The influence of this laughter, as well as the other observable audience responses of applause-cheering and booing, may potentially be seen as extending beyond the studio audience to those watching on television or streaming the debates. While not necessarily making Trump a more likable candidate, these humor-based attacks may have diminished Clinton's prestige and electoral support.

Trump's sarcastic and hostile humor, when combined with his multiple interruptions used to discombobulate, may be seen as a successful strategy to focus scrutiny on Clinton with audience collaboration through their laughter, while avoiding examination of his substantive shortcomings. While Clinton's humor responded in kind, she was not able to respond in volume; this may have had greater and more strategically debilitating results on the election by focusing on style, not policy substance. Whereas entering into the debates, the stage appeared to be Clinton's domain, stylistically Trump made it his own through the studio audiences' support.

NOTES

1. James Fallows, "Who Will Win?" *The Atlantic*, October 2016, 64–79.

2. Darrell M. West, "Cheers and Jeers: Candidate Presentations and Audience Reactions in the 1980 Presidential Campaign," *American Politics Research* 12, no. 1 (1984): 23–50.

3. Marc Mehu et al., "Reliable Facial Muscle Activation Enhances Recognizability and Credibility of Emotional Expression," *Social Psychological and Personality Science* 2, no. 3 (2011): 262–271; Robert Lynch, "It's Funny Because We Think It's True: Laughter Is Augmented by Implicit Preferences," *Evolution and Human Behavior* 31, no. 2 (2010): 141–148.

4. John Morreall, *Comic Relief: A Comprehensive Philosophy of Humor* (Malden, MA: Wiley-Blackwell, 2009).

5. Peter Bull and Karolis Miskinis, "Whipping It Up! An Analysis of Audience Responses to Political Rhetoric in Speeches from the 2012 American Presidential Elections," *Journal of Language and Social Psychology* 34, no. 5 (2015): 521–538; Hyangmi Choi, Peter Bull, and Darren Reed, "Audience Responses and the Context of Political Speeches," *Journal of Social and Political Psychology* 4, no. 2 (2016): 601–622; Steven E. Clayman, "Booing: The Anatomy of a Disaffiliative Response," *American Sociological Review* 58, no. 1 (1993): 110–130; Patrick A. Stewart, Austin D. Eubanks, and Jason Miller, "'Please Clap': Applause, Laughter, and Booing during the 2016 GOP Presidential Primary Debates," *PS: Political Science & Politics* 49, no. 4 (2016): 696–700; Patrick A. Stewart, *Debatable Humor: Laughing Matters on the 2008 Presidential Primary Campaign* (Lanham, MD: Lexington Books, 2012).

6. Andrew J. Dowdle et al., *The Invisible Hands of Political Parties in Presidential Elections: Party Activists and Political Aggregation from 2004 to 2012* (New York: Palgrave Macmillan, 2013).

7. Choi, Bull, and Reed, "Audience Responses," 601–622.

8. Bull and Miskinis, "Whipping It Up!" 521–538; Clayman, "Booing," 110–130.

9. Choi, Bull, and Reed, "Audience Responses," 601–622.

10. Stewart, Eubanks, and Miller, "'Please clap'," 696–700; Stewart, *Debatable Humor*; Patrick A. Stewart, "Polls and Elections: Do the Presidential Primary Debates Matter? Measuring Candidate Speaking Time and Audience Response during the 2012 Primaries," *Presidential Studies Quarterly* 45, no. 2 (2015): 361–381.

11. William O. Dailey, Edward A. Hinck, and Shelly S. Hinck. "Audience Perceptions of Politeness and Advocacy Skills in the 2000 and 2004 Presidential Debates," *Argumentation and Advocacy* 41, no. 4 (2005): 196–210.

12. Stewart, *Debatable Humor*.

13. Stewart, Eubanks, and Miller, "'Please clap'," 696–700; Ibid.; Stewart, "Polls and Elections," 361–381.

14. Jo-Anne Bachorowski and Michael J. Owren, "Not all Laughs are Alike: Voiced but Not Unvoiced Laughter Readily Elicits Positive Affect," *Psychological Science* 12, no. 3 (2001): 252–257; Karl Grammer and Irenäus Eibl-Eibesfeldt, "The Ritualisation of Laughter," *Natürlichkeit der Sprache und der Kultur* (1990): 192–214; Willibald Ruch and Paul Ekman, "The Expressive Pattern of Laughter," *Emotion, Qualia, and Consciousness* (2001): 426–443.

15. Diana P. Szameitat et al., "Differentiation of Emotions in Laughter at the Behavioral Level," *Emotion* 9, no. 3 (2009): 397–405.

16. Mehu et al., "Reliable Facial Muscle Activation," 262–271.

17. Bachorowski and Owren, "Not All Laughs Are Alike," 252–257; Ruch and Ekman, "The Expressive Pattern of Laughter," 426–443; Carolyn McGettigan et al., "Individual Differences in Laughter Perception Reveal Roles for Mentalizing and Sensorimotor Systems in the Evaluation of Emotional Authenticity," *Cerebral Cortex* 25, no. 1 (2015): 246–257; Paul G. Devereux and Gerald P. Ginsburg, "Sociality Effects on the Production of Laughter," *Journal of General Psychology* 128, no. 2 (2001): 227–240; Robert R. Provine, "Contagious Laughter: Laughter Is a Sufficient Stimulus for Laughs and Smiles," *Bulletin of the Psychonomic Society* 30, no. 1 (1992): 1–4.

18. Mark Van Vugt et al., "Laughter as Social Lubricant: A Biosocial Hypothesis about the Pro-Social Functions of Laughter and Humor," Centre for the Study of Group Processes Working Paper, University of Kent (2014).

19. Robert R. Provine, "Laughter as a Scientific Problem: An Adventure in Sidewalk Neuroscience," *Journal of Comparative Neurology* 524, no. 8 (2015): 1532–1539.

20. Elaine Hatfield et al., "New Perspectives on Emotional Contagion: A Review of Classic and Recent Research on Facial Mimicry and Contagion," *Interpersona* 8, no. 2 (2014): 159.

21. Devereux and Ginsburg, "Sociality Effects on the Production of Laughter," 227–240; Elaine Hatfield, John T. Cacioppo, and Richard L. Rapson, "Emotional Contagion," *Current Directions in Psychological Science* 2, no. 3 (1993): 96–99.

22. Provine, "Contagious laughter," 1–4.

23. Irenäus Eibl-Eibesfeldt, *Human Ethology* (New York: Aldine De Gruyter, 1989); Frank K. Salter, *Emotions in Command: Biology, Bureaucracy, and Cultural Evolution* (New Brunswick, NJ: Transaction Publishers, 2007); Tyler F. Stillman, Roy F. Baumeister, and C. Nathan DeWall, "What's so Funny about Not Having Money? The Effects of Power on Laughter," *Personality and Social Psychology Bulletin* 33, no. 11 (2007): 1547–1558.

24. Devereux and Ginsburg, "Sociality Effects," 227–240.

25. Eibl-Eibesfeldt, *Human Ethology*; Richard Alexander, "Ostracism and Indirect Reciprocity: The Reproductive Significance of Humor," *Ethology and Sociobiology* 7 (1986); Jaak Panksepp, *Affective Neuroscience: The Foundations of Human and Animal Emotions* (New York: Oxford University Press, 1998).

26. Robert R. Provine, "Yawns, Laughs, Smiles, Tickles, and Talking: Naturalistic and Laboratory Studies of Facial Action and Social Communication," in *The Psychology of Facial Expression*, eds. José Miguel and Fernández-Dols (New York: Cambridge University Press, 1997), 158–175.

27. Michael J. Platow et al., "'It's Not Funny if They're Laughing': Self-Categorization, Social Influence, and Responses to Canned Laughter," *Journal of Experimental Social Psychology* 41, no. 5 (2005): 542–550.

28. Thomas E. Ford and Mark A. Ferguson, "Social Consequences of Disparagement Humor: A Prejudiced Norm Theory," *Personality & Social Psychology Review (Lawrence Erlbaum Associates)* 8, no. 1 (2004): 79–94; Rod A. Martin, *The Psychology of Humor: An Integrative Approach* (Amsterdam: Elsevier, 2007).

29. Alan J. Fridlund, *Human Facial Expression: An Evolutionary View* (San Diego: Academic Press, 1994).

30. Debra L. Long and Arthur C. Graesser, "Wit and Humor in Discourse Processing," *Discourse Processes* 11, no. 1 (1988): 35–60.

31. Ibid.

32. Patrick A. Stewart, "The Influence of Self- and Other-Deprecatory Humor on Presidential Candidate Evaluation during the 2008 Election," *Social Science Information* 50 (2011): 201–222.

33. John C. Meyer, "Humor as a Double Edged Sword: Four Functions of Humor in Communication," *Communication Theory* 10, no. 3 (2000): 310–331.

34. Gil Greengross and Geoffrey F. Miller, "Dissing Oneself Versus Dissing Rivals: Effects of Status, Personality, and Sex on the Short-Term and Long-Term Attractiveness of Self-Deprecating and Other-Deprecating Humor," *Evolutionary Psychology* 6, no. 3 (2008): 393–408.

35. Ibid.

36. Meyer, "Humor as a Double-Edged Sword," 310–331.

37. Martin, *The Psychology of Humor*; Rod A. Martin et al., "Individual Differences in Uses of Humor and their Relation to Psychological Well-being: Development of the Humor Styles Questionnaire," *Journal of Research in Personality* 37, no. 1 (2003): 48–75.

38. Eibl-Eibesfeldt, *Human Ethology*; Panksepp, *Affective Neuroscience*; Konrad Lorenz, *On Aggression* (New York: Psychology Press, 2002).

39. Marc Mehu and Robin I. M. Dunbar, "Relationship between Smiling and Laughter in Humans (Homo Sapiens): Testing the Power Asymmetry Hypothesis," *Folia Primatol* 79, no. 5 (2008): 269–280.

40. Roger D. Masters, "Ostracism as a Social and Biological Phenomenon: An Introduction," *Ethology and Sociobiology* 7, no. 3–4 (1986): 149–158.

41. Leslie M. Janes and James M. Olson, "Jeer Pressures: The Behavioral Effects of Observing Ridicule of Others," *Personality and Social Psychology Bulletin* 26, no. 4 (2000): 474–485.

42. Masters, "Ostracism," 149–158; Glenn E. Weisfeld, "The Adaptive Value of Humor and Laughter," *Ethology & Sociobiology* 14, no. 2 (1993): 141–169.

43. Caleb Warren and A. Peter McGraw, "Opinion: What Makes Things Humorous," *Proceedings of the National Academy of Sciences of the United States of America* 112, no. 23 (2015): 7105–7106.

44. Robin L. Nabi, Emily Moyer-Guseé, and Sahara Byrne, "All Joking Aside: A Serious Investigation into the Persuasive Effect of Funny Social Issue Messages," *Communication Monographs* 74, no. 1 (2007): 29–54.

45. Stewart, *Debatable Humor*; Steven Fein, George R. Goethals, and Matthew B. Kugler, "Social Influence on Political Judgments: The Case of Presidential Debates," *Political Psychology* 28, no. 2 (2007): 165–192.

46. David L. Paletz, "Political Humor and Authority: From Support to Subversion," *International Political Science Review/Revue internationale de science politique* 11, no. 4 (1990): 483–493.

47. S. Robert Lichter, Jody C Baumgartner, and Jonathan S. Morris, *Politics Is a Joke!: How TV Comedians are Remaking Political Life* (Boulder, CO: Westview Press, 2015).

48. Stewart, *Debatable Humor*.

49. Lilliana Mason, "The Rise of Uncivil Agreement: Issue Versus Behavioral Polarization in the American Electorate," *American Behavioral Scientist* 57, no. 1 (2013): 140–159; Shanto Iyengar, Gaurav Sood, and Yphtach Lelkes, "Affect, Not Ideology: A Social Identity Perspective on Polarization," *Public Opinion Quarterly* 76, no. 3 (2012): 405–431.

50. Stewart, *Debatable Humor*; Reagan G. Dye, "Applause, Laughter, Chants, and Cheers: An Analysis of the Rhetorical Skill of the 'Great Communicator'" (MA thesis, University of Arkansas, 2018).

51. Dailey, Hinck, and Hinck, "Audience Perceptions," 196–210.

52. Thomas Flamson and H. Clark Barrett, "The Encryption Theory of Humor: A Knowledge-Based Mechanism of Honest Signaling," *Journal of Evolutionary Psychology* 6, no. 4 (2008): 261–281.

53. Stewart, *Debatable Humor*.

54. Lichter, Baumgartner, and Morris, *Politics Is a Joke!*

55. Peter Bull, "Claps and Claptrap: The Analysis of Speaker-Audience Interaction in Political Speeches," *Journal of Social and Political Psychology* 4, no. 1 (2016): 473–492.

56. Salter, *Emotions in Command*; Provine, "Yawns," 158–175.

REFERENCES

Alexander, Richard. "Ostracism and Indirect Reciprocity: The Reproductive Significance of Humor." *Ethology and Sociobiology* 7, no. 3–4 (1986): 253–270.

Bachorowski, Jo-Anne, and Michael J. Owren. "Not all Laughs are Alike: Voiced but Not Unvoiced Laughter Readily Elicits Positive Affect." *Psychological Science* 12, no. 3 (May 2001): 252–257.

Bull, Peter, and Karolis Miskinis. "Whipping it Up! An Analysis of Audience Responses to Political Rhetoric in Speeches from the 2012 American Presidential Elections." *Journal of Language and Social Psychology* 34, no. 5 (2014): 521–538.

Choi, Hyangmi, Peter Bull, and Darren Reed. "Audience Responses and the Context of Political Speeches." *Journal of Social and Political Psychology* 4, no. 2 (2016): 601–622.

Clayman, S. E. "Booing: The Anatomy of a Disaffiliative Response." *American Sociological Review* 58, no. 1 (1993): 110–130.

Dailey, William O., Edward A. Hinck, and Shelly S. Hinck. "Audience Perceptions of Politeness and Advocacy Skills in the 2000 and 2004 Presidential Debates." *Argumentation and Advocacy* 41, no. 4 (Spring 2005): 196–210.

Devereux, Paul G., and Gerald P. Ginsburg. "Sociality Effects on the Production of Laughter." *Journal of General Psychology* 128, no. 2 (April 2001): 227–240.

Dowdle, Andrew, Scott Limbocker, Song Yang, Karen Sebold, and Patrick A. Stewart. *The Invisible Hands of Political Parties in Presidential Elections: Party Activists and Political Aggregation from 2004 to 2012*. Basingstoke, UK: Palgrave Macmillan, 2013.

Dye, Reagan G. "Applause, Laughter, Chants, and Cheers: An Analysis of the Rhetorical Skill of the 'Great Communicator'." Masters of Arts in Political Science, University of Arkansas, Fayetteville, Forthcoming.

Eibl-Eibesfeldt, Irenäus. *Human Ethology*. Foundations of Human Behavior. New York: Aldine De Gruyter, 1989.

Fallows, James. "Who Will Win?" *The Atlantic* (October 2016): 64–79.

Fein, Steven, George R. Goethals, and Matthew B. Kugler. "Social Influence on Political Judgments: The Case of Presidential Debates." *Political Psychology* 28, no. 2 (April 2007): 165–192.

Flamson, Thomas, and H. Clark Barrett. "The Encryption Theory of Humor: A Knowledge-Based Mechanism of Honest Signaling." *Journal of Evolutionary Psychology* 6, no. 4 (2008): 261–281.

Ford, Thomas E., and Mark A. Ferguson. "Social Consequences of Disparagement Humor: A Prejudiced Norm Theory." *Personality & Social Psychology Review (Lawrence Erlbaum Associates)* 8, no. 1 (February 2004): 79–94.

Fridlund, Alan J. *Human Facial Expression: An Evolutionary View*. San Diego: Academic Press, 1994.

Grammer, Karl, and Irenäus Eibl-Eibesfeldt. "The Ritualisation of Laughter." *Natürlichkeit Der Sprache Und Der Kultur* 18 (1990): 192–214.

Greengross, Gil, and Geoffrey F. Miller. "Dissing Oneself Versus Dissing Rivals: Effects of Status, Personality, and Sex on the Short-Term and Long-Term

Attractiveness of Self-Deprecating and Other-Deprecating Humor." *Evolutionary Psychology* 6, no. 3 (2008): 393–408.

Hatfield, Elaine, Lisamarie Bensman, Paul D. Thornton, and Richard L. Rapson. "New Perspectives on Emotional Contagion: A Review of Classic and Recent Research on Facial Mimicry and Contagion." *Interpersona* 8, no. 2 (2014): 159.

Hatfield, Elaine, J. T. Cacioppo, and R. L. Rapson. "Emotional Contagion." *Current Directions in Psychological Science* 2, no. 3 (1993): 96–99.

Iyengar, Shanto, Gaurav Sood, and Yphtach Lelkes. "Affect, Not Ideology: A Social Identity Perspective on Polarization." *Public Opinion Quarterly* 76, no. 3 (2012): 405–431.

Janes, Leslie M., and James M. Olson. "Jeer Pressures: The Behavioral Effects of Observing Ridicule of Others." *Personality and Social Psychology Bulletin* 26, no. 4 (April 2000): 474–485.

Kimmel, Christopher M., Patrick A. Stewart, and William D. Schreckhise. "Of Closed Minds and Open Mouths: Indicators of Supreme Court Justice Votes during the 2009 and 2010 Sessions." *The Forum* 10, no. 2. Berlin: De Gruyter, 2012.

Lichter, S. Robert, Jody Baumgartner, and Jonathan S. Morris. *Politics Is a Joke!: How TV Comedians are Remaking Political Life*. Boulder, CO: Westview Press, 2015.

Long, Debra L., and Arthur C. Graesser. "Wit and Humor in Discourse Processing." *Discourse Processes* 11, no. 1 (1988): 35–60.

Lorenz, Konrad. *On Aggression*. New York: Psychology Press, 2002.

Lynch, Robert. "It's Funny because We Think It's True: Laughter Is Augmented by Implicit Preferences." *Evolution and Human Behavior* 31, no. 2 (2010): 141–148.

Martin, Rod A. *The Psychology of Humor: An Integrative Approach*. Amsterdam: Elsevier, 2007.

Martin, Rod A., Patricia Puhlik-Doris, Gwen Larsen, Jeanette Gray, and Kelly Weir. "Individual Differences in Uses of Humor and their Relation to Psychological Well-being: Development of the Humor Styles Questionnaire." *Journal of Research in Personality* 37, no. 1 (2003): 48–75.

Mason, Lilliana. "The Rise of Uncivil Agreement: Issue Versus Behavioral Polarization in the American Electorate." *American Behavioral Scientist* 57, no. 1 (2013): 140–159.

Masters, Roger D. "Ostracism as a Social and Biological Phenomenon: An Introduction." *Ethology and Sociobiology* 7, no. 3–4 (1986): 149–158.

McGettigan, Carolyn, Eamon Walsh, Rosemary Jessop, Zarinah K. Agnew, Dita A. Sauter, Jane E. Warren, and Sophie K. Scott. "Individual Differences in Laughter Perception Reveal Roles for Mentalizing and Sensorimotor Systems in the Evaluation of Emotional Authenticity." *Cerebral Cortex* 25, no. 1 (January 2015): 246–257.

Mehu, Marc, and Robin I. M. Dunbar. "Relationship between Smiling and Laughter in Humans (Homo Sapiens): Testing the Power Asymmetry Hypothesis." *Folia Primatol* 79, no. 5 (2008): 269–280.

Mehu, Marc, Marcello Mortillaro, Tanja Bänziger, and Klaus R. Scherer. "Reliable Facial Muscle Activation Enhances Recognizability and Credibility of Emotional

Expression." *Social Psychological and Personality Science* 2, no. 3 (2011): 262–271.

Meyer, John C. "Humor as a Double-Edged Sword: Four Functions of Humor in Communication." *Communication Theory* 10, no. 3 (2000): 310–331.

Morreall, John. *Comic Relief: A Comprehensive Philosophy of Humor.* Malden, MA: Wiley-Blackwell, 2009.

Nabi, Robin L., Emily Moyer-Gusé, and Sahara Byrne. "All Joking Aside: A Serious Investigation into the Persuasive Effect of Funny Social Issue Messages." *Communication Monographs* 74, no. 1 (March 2007): 29–54.

Paletz, David L. "Political Humor and Authority: From Support to Subversion." *International Political Science Review/Revue Internationale De Science Politique* 11, no. 4 (1990): 483–493.

Panksepp, Jaak. *Affective Neuroscience : The Foundations of Human and Animal Emotions.* Series in Affective Science. New York: Oxford University Press, 1998.

Platow, Michael J., S. Alexander Haslam, Amanda Both, Ivanne Chew, Michelle Cuddon, Nahal Goharpey, Jacqui Maurer, Simone Rosini, Anna Tsekouras, and Diana M. Grace. "'It's Not Funny if They're Laughing': Self-Categorization, Social Influence, and Responses to Canned Laughter." *Journal of Experimental Social Psychology* 41, no. 5 (2005): 542–550.

Provine, Robert R. "Laughter as a Scientific Problem: An Adventure in Sidewalk Neuroscience." *Journal of Comparative Neurology* 524, no. 8 (2016): 1532–1539.

Provine, Robert R. "Contagious Laughter: Laughter is a Sufficient Stimulus for Laughs and Smiles." *Bulletin of the Psychonomic Society* 30, no. 1 (January 1992): 1–4.

———. "Yawns, Laughs, Smiles, Tickles, and Talking: Naturalistic and Laboratory Studies of Facial Action and Social Communication." In *The Psychology of Facial Expression*, edited by Fernández-Dols and José Miguel, 158–175. New York: Cambridge University Press; Editions de la Maison des Sciences de l'Homme, 1997.

Ruch, Willibald, and Paul Ekman. "The Expressive Pattern of Laughter." In *Emotion, Qualia, and Consciousness* (2001): 426–443.

Salter, Frank K. *Emotions in Command: Biology, Bureaucracy, and Cultural Evolution.* New Brunswick, NJ: Transaction Publishers, 2007.

Stewart, Patrick A. *Debatable Humor: Laughing Matters on the 2008 Presidential Primary Campaign.* Lanham, MD: Lexington Books, 2012.

———. "The Influence of Self- and Other-Deprecatory Humor on Presidential Candidate Evaluation during the 2008 Election." *Social Science Information* 50, no. 2 (2011): 201–222.

———. "Polls and Elections: Do the Presidential Primary Debates Matter? Measuring Candidate Speaking Time and Audience Response during the 2012 Primaries." *Presidential Studies Quarterly* 45, no. 2 (2015): 361–381.

Stewart, Patrick A., Austin D. Eubanks, and Jason Miller. "'Please Clap': Applause, Laughter, and Booing during the 2016 GOP Presidential Primary Debates." *PS: Political Science & Politics* 49, no. 4 (2016): 696–700.

Stillman, Tyler F., Roy F. Baumeister, and C. Nathan DeWall. "What's so Funny about Not Having Money? The Effects of Power on Laughter." *Personality and Social Psychology Bulletin* 33, no. 11 (2007): 1547–1558.

Szameitat, Diana P., Kai Alter, André J. Szameitat, Chris J. Darwin, Dirk Wildgruber, Susanne Dietrich, and Annette Sterr. "Differentiation of Emotions in Laughter at the Behavioral Level." *Emotion* 9, no. 3 (June 2009): 397–405.

Van Vugt, Mark, Charlie Hardy, Julie Stow, and Robin Dunbar. "Laughter as Social Lubricant: A Biosocial Hypothesis about the Pro-Social Functions of Laughter and Humor." Centre for the Study of Group Processes Working Paper, University of Kent (2014).

Warren, Caleb, and A. Peter McGraw. "Opinion: What Makes Things Humorous." *Proceedings of the National Academy of Sciences of the United States of America* 112, no. 23 (June 9, 2015): 7105–7106.

Weisfeld, Glenn E. "The Adaptive Value of Humor and Laughter." *Ethology & Sociobiology* 14, no. 2 (March 1993): 141–169.

West, Darrell M. "Cheers and Jeers Candidate Presentations and Audience Reactions in the 1980 Presidential Campaign." *American Politics Research* 12, no. 1 (1984): 23–50.

Chapter 8

The Joke Is On You

Satire and Blowback

Sophia A. McClennen

Much research on satire and politics[1] has emphasized the productive and progressive ways that satire can encourage an active and engaged citizenry. There has been less attention, however, to satire's potential for blowback—for destroying the very social fabric it purports to support. This chapter begins by arguing that research on comedy has missed the fact that there are four key stakeholders for jokes: (1) the satirist, (2) the intended audience, (3) the butt of the joke, and (4) the allies of the butt of the joke. It then goes on to examine the specific ways that satire may play a role in heightening intergroup conflict because of the particular effects it can have on the allies of the butt of the joke. Looking at two extreme cases of satirical blowback, the Danish cartoon controversy and the attacks on *Charlie Hebdo*, this chapter makes the case that further research on the effects of satire on the allies of the butt of the joke is necessary to fully comprehend the social impact of satirical comedy. In particular, I will use research on meta-dehumanization—the perception that another group is dehumanizing your community—to show that certain types of satire can lead to violent outcomes. The chapter will close by considering the risks taken when we use satirical comedy to create a community of "it getters" in a context of intense social factions.

SKEPTICISM OF SOCIAL BENEFITS OF COMEDY

Despite the wide range of scholarly arguments in favor of the positive benefits of comedy, there has been a long tradition of denigrating comedy as antisocial, immature, scornful, and irrational. Plato, one of the most influential critics of laughter, described humor as an emotion that overrides rational self-control. Plato was also one of the first scholars to note the way that humor

can exacerbate social division. He writes in the *Republic* that the Guardians
of the state should avoid laughter, "for ordinarily when one abandons himself
to violent laughter, his condition provokes a violent reaction."[2]

Similarly, Descartes in *Passions of the Soul* identified three of the six
basic emotions in laughter—wonder, love, (mild) hatred, desire, joy, and
sadness. While he notes that there are other causes of laughter than hatred, he
describes laughter as primarily an expression of scorn and ridicule:

> Derision or scorn is a sort of joy mingled with hatred, which proceeds from our
> perceiving some small evil in a person whom we consider to be deserving of it;
> we have hatred for this evil, we have joy in seeing it in him who is deserving
> of it; and when that comes upon us unexpectedly, the surprise of wonder is the
> cause of our bursting into laughter.[3]

For some, humor is entirely dependent on social divisions with hierar-
chies. Thomas Hobbes in *Treatise on Human Nature and That on Liberty
and Necessity* suggested that humor is predicated on a sense of eminency in
ourselves and infirmity in others: "It is no wonder therefore that men take hei-
nously to be laughed at or derided, that is, triumphed over."[4] Such arguments
frame humor as a strategy to attack the identities of others.

These ideas coalesced into what is now known as *the superiority theory
of humor*. John Morreall cites the work of Roger Scruton who argues that,
"if people dislike being laughed at, it is surely because laughter devalues its
object in the subject's eyes."[5] Charles Gruner characterizes humor as a game
with winners and losers and considers it essentially a competition.[6] The basic
idea behind this theory is that humor depends on offering the jokester a superior position vis-à-vis the target of their humor.

While notions of superiority still hold in many theories of humor, especially those related to satire and sarcastic irony, it is important to note that
two other theories of humor explain comedy in ways that are not directly
tied to creating hierarchical divisions. The *relief theory* focuses on the idea
of laughter as a nervous system response. According to Morreall, "we can
note that today almost no scholar in philosophy or psychology explains
laughter or humor as a process of releasing pent-up nervous energy."[7]
In contrast, the *incongruity theory*, which argues that laughter originates
from the perception of something incongruous, is currently the dominant
theory of humor in philosophy and psychology.[8] Under this theory, humor
lies in the gap between what is expected and what is perceived. Morreall
argues for it as a more comprehensive theory of humor since it also applies
to wordplay and puns.

Other theories of humor have focused less on how it works and more on its
social effects. Psychologists have argued for the stress relieving benefits of

jokes and humor and of its ability to offer the jokester and audience a chance to rethink stark social distinctions and appreciate ambiguity and diversity. Morreall also argues for humor as a valuable element in building trust and reducing conflict, and he suggests that humor can be effectively used to defuse difficult conversations. Humor can call attention to norms of behavior and productively mock them, and it can expose hypocrisy.

The catch, though, as will be discussed in more detail below on the specific distinction of satirical humor, is that what may seem incongruous or critically productive to the intended audience of the joke may feel like superiority to the butt of the joke and its allies. In fact, most theorists who advocate for the positive benefits of humor set aside a category of humor that is negative, antisocial, and derogatory. Meanwhile critics of humor often fail to see its potential to function to relieve stress, build community, and help offer critical perspective on society. But, because humor is not literal and because it often depends on the position of the stakeholder to the joke, its meaning can change and its social impact can vary. Its symbolic fluidity is exactly what makes it both critically productive and socially divisive. Morreall, for example, generally dislikes mocking humor, but concedes that mocking Adolf Hitler was not just appropriate, but also effective—a capitulation that shows that most theorists of humor judge the joke not by how it works but by whether or not they agree with its target. As a further sign of the ethical fluidity of humor, some comedy, especially satirical comedy, is aimed at human folly or faulty thinking. It is aimed at ideas. And yet, those people who harbor those ideas will, indeed, feel like the butt of the joke. Thus, one of the core issues that remains tricky for scholars of humor is the fact that, while some comedy is generally positive for all (like a silly pun) and some is generally negative for all (like a racist joke), in most cases the effects of comedy vary depending on the subject position of the person perceiving the joke. This means that overarching theories of the positive or negative effects of comedy must attend to the differences in stakeholder positions.

Thus far the majority of scholarship on the stakeholders to comedy have framed their work on Sigmund Freud's comedic triad of the jokester, the target, and the intended audience. For Freud, the communications structure of the comedic triad was inherently aggressive:

> Generally speaking, a tendentious joke calls for three people: in addition to the one who makes the joke, there must be a second who is taken as the object of the hostile or sexual aggressiveness, and a third in whom the joke's aim of producing pleasure is fulfilled.[9]

As Deniz Göktürk points out, Freud's description of comedy as an aggressive triad challenges us to ask ourselves:

Who is laughing with whom at whom, and why? What kinds of bonds are forged between the tellers of jokes and their listeners? Are hidden aggressions expressed indirectly through the joke? Who is the object of attack, or the butt of the joke?[10]

And as Judith Yaross Lee argues:

One does not need a Freudian claim about the unconscious [. . .] for this model to suggest that whether a target takes an attack with good humor will depend on how sharply it stings—and whether the sting feels metaphorical or seems really to cut.[11]

Yet, it is my claim that there are not three, but rather four key stakeholders to a joke: the jokester, the intended audience, the butt of the joke, and the allies of the butt of the joke. The category of the allies to the butt of the joke is critical, especially in comedy that seems not only to target an individual but rather a representative of a group. It is this fourth category, for instance, that becomes enraged when Stephen Colbert mocks President Donald Trump. Trump himself has shown thin skin, but it has also been his supporters who have bristled at Trump mockery. And, even more important, Trump's allies have used these jokes to confirm their sense that Colbert's audience devalues them. The point is that in each joke the butt is generally not alone. If one is mocking a figure of authority, for example, those who like authority will also feel targeted. It is curious that this fourth stakeholder has been almost entirely ignored in research. And yet, if we are to truly understand the potential risks to comedy, it is this fourth category that might prove most instrumental in understanding how comedy can backfire into conflict.

Perhaps more than any other genre of comedy, satire is the form most likely to produce extreme rewards and extreme risks. And that is because the butt of the joke in satire is *both* symbolic and real. Appreciating the critical gap between the literal target of the joke and the figurative one requires advanced cognitive abilities to detect irony. This is why research on sarcasm and the brain shows that those who use and appreciate sarcasm have a range of cognitive benefits. Katherine P. Rankin did a neurological study that determined that detecting sarcasm requires advanced abilities to appreciate context and "figure[e] out what others are thinking."[12] Li Huang, Francesca Gino, and Adam Galinsky did a study that found that "both the construction and interpretation of sarcasm lead to greater creativity because they activate abstract thinking."[13] Overall a number of studies have shown that "Sarcasm seems to exercise the brain more than sincere statements do. Scientists who have monitored the electrical activity of the brains of test subjects exposed to sarcastic statements have found that brains have to work harder to understand sarcasm."[14]

As Lee explains, satire has a unique ability to spark intense outrage because appreciating the joke requires an ability to simultaneously process both its literal and symbolic meanings, and not everyone can do that. Comedian Dave Chappelle, for example, often did skits that required fairly sophisticated critical thinking since he often used racist comments to undermine racist thinking. In comedy like this not everyone will get the joke, and even more important not everyone will *totally* get the joke. This was what Heather Lamarre, Kristen Landreville, and Michael Beam found in their study of Republican students' misreading of Stephen Colbert's in-character satire. Their research shows that perception of in-character satire varies based on political beliefs. Republican students simply didn't understand the joke. In their study, though, the conservative students did not feel that their beliefs were the butt of the joke either. They were just unable to detect the irony of the comedy.[15]

But it is not just cognitive abilities that are tested in satire, Lee claims, it is the subject position vis-a-vis the joke that most matters. "Few people seem to manage the task well when they or their values are the targets" she argues.[16] The key point for the purposes of this chapter is that when a subject perceives that their values are being questioned via satirical comedy, they will react more aggressively. This is so because most humor, and especially satirical humor, tends to be boundary reinforcing, dividing between the "it getters" and the "allies of the butt" and thereby underscoring group affiliation in ways that are both community reinforcing and socially divisive. Göktürk underscores the fact that while humor can have benefits to those in on the joke, there is little question that it highlights differences across social identities: "We have inherited brains that are inherently sensitive to group affiliation. We find meaning in our lives through social identities, and we experience comfort with those who share these identities. However, when creating an 'us,' the brain seems to seek out a 'them,' bringing online a series of psychological processes—including fear and distrust—that colors our view of out-group members."

Satire is often accused of elitism because at its core it generally focuses on criticizing ideas the satirist characterizes as stupid, illogical, arrogant, or manipulative. It has a biting edge not found in the gentle silliness of comedy that allows everyone to laugh at their common humanity. The upside of satire is that it is especially effective at helping the audience critique the status quo and reject commonly held beliefs that are socially damaging. And, of course, not all satire has the same bite. Colbert's satirical comedy, for example, has far more of a playful edge than the searing mockery of Bill Maher or the righteous rage of Samantha Bee. But in the end, regardless of its edge, satire is about criticizing attitudes, beliefs, worldviews, and behaviors that the satirist wants to target. George A. Test argues in *Satire: Spirit and Art* that satire ultimately judges, it asserts that some person, group, or attitude is not what it should be. However restrained, muted, or disguised a playful judgment may be, whatever form it takes, such an act undermines, threatens, and perhaps violates the target, making the act an attack.[17]

STAKEHOLDER RISKS TO SATIRE

Interestingly the research on satire and blowback has focused primarily on the effects for the intended audience and secondarily on the negative effects for the satirist. In addition, the idea that satire is inherently critical and judgmental has begged the question that there are also negative effects for the butt of the joke, though the butt has been less commonly the subject of research. One major study focused on audience effects is *Politics Is a Joke!* by S. Robert Lichter, Jody C Baumgartner, and Jonathan S. Morris. Surveying years of joke data they conclude that the inherent negativity of late-night humor "is helping late night television comics remake American political life."[18] While they don't focus uniquely on satirical comedy, their overall argument is that late-night humorists have had a direct effect on increased cynicism toward politics in the American public. As I argued with Remy Maisel in *Is Satire Saving Our Nation?* critics of satire:

> worry that satire is (1) too cynical, (2) too persuasive, (3) not persuasive enough, (4) too confusing, (5) too pedantic, (6) too popular, (7) too subtle, (8) too brash, (9) too close to news, (10) not newsy enough, (11) too fun, and (12) not funny enough.[19]

Less research, however, has looked into the potentially negative role that satire might have in creating social division for those in on the joke. The bulk of recent studies, as cited above, looks more generally at satire's role in increasing apathy, cynicism, distraction, and negativity in the audience. And yet, the very nature of satire is designed to heighten we/they thinking and social boundary divisions. Thus far, that element of satirical blowback has been almost completely ignored.

The second category of stakeholder that has received scholarly attention is that of the satirists themselves. In general, this work has focused on the risks the satirist takes by making fun of those in power. In Jon Stewart's endorsement for Egyptian comedian Bassem Youssef's book about his experiences as a satirist in post-Arab Spring Egypt he writes: "Comedy shouldn't take courage, but it made an exception for Bassem." Stewart, of course, is right. Comedy shouldn't take courage. And yet, there are numerous examples of satirists who have been threatened in various ways. In 2013, Youssef was arrested for mocking Muslim Brotherhood leader, Mohammad Morsi and insulting Islam. But when Youssef kept up his critical satire after a military coup that later led to the presidency of Abdul El-Sisi, political pressures became too much and his show was canceled and he was forced into exile. In two other extreme cases—that of the Danish cartoon controversy of 2005 and the attacks on Charlie Hebdo in Paris in 2015, which will be described in more detail below—cartoonists were the direct victims of violence and threats of violence for their satirical work.

These sorts of clear and present violent threats to satirists differ in scope and intensity from threats that derive more from the fact that the satirist is often dependent on the media industry for a platform for their work. Bill Maher lost his show, *Politically Incorrect*, on ABC after making what some perceived as an insensitive comment after the 9/11 attacks. Colbert has come under an FCC investigation for off-color remarks on his show.[20] *The Smothers Brothers* was eventually canceled because CBS found their content politically offensive.[21] There are countless examples of pressures faced by satirical comedians due to their content. There has been less interest, however, in the psychological blowback faced by comedians whose humor depends on we/they thinking. And, as mentioned, there has been almost no interest in the effects of satire on the butt or the allies of the butt of the joke.

For these reasons, I propose the following table as a rough schematic that can allow for a more complete picture of the various types of blowback risks to satirical comedy. As I'll explain below, it may well be the risks of meta-dehumanization—where the allies of the butt of the joke believe that those in on the joke are degrading their humanity—that may explain some of the most violent responses to satirical comedy.

One of the critical challenges to assessing the risks of satire is the way that groups can misread the joke. Because much satire is aimed at ideas over individuals, for instance, a joke mocking religious extremism can feel like a biting attack on one's identity. This is a constant feature of ironic comedy, especially when it is in the form of caricatures, parodies, and cartoons because in those instances ideas are often represented in human form.

The critical issue is that satire can often feel like "one-sided" comedy: what is community building for one group feels like harassment or bullying to the other. As Moira Smith argues "these cases constitute both harassment and humor."[22] She points out that the preferred term today is "laughing with" someone but that in general the laughter is more commonly "at" another, and often at another that is linked to a larger group identity. Smith underscores the fact that certain comedy does not just reinforce boundaries, it heightens them depending on whether the stakeholder is laughing or "unlaughing." She cites the work of Michael Billig who coined the term "unlaughter" to characterize

Table 8.1   Stakeholder Risks to Satire

Stakeholder	Risks
Satirist	Censorship, repression, threats, violence, job pressures, pressures from advertisers or other financial sponsors of their work, sense of superiority over that which is mocked, stereotyping and dehumanization of butt of the joke, increased we/they thinking
Intended Audience	Apathy, cynicism, distraction, negativity, increased polarization, sense of superiority over that which is mocked, confirmation bias, out-group homogeneity bias, stereotyping and dehumanization of butt of the joke, increased we/they thinking
Butt of the Joke	Anger, shame and embarrassment, increased we/they thinking, increased attachment to satirized behaviors, victim of stereotyping and dehumanization, desire for retaliation
Allies of the Butt of the Joke	Increased we/they thinking, motivated reasoning, out-group homogeneity bias, meta-stereotyping and meta-dehumanization of satirist and intended audience, Desire to defend victimized butt of joke

"a display of not laughing when laughter might otherwise be expected, hoped for or demanded."[23] Those laughing are pitted against those unlaughing.

This means that group identities often feel like the target of the joke. Comedy has a public performative quality that puts group responses on display. Thus, it tends to have the potential to heighten meta-perceptions (i.e., how we perceive others to perceive us) and therefore to play a significant role in shaping views in-groups have of out-groups. In fact, as Nour Kteily, Gordon Hodson, and Emile Bruneau found in their study of the role of meta-dehumanization and intergroup conflict, it is often one group's ideas of how another group defines them that can have the most significant impact on potential intergroup conflict.[24]

These perceptions can then be further heightened in communities that are already inclined to defensive, victimized thought patterns as seen in political ideologies such as social dominance orientation, right-wing authoritarianism, religious fundamentalism, and conservatism. For instance, research by Dannagal Young, Benjamin Bogozzi, Abigail Goldring, Shannon Paulsen, and Erin Drouin found that conservatives had a lower ability to appreciate ironic and exaggerated humor than liberals.[25] Other research on political conservatives has found that they share psychological factors of fear and aggression, dogmatism and intolerance of ambiguity, uncertainty avoidance, need for cognitive closure, and terror management.[26] This last feature, terror management, is linked to the idea that political conservatives are inclined to punish outsiders and those who threaten the status of cherished world views—a factor that will play heavily in the two satirical blowback cases I will analyze next.

TWO CASES OF SATIRE AND VIOLENCE

While it seems clear that satirical comedy can have a range of negative consequences for all stakeholders, two recent cases of violent responses to satire stand out. On September 30, 2005, the Danish newspaper *Jyllands-Posten* published twelve cartoons, many of which depicted the prophet Muhammad. According to the editors of the magazine, the idea was to promote debate about self-censorship and to encourage dialogue on the complexities of critiquing Islam. Shortly after the release of the cartoons, Muslim groups in Denmark complained and the story of the cartoons reached a global audience, leading to protests around the world and a number of violent demonstrations in predominantly Muslim countries. In the wake of the protests and ensuing debates, a number of other newspapers reprinted the cartoons leading to further outrage. Ultimately the cartoon controversy led to two hundred reported deaths linked to protests, attacks on Danish and other European embassies and diplomatic missions, attacks on churches and Christians, and a major international boycott of Danish goods.

The French satirical magazine *Charlie Hebdo* was one of the European outlets that republished the twelve *Jyllands-Posten* cartoons. *Charlie Hebdo*'s editors had long been involved with a series of scandals over publishing offensive material, including a controversial cartoon mocking Charles de Gaulle. Their February 9, 2006, issue carried the title "Muhammad overwhelmed by fundamentalists" and the front page had a cartoon of a weeping Muhammad saying, "it's hard being loved by jerks." In November 2011, the offices of the magazine were firebombed and its website was hacked in an attack presumably linked to the November 3rd issue of the magazine entitled "Charia Hebdo," which responded to recent news that Libya had instituted Islamic sharia law and Islamists had won a victory in Tunisia. Then in September 2012, the newspaper published a series of satirical cartoons of Muhammad, some of which featured nude caricatures of the prophet, in an issue released shortly after a series of attacks on US embassies in the Middle East. On January 7, 2016, two gunmen entered the Paris headquarters of *Charlie Hebdo* and opened fire killing twelve members of the staff. During the attacks, the gunmen shouted "the Prophet is avenged." The attackers were later identified as Saïd Kouachi and Chérif Kouachi, French Muslim brothers of Algerian descent.

Both of these cases share much in common. They are each stories of extreme violence in response to satirical cartoons depicting the prophet Muhammad and they both tended to reinforce the idea that there is a significant cultural breakdown between the west and the Islamic world. Critics of the attacks used the events to highlight the idea that the west protects freedom of speech. Critics of the cartoons suggested that the publication of them was intended to humiliate Muslims and possibly even provoke violence. Commentary after these incidents was largely focused on the idea that the cartoons themselves revealed stark differences across cultures. But, as I will elaborate fully below, the issue was not so much one of a cultural clash, but rather of the blowback caused by meta-perceptions, of the ideas different groups had of what the other group thought of them.

One of the more noteworthy outcomes of these incidents was the fact that satire itself came under attack as too caustic, too provocative, and too hostile. As Lee writes, "The satiric spark warms some with pleasure yet sears others with pain."[27] Lee further notes that there was far more violence after the cartoons came out than after the photos of Abu Ghraib. For some, the cartoons seemed to dare the Muslim community to take the joke, for if they couldn't take it, it was a sign of their inability to deal with humor. For Smith, the cartoons were boundary heightening: dividing groups into those that had a sense of humor and those that were humorless.[28] Zimbardo wonders whether the cartoons were intended to push the allies of the butt of the joke to display their sense of offense and thereby affirm their distance from those laughing at the joke: "There may be a deliberate provocation of unlaughter, in order to heighten social boundaries and gauge the butt of jokes' suitability for full inclusion or membership in the group."[29]

And yet those scholars who focus on satire as the problem miss two key features of these cases that may explain why they developed into extreme violence. (1) These were cartoons produced by what the allies of the butt of the joke perceive to be a condescending out-group. That is, these cartoons were made by westerners and the allies of the butt of the joke already assume that the west has a low opinion of them. And (2) the cartoons depicted the Prophet, an aesthetic choice that would naturally feel like an insult to their humanity and an affront to their religion.

In order to fully process these distinctions, it is critical to recall that in the realm of anti-extremist Islamic satire the images from *Charlie Hebdo* and *Jyllands-Posten* are relatively tame. Analysts framing this as a free speech/respect for Islam issue missed the fact that within the Muslim world there is a significant amount of anti-extremist Islam satire and comedy. As John Hall reports: television networks in the Middle East offer viewers "a Looney Tunes-style cartoon poking fun at militant Islamists fighting for ISIS in Syria and Iraq." These cartoons depict the group "as narcissistic, deluded and obsessed with a literal interpretation of Islam that forces them go to ridiculous lengths to ensure they do not use any item that wasn't available in the 7th Century."[30]

Nabil Assaf, writer and producer on Lebanon's ISIS-mocking *Ktir Salbe Show*, explains that the Islamic community has worked to condemn extremists and that they consider satire as a key part of that critique: "These people are not a true representation of Islam and so by mocking them, it is a way to show we are against them."[31] Another excellent example of this type of satire is the Iraqi state TV show, *State of Myths*, which depicts ISIS leader Al'Baghdadi as being hatched from an egg. After using satire to diminish the extremist leader, they then show him killing every single one of his men. The show bravely uses satirical humor to help deflect the state of fear caused by extremists. In another example, Palestinian TV channel *al-Falastiniya* aired a skit showing two militants killing Muslim civilians for their lack of knowledge on the number of times to kneel during prayers. Next a Jordanian Christian approaches and the militants fight over who gets to shoot him—competing for who gets the "blessing" for himself. While they fight over him, the frightened Jordanian suffers a fatal heart attack, leaving the militants disappointed at not being able to take credit for his death.

There is also a whole host of satire aimed at the extreme and grotesque propaganda produced by ISIS and al-Qaeda. This is satire that uses shock tactics that come dangerously close to that which they are parodying—and it is not for the faint of heart. One of these is @CaliphIbrahimAR described as a self-appointed Caliph. Another comes from @Shkh_AL_Adnani who once posted a tweet with a photo of two dead militants shown with their pants down and the line: "Mashallah! Our brothers took off their clothes and patiently await their virgins. Any minute now."

Thus, the notion that the problem here was satire is a mistake since as Ed Krayeski explains, "satirizing radical Islam is not the exclusive domain of white Western Europeans." In fact, there is far more satire of Islamic extremists coming out of the Muslim world than the West. Marwan Kraidy points out that this satire is widely available throughout the region from state produced TV available via satellite to independently made YouTube videos.[32] Twitter users also regularly jump in to mock the extremists. One example is the hashtag #ISISmovies which is used by both Muslims and non-Muslims alike to offer mock extremist movie titles like *To Kill a Mocking Kurd*.

This means that the notion that the violence connected to the cartoon controversies was driven by satire itself is a mistake. The European satirists were working within a far wider, global network of artists interested in using irony, humor, and mockery to attack the ideology of extremists. And all of these artists are crossing lines and provoking their audiences: it's not easy to mock beheadings and indiscriminate murder without ruffling feathers.

These examples from across the Muslim world also help underscore the specific reasons why the European cartoons provoked violent reactions: they were produced in the West and they included depictions of the Prophet—two critical elements in enhancing a sense of meta-dehumanization. Ana Soage underscored the way that the depiction of the Prophet was a trigger for the Islamic community, "the targeting of a religious symbol like Muhammad, the only prophet that Muslims do not share with Jews and Christians, was perceived as the last in a long list of humiliations and assaults."[33]

ROLE OF META-DEHUMANIZATION

Suzan J. Harkness, Mohamed Magid, Jameka Roberts, and Michael Richardson explain in their study of the fallout from the Danish cartoons that it is a mistake to lump all Muslims together when analyzing reactions to the cartoons since the Muslim community had a range of responses. Moderates tended to be more in favor of free speech and simply ignoring the cartoons, more devout Muslims wanted boycotts, nonviolent protests, and an apology, and extremists had more openly violent responses.[34] Yet, across the board there was a common perception among all religious beliefs that the cartoons underscored a cultural clash.

The problem, however, is that characterizing the fallout of the cartoon controversy as a cultural clash does not allow us to understand the specific ways that these cartoons led to violence when other types of cartoons that similarly highlight cultural difference might not. Rather than understanding the conflict over the cartoons as an example of cultural difference, some research suggests that the critical part of the story is the way that the cartoons contributed to meta-dehumanization. The study by Kteily, Hodson, and Bruneau found that "informing people that they are dehumanized by an out-group led in turn to greater dehumanization of that outgroup."[35] Studying a range of cases, they investigated how we react when we perceive (or learn) that other groups see our own group as less than human. They were able to trace a process of heightened dehumanization, cascading as a domino effect: "For example, when learning that Muslims or Arabs dehumanize 'Americans,' Americans in turn come to see Muslims or Arabs as less human. This in turn is associated with greater willingness to engage in severe retribution (e.g., torture, drone strikes)."[36] They further found that meta-perceptions (i.e., how we perceive others to perceive us) are as important as our beliefs about a group.

Their study highlights two types of dehumanization: (1) animalistic, which suggests that others have lower refinement, civility or cognitive aptitude, and (2) mechanistic, which denies traits that might be shared with animals like warmth and emotionality.[37] The key, they argue, is that meta-dehumanization

is distinct from meta-prejudice.[38] Meta-prejudice also plays a role in dividing groups and assigning them different characteristics, but it differs from
meta-dehumanization because it is not predicated on seeing the other as less
than human. As Kteily, Hodson, and Bruneau argue, it is the perception that
another group sees one's group as less than human that produces violent conflict. In their study, they looked not at the views of those in the Muslim world
toward the *Charlie Hebdo* cartoons, but rather to the effects that the attacks
on *Charlie Hebdo* had on US perceptions of ISIS and Muslims in general.
They found that the *Charlie Hebdo* attacks led to meta-dehumanization and
to views favoring "militaristic counter-terrorism, opposition to immigration,
signing anti-ISIS petitions, and punitiveness towards the Hebdo attackers."[39]
Their research highlights the way that meta-dehumanization has an escalating
circular effect that is not limited to the perceptions of only one group. In fact,
they were able to document "a novel *dehumanization specific pathway* from
meta-perception to action (including aggressive intergroup attitudes and
behavior)."[40]

This research helps make sense of the intense blowback cause by these
two cartoon controversies and it helps explain why an Iraqi TV show that
depicts Al'Baghdadi as being hatched from an egg does not provoke the same
outcome. Recall that in many cases the protesters of the Danish cartoons had
not even seen the cartoons at all.[41] And as Smith points out, there was a clear
effort on the part of some Muslim extremists to weaponize the story of the
cartoons. She notes that in the dossiers of cartoons that circulated in the wake
of the *Jyllands-Posten* scandal there were a number of additional images
besides those that the Danish paper had published. These additions were even
more specifically dehumanizing. They included a cartoon showing a Muslim
man kneeling in prayer being raped by a dog and a photograph of a man
wearing a pig mask who was alleged to be a representation of the Prophet.
The point is that it was not the cartoons per se that were being protested; it
was backlash for meta-perceptions, that is ideas the protesters had of what the
other group thought of them.

And for those who did see the cartoons, it is further important to note that
by the nature of their genre, satirical cartoons are inclined to produce exaggerated, extreme, perhaps dehumanized images. In an address announcing a
UN effort to try to mobilize cartooning for peace, Kofi Annan cautioned that
cartoons can often lead to social division: "few things can hurt you more
directly than a caricature of yourself, of a group you belong to, or a person
you deeply respect."[42] Annan pointed to the visceral way that cartoons can
impact viewers, "because an image generally has a stronger, more direct
impact on the brain than a sentence does, and because many more people
will look at a cartoon than read an article."[43] Satirical cartoons often use
personification to critique ideas, they often depict human figures in symbolic

ways, and they often rely on using gross exaggerations to make their point. But when the cartoonists chose to depict the prophet Muhammad as a symbol of Muslim extremism, they clearly made an aesthetic choice that would inevitably provoke. As Matthieu Madenian, a contributor to *Charlie Hebdo*, put it, one of the fun aspects of satire is causing offense. He describes the team at *Charlie Hebdo* as "an unlikely gathering of sexually obsessed cartoonists, anti-globalisation economists and clergy ravagers brought together by the desire to laugh, denounce things, and above all to enjoy causing offense."[44]

One of the most unsettling elements of these two cases is the fact that many of those who felt like the target of the joke where not, ostensibly, the intended target. Thus, one critical issue to take into account in analyzing the risks of satire is the fact that some groups will misperceive themselves as targets because they will feel that their belief systems are under attack or they will feel a need to show solidarity as allies of the intended butt of the joke. For those favoring the satire of the cartoons, the object of them was Islamic extremism and intolerance of western principles of free speech. Kurt Westergaard, the cartoonist who depicted the prophet Muhammad with a bomb in his turban for *Jyllands-Posten*, defended his work and argued: "The cartoon is not directed at a whole, but against the part of it that obviously can inspire terrorism, death and destruction."[45] In another example, cartoonist Art Spiegelman said that if Westergaard's drawing "had simply not appeared under the rubric of 'Muhammad's Face,' it would have been more immediately seen to specifically represent the murderous aspect of fundamentalism, that . . . made this drawing a self-fulfilling prophecy."[46]

But that's the point. The cartoons did depict the Prophet—a move that meant that anyone practicing Islam would have a hard time seeing beyond that image and deriving any deeper meaning. Speigelman's inability to note the trigger of using a depiction of the prophet Muhammad underscores the gap between stakeholder positions in satire. Because the cartoons in both *Jyllands-Posten* and *Charlie Hebdo* chose to criticize Islamic extremism by depicting the Prophet, an act considered by most Muslims to be forbidden by their religion, they were designed to develop stark oppositions between the intended audience and the allies of the butt of the joke. For the cartoonists, the butt of the joke was extremism, but for the allies, the butt was the Prophet himself. That the cartoonists chose not to depict Al'Baghdadi or another noteworthy extremist leader, for example, is telling and explains much about the ways that the cartoons led to violent blowback. As Kteily, Hodson, and Bruneau find in their research on meta-dehumanization, differences in out-group dehumanization are mediated by (1) a general desire to reciprocate the out-group's perceptions of the in-group, and (2) perceived identity threat.[47] That the dehumanizing cartoons also included depictions of the Prophet added a layer of identity threat that logically led to greater blowback. The critical component is that those offended by the cartoons felt like victims—an attitude Bruneau has also found in the terrorist mindset, which tends to see itself as part of an aggrieved minority.[48] But the real catch, Bruneau argues, is the role of empathy. His research shows that when a member of a community feels empathy for his own group it leads to "*less* willingness to help the outgroup and *more* willingness to harm." In the case of the violent responses to the *Jyllands-Posten* and *Charlie Hebdo* cartoons, the allies of the butt of the joke displayed a combination of in-group empathy, meta-dehumanization, and identification as an aggrieved minority—feelings that unsurprisingly led to violence.

CONCLUSIONS

It is commonly argued that "good" comedy punches up and "bad" comedy punches down. But, as I've argued here, the perception of whether the punch is up or down varies by stakeholder. For the cartoonists and their advocates, it was modern secular society that was under attack—victimized by Islamic fundamentalism. As Flemming Rose explained in a piece entitled, *Why I Published Those Cartoons*:

> The modern secular society is dismissed by some Muslims. They demand special treatment when they insist on special consideration of their religious feelings. This is incompatible with secular democracy and freedom of speech, where one should be ready to stand scorn, mockery and ridicule.[49]

For the Europeans creating the cartoons, the idea was to energize their respective communities. Jane Weston Vauclair points out that one of the core identities for the *Charlie Hebdo* satirists was their desire to poke fun at taboo subjects, something they did thinking they were speaking to a fairly small audience. *Charlie Hebdo* was, after all, on the verge of bankruptcy just prior to the attacks. In an interview with the magazine's editor Stephane Charbonnier, who was later murdered in the attacks, Charb explained, "I don't think we're going to change the minds of people who stumble on *Charlie Hebdo*, I think we're speaking to people who already agree with us, it comforts people who are isolated in their milieu."[50] For Charb as for Rose, their audience was an isolated, frustrated group of European citizens tired of seeing secularism and Enlightenment ideals under attack. They felt they were directing their jokes at an ostracized minority. The great irony, then, is that cartoons meant to build community and help promote solidarity among an in-group led to violent blowback when perceived by an out-group.

Debates on the blowback from the cartoon controversies led many to think that it was necessary to draw a line between acceptable and unacceptable comedy. On its face, it's a plan that makes sense, but, as with all freedom of expression debates, the devil is in the details. As Lee puts it, "there is no absolute agreement on the boundary between humor and offensiveness."[51] What we can do, then, is have a more sophisticated understanding of the effects of comedy on all four of the key stakeholders. That understanding can lead to greater awareness of the fact that each time a satirist builds a community of "it getters" they may also be aggravating the allies of the butt of their jokes. And, as this article has shown, the extent of that aggravation and its propensity for violence may well be fairly predictable.

NOTES

1. Geoffrey Baym, *From Cronkite to Colbert* (Oxford: Oxford University Press, 2009); Amber Day, *Satire and Dissent* (Bloomington: Indiana University Press, 2011); Jeffrey P. Jones, *Entertaining Politics* (Lanham, MD: Rowman & Littlefield, 2010); Sophia A. McClennen, *America According to Colbert* (Basingstoke, UK: Palgrave Macmillan, 2011); Sophia A. McClennen and Remy M. Maisel, *Is Satire Saving Our Nation?* (Basingstoke, UK: Palgrave Macmillan, 2014).

2. Plato, *The Republic* (Chicago: Perseus at the University of Chicago, 2010).

3. René Descartes, *Delphi Collected Works of René Descartes* (Hastings, East Sussex, UK: Delphi Publishing, 2017).

4. Thomas Hobbes, *The Treatise on Human Nature and that on Liberty and Necessity with a Supplement* (London: J. Johnson and Company, 1812).

5. In Morreall 1987, 168.

6. Charles R. Gruner, *The Game of Humor* (Abingdon, UK: Routledge, 1999).

7. John Morreall, "Philosophy of Humor," *The Stanford Encyclopedia of Philosophy*, last modified Winter 2016, https://plato.stanford.edu/archives/win2016/entries/humor/.

8. Ibid.

9. Sigmund Freud, *Jokes and Their Relation to the Unconscious* (New York: W. W. Norton & Company, 1990), 118.

10. Deniz Göktürk, "Jokes and Butts: Can We Imagine Humor in a Global Public Sphere?" *PMLA* 123, no. 5 (October 2008): 1707.

11. Ibid.

12. Dan Hurley, "The Science of Sarcasm (Not That You Care)," *The New York Times*, June 3, 2008.

13. Li Huang, Francesca Gino, and Adam D. Galinsky, "The Highest Form of Intelligence: Sarcasm Increases Creativity for Both Expresses and Recipients," *Organizational Behavior and Human Decision Processes* 131 (November 2015): 162.

14. Richard Chin, "The Science of Sarcasm? Yeah Right," *Smithsonian. com*, November 14, 2011, https://www.smithsonianmag.com/science-nature/the-science-of-sarcasm-yeah-right-25038/#0tDr8L5CLumRX7Ku.99.

15. Heather L. LaMarre, Kristen D. Landreville, and Michael Beam, "The Irony of Satire," *The International Journal of Press/Politics* 14, no. 2 (April 1, 2009): 212.

16. Ibid., viii.

17. Ibid., 5.

18. Robert S. Lichter, Jody C Baumgartner, and Jonathan S. Morris, *Politics Is a Joke!* (Abingdon, UK: Routledge, 2014), 9.

19. McClennen, *Is Satire Saving Our Nation?*

20. Nick Statt, "FCC opens investigation into Stephen Colbert's controversial Trump insult," *The Verge*, May 5, 2017.

21. Maureen Muldaur, dir. *Smothered: The Censorship Struggles of the Smothers Brothers Comedy Hour*, Muldaur Media Ltd., December 4, 2002.

22. Moira Smith, "Humor, Unlaughter, and Boundary Maintenance," *Journal of American Folklore* 122, no. 484 (Spring 2009): 162.

23. Ibid.

24. Emile Bruneau, Gordon Hodson, and Nour Kteily, "They See Us As Less Than Human: Meta-Dehumanization Predicts Intergroup Conflict Via Reciprocal Dehumanization," *Journal of Personality and Social Psychology* 110, no. 3 (March 2016): 343.

25. Dannagal G. Young et al., "Psychology, Political Ideology, and Humor Appreciation: Why is Satire So Liberal?" *Psychology of Popular Media Culture*, 2017.

26. Kathleen Maclay, "Researchers help define what makes a political conservative," *UCBerkeleyNews*, July 22, 2003.

27. Freud, *Jokes and Their Relation to the Unconscious.*

28. Smith, "Humor, Unlaughter, and Boundary Maintenance," 162.

29. Zara Zimbardo, "Cultural Politics of Humor in (De)Normalizing Islamophobic Stereotypes," *Islamaphobia Studies Journal* 2, no. 1 (Spring 2014): 64.

30. John Hall, "ISIS Jihadis Blowing Themselves Up and Rejecting Radio as Un-Islamic – Welcome to Iraqi TV's Cartoon Satire on Terror," *DailyMail.com*, September 1, 2014.

31. Ibid.

32. Marwan Kraidy, "Anti-ISIS Satire Lampoons Militant Group's Hypocrisy," interview by Audie Cornish, *All Things Considered*, NPR, November 10, 2014. http://wamc.org/post/anti-isis-satire-lampoons-militant-groups-hypocrisy.

33. Ana Belen Soage, "The Danish Caricatures Seen from the Arab World," *Politics, Religion & Ideology* 7, no. 3 (September 2006): 363.

34. Suzan J. Harkness, Mohamed Magid, Jameka Roberts, and Michael Richardson, "Crossing the Line? Freedom of Speech and Religious Sensibilities," *PSL Political Science & Politics* 40, no. 2 (April 2007): 276.

35. Emile Bruneau, Gordon Hudson, and Nour Kteily, "They See Us As Less Than Human."

36. Ibid.

37. Ibid., 9.

38. Ibid., 10.

39. Ibid., 46.

40. Ibid., 60.

41. Smith, "Humor, Unlaughter, and Boundary Maintenance."

42. Avy Mallik, "The Ethical Responsibility of Political Cartooning," *UN Chronicle* 43, no. 4 (December 2006).

43. Ibid.

44. Mathieu Madénian, "My Postcard Published in Charlie Hebdo Today," *Facebook*, January 14, 2015, https://www.facebook.com/mathieumadenian/posts/10153667851305656.

45. David Keane, "Violence and Freedom of Expression," *Human Rights Quarterly* 30, no. 4 (November 2008): 858.

46. Ibid.

47. Bruneau et al., "They See Us As Less Than Human," 2.

48. Emile Bruneau, "Understanding the Terrorist Mind," *Cerebrum*, November 21, 2016, http://www.dana.org/Cerebrum/2016/Understanding_the_Terrorist_Mind/.

49. Flemming Rose, "Why I Published Those Cartoons," *The Washington Post*, February 19, 2016.

50. Jane Weston Vauclair, "Local Laughter, Global Polemics: Understanding Charlie Hebdo," *European Comic Art* 8, no. 1 (Spring 2015): 8.

51. Judith Yaross Lee, "Assaults on Laughter," *Studies in American Humor* 1, no. 1 (2015): v.

REFERENCES

Baym, Geoffrey. *From Cronkite to Colbert*. Oxford: Oxford University Press, 2009.

Bruneau, Emile. "Understanding the Terrorist Mind." *Cerebrum*, November 21, 2016. http://www.dana.org/Cerebrum/2016/Understanding_the_Terrorist_Mind/.

Bruneau, Emile, Gordon Hodson, and Nour Kteily. "They See Us As Less Than Human: Meta-Dehumanization Predicts Intergroup Conflict Via Reciprocal Dehumanization." *Journal of Personality and Social Psychology* 110, no. 3 (March 2016): 343.

Chin, Richard. "The Science of Sarcasm? Yeah Right." *Smithsonian.com*, November 14, 2011. https://www.smithsonianmag.com/science-nature/the-science-of-sarcasm-yeah-right-25038/#0tDr8L5CLumRX7Ku.99.

Day, Amber. *Satire and Dissent*. Bloomington: Indiana University Press, 2011.

Descartes, René. *Delphi Collected Works of René Descartes*. Hastings, East Sussex, UK: Delphi Publishing, 2017.

Freud, Sigmund. *Jokes and Their Relation to the Unconscious*. New York: W. W. Norton & Company, 1990.

Göktürk, Deniz. "Jokes and Butts: Can We Imagine Humor in a Global Public Sphere?" *PMLA* 123, no. 5 (October 2008): 1707.

Gruner, Charles R. *The Game of Humor*. Abingdon, UK: Routledge, 1999.

Hall, John. "ISIS Jihadis Blowing Themselves Up and Rejecting Radio as Un-Islamic—Welcome to Iraqi TV's Cartoon Satire on Terror." *DailyMail.com*, September 1, 2014.

Harkness, Susan J., Mohamed Magid, Jameka Roberts, and Michael Richardson. "Crossing the Line? Freedom of Speech and Religious Sensibilities." *PSL Political Science & Politics* 40, no. 2 (April 2007): 276.

Hobbes, Thomas. *The Treatise on Human Nature and that on Liberty and Necessity with a Supplement*. London: J. Johnson and Company, 1812.

Huang, Li, Francesca Gino, and Adam D. Galinsky. "The Highest Form of Intelligence: Sarcasm Increases Creativity for Both Expresses and Recipients." *Organizational Behavior and Human Decision Processes* 131 (November 2015): 162.

Hurley, Dan. "The Science of Sarcasm (Not That You Care)." *The New York Times*, June 3, 2008.

Jones, Jeffrey. *Entertaining Politics*. Lanham, MD: Rowman & Littlefield, 2010.

Keane, David. "Violence and Freedom of Expression." *Human Rights Quarterly* 30, no. 4 (November 2008): 858.

Kraidy, Marwan. "Anti-ISIS Satire Lampoons Militant Group's Hypocrisy." Interview by Audie Cornish. *All Things Considered*. NPR, November, 10, 2014. http://wamc.org/post/anti-isis-satire-lampoons-militant-groups-hypocrisy.

LaMarre, Heather L., Kristen D. Landreville, and Michael Beam. "The Irony of Satire." *The International Journal of Press/Politics* 14, no. 2 (April 1, 2009): 212.

Lee, Judith Yaross. "Assaults of Laughter." *Studies in American Humor* 1, no. 1 (2015): v–xiv.

Lichter, Robert S., Jody C Baumgartner, and Jonathan S. Morris. *Politics Is a Joke!* Abingdon, UK: Routledge, 2014.

Maclay, Kathleen. "Researchers help define what makes a political conservative." *UCBerkeleyNews*, July 22, 2003.

Madénian, Mathieu. "My Postcard published in Charlie Hebdo today." *Facebook*, January 14, 2015. https://www.facebook.com/mathieumadenian/posts/10153667851305656.

Mallik, Avy. "The Ethical Responsibility of Political Cartooning." *UN Chronicle* 43, no. 4 (December 2006).

McClennen, Sophia A. *America According to Colbert*. Basingstoke, UK: Palgrave Macmillan, 2011.

McClennen, Sophia A., and Remy M. Maisel. *Is Satire Saving Our Nation?* Basingstoke, UK: Palgrave Macmillan, 2014.

Morreall, John. "Philosophy of Humor." *The Stanford Encyclopedia of Philosophy*. Last modified Winter 2016. https://plato.stanford.edu/archives/win2016/entries/humor/.

Muldaur, Maureen, dir. *Smothered: The Censorship Struggles of the Smothers Brothers Comedy Hour*. Muldaur Media, Ltd. December 4, 2002.

Plato. *The Republic*. Chicago: Perseus at the University of Chicago, 2010.

Rose, Flemming. "Why I Published Those Cartoons." *The Washington Post*, February 19, 2016.

Smith, Moira. "Humor, Unlaughter, and Boundary Maintenance." *Journal of American Folklore* 122, no. 484 (Spring 2009): 162.

Soage, Ana Belen. "The Danish Caricatures Seen from the Arab World." *Politics, Religion & Ideology* 7, no. 3 (September 2006): 363.

Statt, Nick. "FCC opens investigation into Stephen Colbert's controversial Trump insult." *The Verge*, May 5, 2017.

Vauclair, Jane Weston. "Local Laughter, Global Polemics: Understanding Charlie Hebdo." *European Comic Art* 8, no. 1 (Spring 2015): 8.

Young, Dannagal G., Benjamin E. Bagozzi, Abigail Goldring, Shannon Poulsen, and Erin Drouin. "Psychology, Political Ideology, and Humor Appreciation: Why is Satire So Liberal?" *Psychology of Popular Media Culture*, 2017. http://dx.doi.org/10.1037/ppm0000157

Zimbardo, Zara. "Cultural Politics of Humor in (De)Normalizing Islamophobic Stereotypes." *Islamaphobia Studies Journal* 2, no. 1 (Spring 2014): 64.

Chapter 9

What Is Funny to Whom?

Applying an Integrative Theoretical Framework to the Study of Political Humor Appreciation

Christiane Grill

For centuries, political humor has been a vital element in democratic societies. Political humor paves the way to playfully criticize governments, institutions, and policies, and thus serves as an important form of political expression in healthy democracies.[1] It is therefore hardly surprising that political humor has attracted a fair share of scientific interest in the past. So far, media and political communication scholars have investigated correlates and effects of exposure to political humor, thereby opening up two strands of research. Political humor has been found to increase awareness for and attention to political campaigns, actors, and issues,[2] resulting in higher rates of political knowledge.[3] Furthermore, empirical studies have shown that political humor affects democratic health. On the one hand, exposure to political humor may foster political participation and political discussions[4] and may improve self-assessed political efficacy.[5] On the other hand, exposure to political humor might promote cynicism and resentment toward political life.[6]

Despite substantial research on the correlates and effects of political humor and satire, it is still unclear why some members of the audience appreciate certain political jokes more than others.[7] Such an analysis is certainly worthwhile, as empirical studies on the impact of political humor have revealed diverging patterns of effects on the audience. Thus, scholars have suggested taking a step back and focusing first on the understanding of political humor appreciation. A profound understanding of humor appreciation—so scholars argue—is central for explaining why political humor affects its audience differently.[8] Therefore, this work sets out to examine the explanatory factors behind why political humor might be appreciated by some and not by others.

In so doing, this study aims at providing an integrative theory-rich approach for understanding political humor appreciation. This work thereby extends the extant theoretical and empirical work on political humor on two levels.

First, research on humor appreciation has thus far been limited to isolated studies, which produced not more than a few islands of analysis. Some studies drew on the disposition theory of humor as a solid theoretical framework for the analysis of political humor appreciation,[9] while others dovetailed humor appreciation with ego and issue involvement[10] as well as with the intellectual appreciation of the joke.[11] However, these theoretical approaches have until now never been applied in an integrative manner. This study thus draws on the aforementioned theoretical approaches to provide an integrated theoretical framework for the analysis of political humor appreciation. It builds a bridge between the extant theoretical explanations for humor appreciation. Ultimately, this work is able to shed light on the explanatory power of the different approaches.

Second, this study speaks to the need to go beyond US-American late-night comedy shows. Political humor and satire research is particularly rich in the United States where it has been focusing on the late-night shows *The Daily Show with Jon Stewart* and *The Colbert Report*. However, political humor is not a monolithic construct and comes in exceedingly diverse forms. Hence, different comedic types have to be consulted for the study of political humor.[12] Therefore, this study breaks with the tradition of looking at US-American political comedy and instead connects its analysis to an European political comedy format. Specifically, this study aims at analyzing humor appreciation for a national and culturally specific comedic form.

By providing empirical evidence from a survey ($N = 358$) on humor appreciation conducted in Austria, this work offers an integrated theoretical framework for the analysis of political humor, and in so doing deepens insights into political humor appreciation.

DISPOSITIONS AND POLITICAL
HUMOR APPRECIATION

Early work on humor appreciation adopted a reference group and identification class theory of humor.[13] To this end, scholars established the idea of affiliated and unaffiliated entities arguing that only jokes at the expense of unaffiliated objects result in feelings of mirth and humor. However, categorizing affiliated objects into, for instance, racial, national, political, religious, or socioeconomic classes only supports the explanation of humor appreciation if these categorizations adequately classify dispositions. Enjoyment derived from negative affective dispositions toward the degraded and

debased object and feelings of superiority form the bases of humor appreciation.[14] Empirical studies within this theoretical realm analyzing resentments
toward jokes about the in-group and appreciation of jokes about the out-group
revealed that the depreciated in-group showed less humor appreciation than
the superior out-group did.[15]

While the reference group membership toward affiliation or identification
focuses on a dichotomization of disparaged entities, the disposition theory of
humor allows for a "continuum of affective disposition ranging from extreme
negative affect through a neutral point of indifference to extreme positive
effect."[16] The disposition theory of humor states as its core argument that
antipathy or resentment toward the joke's disparaged object as well as sym-
pathy or liking toward the disparaging object shape the individual's response
to the humorous stimulus.[17] Specifically, the theory posits that humor appreciation is positively correlated with the favorableness of the joke's victor and
at the same time is negatively correlated with the favorableness of the joke's
victim.[18] Meaning, positive affective dispositions toward the disparaging
entity as well as negative affective dispositions toward the disparaged entity
result in greater humor appreciation.[19]

Even though Wolff and his colleagues and Zillmann and his colleagues[20]
explicitly stated that other affiliated objects to which someone can hold
positive dispositions also have an effect on humor appreciation, so far only
affective dispositions toward the disparaged and disparaging entities have
been taken into consideration. Instead of yet again looking at dispositions
toward political figures, this study opens up a new perspective by focusing
on dispositions toward political issues being disparaged. To that end, this
work draws on a study by Stewart. Stewart[21] proposed that one's personal
disposition toward political affairs—in the sense of being generally interested
in them—is a necessary precondition for humor appreciation. Consequently,
Stewart hypothesized a positive correlation between interest in specific political affairs and the appreciation of the humor being provided in the comedic
form. However, only partial support for a positive relationship between interest in political affairs and humor appreciation was found. The lack of a robust
finding was attributed to the confounding stimuli used, those being self-
deprecatory and other-deprecatory jokes made by President Barack Obama
and his opponent, John McCain. Consequently, further empirical evidence
is needed in this regard. In line with Stewart's take on defining a disposition
toward political affairs as being interested in them, this work posits the following first hypothesis:

H1: Being interested in the politics being disparaged hampers political humor
appreciation. In contrast, being interested in other politics not being disparaged
motivates political humor appreciation.

INVOLVEMENT AND POLITICAL
HUMOR APPRECIATION

In 1960, Levine and Redlich[22] already stated that perceived humor depends upon a range of factors. However, thus far, the majority of research on political humor appreciation has drawn on the disposition theory of humor. While the concepts of involvement and information appreciation have also been connected to humor appreciation in the past, empirical studies on the relationships between involvement, information appreciation, and humor appreciation are rare. Therefore, this work once again turns to these concepts to illustrate their fruitful integration into the theoretical explanations for political humor appreciation.

While the concept of involvement is well established in persuasion theory, it has been marginally applied to the explanation of humor appreciation.[23] In persuasion theory, a distinction is drawn between ego and issue involvement. Ego involvement or personal involvement refers to the involvement of oneself including all physical characteristics, things that belong to oneself, social values one upholds, as well as entities with which someone identifies.[24] Issue or topic involvement is defined as the importance—synonymously used with salience—of issues, opinions, or positions taken.[25]

While manifold studies building on persuasion theory revealed that increased ego as well as issue involvement goes along with increased resistance to persuasion,[26] empirical evidence on the influence of ego and issue involvement on humor appreciation is marginal at best. As one of the first, Priest[27] casually noted that high salience of an issue in the sense of being strongly involved in a specific issue might contribute to differences in humor appreciation. Grote and Cvetkovich[28] were the first who empirically demonstrated that there is a positive relation between personal involvement in an issue and appreciating jokes on the respective issue. Later on, a series of studies by Powell[29] analyzed the influence of ego and issue involvement on persuasive outcomes of satire. Specifically, Powell argued that increased levels of ego as well as issue involvement not only result in an improved cognitive processing of satirical information and higher comprehension of the message but also in greater appreciation of the humorous information.[30] While the results on the satire's effect on message comprehension were inconclusive and not deemed replicable,[31] the study provided clear empirical evidence that involvement affects humor appreciation. However, as these results were obtained via experimental designs using a small sample of students, the relation between involvement and humor appreciations warrants following up.

Building on extant empirical findings on the influence of ego and issue involvement on humor appreciation, this work hypothesizes:

H2: Ego involvement positively affects humor appreciation: Increased ego involvement results in higher humor appreciation.

H3: Issue involvement facilitates humor appreciation in the sense of higher personal salience of an issue significantly predicts humor appreciation.

INFORMATION APPRECIATION AND POLITICAL HUMOR APPRECIATION

Lastly, this study also draws on information appreciation. Already in 1972, Grote and Cvetkovic[32] highlighted the importance of intellectually appreciating a joke in order to rate it as funny and humorous. Furthermore, scholars widely agree on the fact that the appreciation of a joke is decisive for the understanding of humor.[33] One of the rare studies to date addressing the informative component of political humor revealed that political satire gratifies the viewers' desire to learn something from a joke.[34] However, research lacks empirical evidence on the relationship between humor appreciation and information appreciation. Based on the theoretical understanding of information appreciation, this work hypothesizes the following:

H4: Appreciating the information provided by political humor results in greater humor appreciation.

METHOD

An online survey ($N = 358$) was fielded by a large public university between May and June 2014 in Vienna, Austria. The survey was programmed with EFS survey software and administered online among a quota-based sample. The sample can be deemed representative for the country's population in terms of gender (44.3% male) and education (3.6% graduate school, 18.9% vocational school, 57.9% A-level, 19.5% university degree). Participants ranged from 14 to 76 years in age ($M = 28.77$, $SD = 12.25$). In total, 40.8 percent of the participants were students. The survey took around twenty minutes to complete. Respondents received a small monetary incentive.

After a brief introduction and filling in a consent form, all subjects completed the first part of a questionnaire that included a range of different variables. Two humorous video clips followed this first part of the questionnaire. In order to prevent any bias in the perception of the two video clips, the order of presenting these two video clips occurred randomly. After watching each video clip, survey respondents received additional questionnaires in which they answered questions along a semantic differential scale regarding the perception of each video clip.

Video Clips

The two video clips were approximately four minutes in length and originally produced for the Austrian national late-night show *Willkommen Österreich*; more precisely for the special segment *Maschek* which is part of the late-night show. *Maschek* is a comedic segment in which three comedians synchronize footage of real-life political incidents with funny voices. One video clip portrayed a battle of words in parliament between the chancellor and the leader of the right-wing party concerning a financial scandal involving one of the largest national banks in the country. The other video clip with a more international frame dealt with Europe's shortcoming in gas supply originated by the Ukrainian-Russian crisis and Russia's threat of terminating gas delivery to Europe. Although this video clip had a clear affiliation with an international political issue, mockery strongly emphasized the country's national perspective toward the Ukrainian-Russian gas conflict. In both video clips, all political figures were mocked regardless of any party affiliation. Hence, the humorous stimuli did not provide a clear picture of the jokes' disparaged and disparaging political actors. Instead, the political issues per se were the central points of humorous mockery and disparagement in the video clips.

The two video clips were deliberately chosen in order to test humor appreciation for disparaged political issues differing in salience. A pretest confirmed that the political issues being disparaged in the video clips indeed differed in public salience. While more than half of all respondents (55.3%) assessed the Ukrainian-Russian crisis as the most important problem, which Austria was facing currently, 12.6 percent of all respondents rated the financial scandal involving one of the country's largest banks as the most important national problem.

A manipulation check for perceived humor was conducted to make sure that viewers rated the video clips funny and humorous. As Table 9.1 shows, viewers perceived both video clips equally funny and humorous.

Measures

Humor Appreciation

Immediately after watching each video clip, participants were asked a series of semantic differentials in order to evaluate their impressions of the video clips. A measure of humor appreciation for each video clip was created by combining responses to the two item pairs "serious—funny" and

Table 9.1   Single Semantic Differentials as well as Humor Appreciation and Information Appreciation by Video Clips

	Video: National Bank		Video: Gas Crisis	
	M	SD	M	SD
Serious—funny	5.99	2.00	5.87	1.76
Humorless—humorous	5.85	2.09	5.80	1.97
Humor appreciation	5.91	1.86	5.82	1.73
Simple—complex	3.29*	1.81	3.72*	1.89
Irrelevant—informative	3.49*	1.80	4.17*	1.86
Superficial—profound	3.66*	1.78	4.00*	1.70
One-sided—balanced	4.14	1.81	4.18	1.74
Information appreciation	3.65*	1.45	4.01*	1.53

Note: N = 358, scale, 1–8. *Means differ at $p < .001$.

"humorless—humorous" on an 8-point scale (e.g., 1 = extremely serious, 8 = extremely funny) (video clip $_{national\ bank}$: Pearson's $r = .611$, $p < .001$; video clip $_{gas\ crisis}$: Pearson's $r = .666$, $p < .001$). These perceived humor items have proven their validity in different studies.[35]

Dispositions toward Political Issues

In line with Stewart's[36] suggestion to measure interest in a political issue as a personal disposition toward the respective issue, subjects were asked about how much they were interested in domestic politics ($M = 5.24$, $SD = 2.01$) and in international affairs ($M = 5.69$, $SD = 1.91$) on an 8-point scale (1 = not at all interested, 8 = very much interested).

Ego Involvement

As the humorous video clips concerned national versus international political affairs, a measurement identifying different levels of citizenship was included. For this reason, subjects were asked about how much they identified with being Austrian (identification: national citizen: $M = 5.62$, $SD = 2.72$), being European (identification: European citizen: $M = 6.22$, $SD = 1.77$), and being a global citizen (identification: global citizen: $M = 5.88$, $SD = 2.03$) on an 8-point scale ranging from 1 (not at all) to 8 (very much).

Issue Involvement

For the measurement of issue involvement, the traditional *most important problem facing the country today* question commonly used in agenda-setting studies was used.[37] More specifically, subjects were asked to pinpoint the three most important problems the country was facing at this point in time. The open-ended answers were then recoded into a measurement indicating the ranked saliences of the domestic financial scandal as well as of the international Ukrainian-Russian crisis. Overall, nearly two-thirds of all respondents assessed the Ukrainian-Russian crisis as one of most important problem, which Austria was facing currently. Of these respondents, half of them considered it the most important problem. The other half equally assessed it as the second and third most important problem the country was facing. In contrast, only a quarter of all respondents rated the financial scandal involving one of the country's largest banks as one of the most important national problems. Of these respondents, half of them considered it the most important problem while the rest of the respondents assessed the national financial scandal in equal amounts as the second and third most important problem the country was facing.

Information Appreciation

In order to measure the intellectual appreciation of the information provided by the two video clips, bipolar semantic item pairs were measured.[38] A scale for information appreciation was constructed by using the item pairs "simple—complex," "irrelevant—informative," "superficial—profound," and "one-sided—balanced." Again, an 8-point scale (e.g., 1 = extremely irrelevant, 8 = extremely informative) was used. The measure for information appreciation proved to be reliable (video clip $_{national\ bank}$: $M = 3.65$, $SD = 1.45$, Cronbach's α = .817; video clip $_{gas\ crisis}$: $M = 4.01$, $SD = 1.53$, Cronbach's α = .866).

Demographics

As control variables, gender (44.3% male), age (range: 14–76 years, $M = 28.77$, $SD = 12.25$), and education (3.6% graduate school, 18.9% vocational school, 57.9% A-level, 19.5% university degree) were included.

Analysis

In order to assess the extent to which the hypothesized factors predict humor appreciation, ordinary least squares (OLS) regressions were calculated. Five blocks of variables were introduced into the regression models: sociodemographics, dispositions, ego involvement, issue involvement, and information appreciation. All predictor variables were mean centered which does not affect the regression coefficients but removes multicollinearity between predictors. Variance inflation factor tests for all independent variables indicated no multicollinearity problems for the regression models for both video clips (video clip $_{national\ bank}$: average VIF = 1.378; video clip $_{gas\ crisis}$: average VIF = 1.373).

RESULTS

The OLS regression models explaining political humor appreciation are outlined in Table 9.2, which displays unstandardized regression coefficients and standard errors. Model 1 shows the results for the humorous video clip on the national bank scandal. The model reveals that the first block of variables—sociodemographics, namely gender, age, and education—accounted for 2.1 percent of incremental, explained variance (incremental R^2 = .021, $F(3,305)$ = 2.147, $p < .1$). Only age—more precisely, being younger—significantly predicted humor appreciation (B = −.026, $p < .05$) The second block of variables—dispositions toward the political issues—accounted for an additional 4.4 percent ($p < .05$) of incremental, explained variance (incremental R^2 = .044, $F(5,303)$ = 4.182, $p < .05$). Whereas interest in domestic affairs did not predict appreciating the humor in the video clip on the national bank scandal, interest in foreign affairs turned out to positively predict humor appreciation (B = .245, $p < .05$).

The third block of variables aiming at predicting humor appreciation was ego involvement. Ego involvement accounted for an additional 11.3 percent ($p < .001$) of incremental, explained variance (incremental R^2 = .113, $F(8,300)$ = 8.118, $p < .001$). Within this block of variables, identification as an Austrian citizen positively predicted humor appreciation (B = .222, $p < .001$).

As the fourth block of variables, issue involvement was introduced into the regression model which accounted for .4 percent of incremental, explained variance (incremental R^2 = .004, $F(9,299)$ = 7.410, $p < .001$). The salience of the national bank scandal among the public did not predict humor appreciation.

The last block of variables—information appreciation—accounted for 8.9 percent of incremental, explained variance (incremental R^2 = .089, $F(10,298)$ = 11.114, $p < .001$). Information appreciation significantly and positively predicted the perceived humorousness of the video clip on the national bank scandal thereby revealing to be the strongest predictor (B = .386, $p < .001$) for humor appreciation overall. In total, the OLS regression model for the humorous video clip on the domestic political affair accounted for 27.2 percent of variance in the dependent variable (Adjusted R^2 = .247, $p < .001$).

With respect to the hypotheses, this model demonstrated that being interested in the politics being disparaged does not affect political humor appreciation. However, being interested in other politics not being disparaged motivates political humor appreciation (*H1*). Ego involvement—identifying oneself as Austrian—had a positive relationship with the perceived humorousness of the video clip on a national bank scandal (*H2*). Issue involvement did not predict humor appreciation, which is not surprising as the disparaged issue was not highly salient among the public (*H3*). Appreciating the information provided by political humor resulted in greater humor appreciation (*H4*).

Model 2 in Table 9.2 shows the results for humor appreciation of the video clip on the international Ukrainian-Russian gas conflict. The model demonstrates that the first block of variables—sociodemographics, namely gender, age, and education—accounted for 2.1 percent of incremental, explained variance (incremental $R^2 = .021$, $F(3,308) = 2.233$, $p < .1$). Heightened levels of education slightly predicted increased humor appreciation ($B = .212$, $p < .1$). The second block of variables—dispositions toward politics—accounted for 3.0 percent of incremental, explained variance (incremental $R^2 = .030$, $F(5,306) = 3.332$, $p < .05$). As in the first model, interest in domestic affairs did not predict humor appreciation. Interest in foreign affairs significantly and positively predicted humor appreciation ($B = .204$, $p < .05$). Ego involvement, which was introduced as the third block of variables, accounted for 1.6 percent of incremental, explained variance (incremental $R^2 = .016$, $F(8,303) = 2.768$, $p > .1$). Identifying oneself as an Austrian citizen predicted humor appreciation ($B = .099$, $p < .05$). Introducing issue involvement into the regression model accounted for 2.5 percent of incremental, explained variance (incremental $R^2 = .025$, $F(9,302) = 3.451$, $p < .05$). Heightened public salience of the disparaged political issue predicted humor appreciation ($B = .135$, $p < .05$).

Information appreciation—as the last block of variables—accounted for 19.1 percent of incremental, explained variance (incremental $R^2 = .191$, $F(10,301) = 11.938$, $p < .001$). As in model 1, also in model 2, information appreciation significantly and positively predicted the perceived humorousness of the video clip on the international Ukrainian-Russian gas conflict thereby being the strongest predictor ($B = .493$, $p < .001$) for humor appreciation overall. In total, the OLS regression model for the humorous video clip on international Ukrainian-Russian gas conflict accounted for 28.4 percent of variance in the dependent variable (Adjusted $R^2 = .260$, $p < .001$).

Regarding the hypotheses, this model demonstrated that being interested in the politics being disparaged does not affect political humor appreciation and that being interested in other politics not being disparaged motivates political humor appreciation (*H1*). In addition, ego involvement positively affects humor appreciation: increased ego involvement results in higher humor appreciation (*H2*). Issue involvement facilitates humor appreciation in the sense of higher personal importance of an issue significantly predicts humor appreciation (*H3*). Appreciating the information provided by political humor results in greater humor appreciation (*H4*).

Table 9.2 OLS Regression Models Predicting Humor Appreciation

	Model 1: video clip _national bank_					Model 2: video clip _gas crisis_				
	r	Sig.	B	Sig.	SE	r	Sig.	B	Sig.	SE
Constant			5.970	***	0.139			5.887	***	0.126
Block 1: Demographics										
Gender (1 = female)	-0.002		-0.146		0.193	-0.040		-0.107		0.176
Age	-0.117	**	-0.026	**	0.008	-0.045		-0.012		0.008
Education	0.045		0.203	*	0.128	0.129	**	0.212	*	0.117
Incremental R square			0.021	*				0.021	*	
Block 2: Dispositions toward political issues										
Interest in domestic affairs	0.132	**	-0.004		0.064	0.103	*	-0.060		0.058
Interest in foreign affairs	0.165	**	0.245	**	0.070	0.194	***	0.204	**	0.064
Incremental R square			0.044	**				0.030	**	
Block 3: Ego involvement										
Identification: national citizen	0.255	***	0.222	***	0.038	0.046		0.099	**	0.035
Identification: European citizen	0.090		-0.014		0.064	0.066		0.008		0.059
Identification: global citizen	0.000		-0.088		0.054	0.025		-0.057		0.049
Incremental R square			0.113	***				0.016		
Block 4: Issue involvement										
Issue salience	-0.040		-0.119		0.116	0.163	**	0.135	**	0.067
Incremental R square			0.004					0.025	**	
Block 5: Information appreciation										
Information appreciation	0.396	***	0.386	***	0.064	0.488	***	0.493	***	0.055
Incremental R square			0.089	***				0.191	***	
Adjusted R square	24.7%***					26.0%***				

Note: Pearson's correlation coefficient as well as unstandardized regression coefficients and standard errors are reported. $* p < .1$, $** p < .05$, $*** p < .001$.

Post Hoc Analysis

As the OLS regression models revealed that information appreciation was the strongest predictor for political humor appreciation, post hoc analyses on the perceptions of the video clips, on the relation between information appreciation and humor appreciation as well as on the relationships between the dependent and independent variables were performed.

Regarding the audience's perception of the video clips, further independent samples t-tests showed significant differences concerning the semantic differential pairs "simple—complex" ($t(321) = -4.57$, $p < .001$), "irrelevant—informative" ($t(325) = -7.76$, $p < .001$) and "superficial—profound" ($t(322) = -3.74$, $p < .001$) (see Table 9.1). The video clip on the international Ukrainian-Russian gas conflict was perceived as significantly more complex ($M = 3.72$, $SD = 1.89$), informative ($M = 4.17$, $SD = 1.86$), and profound ($M = 4.00$, $SD = 1.70$) than the video clip on the national bank scandal (complex: $M = 3.29$, $SD = 1.81$; informative: $M = 3.49$, $SD = 1.80$; profound: $M = 3.66$, $SD = 1.78$). Participants rated both video clips equally balanced (video clip $_{national\ bank}$: $M = 4.14$, $SD = 1.81$; video clip $_{gas\ crisis}$: $M = 4.18$, $SD = 1.74$; $t(326) = -.39$, $p > .05$). Overall, Table 9.1 also reveals that information appreciation significantly differed between the two video clips ($t(328) = -5.83$, $p < .001$). Specifically, the information provided in the video clip on the international Ukrainian-Russian gas conflict was generally more appreciated ($M = 4.01$, $SD = 1.53$) than the information about the financial scandal ($M = 3.65$, $SD = 1.45$).

Furthermore, zero-order correlations between the single semantic differential pairs for both video clips demonstrated that the perceptions of funny and humorous positively and significantly correlated with the semantic item pairs concerning information appreciation. In particular, concerning the video clip on the international Ukrainian-Russian gas conflict, the table displays highly significant and strong correlations between all item pairs.

Furthermore, zero-order correlations between the dependent and independent variables (Table 9.3) revealed that in line with extant research, humor appreciation and information appreciation positively correlated with each other (video clip $_{national\ bank}$: $r = .40$, $p < .01$; video clip $_{gas\ crisis}$: $r = .488$, $p < .01$). Concluding, these results not only demonstrate a strong relation between humor and information appreciation but also hint at the fact that appreciating a joke's information might be decisive for rating it funny and humorous.

Moreover, zero-order correlations (Table 9.3) revealed that for the humorous video clip on the domestic political affair—concerning the financial

Table 9.3   Zero-order Correlations between Semantic Differentials for Videos (National Bank on Top and Gas Crisis on Bottom)

		1	2	3	4	5	6
National Bank							
1	Serious—funny	1.00					
2	Humorless—humorous	0.61***	1.00				
3	Simple—complex	0.09*	0.29***	1.00			
4	Irrelevant—Informative	0.13**	0.35***	0.53***	1.00		
5	Superficial—profound	0.17**	0.38***	0.520***	0.630***	1.000	
6	One-Sided—balanced	0.26***	0.55***	0.42***	0.53***	0.56***	1.00
Gas Crisis							
1	Serious—funny	1.00					
2	Humorless—humorous	0.69***	1.00				
3	Simple—complex	0.20***	0.37***	1.00			
4	Irrelevant—Informative	0.33***	0.51***	0.58***	1.00		
5	Superficial—profound	0.29***	0.46***	0.59***	0.73***	1.00	
6	One-Sided—balanced	0.34***	0.50***	0.49***	0.63***	0.69***	1.00

Note: N = 358. * $p < .1$, ** $p < .05$, *** $p < .001$.

scandal of one of the country's largest banks—the low issue salience did neither interlink with humor appreciation ($r = -.04$, $p > .05$) nor with information appreciation ($r = -.03$, $p > .05$). In contrast, the issue salience of the international Ukrainian-Russian gas conflict moderately correlated with humor appreciation ($r = .16$, $p < .05$) as well as with information appreciation ($r = .14$, $p < .05$). These correlations indicate that, as the foreign affair was perceived more salient, also the information provided by political humor was more appreciated. Hence, the salience of an issue seems to vary positively with information appreciation.

In addition, zero-order correlations between the dependent variable—humor appreciation—and the independent variables (Table 9.3) revealed that humor appreciation was positively correlated with dispositions toward political issues. Appreciating the humor provided by the video clip on the national bank scandal had a positive relationshi with interest in domestic affairs ($r = .13$, $p < .05$) and interest in foreign affairs ($r = .17$, $p < .05$). Humor appreciation of the video clip on the international Ukrainian-Russian gas conflict was correlated somewhat with interest in domestic affairs ($r = .10$, $p < .1$) and highly significantly correlated with interest in foreign affairs ($r = .19$, $p < .001$). Lastly, the perceived humorousness of the video clip on the national bank scandal went along with being younger ($r = -.12$, $p < .05$) and stronger feelings toward nationality ($r = .26$, $p < .001$). Humor appreciation of the video clip on the international gas conflict was moderately correlated with education ($r = -.13$, $p < .05$).

DISCUSSION

In the past, political humor research has primarily focused on assessing correlates and effects of exposure to political humor. Examining the variables predicting political humor appreciation—in other words, examining why some members of the audience enjoy certain types of political jokes more than others do—has thus far only evoked marginal scholarly attention. Consequentially, the present study aimed at contributing to this research gap by providing an integrative theory-rich approach for the understanding of political humor appreciation. Overall, the goal of the study was—put bluntly—to shed light on the question: What is funny to whom? In so doing, this work set out to assess the extent to which the different theoretical approaches help in explaining political humor appreciation. By drawing on multifaceted theoretical approaches, this study was able to offer an integrated theoretical framework for the analysis of political humor appreciation. Such an analytical step in the study of political humor is all the more important as extant empirical evidence revealed diverging effect patterns of exposure to political humor on its audience. Thus, scholars have been stressing the value of comprehending political humor appreciation as a vital mediating factor for understanding the effects of political humor.[39]

Overall, this work extended the extant theoretical and empirical work on political humor in two ways. First, the majority of research on political humor appreciation has thus far drawn on the disposition theory of humor. Even though scholars have been arguing that perceived humor depends upon a range of factors—not only affective dispositions toward the disparaged and disparaging political actors—empirical evidence on other possible explanatory factors is rare at best. Therefore, this work also included ego and issue involvement and information appreciation in the analysis of the driving forces for humor appreciation. In doing so, the study was able to apply an integrative theory-rich approach toward the analysis of humor appreciation. Second, this study broke with the tradition of looking at US-American political comedy. The lion's share of studies on humorous political communication have thus far been primarily concerned with the US-American news parody shows, *The Daily Show with Jon Stewart* and *The Colbert Report,* and their adoptions in non-English speaking countries. This study instead connected the analysis to a European political comedy format. Moreover, while prior studies employed unambiguous images of the disparaged and the disparaging political figures,[40] this study analyzed video clips in which the appearing political figures were mocked regardless of any party affiliation. Instead, political issues were the center of humorous mockery and disparagement. Overall, this approach speaks well to the notion that political humor is not monolithic and different humorous types need to be analyzed for the study of political humor.[41]

Overall, the findings provided empirical evidence that being interested in the type of politics being disparaged does not affect political humor appreciation. However, a positive disposition—in the sense of being interested—toward other politics not being disparaged motivates political humor appreciation. In other words, the results demonstrated that jokes about not affiliated political affairs are valued while jokes about affiliated political affairs are not. Moreover, the analysis revealed that another decisive predictor for perceived humor is involvement. Ego involvement—in the sense of identifying oneself with an entity—and issue involvement—referring to the importance or salience of an issue—significantly predict humor appreciation. Lastly, the results indicated that the most important predictor for humor appreciation is information appreciation. The results pointed toward a significant relationship between the intellectual appreciation of the humorous content and the appreciation of political humor. Perceiving political humor as informative, profound, balanced, and complex significantly shape the way the audience rates the humorousness and funniness of a joke. Unfortunately, the methodological design of the study was not able to explain why the information provided in the video clip on the international Ukrainian-Russian gas conflict was generally more appreciated than the information about the financial scandal. As the zero-order correlations revealed, the salience of a political issue varies positively with information appreciation. Hence, a possible explanation for the different levels of information appreciation for the two video clips might be that the heightened public salience of the respective political affair resulted in greater appreciation of the information provided by the video clip.

Concerning limitations of this study, three caveats should be mentioned. First, the study did not include a measurement for the likeability of the political figures presented in the video clips, which is the core measurement in classic studies concerning the disposition theory of humor. However, these studies used clear images of the victims and heroes in the jokes. In contrast, this study used humorous video clips in which a broad range of different politicians appeared and mocked a policy issue. In practice, this means that the study was unable to analyze the extent to which the likeability of the politicians explains variance in the dependent variable being humor appreciation.

Second, the presentation of the video clips and their nature must be addressed. Both video clips were presented to all survey respondents. Although the order of presentation occurred randomly and the video clips were played after a short time delay in between, a certain biasing effect cannot be precluded. In addition, the international political affair was primarily reflected from a national perspective, which may have blurred the issue's international meaningfulness.

Third, this survey was conducted in late spring of 2014, which was a period characterized by highly salient international affairs issues (e.g., civil war in Syria, mass kidnapping of Nigerian girls by the terrorist group Boko Haram). This can in turn effectively mean that during this time interest in foreign affairs was remarkably high, which may have led to a dilution of the predictive power of interest in international political affairs on humor appreciation.

Notwithstanding these caveats, this work provides three conclusions on humor appreciation. The first lesson, which might pave the way for a better understanding of humor appreciation, concerns dispositions toward the disparaged object. The results of this study demonstrated that positive dispositions toward political issues not being the target of the joke result in greater humor appreciation. The second lesson focuses on ego and issue involvement. Being personally involved with the target of the political joke as well as ascribing heightened personal relevance to the disparaged entity result in greater feelings of enjoyment and mirth. The third lesson of this study links to information appreciation. Appreciating the information provided by political humor is decisive for rating it as funny, humorous, and entertaining. This result speaks well to the possible backlash effects of political humor. Based on the results of this study, a possible explanation for the backlash effect of humor might be the intellectual resentment of the humorous content and furthermore the devaluation of the content as being irrelevant, superficial, one-sided, and dumb.

Future research should continue to apply and validate these theoretical concepts. A first step might be to vary the issue's salience and affiliation; namely employing a highly salient national and a low salient international political issue. Additionally, future empirical studies should also embrace the mediating and moderating effects of humor appreciation and information appreciation on the effects which political humor may have on its audience. Such studies would not only allow for an in-depth analysis as to why audiences perceive humor in political comedies differently, but would also allow research to examine the reasons why political humor evokes inconclusive effect patterns on its audience.

NOTES

1. Dannagal Goldthwaite Young, "Humor and Satire, Political," in *The International Encyclopedia of Political Communication*, eds. Gianpietro Mazzoleni, Kevin G. Barnhurst, Ken'ichi Ikeda, Rousiley C. M. Maia, and Hartmut Wessler (Hoboken, NJ: John Wiley & Sons, 2015), 4–5, https://doi.org/10.1002/9781118541555.

2. Sarah Esralew and Dannagal Goldthwaite Young, "The Influence of Parodies on Mental Models: Exploring the Tina Fey-Sarah Palin Phenomenon," *Communication*

Quarterly 60, no. 3 (2012): 345–46, https://doi.org/10.1080/01463373.2012.6887 91; Lauren Feldman and Dannagal Goldthwaite Young, "Late-Night Comedy as a Gateway to Traditional News: An Analysis of Time Trends in News Attention among Late-Night Comedy Viewers during the 2004 Presidential Primaries," *Political Communication* 25, no. 4 (2008): 409, https://doi.org/10.1080/10584600802427013; Michael A. Xenos and Amy B. Becker, "Moments of Zen: Effects of the Daily Show on Information Seeking and Political Learning," *Political Communication* 26, no. 3 (2009): 324–25, https://doi.org/10.1080/10584600903053569; Dannagal Goldthwaite Young, "Late-Night Comedy in Election 2000: Its Influence on Candidate Trait Ratings and the Moderating Effects of Political Knowledge and Partisanship," *Journal of Broadcasting & Electronic Media* 48, no. 1 (2004): 13, https://doi.org/10.1207/s15506878jobem4801_1; Dannagal Goldthwaite Young, "Late-Night Comedy and the Salience of the Candidates' Caricatured Traits in the 2000 Election," *Mass Communication and Society* 9, no. 3 (2006): 351–56, https://doi.org/10.1207/s15327825mcs0903_5; Dannagal Goldthwaite Young, "The Privileged Role of the Late-Night Joke: Exploring Humor's Role in Disrupting Argument Scrutiny," *Media Psychology* 11, no. 1 (2008): 133, https://doi.org/10.1080/15213260701837073.

3. Xiaoxia Cao, "Political Comedy Shows and Knowledge about Primary Campaigns: The Moderating Effects of Age and Education," *Mass Communication and Society* 11, no. 1 (2008): 51–57, https://doi.org/10.1080/15205430701585028; Dannagal Goldthwaite Young and Russell M. Tisinger, "Dispelling Late-Night Myths: News Consumption among Late-Night Comedy Viewers and the Predictors of Exposure to Various Late-Night Shows," *Harvard International Journal of Press/Politics* 11, no. 3 (2006): 121–27, https://doi.org/10.1177/1081180X05286042.

4. Xiaoxia Cao and Paul R. Brewer, "Political Comedy Shows and Public Participation in Politics," *International Journal of Public Opinion Research* 20, no. 1 (2008): 95–96, https://doi.org/10.1093/ijpor/edm030; Lindsay H. Hoffman and Dannagal Goldthwaite Young, "Satire, Punch Lines, and the Nightly News: Untangling Media Effects on Political Participation," *Communication Research Reports* 28, no. 2 (2011): 164–65, https://doi.org/10.1080/08824096.2011.565278.

5. Paul R. Brewer, Dannagal Goldthwaite Young, and Michelle Morreale, "The Impact of Real News about 'Fake News': Intertextual Processes and Political Satire," *International Journal of Public Opinion Research* 25, no. 3 (2013): 335–38, https://doi.org/10.1093/ijpor/edt015.

6. Jody C Baumgartner, "No Laughing Matter? Young Adults and the 'Spillover Effect' of Candidate-Centered Political Humor," *Humor* 26, no. 1 (2013): 36–37, https://doi.org/10.1515/humor-2013-0003; Jody C Baumgartner and Jonathan S. Morris, "The Daily Show Effect: Candidate Evaluations, Efficacy, and American Youth," *American Politics Research* 34, no. 3 (2006): 351–57, https://doi.org/10.1177/1532673X05280074; Jody C Baumgartner and Jonathan S. Morris, "One 'Nation,' under Stephen? The Effects of the Colbert Report on American Youth," *Journal of Broadcasting and Electronic Media* 52, no. 4 (2008): 633, https://doi.org/10.1080/08838150802437487; Amy B. Becker, "Comedy Types and Political Campaigns: The Differential Influence of Other-Directed Hostile Humor and Self-Ridicule on Candidate Evaluations," *Mass Communication and Society* 15, no. 6

(2012): 792, https://doi.org/10.1080/15205436.2011.628431; Goldthwaite Young, "Late-Night Comedy in Election 2000: Its Influence on Candidate Trait Ratings and the Moderating Effects of Political Knowledge and Partisanship," 14–16.

7. Josh Compton, "Introduction: Surveying Scholarship on The Daily Show and The Colbert Report," in *The Stewart/Colbert Effect: Essays on the Real Impacts of Fake News*, ed. Amarnath Amarasingam (Jefferson, NC: McFarland, 2011), 10–12.

8. Amy B. Becker, "Playing with Politics: Online Political Parody, Affinity for Political Humor, Anxiety Reduction, and Implications for Political Efficacy," *Mass Communication and Society* 17, no. 3 (2014): 431, https://doi.org/10.1080/1520543 6.2014.891134; R. Lance Holbert et al., "Affinity for Political Humor: An Assessment of Internal Factor Structure, Reliability, and Validity," *Humor* 26, no. 4 (2013): 551–52, https://doi.org/10.1515/humor-2013-0034.

9. Amy B. Becker, "Humiliate My Enemies or Mock My Friends? Applying Disposition Theory of Humor to the Study of Political Parody Appreciation and Attitudes Toward Candidates," *Human Communication Research* 40, no. 2 (2014): 138–40, https://doi.org/10.1111/hcre.12022; R. Lance Holbert, "A Typology for the Study of Entertainment Television and Politics," *American Behavioral Scientist* 49, no. 3 (2005): 442–43, https://doi.org/10.1177/0002764205279419.

10. Lawrence LaFave, "Humor Judgments as a Function of Reference Groups and Identification Classes," in *The Psychology of Humor: Theoretical Perspectives and Empirical Issues*, ed. Jeffrey H. Goldstein (Cambridge, MA: Academic Press, 1972), 196–98; Larry Powell, *Ego-Involvement: A Mediating Factor in Satirical Persuasion* (Gainesville: University Press of Florida, 1975), 23–24; Larry Powell, "Satire and Speech Trait Evaluation," *Western Journal of Speech Communication* 41, no. 2 (1977): 117–18, https://doi.org/10.1080/10570317709389604; Larry Powell, "Voter Needs and Evaluations of Satire," *Journalism Quarterly* 55, no. 2 (1978): 311–12.

11. Jacob Levine and Fredrick C. Redlich, "Intellectual and Emotional Factors in the Appreciation of Humor," *The Journal of General Psychology* 62, no. 1 (1960): 25–27.

12. Geoffrey Baym and Jeffrey P. Jones, "News Parody in Global Perspective: Politics, Power, and Resistance," *Popular Communication* 10, no. 1–2 (2012): 4–5; R. Lance Holbert et al., "Adding Nuance to the Study of Political Humor Effects: Experimental Research on Juvenalian Satire versus Horatian Satire," *American Behavioral Scientist* 55, no. 3 (2011): 189, https://doi.org/10.1177/0002764210392156; R. Lance Holbert, "Developing a Normative Approach to Political Satire: An Empirical Perspective," *International Journal of Communication* 7, no. 1 (2013): 307–08, https:// doi.org/1932–8036/20130005.

13. Lawrence LaFave, Jay Haddad, and William A. Maesen, "Superiority, Enhanced Self-Esteem, and Perceived In-Congruity Humour Theory," in *Humour and Laughter: Theory, Research, and Applications*, eds. Anthony J. Chapman and Hugh C. Foot (London: Wiley, 1976), 65–67; Harold A. Wolff, Carl E. Smith, and Henry A. Murray, "The Psychology of Humor," *The Journal of Abnormal and Social Psychology* 28, no. 4 (1934): 342–44.

14. Wolff, Smith, and Murray, "The Psychology of Humor," 343–44; Dolf Zillmann and Joanne R. Cantor, "A Disposition Theory of Humor and Mirth," in *Humor*

and Laughter: Theory, Research, and Application, eds. A. J. Chapman and H. C. Foot (London: John Wiley & Sons, 1976), 99–101.

15. LaFave, Haddad, and Maesen, "Superiority, Enhanced Self-Esteem, and Perceived In-Congruity Humour Theory," 65–67; Paul E. McGhee and Sally A. Lloyd, "A Developmental Test of the Disposition Theory of Humor," *Child Development* 52, no. 3 (1981): 925–26, https://doi.org/10.2307/1129096; Robert F. Priest, "Election Jokes: The Effects of Reference Group Membership," *Psychological Reports* 18 (1966): 600–01, https://doi.org/10.2466/pr0.1966.18.2.600; Robert F. Priest and Joel Abrahams, "Candidate Preference and Hostile Humor in the 1968 Elections," *Psychological Reports* 26, no. 3 (1970): 779–80; Wolff, Smith, and Murray, "The Psychology of Humor," 343–44.

16. Zillmann and Cantor, "A Disposition Theory of Humor and Mirth," 100–01.

17. Zillmann and Cantor, "A Disposition Theory of Humor and Mirth," 101–02.

18. Dolf Zillmann, "Humor and Comedy," in *Media Entertainment: The Psychology of Its Appeal*, eds. Dolf Zillmann and Peter Vorderer (Mahwah, NJ: Lawrence Erlbaum, 2000), 40–41.

19. Becker, "Humiliate My Enemies or Mock My Friends? Applying Disposition Theory of Humor to the Study of Political Parody Appreciation and Attitudes toward Candidates," 138; Joanne R. Cantor, "What Is Funny to Whom? The Role of Gender," *Journal of Communication* 26, no. 3 (1976): 164–65; Zillmann, "Humor and Comedy," 37–39; Dolf Zillmann and Jennings Bryant, "Retaliatory Equity as a Factor in Humor Appreciation," *Journal of Experimental Social Psychology* 10, no. 5 (1974): 481–83, https://doi.org/10.1016/0022-1031(74)90016-X; Dolf Zillmann, Jennings Bryant, and Joanne R. Cantor, "Brutality of Assault in Political Cartoons Affecting Humor Appreciation," *Journal of Research in Personality* 7, no. 4 (1974): 334–35, https://doi.org/10.1016/0092-6566(74)90055-5; Dolf Zillmann and Joanne R. Cantor, "Directionality of Transitory Dominance as a Communication Variable Affecting Humor Appreciation," *Journal of Personality and Social Psychology* 24, no. 2 (1972): 192, https://doi.org/10.1037/h0033384; Zillmann and Cantor, "A Disposition Theory of Humor and Mirth," 99–101.

20. Wolff, Smith, and Murray, "The Psychology of Humor," 342–44; Zillmann and Cantor, "A Disposition Theory of Humor and Mirth," 101–02; Zillmann, Bryant, and Cantor, "Brutality of Assault in Political Cartoons Affecting Humor Appreciation," 334–35.

21. Patrick A. Stewart, "The Influence of Self- and Other-Deprecatory Humor on Presidential Candidate Evaluation during the 2008 US Election," *Social Science Information* 50, no. 2 (2011): 207, https://doi.org/10.1177/0539018410396616.

22. Levine and Redlich, "Intellectual and Emotional Factors in the Appreciation of Humor," 25–27.

23. Richard E. Petty, John T. Cacioppo, and Curtis Haugtvedt, "Ego-Involvement and Persuasion: An Appreciative Look at the Sherif's Contribution to the Study of Self-Relevance and Attitude Change," in *Social Judgment and Intergroup Relations: Essays in Honor of Muzafer Sherif*, eds. D. Granberg and G. Sarup (New York: Springer, 1992), 149–51; Muzafer Sherif and Carl Hovland, *Social Judgment: Assimilation and Contrast Effects in Communication and Attitude Change* (New Haven, CT: Yale University Press, 1961), 10–12.

24. Muzafer Sherif and Hadley Cantril, *The Psychology of Ego-Involvements: Social Attitudes and Identifications* (New York: John Wiley & Sons, 1947), 17–19.

25. Herbert E. Krugman, "The Measurement of Advertising Involvement," *The Public Opinion Quarterly* 64, no. 4 (1966): 584–85.

26. Sherif and Hovland, *Social Judgment: Assimilation and Contrast Effects in Communication and Attitude Change*, 10–12.

27. Priest, "Election Jokes: The Effects of Reference Group Membership," 600–01.

28. Barbara Grote and George Cvetkovich, "Humor Appreciation and Issue Involvement," *Psychonomic Science* 27, no. 4 (1972): 199, https://doi.org/10.3758/BF03328936.

29. Powell, *Ego-Involvement: A Mediating Factor in Satirical Persuasion*, 24–27; Powell, "Satire and Speech Trait Evaluation," 117–19; Powell, "Voter Needs and Evaluations of Satire," 311–12.

30. Powell, "Voter Needs and Evaluations of Satire," 311–12.

31. Holbert, "Developing a Normative Approach to Political Satire: An Empirical Perspective," 307.

32. Grote and Cvetkovich, "Humor Appreciation and Issue Involvement," 199.

33. Charles R. Gruner, "Satire as Persuasion" (presentation, Annual Meeting of the Speech Communication Association, 1992); Levine and Redlich, "Intellectual and Emotional Factors in the Appreciation of Humor," 25–27; Heather LaMarre, "When Parody and Reality Collide: Examining the Effects of Colbert's Super PAC Satire on Issue Knowledge and Policy Engagement across Media Formats," *International Journal of Communication* 7, no. 1 (2013): 407–09, https://doi.org/10.1932–8036/20130005; Francis L. F. Lee, "The Impact of Online User-Generated Satire on Young People's Political Attitudes: Testing the Moderating Role of Knowledge and Discussion," *Telematics and Informatics* 31, no. 3 (2014): 406–07, https://doi.org/10.1016/j.tele.2013.08.002; Jörg Matthes and Adrian Rauchfleisch, "The Swiss 'Tina Fey Effect': The Content of Late-Night Political Humor and the Negative Effects of Political Parody on the Evaluation of Politicians," *Communication Quarterly* 61, no. 5 (2013): 603, https://doi.org/10.1080/01463373.2013.822405; Young, "Late-Night Comedy and the Salience of the Candidates' Caricatured Traits in the 2000 Election," 360.

34. Dannagal Goldthwaite Young, "Laughter, Learning, or Enlightenment? Viewing and Avoidance Motivations behind The Daily Show and The Colbert Report," *Journal of Broadcasting and Electronic Media* 57, no. 2 (2013): 163–64, https://doi.org/10.1080/08838151.2013.787080.

35. Becker, "Humiliate My Enemies or Mock My Friends? Applying Disposition Theory of Humor to the Study of Political Parody Appreciation and Attitudes toward Candidates," 145; Amy B. Becker and Beth A. Haller, "When Political Comedy Turns Personal: Humor Types, Audience Evaluations, and Attitudes," *Howard Journal of Communications* 25, no. 1 (2014): 43, https://doi.org/10.1080/10646175.2013.835607.

36. Stewart, "The Influence of Self- and Other-Deprecatory Humor on Presidential Candidate Evaluation during the 2008 US Election," 207.

37. Maxwell McCombs, "A Look at Agenda-Setting: Past, Present and Future," *Journalism Studies* 6, no. 4 (2005): 547, https://doi.org/10.1080/14616700500250438.

38. Maxwell McCombs, *Setting the Agenda: Mass Media and Public Opinion* (Hoboken, NJ: John Wiley & Sons, 2014), 114–17; Judith Lynne Zaichkowsky, "Measuring the Involvement Construct," *Journal of Consumer Research* 12, no. 3 (1985): 341, https://doi.org/10.1086/208520.

39. Becker, "Playing with Politics: Online Political Parody, Affinity for Political Humor, Anxiety Reduction, and Implications for Political Efficacy," 439–40; Holbert et al., "Affinity for Political Humor: An Assessment of Internal Factor Structure, Reliability, and Validity," 567–68.

40. Baumgartner, "No Laughing Matter? Young Adults and the 'Spillover Effect' of Candidate-Centered Political Humor," 34–35; Baumgartner and Morris, "The Daily Show Effect: Candidate Evaluations, Efficacy, and American Youth," 347–48; Baumgartner and Morris, "One 'Nation,' under Stephen? The Effects of the Colbert Report on American Youth," 628; LaMarre, "When Parody and Reality Collide: Examining the Effects of Colbert's Super PAC Satire on Issue Knowledge and Policy Engagement across Media Formats," 402–03.

41. R. Lance Holbert et al., "Adding Nuance to the Study of Political Humor Effects: Experimental Research on Juvenalian Satire versus Horatian Satire," 189; Holbert, "Developing a Normative Approach to Political Satire: An Empirical Perspective," 307–08.

REFERENCES

Baumgartner, Jody C. "No Laughing Matter? Young Adults and the 'Spillover Effect' of Candidate-Centered Political Humor." *Humor* 26, no. 1 (2013): 23–43. https://doi.org/10.1515/humor-2013-0003.

Baumgartner, Jody C, and Jonathan S. Morris. "One 'Nation,' under Stephen? The Effects of the Colbert Report on American Youth." *Journal of Broadcasting and Electronic Media* 52, no. 4 (2008): 622–43. https://doi.org/10.1080/08838150802437487.

———. "The Daily Show Effect: Candidate Evaluations, Efficacy, and American Youth." *American Politics Research* 34, no. 3 (2006): 341–67. https://doi.org/10.1177/1532673X05280074.

Baym, Geoffrey, and Jeffrey P. Jones. "News Parody in Global Perspective: Politics, Power, and Resistance." *Popular Communication* 10, no. 1–2 (2012): 2–13.

Becker, Amy B. "Comedy Types and Political Campaigns: The Differential Influence of Other-Directed Hostile Humor and Self-Ridicule on Candidate Evaluations." *Mass Communication and Society* 15, no. 6 (2012): 791–812. https://doi.org/10.1080/15205436.2011.628431.

———. "Humiliate My Enemies or Mock My Friends? Applying Disposition Theory of Humor to the Study of Political Parody Appreciation and Attitudes toward Candidates." *Human Communication Research* 40, no. 2 (2014): 137–60. https://doi.org/10.1111/hcre.12022.

———. "Playing with Politics: Online Political Parody, Affinity for Political Humor, Anxiety Reduction, and Implications for Political Efficacy." *Mass Communication and Society* 17, no. 3 (2014): 424–45. https://doi.org/10.1080/15205436.2014.891 134.

Becker, Amy B., and Beth A. Haller. "When Political Comedy Turns Personal: Humor Types, Audience Evaluations, and Attitudes." *Howard Journal of Communications* 25, no. 1 (2014): 34–55. https://doi.org/10.1080/10646175.2013.835607.

Brewer, Paul R., Dannagal Goldthwaite Young, and Michelle Morreale. "The Impact of Real News about 'Fake News': Intertextual Processes and Political Satire." *International Journal of Public Opinion Research* 25, no. 3 (2013): 323–43. https://doi.org/10.1093/ijpor/edt015.

Cantor, Joanne R. "What Is Funny to Whom? The Role of Gender." *Journal of Communication* 26, no. 3 (1976): 164–72.

Cao, Xiaoxia. "Political Comedy Shows and Knowledge about Primary Campaigns: The Moderating Effects of Age and Education." *Mass Communication and Society* 11, no. 1 (2008): 43–61. https://doi.org/10.1080/15205430701585028.

Cao, Xiaoxia, and Paul R. Brewer. "Political Comedy Shows and Public Participation in Politics." *International Journal of Public Opinion Research* 20, no. 1 (2008): 90–99. https://doi.org/10.1093/ijpor/edm030.

Compton, Josh. "Introduction: Surveying Scholarship on The Daily Show and The Colbert Report." In *The Stewart/Colbert Effect: Essays on the Real Impacts of Fake News*, edited by Amarnath Amarasingam, 9–23. Jefferson, NC: McFarland, 2011.

Esralew, Sarah, and Dannagal Goldthwaite Young. "The Influence of Parodies on Mental Models: Exploring the Tina Fey-Sarah Palin Phenomenon." *Communication Quarterly* 60, no. 3 (2012): 338–52. https://doi.org/10.1080/01463373.20 12.688791.

Feldman, Lauren, and Dannagal Goldthwaite Young. "Late-Night Comedy as a Gateway to Traditional News: An Analysis of Time Trends in News Attention among Late-Night Comedy Viewers during the 2004 Presidential Primaries." *Political Communication* 25, no. 4 (2008): 401–22. https://doi.org/10.1080/10584600802427013.

Grote, Barbara, and George Cvetkovich. "Humor Appreciation and Issue Involvement." *Psychonomic Science* 27, no. 4 (1972): 199–200. https://doi.org/10.3758/BF03328936.

Gruner, Charles R. "Satire as Persuasion." Presentation at the *Annual Meeting of the Speech Communication Association*, 1992.

Hoffman, Lindsay H., and Dannagal Goldthwaite Young. "Satire, Punch Lines, and the Nightly News: Untangling Media Effects on Political Participation." *Communication Research Reports* 28, no. 2 (2011): 159–68. https://doi.org/10.1080/0882 4096.2011.565278.

Holbert, R. Lance. "A Typology for the Study of Entertainment Television and Politics." *American Behavioral Scientist* 49, no. 3 (2005): 436–53. https://doi.org/10.1177/0002764205279419.

———. "Developing a Normative Approach to Political Satire: An Empirical Perspective." *International Journal of Communication* 7, no. 1 (2013): 305–23. https://doi.org/1932–8036/20130005.

Holbert, R. Lance, Jay Hmielowski, Parul Jain, Julie Lather, and Alyssa Morey. "Adding Nuance to the Study of Political Humor Effects: Experimental Research on Juvenalian Satire versus Horatian Satire." *American Behavioral Scientist* 55, no. 3 (2011): 187–211. https://doi.org/10.1177/0002764210392156.

Holbert, R. Lance, Jayeon Lee, Sarah Esralew, Whitney O. Walther, Jay D. Hmielowski, and Kristen D. Landreville. "Affinity for Political Humor: An Assessment of Internal Factor Structure, Reliability, and Validity." *Humor* 26, no. 4 (2013): 551–72. https://doi.org/10.1515/humor-2013–0034.

Krugman, Herbert E. "The Measurement of Advertising Involvement." *The Public Opinion Quarterly* 64, no. 4 (1966): 583–96.

LaFave, Lawrence. "Humor Judgments as a Function of Reference Groups and Identification Classes." In *The Psychology of Humor: Theoretical Perspectives and Empirical Issues*, edited by Jeffrey H. Goldstein, 195–210. Cambridge, MA: Academic Press, 1972.

LaFave, Lawrence, Jay Haddad, and William A. Maesen. "Superiority, Enhanced Self-Esteem, and Perceived In-Congruity Humour Theory." In *Humour and Laughter: Theory, Research, and Applications*, edited by Anthony J. Chapman and Hugh C. Foot, 63–91. London: Wiley, 1976.

LaMarre, Heather. "When Parody and Reality Collide: Examining the Effects of Colbert's Super PAC Satire on Issue Knowledge and Policy Engagement across Media Formats." *International Journal of Communication* 7, no. 1 (2013): 394–413. https://doi.org/10.1932–8036/20130005.

Lee, Francis L. F. "The Impact of Online User-Generated Satire on Young People's Political Attitudes: Testing the Moderating Role of Knowledge and Discussion." *Telematics and Informatics* 31, no. 3 (2014): 397–409. https://doi.org/10.1016/j.tele.2013.08.002.

Levine, Jacob, and Fredrick C. Redlich. "Intellectual and Emotional Factors in the Appreciation of Humor." *The Journal of General Psychology* 62, no. 1 (1960): 25–35.

Matthes, Jörg, and Adrian Rauchfleisch. "The Swiss 'Tina Fey Effect': The Content of Late-Night Political Humor and the Negative Effects of Political Parody on the Evaluation of Politicians." *Communication Quarterly* 61, no. 5 (November 1, 2013): 596–614. https://doi.org/10.1080/01463373.2013.822405.

McCombs, Maxwell. "A Look at Agenda-Setting: Past, Present and Future." *Journalism Studies* 6, no. 4 (2005): 543–57. https://doi.org/10.1080/14616700500250438.

———. *Setting the Agenda: Mass Media and Public Opinion.* Hoboken, NJ: John Wiley & Sons, 2014.

McGhee, Paul E., and Sally A. Lloyd. "A Developmental Test of the Disposition Theory of Humor." *Child Development* 52, no. 3 (1981): 925–31. https://doi.org/10.2307/1129096.

Petty, Richard E., John T. Cacioppo, and Curtis Haugtvedt. "Ego-Involvement and Persuasion: An Appreciative Look at the Sherif's Contribution to the Study of Self-Relevance and Attitude Change." In *Social Judgment and Intergroup Relations: Essays in Honor of Muzafer Sherif*, edited by D. Granberg and G. Sarup, 147–75. New York: Springer, 1992.

Powell, Larry. *Ego-Involvement: A Mediating Factor in Satirical Persuasion*. Gaines-ville: University Press of Florida, 1975.

———. "Satire and Speech Trait Evaluation." *Western Journal of Speech Communication* 41, no. 2 (1977): 117–25. https://doi.org/10.1080/10570317709389604.

———. "Voter Needs and Evaluations of Satire." *Journalism Quarterly* 55, no. 2 (1978): 311–18.

Priest, Robert F. "Election Jokes: The Effects of Reference Group Membership." *Psychological Reports* 18 (1966): 600–02. https://doi.org/10.2466/pr0.1966.18.2.600.

Priest, Robert F., and Joel Abrahams. "Candidate Preference and Hostile Humor in the 1968 Elections." *Psychological Reports* 26, no. 3 (1970): 779–83.

Sherif, Muzafer, and Hadley Cantril. *The Psychology of Ego-Involvements: Social Attitudes and Identifications*. New York: John Wiley & Sons, 1947.

Sherif, Muzafer, and Carl Hovland. *Social Judgment: Assimilation and Contrast Effects in Communication and Attitude Change*. New Haven, CT: Yale University Press, 1961.

Stewart, Patrick A. "The Influence of Self- and Other-Deprecatory Humor on Presidential Candidate Evaluation during the 2008 US Election." *Social Science Information* 50, no. 2 (2011): 201–22. https://doi.org/10.1177/0539018410396616.

Wolff, Harold A., Carl E. Smith, and Henry A. Murray. "The Psychology of Humor." *The Journal of Abnormal and Social Psychology* 28, no. 4 (1934): 341–65.

Xenos, Michael A., and Amy B. Becker. "Moments of Zen: Effects of the Daily Show on Information Seeking and Political Learning." *Political Communication* 26, no. 3 (2009): 317–32. https://doi.org/10.1080/10584600903053569.

Young, Dannagal Goldthwaite. "Humor and Satire, Political." In *The International Encyclopedia of Political Communication*, edited by Gianpietro Mazzoleni, Kevin G. Barnhurst, Ken'ichi Ikeda, Rousiley C. M. Maia, and Hartmut Wessler, 1–7. Hoboken, NJ: John Wiley & Sons, 2015.

———. "Laughter, Learning, or Enlightenment? Viewing and Avoidance Motivations behind The Daily Show and The Colbert Report." *Journal of Broadcasting and Electronic Media* 57, no. 2 (2013): 153–69. https://doi.org/10.1080/08838151.2013.787080.

———. "The Privileged Role of the Late-Night Joke: Exploring Humor's Role in Disrupting Argument Scrutiny." *Media Psychology* 11, no. 1 (2008): 119–42. https://doi.org/10.1080/15213260701837073.

———. "Late-Night Comedy and the Salience of the Candidates' Caricatured Traits in the 2000 Election." *Mass Communication and Society* 9, no. 3 (2006): 339–66. https://doi.org/10.1207/s15327825mcs0903_5.

———. "Late-Night Comedy in Election 2000: Its Influence on Candidate Trait Ratings and the Moderating Effects of Political Knowledge and Partisanship." *Journal of Broadcasting & Electronic Media* 48, no. 1 (2004): 1–22. https://doi.org/10.1207/s15506878jobem4801_1.

Young, Dannagal Goldthwaite, and Russell M. Tisinger. "Dispelling Late-Night Myths: News Consumption among Late-Night Comedy Viewers and the Predictors of Exposure to Various Late-Night Shows." *Harvard International Journal of Press/Politics* 11, no. 3 (2006): 113–34. https://doi.org/10.1177/1081180X05286042.

Zaichkowsky, Judith Lynne. "Measuring the Involvement Construct." *Journal of Consumer Research* 12, no. 3 (1985): 341–52. https://doi.org/10.1086/208520.

Zillmann, Dolf. "Humor and Comedy." In *Media Entertainment. The Psychology of Its Appeal*, edited by Dolf Zillmann and Peter Vorderer, 37–57. Mahwah, NJ: Lawrence Erlbaum, 2000.

Zillmann, Dolf, and Jennings Bryant. "Retaliatory Equity as a Factor in Humor Appreciation." *Journal of Experimental Social Psychology* 10, no. 5 (1974): 480–88. https://doi.org/10.1016/0022–1031(74)90016-X.

Zillmann, Dolf, Jennings Bryant, and Joanne R. Cantor. "Brutality of Assault in Political Cartoons Affecting Humor Appreciation." *Journal of Research in Personality* 7, no. 4 (1974): 334–45. https://doi.org/10.1016/0092–6566(74)90055-5.

Zillmann, Dolf, and Joanne R. Cantor. "A Disposition Theory of Humor and Mirth." In *Humor and Laughter: Theory, Research, and Application*, edited by A. J. Chapman and H. C. Foot, 97–115. London: John Wiley & Sons, 1976.

———. "Directionality of Transitory Dominance as a Communication Variable Affecting Humor Appreciation." *Journal of Personality and Social Psychology* 24, no. 2 (1972): 191–98. https://doi.org/10.1037/h0033384.

Section IV

IT'S GONE GLOBAL

*International Perspectives
on Political Comedy*

Chapter 10

Political Entertainment in Comparative Perspective

Exploring the Applicability of the Gateway Hypothesis across Media Systems

Michael A. Xenos, Patricia Moy,
Gianpietro Mazzoleni, and Julian Mueller-Herbst

Few boundaries remain in the study of political entertainment.[1] Though myriad intellectual puzzles remain and a variety of theoretical challenges continue to beckon, research in this area has made tremendous strides in a remarkable span of time. The prevailing view of the late 1990s and early 2000s meant scholars had to make a strong case for studying "soft news" or political humor.[2] Fortunately, as growing numbers of American political communication researchers turned their attention to political entertainment programming, particularly late-night comedy shows and political satire programs like *The Daily Show* and *The Colbert Report*, concerted efforts to integrate scholarship from various epistemological perspectives broke further boundaries.[3] Collectively, these efforts have paved the way for a discernible literature, which includes multiple research traditions and focuses squarely on substantial theoretical and critical refinement.

Still absent from this growing corpus, however, is comparative research that systematically approaches variations in political entertainment and related phenomena. To be sure, the dramatic growth in empirical studies of political entertainment and its effects has included many investigations that go beyond the familiar US-based programs that once dominated the literature as a whole.[4] Indeed, a recent special issue of *Popular Communication* (later republished as an associated edited volume) was explicitly dedicated to exploring political humor in a global context, featuring roughly a dozen explorations of political comedy programming outside of the familiar US/Comedy Central context, and new studies based on non-US data are becoming normalized. As Baym and Jones have argued, this recent turn in the literature reminds us of the rich history of political satire across the globe, while also provides numerous opportunities for us to consider its many forms and functions.[5] In other words, just as it is possible to find examples of political humor spanning as far back as ancient Greece, the general phenomenon of political humor as an avenue for critical voices and a potential stimulant of political engagement also likely travels geographically. As Baym and Jones put it, a transnational examination of political humor suggests that "in each instance, part of the power of news parody seems to lie in its portability, its ability to cross national, cultural, and linguistic boundaries." Though focused on a particular style of political entertainment—satirical news parody (as exemplified by *The Daily Show* in the United States)—this statement suggests that political humor can function in some critical ways: it can provide not only unique opportunities to criticize those in power, but also accessible cognitive entry-points into politics.

Transnational research, however, is not always comparative research. Transnational research raises important new questions and invites us to consider familiar questions in new contexts, but without the unique analytical leverage provided by comparative designs in which the same measurement and analytic strategies are applied across national contexts, it is ill-equipped to answer them.

The growing significance of comparative political communication, reflected in both theorizing and empirical research, has not gone unnoticed. Indeed, with a nod to Young and Gray's sibling-rivalry metaphor, it is worth noting that the growth curve of political entertainment research positions it as junior to, but still a contemporary of, comparative political communication. According to the narrative articulated through the most influential state-of-the-field essays, comparative political communication was an "infant" in the mid-1970s and blossomed into "early adulthood" in the 1990s. It was not until the early 2000s that Gurevitch and Blumler jubilantly declared that comparative work had become "almost . . . fashionable!" if still short of complete maturity.[6] Throughout that trajectory, political communication scholars have used comparative methods with increasing sophistication to create "double value," that is, refining theories about political communication processes themselves while also contributing insights to broader scholarship on the specific systems examined.[7] In light of these overlapping development paths, the relative absence of comparative research on the effects of political humor presents itself as a particularly notable missed opportunity. Perhaps this is understandable given the same dynamics that have sometimes strained the relationship between political entertainment research and other strands of work in communication as a whole. Naturally we must also consider the fundamental difficulties of doing comparative research on any social or political phenomenon. Understanding why this barrier seems to persist, however, does not deny the potential gains that could be realized by more systematic comparative research on political entertainment.

Against this backdrop, we take aim at this remaining structural limitation of political entertainment research by using a comparative approach to reexamine one of the most central strands of work on media effects in this area—effects on political knowledge. Our goals arise directly from the promise of "double value" highlighted by Gurevitch and Blumler.[8] First, we seek to explore questions about the fundamental dynamics through which viewing televised political entertainment content may be associated with acquiring relevant factual information about the political world, at least or especially among certain subgroups of viewers. At the same time, drawing on the relatively solid foundation of research on political learning and the "gateway hypothesis" built up around mainly US-focused studies on the effects of exposure to political satire and political entertainment,[9] our comparative approach may help shed light on how various media systems operate. Our unified approach to examining relationships between political entertainment viewing and political knowledge includes four different countries that span the full range of media systems as identified by Hallin and Mancini[10]: the United States and the United Kingdom (Liberal), Italy (Polarized Pluralist), and Germany (Democratic Corporatist). Our careful consideration of the relevant available content and creation of comparable tests of the same hypothesis in each country show that despite wide variation in the kinds of political entertainment programming available in each system, a strong generalizable pattern of gateway effects across the four country cases is observable, with Germany as a notable outlier.

The remainder of the chapter is organized as follows. First, we set the stage for our investigations by reviewing the theoretical and empirical literature regarding political entertainment programming and learning effects to derive our principal hypothesis. This section concludes by outlining the specific appropriateness of learning effects for comparative study and specifying the research questions that guide our investigations. Next, we introduce the relevant features of the media systems in which we gathered data, focusing on the most prominent forms of political entertainment programming found in each that create the conditions for learning from political humor. This is followed by a description of the surveys we conducted in each country, including the measures featured in our analysis of learning effects. After presenting results from a series of hierarchical ordinary least squares regression models, we return to the larger context of political entertainment research and articulate how our findings contribute to the literature on learning effects from humorous political content. We conclude with a discussion of the value of comparative designs for scholarship on political entertainment, outlining a series of promising future paths for this kind of research.

THE GATEWAY HYPOTHESIS IN
COMPARATIVE PERSPECTIVE

Seeking to understand the political impacts of political entertainment content, researchers have investigated an array of individual-level effects. In addition to knowledge and learning effects, researchers have explored effects on political attitudes and opinions, and effects on political engagement and related predispositions such as cynicism and trust.[11] With its roots in Baum's work on "soft news" in the early 2000s, research on potential impacts on awareness and knowledge of specific political issues is arguably the longest running strand of research into the effects of exposure to political entertainment.[12] This is unsurprising given the fundamental role political knowledge and awareness play in a variety of normative democratic theories.

One factor contributing to the richness of this particular literature is the debate about the nature and extent of political entertainment's ability to foster awareness and understanding among its viewers. Some studies, focusing on a direct path to awareness and knowledge flowing to viewers in general, or the less attentive, have identified positive effects. For example, Baum's early studies focused on associations between exposure to "soft news" programming and respondent knowledge and awareness related to specific foreign and domestic policy issues.[13] Later studies identified positive relationships between viewership of late-night comedy programs and campaign-related individual outcomes like factual knowledge about political candidates and levels of political expertise.[14] Outside of the campaign setting, experimental research has shown that viewers of political interview segments on satire programs such as *The Daily Show* and *The Colbert Report* were able to recall more information than viewers exposed to comparable interviews on non-humorous programs.[15]

Skeptics, however, have questioned the quality and extent of knowledge gain attributable to "soft news" and other infotainment formats that mix entertainment with political information and commentary. Research along these lines suggests that political learning attributable to political entertainment exposure is often focused on "light" political information such as scandals and relatively easy factual questions,[16] and that it is reflected more in "recognition" than "recall" of relevant information.[17] Further contributing to doubts about political entertainment's educative potential, a study directly comparing learning effects from news and entertainment media showed the former to be much more effective in helping viewers acquire factual political information, and that the latter was more strongly associated with online rather than memory-based information processing.[18]

This debate can be resolved if we relax assumptions about political entertainment *directly* imparting political knowledge and understanding, while focusing on an often overlooked nuance within the "gateway hypothesis." As formulated by Baum, the gateway hypothesis posits that political entertainment is of particular utility to those with lower levels of political interest. With the promise of a good laugh, political entertainment is believed to essentially lure low-interest individuals into awareness of, and attentiveness to, specific political issues. These processes are then expected to facilitate "an equalizing effect over time," enabling those with less intrinsic interest in politics to acquire public affairs knowledge levels closer to their more interested counterparts, ostensibly from a range of sources beyond the original entertaining or humorous content.[19] From this perspective, there is little expectation that political entertainment imparts political information on its own; rather, it helps spark attention to other forms of more information-rich political content such as hard news programs, as well as other sources of political information from which relevant information may be acquired.[20] Such an approach aligns with research suggesting that traditional news programs are more information-rich and educative than "soft news" and political entertainment shows.[21] In addition, it speaks to surveys and experimental studies that have focused on the potential of political comedy to stimulate attentiveness to news among the less politically interested.[22]

Synthesized this way, the body of research exploring the effects of political entertainment viewing on political awareness and knowledge offers us a relatively solid point of departure for comparative study. Specifically, based on the gateway hypothesis, exposure to political entertainment should be associated with modest but distinct gains in political knowledge, with these effects significantly concentrated among those with relatively low levels of intrinsic interest in politics.[23] Though numerous studies have provided tests of this theoretical proposition in the US context, we know of no concrete attempts to replicate these findings in other media systems.

In sum, our decision to foreground the gateway hypothesis in this comparative study stems from a few considerations. First, the relatively universal value of political knowledge across a variety of democratic visions (liberal, participatory, and deliberative) makes a study of political knowledge highly compelling. Second, although gateway effects are relatively small and concentrated among those with below-average levels of political interest, they provide the most stable base for leveraging comparative contrasts. Third, and in a related vein, studying gateway effects across different media systems allows us to circumvent those perennial issues associated with studying phenomena that vary in cultural and linguistic nuance. Instead of needing to determine *how* something is funny in other cultures or having to understand the specific critical contexts of humorous political content, we are concerned only with establishing that specific content is widely considered entertaining and that it includes information about prominent political issues of the day.

Fourth, the emerging literature on non-US examples of political entertainment has emphasized content and case studies, and few such studies have focused directly on effects. Together, these considerations allow us to leverage a reasonably solid pattern from the US context into a study of how political humor may be implicated in a central democratic process across a range of media systems.

Focused on exploring the "portability" of gateway effects, found primarily in the United States, we pose the following research questions that allow us to illuminate not only the effects themselves, but also how different media systems might function.

RQ1: To what extent are the principal forms of political entertainment associated with gateway effects—political satire and infotainment—observable across media systems?

RQ2: To what extent is a positive association between exposure to political entertainment and political knowledge, contingent on lower levels of political interest (gateway hypothesis), observable across a variety of media systems?

POLITICAL SATIRE AND POLITICAL ENTERTAINMENT IN THE UNITED STATES, UNITED KINGDOM, GERMANY, AND ITALY

This section introduces relevant aspects of our four country cases, while shedding light on our first research question. As noted earlier, these four countries allow us to test our central hypothesis and explore our research questions in settings that span the major media system types identified by Hallin and Mancini.[24] Examining these countries also allows us to (1) identify the relevant television programs, the viewership for which we include as principal independent variables in our survey analyses; (2) provide important context for interpreting the survey findings; and (3) reveal important insights into the conditions for the possibility of gateway effects in each case.

Overall, with respect to the first research question, each media system investigated here provides at least the minimal conditions for potential gateway effects. That is, we can identify at least some relatively popular programming in each country that treats political topics in a comedic or entertaining format. There are, however, important differences. Although all countries feature a reasonable amount of "infotainment" programming (most commonly, late-night or prime time talk or interview formats), only a majority (all but the United Kingdom) prominently featured "political satire" in the form of news parody or satirical news commentary. Moreover, consistent with emerging transnational research, the cases present a wide array of local variants, including seemingly singular examples as well as shows that appear to purposefully mirror formats familiar to US audiences.

United States

In many ways, the United States stands as our reference case. It serves as the setting in which our principal hypothesis was developed and has seen the most extensive testing. As perhaps the most notable exemplar of a "liberal" system, the United States features a market-oriented media system that prizes independent or neutral news in service of a highly individualistic pluralism. Following established patterns in the literature, we identify two distinct forms of political entertainment that we believe contribute to gateway effects in the United States: infotainment (often labeled "late-night comedy" in the United States), and political satire. The former category is represented by *The Tonight Show with Jay Leno*, *The Late Show with David Letterman*, and *Jimmy Kimmel Live!* The latter includes the core political satire programs represented in much of the US literature: *The Daily Show with Jon Stewart* and *The Colbert Report*.

United Kingdom

As another example of a "liberal" media system, the United Kingdom has features similar to those in the US system, with a few exceptions. These include a much stronger system of public broadcasting, a parliamentary system of governance (with associated differences in the role of political parties), and a slightly less individualized pluralism. Despite Baym and Jones pointing out that the United Kingdom enjoys one of the richest traditions of televised political humor, stretching back to *That Was the Week That Was* in the early 1960s,[25] this case presented us with a slight challenge in terms of identifying opportunities for gateway effects. Unlike the other three country cases, the United Kingdom was the only media system in which we were unable to identify prominent examples of both reasonably popular infotainment and reasonably popular political satire programming. The first category, in which we were merely looking for programs that mix entertainment and political content (often, though not always, in the basic format established by US late-night comedy programs), offered a number of possibilities. In terms of infotainment, we base our analysis on viewership of *The One Show* (a magazine program that regularly features political topics and guest interviews), *Piers Morgan's Life Stories* (an entertaining interview program in which guests are often political figures and political topics are often discussed), and the news and public affairs focused panel show, *Have I Got News For You!*

Germany

In our analysis, Germany represents the "democratic corporatist" media system type described by Hallin and Mancini. Relative to the other cases, Germany enjoys a vibrant traditional news media system, with high newspaper readership and a strong party press. Public broadcasting is strong in this case, but an increasing presence of more market-driven news media is also notable. The German media system includes a vibrant selection of infotainment programs that mix discussion of the issues of the day with various forms of light or entertaining content. Relevant programs include some mainly interview-driven programs such as *Hart Aber Fair* and *Anne Will*, talk shows focused on public affairs content such as *Harald Schmidt*, as well as programs like *TV Total*, a late-night comedy talk show very similar in structure to late-night programs in the United States. In terms of satirical content, Germany is home to one of the better-known examples of portability in terms of the satirical news parody format. In this category, *Heute Show* (literally translated, "Daily Show") is very much a German version of *The Daily Show with Jon Stewart*. This category also includes the satirical program, *Neues aus der Anstalt*.

Italy

Rounding out the major media system categories, Italy exemplifies the "polarized pluralist" media system, characterized by relatively low newspaper circulation as compared to the other system types, and high levels of political parallelism. Like Germany, Italy features established public media alongside a growing presence of more market-oriented outlets. Consistent with previous research,[26] Italy's media system includes a rich array of what we categorize as infotainment and political satire. In the former category are evening and late-night political talk shows, including *Che tempo che fa*, *Ballaro*, *Servizio Pubblico*, and *Matrix*. In the realm of satire, Italy is home to news parody and news satire programs such as *Striscia la Notizia* (which translates as "The News Slither") and *La Iene* ("The Hyenas"). In addition, Italian audiences at the time of our study were able to tune into *Crozza Italia* featuring provocative news satire from Italian comedian Maurizio Crozza.

SURVEY DATA

The principal source of data for our analysis is a collection of four online surveys we conducted from February through March of 2012 in each country. The surveys were designed to be identical in each case, with variations only where absolutely necessary. Beyond language, variations were limited to items referring to the unique television programs, political knowledge questions, and the ways in which educational attainment was measured. We contracted with Survey Sampling International (SSI) to recruit respondents from online panels that SSI maintains in each country, with recruitment carefully managed by SSI to create samples that mirror core census-level demographics in each country (i.e., age, gender, and educational attainment). In all, 3,323 individuals completed our surveys, with $n = 762$ in the United States, 971 in the United Kingdom, 712 in Germany, and 878 in Italy. The remainder of this section describes the key variables used to explore our research questions.

Criterion Variables

Our central outcome variable in each country is political knowledge, which operationally was a mix of more traditional "hard news" information and issues as well as some "soft news" material. Respondents were given six factual questions to answer, with the sum of correct answers serving as an index of political knowledge.[27] With the exception of items designed to tap familiarity with individuals who are generally in the news (e.g., the names or offices of leading government officials), items focused on topics prevalent in traditional news outlets within a few months of data collection. To discourage the Googling of answers, respondents were given only fifteen seconds to respond to these questions. In the United States, items included a question about the country in which Osama bin Laden was killed in the previous year, and one about politician Newt Gingrich's half-million dollar revolving credit account with a major jewelry retailer. In the United Kingdom, questions included as soft news items on topics such as Cabinet member Chris Huhne's resignation when the public learned how he avoided justice in a 2003 speeding ticket case, and meatier questions on topics like Michael Higgins' victory in the Irish presidential election. German items included topics such as the death of the Berlin Zoo's beloved polar bear, "Knut," as well as the then recent election of Germany to the UN Security Council. In Italy topics included which localities did and did not hold elections in the previous year, as well as sexual scandals involving Silvio Berlusconi at the time. Mean scores on the six-item knowledge index were highest in the United Kingdom ($M = 2.70$, $S.D. = 1.65$) and Italy ($M = 2.67$, $S.D. = 1.48$), followed by Germany ($M = 1.94$, $S.D. = 1.36$), then the United States ($M = 1.44$, $S.D. = 1.15$).

Independent Variables

Independent variables used in our models are organized into three blocks. The first block, comprising demographic variables, included age, gender, and education. Analyses confirmed that the central tendencies and distributions of these variables mirror those found in each country.

The second block included political interest and media exposure variables. *Political interest* was tapped by asking individuals to reflect, at the start of the survey, on the extent to which they pay attention to politics and public affairs. Responses ranged from "not at all interested" (1) to "extremely interested" (5) with the following means and standard deviations: United States ($M = 3.19$, *S.D.* = 1.25); United Kingdom ($M = 2.90$, *S.D.* = 1.20); Germany ($M = 3.19$, *S.D.* = 1.01); and Italy ($M = 2.95$, *S.D.* = 1.09).

Media exposure items asked respondents to report their frequency of watching specific programs, with responses ranging from "never" (0) to "regularly" (3). Responses were averaged to create indices for exposure to five different types of television programming. *News exposure* was measured by a series of items based on prominent national news programs available in each country. Programs included all nationally available public, private, and where appropriate, cable news shows. Means and standard deviations for this variable in each country were as follows: United States ($M = 1.35$, *S.D.* = 0.83); United Kingdom ($M = 1.45$, *S.D.* = 0.74); Germany ($M = 1.68$, *S.D.* = 0.71); and Italy ($M = 1.68$, *S.D.* = 0.68). *Entertainment exposure* was measured using selections of the most popular entertainment programs in each country serving as reference points (e.g., *Dancing with the Stars* and *NCIS* in the United States). Means and standard deviations for *entertainment exposure* in each country were as follows: United States ($M = 1.12$, *S.D.* = 0.96); United Kingdom ($M = 1.27$, *S.D.* = 0.83); Germany ($M = 1.56$, *S.D.* = 1.07); and Italy ($M = 0.97$, *S.D.* = 1.07). *Infotainment* exposure and *political satire* exposure was based on reported exposure to programs as described in the previous section. Means and standard deviations for *infotainment* exposure in each country were as follows: United States ($M = 0.85$, *S.D.* = 0.87); United Kingdom ($M = 1.32$, *S.D.* = 0.82); Germany ($M = 0.92$, *S.D.* = 0.71); and Italy ($M = 1.70$, *S.D.* = 0.73). Means and standard deviations for *political satire* exposure in each country were as follows: United States ($M = 0.86$, *S.D.* = 1.02); United Kingdom *N/A*; Germany ($M = 0.85$, *S.D.* = 1.03); and Italy ($M = 1.43$, *S.D.* = 0.86).

The third block included interaction terms between political interest and each type of political entertainment content (political interest × political entertainment exposure, and political interest × political satire exposure).

TESTING THE GATEWAY HYPOTHESIS
IN EACH COUNTRY

To shed light on our second research question concerning the replicability of gateway effects for political humor in different media systems, we ran hierarchical ordinary least squares regression models in which political knowledge is a function of the three aforementioned blocks, with the final block allowing us to specifically test the gateway hypothesis. Analytically, these product terms enable us to explore whether the effects of exposure to political infotainment and satire are significantly different at different levels of political interest, with negative and significant coefficient estimates suggesting that positive associations between exposure to political entertainment are significantly stronger for those at the lower ends of the distributions of political interest—the classic "equalizing effect" initially identified by Baum. The results from these four models, which all produce significant F statistics and explain between 12 and 29 percent of variations in political knowledge across the country cases, are reported in Table 10.1.

The results for demographic variables in the first block are relatively consistent across countries as well as with well-established patterns in the literature. Age is positively and significantly related to political knowledge in each case, though this relationship is notably stronger in the liberal cases (United States and United Kingdom) as compared to the democratic corporatist and polarized pluralist cases (Germany and Italy). Females score lower than males on our political knowledge index across the board, though this relationship appears to be most pronounced in the US case. Finally, and unsurprisingly, education is a significant positive predictor of political knowledge in

Table 10.1   The Effects of Political Entertainment Exposure on Political Knowledge by Country

	USA	UK	Germany	Italy
Demographics				
Age	.29***	.31***	.13***	.08*
Female	−.18***	−.09*	−.11**	−.08*
Education	.25***	.14***	.09*	.15***
Adjusted R^2	.19	.12	.04	.03
Political Interest and Media Exposure				
Political Interest	.28***	.26***	.33***	.29***
News Exposure	−.09*	−.07	−.00	.04
Entertainment Exposure	−.12***	−.15***	−.10**	−.16***
Infotainment Exposure	−.03	.12**	.04	−.02
Satire Exposure	.10*	---	.10*	.04
Adjusted R^2	.28	.20	.17	.10
"Gateway" Interaction Effects				
Political Interest × Infotainment	−.42***	−.45***	−.14	−.43**
Political Interest × Satire	−.27**	---	.03	−.31*
Total adjusted R^2	.29	.21	.17	.12
N	750	761	705	860

*Cell entries are standardized regression coefficients. * = $p \leq .05$, ** = $p \leq .01$, *** = $p \leq .001$. Coefficients reported for blocks 1 and 2 control for all other variables in each block; interaction terms are entered individually to minimize problems of multicollinearity. Ns reflect list-wise deletion of cases with missing data on one or more variables.*

each case, though again there are variations, with the strongest relationship observed in the United States (β = .25, $p \leq .001$) and the weakest relationship observed in Germany (β = .09, $p \leq .05$).

Differences begin to emerge more prominently in the second block of variables, which includes political interest along with variables tapping exposure to news, entertainment, political entertainment, and political satire programs. To be sure, political interest is a consistently strong predictor of political knowledge, producing the highest average standardized coefficients for any main-effect variable in the models. News exposure, however, only significantly predicts political knowledge in the US case, and there the relationship is actually negative (β = −.09, $p \leq .05$). Consistent with research on the effects of media choice,[28] coefficients for entertainment programming exposure are negative and significant in each country. With respect to infotainment exposure, we only observe a statistically significant relationship with political knowledge in the United Kingdom (β = .12, $p \leq .01$). Political satire exposure appears to be a more robust predictor of political knowledge in two of the three countries in which it was measured, with significant coefficients in the United States (β = .10, $p \leq .05$) and Germany (β = .10, $p \leq .05$).

The third and final block of each model presents the results that relate directly to the replicability of gateway effects across media systems. A clear pattern of gateway effects is observable in all countries except Germany. These effects appear to be strongest for infotainment programming, contingent on levels of political interest, with remarkably similar negative and significant coefficient estimates in the United States (β = −.42, $p \leq .001$), the United Kingdom (β = −.45, $p \leq .001$), and Italy β = −.43, $p \leq .01$). Still, significant and negative coefficients emerge in two of the three countries with political satire programming: the United States (β = −.27, $p \leq .01$) and Italy (β = −.31, $p \leq .05$). Together, these results suggest that the pattern of gateway effects for political entertainment long observed in the US context travels well to a liberal media system context outside of the United States, as well as the polarized pluralist media system of Italy, though apparently not so well to the democratic corporatist system found in Germany. These results also suggest that the observed replicability of gateway effects is more pronounced for the somewhat less cognitively demanding political entertainment formats, as compared to the notoriously more complex and cognitively taxing forms of political humor that take a more satirical approach.

DISCUSSION AND CONCLUSION

In this chapter we sought to produce what is very likely the first comparative analysis of political entertainment exposure effects—specifically, by systematically exploring across all major media system types the replicability of patterns long observed in the United States. As part of this effort, we also hoped to shed light on an additional research question concerning the opportunity structures for such effects across media system types. Our results suggest similar opportunity structures and replicability of effects, with notable exceptions. These exceptions include the relatively low supply of satirical political programming in the UK context, and the somewhat surprising absence of evidence for equalizing effects (in which those with lower levels of political interest appear to acquire knowledge and understanding from political humor that they wouldn't otherwise have) in Germany. In this section, we consider the implications of these findings. In the spirit of Gurevitch and Blumler's notion of "double value," we discuss these implications in terms of those of interest to scholars of political humor, as well as scholars of comparative political communication.

Before considering these implications, however, several caveats need to be addressed. First, though our focus on political knowledge as an outcome variable offers certain advantages for a comparative study, it is not without complications. Because indices of political knowledge are difficult to construct, especially in terms of establishing sets of items that feature a reasonable range of difficulty levels,[29] we attended to these issues as we constructed each instrument. However, we were unable to fully pilot-test our items prior to fieldwork, and therefore could not confirm that these questions would produce ideal discriminant validity. Nonetheless, the consistent and largely expected results for most variables in the model, especially those for demographics and political interest, provide reasonable indirect validation of these measures. While this issue is something to consider, we do not believe it fundamentally undermines our principal findings.

A second limitation concerns the nature of the surveys on which our results are based. Unfortunately, given the resources required to field our study in so many different countries, cross-sectional surveys were the only feasible format available to us for this preliminary investigation. Gateway effects are, at root, learning effects and as such they are best explored through designs that afford greater leverage over causal processes, such as panel surveys or experimental protocols. Given the contingent nature of the gateway hypothesis, however, this issue seems of less concern than it might for a simple relationship between two variables. Moreover, our decision to include the United States as a case was based on the idea that the US results could be used as a reference point. Indeed, that the US results are entirely consistent with those found in prior survey and experimental research is heartening. They suggest that the similar results found in the United Kingdom and Italian cases also reflect dynamics revealed by previous studies with greater purchase over causal processes. So while the present study offers a reasonable and informative first step in comparative studies in political entertainment effects, we strongly endorse the use of more refined study designs in future research into these phenomena.

Despite these limitations, the present study offers insights for both research focused explicitly on political humor, as well as the somewhat broader and more mature field of comparative research in political communication. In terms of political humor research, the present study builds on the somewhat nascent conversation regarding theoretical expectations for political humor in a global context. Our findings suggest important limitations to the portability of political humor and its effects. For example, despite the seemingly inherent broad applicability of political humor content in general as well as specific formats like news parody, we found a relative absence of prominent satirical political humor programs in the British media system. This finding is all the more notable when one considers that compared to our other cases, the UK media system is the most similar to that of the United States, and that the United Kingdom enjoys a long history of political satire.[30]

Likewise, with respect to our key research question, Germany emerged as a case where infotainment and political satire are reasonably popular, but do not appear to perform the same function as they do elsewhere. In other words, political entertainment in Germany does not provide less attentive citizens an entry point into cognitive engagement with politics. This unexpected variation is all the more curious given the extent to which German programs, relative to the British and Italian examples in our data, appear to hew the closest to American formats and formulas (e.g., *Heute Show, TV Total*).

The lack of gateway effects in Germany might be explained by some idiosyncrasies in its media landscape. From an audience perspective, Germans still predominantly rely on television and radio, and to a slightly lesser degree, newspapers as information sources.[31] The strong reliance on traditional news media might indicate that individuals who select to watch political entertainment formats are already more uniformly well-informed. Also supporting this argument is that the most popular radio and TV stations in terms of market share are public broadcasting stations and that the three most watched evening news casts are all aired and produced by the two main public broadcasters.[32] In addition to the German public broadcasting stations' educational mandate, they are well-funded, which facilitates the creation of high-quality content. In fact, out of the assessed infotainment and satire programs in this study, *Anne Will, Hart aber Fair, Neues aus der Anstalt*, and *Heute Show* all air or aired on one of the public service stations. *TV Total* and *Harald Schmidt* are the only private station formats, and at the time of the study it had been less than a year since *Harald Schmidt* had switched from a public broadcaster to a private station. The structural composition of the German TV landscape thus suggests that the high popularity of public broadcasting stations reflects already well-informed audiences that select to watch political entertainment and satire formats.

The lack of gateway effects also might be explained by the content of German political comedy and satire formats. *Anne Will* and *Hart Aber Fair* aim to entertain their audience, but their guests tend to be strictly politicians or public sector figures, who appear in their professional roles on the show for discussion and debates of policy and political events. Deriving full value from these shows requires a certain base level of political knowledge. *Neues aus der Anstalt* takes a humorous, but also very socially critical approach to political issues, but in contrast to *Heute Show* or many of the US formats spends little time explaining political events or contexts. Thus audiences that do not possess the necessary preexisting knowledge might find the show not so entertaining or valuable, as most references will be lost on them. Similarly, *Heute Show* and *Harald Schmidt* cater to a more educated audience

In summary, gateway effects for German political entertainment and satire formats may be absent because the selection mechanism works in the opposite direction. Rather than selecting these shows to learn more about political events, viewers select them precisely because they are already informed and now seek dispersion or some interpretive guidance from these formats. In the German context then, political knowledge is not an outcome, but a prerequisite for political entertainment and satire shows.

Together these findings suggest that while phenomena related to political humor may be portable—that is, they *may* be transported to different media systems and national contexts—comparative research can play an important role in identifying and understanding instances in which such phenomena are absent. Such cases of absence and/or variation raise a host of interesting questions that go beyond the initial open-ended queries concerning the generalizability of political humor phenomena. This last point is related to potential implications of our research for the broader field of comparative political communication. Our empirical findings and the foregoing discussion confirm that if we examine political humor in a global and comparative context, it is possible to view political entertainment media as critical components of processes that lie at the core of comparative political communication research. As shown here, political entertainment is an important factor in the circulation and distribution of political information with discernable variation across national contexts. Viewed from this angle, one may ask similar questions about the anomalies observed in the United Kingdom and Germany, but this time with an interest in political humor expression and effects as potential indicators of broader system dynamics related to democratic health. Such questions would likely be even more interesting when considering the more complex dynamics such as how political humor in different systems may serve as a vehicle for the expression of political dissent and critique.

It is clear that comparative research on political entertainment offers potential insights across multiple specific literatures within the broader field of political communication research.

The research reported here extends political entertainment research into the realm of comparative research, but more important, into comparative research that includes the full spectrum of media system types. It is important to acknowledge that an initial exploration into this territory falls far short of comprehensively answering questions that non-US single-case studies can merely raise. Such answers will require additional research that not only increases the sophistication of research designs through the use of panel survey and experimental methods, but also broadens the array of political entertainment phenomena explored to include more complex processes related to political persuasion and other kinds of attitudinal effects. Scholarship on political entertainment has many opportunities to mature while still hanging on to fashionableness, not unlike its successful and slightly more middle-aged siblings.

NOTES

1. Throughout this chapter, we will use the term "political entertainment" as a general catch-all label that is inclusive of many different forms of such programming. Later, as we present the empirical research anchoring this chapter, we will distinguish between "infotainment," and "satire" programs. In the context of this study, the former is a broader category referring to a number of different program types in which politics and entertainment are merely mixed, whereas the latter will refer specifically to programs that are distinctive in their use of satire and parody. At other times we will occasionally use other labels as appropriate—for example in citing Matthew Baum's work on "soft news."

2. See, for example, Matthew Baum, "Sex, Lies, and War: How Soft News Brings Foreign Policy to the Inattentive Public," *American Political Science Review* 96, no. 1 (2002): 91–109; Matthew Baum, "Soft News and Political Knowledge: Evidence of Absence or Absence of Evidence?" *Political Communication* 20, no. 2 (2003): 173–90; Matthew Baum, *Soft News Goes to War* (Princeton, NJ: Princeton University Press, 2005); Richard Davis and Diana Owen, *New Media and American Politics* (New York: Oxford University Press, 1998).

3. Dannagal G. Young and Jonathan Gray, "Breaking Boundaries: Working across the Methodological and Epistemological Divide in the Study of Political Entertainment," *International Journal of Communication* 7 (2013).

4. Notable examples here include: Gianpietro Mazzoleni and Anna Sfardini, *Politica Pop: da "Porta a Porta" a "L'Isola dei famosi"* [Pop Politics: From "door to door" to "island of the famous"] (Bologna, Italy: Il Mulino, 2009); John Street, Sanna Inthorn, and Martin Scott, "Playing at Politics? Popular Culture as Political

Engagement," *Parliamentary Affairs* 65, no. 2 (2011): 338–58; Jörg Matthew, "Elaboration or Distraction? Knowledge Acquisition from Thematically Related and Unrelated Humor in Political Speeches," *International Journal of Public Opinion Research* 25, no. 3 (2013): 291–302.

5. Geoffrey Baym and Jeffrey Jones, "News Parody in Global Perspective: Politics, Power, and Resistance," *Popular Communication* 10, no. 1–2 (2012): 2–13.

6. Jay G. Blumler and Michael Gurevitch, "Towards a Comparative Framework for Political Communication Research," in *Political Communication: Issues and Strategies for Research*, ed. Stephen H. Chaffee (Beverly Hills, CA: Sage, 1975), 165–84; Michael Gurevitch and Jay Blumler, "Comparative Research: The Extending Frontier," in *New Directions in Political Communication*, eds. David L. Swanson and Dan D. Nimmo (Newbury Park, CA: Sage, 1990); Barbara Pfetsch and Frank Esser, "Comparing Political Communication," in *The Handbook of Comparative Communication Research*, edited by Frank Esser and Thomas Hanitzsch (New York: Routledge, 2013), 25–47; Michael Gurevitch and Jay Blumler, "State of the Art of Comparative Political Communication Research: Posed for Maturity?" in *Comparing Political Communication: Theories, Cases, and Challenges*, ed. Frank Esser and Barbara Pfetsch (New York: Cambridge University Press, 2004), 325–43.

7. Michael Gurevitch and Jay Blumler, "State of the Art of Comparative Political Communication Research: Posed for Maturity?" in *Comparing Political Communication: Theories, Cases, and Challenges*, eds. Frank Esser and Barbara Pfetsch (New York: Cambridge University Press, 2004), 325–343.

8. Ibid.

9. Young Min Baek and Magdalena E. Wojcieszak, "Don't Expect Too Much! Learning From Late-Night Comedy and Knowledge Item Difficulty," *Communication Research* 36, no. 6 (2009): 783–809; Matthew A. Baum, "Soft News and Political Knowledge: Evidence of Absence or Absence of Evidence?" *Political Communication* 20, no. 2 (2003): 173–90; Xiaoxia Cao, "Political Comedy Shows and Knowledge about Primary Campaigns: The Moderating Effects of Age and Education," *Mass Communication and Society* 11, no. 1 (2008): 43–61; Lauren Feldman and Dannagal G. Young, "Late-Night Comedy as a Gateway to Traditional News: An Analysis of Time Trends in News Attention among Late-Night Comedy Viewers During the 2004 Presidential Primaries," *Political Communication* 25, no. 4 (2008): 401–22; Michael A. Xenos and Amy B. Becker, "Moments of Zen: Effects of The Daily Show on Information Seeking and Political Learning," *Political Communication* 26, no. 3 (2009): 317–32.

10. Daniel Hallin and Paolo Mancini, *Comparing Media Systems: Three Models of Media and Politics* (New York: Cambridge University Press, 2004).

11. For reviews of the literature on effects of political entertainment exposure, see: Amy B. Becker and Don J. Waisanen, "From Funny Features to Entertaining Effects: Connecting Approaches to Communication Research on Political Comedy," *Review of Communication* 13, no. 3 (2013): 161–83; Patricia Moy, Michael A. Xenos, and Muzammil Hussain, "News and Political Entertainment Effects on Democratic Citizenship," in *The International Encyclopedia of Media Studies, Volume V: Media Effects/Media Psychology*, ed. Erica Scharrer (Hoboken, NJ: Blackwell Publishing,

2013), 111–31; Michael A. Xenos, "Research on the Political Implications of Political Entertainment," in *Handbook of Digital Politics*, eds. Stephen Coleman and Deen Freelon (Cheltenham, UK: Edward Elgar Publishing, 2015), 340–56.

12. Matthew Baum, "Sex, Lies, and War: How Soft News Brings Foreign Policy to the Inattentive Public," *American Political Science Review* 96, no. 1 (2002): 91–109; Matthew Baum, "Soft News and Political Knowledge: Evidence of Absence or Absence of Evidence?" *Political Communication* 20, no. 2 (2003): 173–90.

13. Ibid.

14. Paul Brewer and Xiaxia Cao, "Candidate Appearances on Soft News Shows and Public Knowledge about Primary Campaigns," *Journal of Broadcasting and Electronic Media* 50, no. 1 (2006): 18–35; Michael Pfau, J. Brian Houston, and Shane M. Semmler, *Mediating the Vote: The Changing Media Landscape in U.S. Presidential Campaigns* (New York: Rowman & Littlefield, 2007).

15. Amy B. Becker, "What About Those Interviews? The Impact of Exposure to Political comedy and Cable News on Factual Recall and Anticipated Political Expression," *International Journal of Public Opinion Research* 25, no. 3 (2013): 344–56.

16. Markus Prior, "Any Good News in Soft News? The Impact of Soft News Preference on Political Knowledge," *Political Communication* 20, no. 3 (2003): 149–71; Young Min Baek and Magdalena Wojcieszak, "Don't Expect Too Much! Learning from Late-Night Comedy and Knowledge Item Difficulty," *Communication Research* 36, no. 6 (2009): 783–809.

17. Barry Hollander, "Late-Night Learning: Do Entertainment Programs Increase Political Campaign Knowledge for Young Viewers?" *Journal of Broadcasting & Electronic Media* 49, no. 4 (2005): 402–415.

18. Young Mie Kim and John Vishak, "Just Laugh! You Don't Need to Remember: The Effects of Entertainment Media on Political Information Acquisition and Information Processing in Political Judgment," *Journal of Communication* 58, no. 2 (2008): 338–60.

19. Matthew Baum, "Sex, Lies, and War: How Soft News Brings Foreign Policy to the Inattentive Public," *American Political Science Review* 96, no. 1 (2002): 91–109; Matthew Baum, "Soft News and Political Knowledge: Evidence of Absence or Absence of Evidence?" *Political Communication* 20, no. 2 (2003): 173–90.

20. See, for example, Michael Xenos and Amy Becker, "Moments of Zen: Effects of The Daily Show on Information Seeking and Political Learning," *Political Communication* 26, no. 3 (2009): 317–32.

21. For example, Markus Prior, "Any Good News in Soft News? The Impact of Soft News Preference on Political Knowledge," *Political Communication* 20, no. 3 (2003): 149–71; Young Mie Kim and John Vishak, "Just Laugh! You Don't Need to Remember: The Effects of Entertainment Media on Political Information Acquisition and Information Processing in Political Judgment," *Journal of Communication* 58, no. 2 (2008): 338–60.

22. Michael Xenos and Amy Becker, "Moments of Zen: Effects of The Daily Show on Information Seeking and Political Learning," *Political Communication* 26, no. 3 (2009): 317–32; Lauren Feldman and Dannagal Young, "Late-Night Comedy as a Gateway to Traditional News: An Analysis of Time Trends in News Attention among Late-Night Comedy Viewers during the 2004 Presidential Primaries,"

Political Communication 25, no. 4 (2008): 401–22; Dannagal Young and Russell M. Tisinger, "Dispelling Late-Night Myths: News Consumption among Late-Night Comedy Viewers and the Predictors of Exposure to Various Late-Night Shows," *The Harvard International Journal of Press/Politics* 11, no. 3 (2006): 113–34.

23. Amy B. Becker, "What About Those Interviews? The Impact of Exposure to Political comedy and Cable News on Factual Recall and Anticipated Political Expression," *International Journal of Public Opinion Research* 25, no. 3 (2013): 344–56.

24. Daniel Hallin and Paolo Mancini, *Comparing Media Systems: Three Models of Media and Politics* (New York: Cambridge University Press, 2004).

25. Geoffrey Baym and Jeffrey Jones, "News Parody in Global Perspective," 2012.

26. Gianpietro Mazzoleni and Anna Sfardini, *Politica Pop: da "Porta a Porta" a "L'Isola dei famosi"* [Pop Politics: From "door to door" to "island of the famous"] (Bologna, Italy: Il Mulino, 2009).

27. Though we analyzed both "hard" and "soft" knowledge items separately, since general patterns were similar across both we will focus on "total" knowledge in the analyses reported here.

28. Markus Prior, *Post-Broadcast Democracy: How Media Choice Increases Inequality in Political Involvement and Polarizes Elections* (New York: Cambridge University Press, 2007).

29. Indeed, we would caution against the utility of these measures for comparisons between the countries studied here, for example. While we believe the measures enable us to determine relationships between media habits and knowledge across the country cases, due to the level-of-difficulty calibration problem, we would not treat them as comparable indicators of relative levels of knowledgeableness of the different populations.

30. Geoffrey Baym and Jeffrey Jones, "News Parody in Global Perspective," 2012.

31. Germany, Statistisches Bundesamt, Destatis Wiesbaden. (May 18, 2015). Zeitverwendungserhebung Aktivitäten in Stunden Und Minuten Für Ausgewählte Personengruppen 2012/2013. Accessed April 1, 2018, https://www.destatis.de/DE/Publikationen/Thematisch/EinkommenKonsumLebensbedingungen/Zeitbudgeterhebung/Zeitverwendung5639102139004.pdf?__blob=publicationFile; AGF Fernsehforschung in Zusammenarbeit mit GfK, Media Perspektiven Basisdaten 2015, S. 73 [8]; B. Van Eimeren and B. Frees, "Rasanter Anstieg des Internetkonsums–Onliner fast drei Stunden täglich im Netz," *Media Perspektiven* 7, no. 8 (2013): 358–72.

32. AGF Fernsehforschung in Zussamenarbeit mit GfK, TV Scope 6.1, 01.02.2018–28.02.2018/. Accessed April 1, 2018, https://www.agf.de/daten/tvdaten/marktanteile/.

REFERENCES

AGF Fernsehforschung in Zusammenarbeit mit GfK, *Media Perspektiven Basisdaten* 2015, S. 73 [8].

AGF Fernsehforschung in Zussamenarbeit mit GfK, *TV Scope* 6.1, 01.02.2018–28.02.2018/. Accessed April 1, 2018. https://www.agf.de/daten/tvdaten/marktanteile/.

Baek, Young Min, and Magdalena E. Wojcieszak. "Don't Expect Too Much! Learning From Late-Night Comedy and Knowledge Item Difficulty." *Communication Research* 36, no. 6 (2009): 783–809.

Baum, Matthew A. "Sex, Lies, and War: How Soft News Brings Foreign Policy to the Inattentive Public." *American Political Science Review* 96, no. 1 (2002): 91–109. http://journals.cambridge.org/production/action/cjoGetFulltext?fulltextid=208462.

———. "Soft News and Political Knowledge: Evidence of Absence or Absence of Evidence?" *Political Communication* 20, no. 2 (2003): 173–90.

———. *Soft News Goes to War: Public Opinion and American Foreign Policy in the New Media Age*. Princeton, NJ: Princeton University Press, 2005.

Baumgartner, Jody C. "Internet Political Ads in 2012: Can Humor Mitigate Unintended Effects of Negative Campaigning?" *Social Science Computer Review* 31, no. 5 (2013): 601–13.

Baumgartner, Jody C, and Jonathan S. Morris. "The Daily Show Effect Candidate Evaluations, Efficacy, and American Youth." *American Politics Research* 34, no. 3 (2006): 341–67.

Baym, Geoffrey, and Jeffrey Jones. "News Parody in Global Perspective: Politics, Power, and Resistance." *Popular Communication* 10, no. 1–2 (2012): 2–13.

Becker, Amy B. "What About Those Interviews? The Impact of Exposure to Political Comedy and Cable News on Factual Recall and Anticipated Political Expression." *International Journal of Public Opinion Research* 25, no. 3 (2013): 344–56.

———. "Political Humor as Democratic Relief? The Effects of Exposure to Comedy and Straight News on Trust and Efficacy." *Atlantic Journal of Communication* 19, no. 5 (2011): 235–50.

Becker, Amy B., and Don J. Waisanen. 2013. "From Funny Features to Entertaining Effects: Connecting Approaches to Communication Research on Political Comedy." *Review of Communication* 13, no. 3 (2013): 161–83.

Blumler, Jay G., and Michael Gurevitch. "Towards a Comparative Framework for Political Communication Research." In *Political Communication: Issues and Strategies for Research*, edited by Stephen H. Chaffee, 165–84. Beverly Hills, CA: Sage, 1975.

Brewer, Paul, and Xiaxia Cao. "Candidate Appearances on Soft News Shows and Public Knowledge about Primary Campaigns." *Journal of Broadcasting and Electronic Media* 50, no. 1 (2006): 18–35.

Cao, Xiaoxia. "Political Comedy Shows and Knowledge about Primary Campaigns: The Moderating Effects of Age and Education." *Mass Communication and Society* 11, no. 1 (2008): 43–61.

Davis, Richard, and Diana Owen. *New Media and American Politics*. New York: Oxford University Press, 1998.

Esser, Frank, and Barbara Pfetsch, eds. *Comparing Political Communication: Theories, Cases, and Challenges*. New York: Cambridge University Press, 2004.

Feldman, Lauren, and Dannagal Goldthwaite Young. "Late-Night Comedy as a Gateway to Traditional News: An Analysis of Time Trends in News Attention among Late-Night Comedy Viewers during the 2004 Presidential Primaries." *Political Communication* 25, no. 4 (2008): 401–22.

Feldman, Lauren, and Dannagal G. Young. "Late-Night Comedy as a Gateway to Traditional News: An Analysis of Time Trends in News Attention among Late-Night Comedy Viewers during the 2004 Presidential Primaries." *Political Communication* 25, no. 4 (2008): 401–22.

Ferree, Myra Marx, William Gamson, Jürgen Gerhards, and Dieter Rucht. *Shaping Abortion Discourse: Democracy and the Public Sphere in Germany and the United States*. New York: Cambridge University Press, 2002.

Germany, Statistisches Bundesamt, Destatis Wiesbaden. (May 18, 2015). Zeitverwendungserhebung Aktivitäten in Stunden Und Minuten Für Ausgewählte Personengruppen 2012/2013. Accessed April 1, 2018. https://www.destatis.de/DE/Publikationen/Thematisch/EinkommenKonsumLebensbedingungen/Zeitbudgeterhebung/Zeitverwendung5639102139004.pdf?__blob=publicationFile.

Gurevitch, Michael, and Jay Blumler. "Comparative Research: The Extending Frontier." In *New Directions in Political Communication*, edited by David L. Swanson and Dan D. Nimmo. Newbury Park, CA: Sage, 1990.

Gurevitch, Michael, and Jay G. Blumler. "State of the Art of Comparative Political Communication Research: Poised for Maturity?" In *Comparing Political Communication: Theories, Cases, and Challenges*, edited by Frank Esser and Barbara Pfetsch, 325–43. New York: Cambridge University Press, 2004.

Hallin, Daniel C., and Paolo Mancini. *Comparing Media Systems: Three Models of Media and Politics*. New York: Cambridge University Press, 2004.

Hollander, Barry A. "Late-Night Learning: Do Entertainment Programs Increase Political Campaign Knowledge for Young Viewers?" *Journal of Broadcasting & Electronic Media* 49, no. 4 (2005): 402–15.

Kim, Young Mie, and John Vishak. "Just Laugh! You Don't Need to Remember: The Effects of Entertainment Media on Political Information Acquisition and Information Processing in Political Judgment." *Journal of Communication* 58, no. 2 (2008): 338–60.

Lamarre, Heather. "When Parody and Reality Collide: Examining the Effects of Colbert's Super PAC Satire on Issue Knowledge and Policy Engagement across Media Formats." *International Journal of Communication* 7, no. 1 (2013): 394–413.

Matthes, Jörg. "Elaboration or Distraction? Knowledge Acquisition from Thematically Related and Unrelated Humor in Political Speeches." *International Journal of Public Opinion Research* 25, no. 3 (2013): 291–302.

Mazzoleni, Gianpietro, and Anna Sfardini. *Politica Pop: da "Porta a Porta" a "L'Isola dei famosi"* [Pop Politics: From "door to door" to "island of the famous"]. Bologna, Italy: Il Mulino (2009).

Moy, Patricia, Michael A. Xenos, and Muzammil Hussain. "News and Political Entertainment Effects on Democratic Citizenship." In *The International Encyclopedia of Media Studies, Volume V: Media Effects/Media Psychology*, edited by Erica Scharrer, 111–31. Hoboken, NJ: Blackwell Publishing, 2013.

Pfau, Michael, J. Brian Houston, and Shane M. Semmler. *Mediating the Vote: The Changing Media Landscape in U.S. Presidential Campaigns*. New York: Rowman & Littlefield, 2007.

Pfetsch, Barbara, and Frank Esser. "Comparing Political Communication." In *The Handbook of Comparative Communication Research*, edited by Frank Esser and Thomas Hanitzsch, 25–47. New York: Routledge, 2013.

Prior, Markus. "Any Good News in Soft News? The Impact of Soft News Preference on Political Knowledge." *Political Communication* 20, no. 2 (2003): 149–71.

Prior, Markus. *Post-Broadcast Democracy: How Media Choice Increases Inequality in Political Involvement and Polarizes Elections*. New York: Cambridge University Press, 2007.

Robinson, John P., and Mark R. Levy. "News Media Use and the Informed Public: A 1990s Update." *Journal of Communication* 46, no. 2 (1996): 129–35.

Street, John, Sanna Inthorn, and Martin Scott. "Playing at Politics? Popular Culture as Political Engagement." *Parliamentary Affairs* 65, no. 2 (2012): 338–58.

van Eimeren, Birgit, and Beate Frees. "Rasanter Anstieg des Internetkonsums– Onliner fast drei Stunden täglich im Netz." *Media Perspektiven* 7, no. 8 (2013): 358–72.

Xenos, Michael A. "Research on the Political Implications of Political Entertainment." In *Handbook of Digital Politics*, edited by Stephen Coleman and Deen Freelon, 340–56. Cheltenham, UK: Edward Elgar Publishing, 2015.

Xenos, Michael A., and Amy B. Becker. "Moments of Zen: Effects of The Daily Show on Information Seeking and Political Learning." *Political Communication* 26, no. 3 (2009): 317–32.

Young, Danagal Goldthwaite, and Russell M. Tisinger. "Dispelling Late-Night Myths: News Consumption among Late-Night Comedy Viewers and the Predictors of Exposure to Various Late-Night Shows." *The Harvard International Journal of Press/Politics* 11, no. 3 (2006): 113–34.

Young, Danagal Goldthwaite, and Jonathan Gray. "Breaking Boundaries: Working across the Methodological and Epistemological Divide in the Study of Political Entertainment." *International Journal of Communication* 7 (2013): 552–55.

Chapter 11

The Causes and Consequences of Affinity for Political Humor

Mark Boukes

Research on political satire has developed quickly over the past two decades. A wide array of studies has been conducted that examine the audiences,[1] content,[2] and effects of this infotainment format.[3] Most of the concepts used and applied in these studies are borrowed from research on traditional journalistic formats and political science; for example, framing, political efficacy, knowledge, and trust. To develop a concept specifically tailored to the genre of political satire, recent research has put forward the concept of *Affinity for Political Humor* (AFPH).[4]

Although probably known by most scholars working on the subject of satire and frequently referenced—by January 2018, Hmielowski et al. (2011) received eighty-six cites, and Holbert et al. (2013) thirteen cites—the concept has hardly been put into actual practice. Only two empirical articles can be found that actively used the scale measuring AFPH. One of the two studies was the article of Hmielowski et al. (2011) itself, in which they introduced the concept. Their study used AFPH to predict the consumption of political satire among respondents of a statewide telephone survey. AFPH, thus, was an independent variable in this study. The other study used AFPH as a moderator.[5] Focusing on a specific subdimension of the AFPH scale, Becker analyzed how AFPH *to reduce anxiety* influenced the relationship between exposure to (in)congruent political satire and political efficacy.

Given the still very limited knowledge about AFPH, the current chapter provides an exploratory study into the causes and consequences of AFPH. Using a set of two studies, I will: (1) analyze the characteristics of citizens that predict their personal AFPH, (2) examine AFPH's ability to predict the exposure to political satire content, and (3) investigate how AFPH affects the appreciation and perceived influence of political satire.

All this has been done in the context of the Netherlands. Research on political satire is still heavily dominated by work from the United States, but the genre is very popular in other contexts as well. Accordingly, academic attention from other sides of the world is highly valuable to better understand the satire phenomenon.[6] Especially in the case of a new concept like AFPH, research from a different context will shed light on the construct's validity under different conditions and may eventually encourage its use in future research.

AFFINITY FOR POLITICAL HUMOR

The latent construct of AFPH has been assessed in terms of internal factor structure, reliability, and validity by Holbert and colleagues (2013).[7] They found that the scale can be employed in two manners: (a) as a one-dimension scale tapping AFPH generally or (b) as four separate dimensions that each capture one aspect of AFPH. These four dimensions were already specified in the first study that introduced AFPH: (1) incongruity, (2) superiority, (3) anxiety reduction, and (4) social connection.[8] The paragraphs below will shortly introduce each of these; thereby, heavily relying on and integrating the works of Hmielowski et al. (2011) and Holbert et al. (2013).

The first lower-order construct under AFPH is *incongruity*. Political satire may point out to its viewers where a disconnection can be found between the real and the unreal, or the normal and the abnormal. Especially, in an age of *alternative facts*, political satire may be helpful for citizens to become aware of the differences between what politicians say and what is actually happening in society. Satire makes its audiences laugh by the unexpectedness of its messages: highlighting inconsistencies in political rhetoric, satire programs humorously demonstrate where the politician or the political system more broadly is dysfunctional.[9]

The second dimension of AFPH is *superiority*. Watching political satire may give its viewers a "sense of victory or triumph" by laughing *at* (i.e., not *with*) another's follies.[10] Disparaging politicians' behavior or communications in a humorous way is common in political satire, and may make viewers feel more secure about their own beliefs (at least if they held a negative opinion toward the satirized politician/party). Enjoyment of jokes, according to this dimension, depends on the action of comparing oneself to the other (i.e., a politician about who the satirist makes a joke) and identifying the weakness of the other.

Anxiety reduction is the third dimension of AFPH. Laughing about politics may release tension that people build up when thinking about an election outcome, policies proposed by Parliament, or the behaviors of a particular president. Humor is a successful coping mechanism to deal with such stressful situations,[11] and this also applies in anxious political situations.

The fourth and last lower-order construct under AFPH is *social connectedness*. Especially in times of strong political polarization,[12] political humor may be a tool that still "bridges" both sides of the political spectrum. Humor allows laughing together, eases conversations, and causes individuals to be perceived as being more socially attractive.[13] Particularly *within* politically homogenous groups, humor may fulfill this role of a social glue: making jokes about "the other" could strengthen the bonds between in-group members.

Who Has an Affinity for Political Humor?

Very little is known about the scale that measures citizens' AFPH. Even basic information, such as which demographics and political characteristics predict people to have a stronger or weaker AFPH are still unknown. Only Hmielowski et al. (2011) have shown, surprisingly, that the scale is *unrelated* to a number of variables such as need for cognition,[14] ideology, and the consumption of traditional news media (i.e., newspaper and television news).

Arguably, frequent viewers of political comedy should have a higher AFPH. Previous studies have shown that AFPH is higher among younger, male, liberal, and frequent news consumers, who watch political satire programs relatively more often.[15] Yet, the consumption of satire is conceptually different from one's AFPH; hence, this study aims to shed more light on the AFPH construct by answering the following research question:

RQ1: Which individual citizen characteristics predict a stronger or weaker Affinity for Political Humor?

Affinity for Political Humor and the Consumption of Political Satire

Originally, the AFPH scale was developed by Hmielowski et al. to assess the factors that predict citizens to consume political satire shows.[16] Their motivation was that scholars know more and more about the factors that mediate or moderate the effects of political satire, but that "an understanding of the general audience remains this area of research's lacuna" (p. 98). Insight into the audience of political satire is crucial, because without this information it is very difficult to assess the relevance and real-world magnitude of effects found in experimental settings: How many and precisely which people do actually watch political satire?

The question, thus, is whether a citizens' AFPH predicts their actual consumption of political satire. Both Hmielowski et al. and Holbert et al. (as a means of validity assessment) revealed this relationship, but are faced with cross-sectional data.[17] Having conducted a survey study, it was impossible to assess the causal direction of the relationship. Measuring AFPH and the consumption of satire programs *The Daily Show* and *The Colbert Report* at the same point in time, it was difficult to disentangle which causes which. Dynamic data in the form of an experiment or panel research are needed to draw strong causal conclusions. To examine the predictive power of AFPH, we test the following hypothesis:

H1: Individuals with a stronger Affinity for Political Humor are more likely to expose themselves to political satire shows.

Affinity for Political Humor and the Consequences of Political Satire Consumption

Not only may AFPH cause the consumption of political satire, it may also moderate its effects. Hmielowski et al. wrote: "We urge future research to assess potential differential effects of a variety of political entertainment messages for those individuals with varied levels of AFPH (i.e., AFPH as potential moderator variable)."[18] This challenge has been taken up by Becker (2014) who showed that the effects of satire exposure may indeed depend on AFPH; her study focused on one particular dimension of the scale (i.e., anxiety reduction).[19]

The current study assesses the impact of AFPH more generally and looks at two potential outcome variables that are in line with the nature of this scale: (a) appreciation of political satire exposure and (b) the perceived influence of political satire. Theoretical frameworks, such as the Orientations-Stimulus-Orientations-Response[20] or the Differential Susceptibility to Media Effects Model,[21] predict that people's existing dispositions influence the way media messages are processed and, therefore, influence the potential effects these may have. In relation to political satire, for example, it has been shown that education may moderate the (indirect) relationship between political satire exposure and political participation.[22]

This study examines the moderating impact on two dependent variables that arguably should be more strongly affected by satire exposure among viewers with a high AFPH. First, one may expect satire exposure to especially yield favorable experiences, such as perceptions of funniness or entertainment, when people score high on AFPH. After all, people who will score lower on this scale may find political satire boring, offending, or difficult to comprehend. Accordingly, we test this hypothesis:

H2: Individuals with a stronger Affinity for Political Humor are more likely to enjoy exposure to political satire than people with a weaker AFPH.

With the development of the literature on political satire, studies have become more fine-grained regarding the exact content features of satire fragments. A regularly made distinction is the one between horatian and juvenalian satire; the first being lighter and having more emphasis on the "funny," whereas the latter provides a more bitter and cynical approach to humor.[23] Research demonstrated that especially the juvenalian types of satire are less likely to be counterargued and, therefore, have a stronger persuasive effect.[24]

Recognizing that political satire may come in different forms, the current study examines the impact of another dimension on which satire clips can be distinguished: the nature of attack. Political satire, almost by definition,[25] criticizes—in one way or the other—the folly of political actors (or news producers)[26]: Jokes may be presented in different degrees of how gentle versus harsh they are in their nature of attack.[27] Hmielowski et al. predicted that the inconsistency presented in political satire should not stray too far from the mundane to still be perceived as being humorous.[28] Yet, the question is whether people who score high on AFPH are more accepting of harsher forms of satire than those who have a lower AFPH. Accordingly, the following research question is examined:

RQ2: Is the relationship between Affinity for Political Humor and enjoyment conditional on the type of satire that is being presented (gentle vs. harsh)?

Previous research found that people perceive a persuasive intent in satire messages.[29] Yet, the perceived influence on oneself was rather weak, especially in case of horatian satire. The question is whether the perceived influence is stronger or weaker for different levels of AFPH. The measurement of AFPH is largely shaped by expectations that political satire may have certain consequences, such as revealing the weaknesses of politicians, providing knowledge, and reducing anxiety.[30] Accordingly, people with a strong AFPH may be more open to the potential effects that satire may have on others or themselves. Whereas people with a weak AFPH could consider humorous formats inappropriate for a serious topic as politics, the opposite probably will be true for citizens with a strong AFPH. Because citizens scoring high on AFPH will especially believe in the (favorable) consequences of political satire, the following hypothesis is tested:

H3: Individuals with a stronger Affinity for Political Humor will perceive a stronger influence of political satire than participations with a weaker AFPH.

METHOD

Data from two studies will be combined in this chapter to examine the research questions and hypotheses presented above. The studies rely on different samples (i.e., random vs. convenience) and experimental techniques (i.e., forced exposure vs. self-selection) to investigate the different causes and consequences of AFPH. Because of the lengthy nature of the AFPH scale (11 survey items), both studies used a condensed version of the measurement (respectively, six items in Study 1 and eight items in Study 2). Although ideally one would measure AFPH with the full scale, shorter scales were employed in the current work due to space constraints. This did not threaten the validity of the studies, because (a) items were consciously chosen that reflected the different dimensions of the AFPH scale, (b) Holbert et al. showed that the full scale could function as a unidimensional latent construct (i.e., all items measure the same latent construct), and (c) some items in the original scale are very similar to each other.

STUDY 1

Sample

The first study recruited participants from the database of a market research agency, *PanelClix*, and used quotas for age, gender, and political preference to assure a sample that was diverse and representative for Dutch society on these characteristics. The study was fielded online on April 3–4, 2014. A total of 667 Dutch adults completed the survey successfully and responded correctly to the instructional manipulation checks built into the questionnaire.[31] Participants were on average 40.37 years old (*SD* = 13.80) and 51.9 percent were female.

Design and Stimuli

Participants were randomly allocated to one of twelve experimental conditions. The experiment followed a 2 (topic: policy *vs.* personal) × 2 (background information provision: yes *vs.* no) × 2 (nature of attack: gentle *vs.* harsh) between-subjects factorial design with four control conditions (i.e., news about policy topic; news about personal topic; "no exposure" condition with questions about policy topic; and "no exposure" condition with questions about personal topic).

Participants in conditions that dealt with policy were exposed to a video clip about the plan of the Dutch government to cut funding for the public broadcasting organization.[32] To assure that participants watched the video they were allocated to, the survey could not be clicked to the next page before the time passed that viewing the complete video would minimally take. This policy proposal was covered neutrally in the (control) news condition of one minute and twelve seconds and was satirized (i.e., humorously critiqued) in the satire conditions either in a gentle manner (i.e., by inserting a ridiculous advertisement for senior toilets in the middle of the news item with funny music in the background; 1:38 minutes) or a harsh manner (i.e., inserting visuals of violent scenes from movies; 1:04 minutes).

Conditions on the personal topic showed a video clip of Mark Rutte (prime minister of the Netherlands) who either apologized for the confusion he caused at a Eurotop (news condition; 36 seconds), who was bullied by his colleague prime minister's at the same Eurotop (gentle satire condition; 39 seconds) or who was involved in a sexual scandal that leaked out to the internet (harsh satire condition; 38 seconds). Participants were either provided with background information about the actual topic or not to support the understanding of satire videos.[33] Overall, the harsh satire items were perceived as more tasteless ($p < .001$) and offensive ($p < .001$) than the gentle satire clips.

The satire stimuli were especially designed for this experiment by Sander van der Pavert, who is the producer of *LuckyTV* and among other things, famous for the clip "Time of my Life" in which Donald Trump and Hillary Clinton sing a duet. *LuckyTV* usually produces satire videos by manipulating existing news videos and putting a humorous twist on these materials by reediting them, inserting certain visuals, or adapting the voiceover (e.g., similar to Bad Lip Reading in the US context, though much more well-known and popular). Thereby, the internal validity is relatively strong compared to studies that, for example, employ stimuli from a newscaster (e.g., CNN) with a satire show (e.g., *The Daily Show*) who differ on many more aspects than just the message that is provided (i.e., different host, different studio, different visuals, etc.).

Measurements

Education

Participants' highest level of obtained education was measured with a 0 to 8 scale adapted to the Dutch educational system ($M = 5.43$, $SD = 1.90$). It ranged from no education (0) to university diploma (8).

Political Ideology

The political preference was measured with a scale that asked participants to position themselves on a scale ranging from −5 (left) to 0 (not left, neither right) to +5 (right). Due to the quota used for the recruitment, equally many citizens with a left-wing as a right-wing political preference were present in the sample ($M = 0.01$, $SD = 2.39$).

Political Interest

The interest participants had in politics was tapped on a 11-point scale ranging from 0 (*totally no interest*) to 10 (*very interested*) ($M = 5.29$, $SD = 2.40$).

Political Knowledge

How knowledgeable people were about politics was assessed with nine multiple choice questions (each: four answer options and a "don't know" option). Among others, questions asked participants to recognize a politician from a photo, of which department Jeroen Dijsselbloem was the minister, the number of seats in Parliament, and which parties formed the government ($M = 5.83$, $SD = 2.69$).

Internal Political Efficacy

People's perceived understanding of political affairs was measured with two items that formed a reliable scale ($α = .87$; $M = 5.33$, $SD = 2.08$): (a) How much do you know about politics compared to other people? (b) I have the feeling that I understand most political affairs well.

News Consumption

One composite measure was created that combined the consumption of news on different platforms: television evening news, newspapers, and news websites. For any of the following sources, participants answered how often they consumed it on a scale from 0 (*never*) to 6 (*seven days per week*). Summing up all the responses resulted in a scale that ranged from 0 to 18 ($M = 11.70$, $SD = 3.87$).

Affinity for Political Humor

The central variable in this study, AFPH, was measured with six 7-point Likert scales that reflected the different dimensions of AFPH: I appreciate political humor, because it: (1) makes me aware that our political system is dysfunctional [*incongruity*], (2) can reveal the weaknesses of our political leaders and institutions, (3) can make me feel more knowledgeable about politics [both: *superiority*], (4) can reduce the anxiety I feel toward politics [*anxiety reduction*], (5) can help me express my political opinions, and (6) allows me to form stronger bonds with other people [both: *social connectedness*]. All items loaded on one dimension in an exploratory factor analysis (Eigenvalue = 3.35, explained variance = 55.86%) and formed a reliable scale (α = .84). The AFPH scale was created by computing the mean of the six items (M = 2.76, SD = 1.00).

Satire Consumption

The consumption of political satire programs was tapped with four items that asked how often participants watched (1) *Koefnoen*, (2) *Dit was het Nieuws*, (3) *De Kwis*, and (4) broadcasted shows of Dutch stand-up comedians who discuss societal and political issues, such as Youp van 't Hek and Theo Maassen. These items were added together in a reliable scale ranging from 0 to 12 (α = .70; M = 3.02, SD = 2.42).

Koefnoen was a prime-time Saturday evening show that presents a variety of satirical sketches about political issues, celebrities, and "the common man." It's comparable to the sketches one sees in *Saturday Night Live*. *Dit was het Nieuws* is the Dutch equivalent of the British *Have I Got News for You*.[34] It is a satirical panel show in which two teams display their knowledge about the news of the week in a humorous manner. Finally, *De Kwis* is a satirical news quiz broadcasted prime-time on the Saturday evening. Every episode another celebrity is invited to answer funny questions about the news of the week. Notably, all these satire shows are aired on the public broadcasting channels.

Enjoyment

Participants ranked the video to which they had been exposed on a number of dimensions that tap into the enjoyment they experienced while watching. Five items, specifically, are used to measure how well they appreciated the video on 11-point scales for the following characteristics: (1) not funny–funny; (2) boring–enjoyable; (3) unpleasant–pleasant; (4) not annoying-annoying; and (5) tasteless–good taste. Together these formed a reliable scale (α = .89; M = 4.21, SD = 2.35).

Perceived Influence

The impact that political satire may have in the perception of viewers was measured with four items: how much (a) do you think others will be influenced by this video, (b) were you incited to think by the video, (c) were you convinced by the video, and (d) were you helped by the video in forming an opinion. The mean value of these four items was calculated to create an overall measurement of perceived influence (α = .77; M = 3.48, SD = 1.97).

STUDY 2

Sample

The second experiment relied on a convenience sample that was recruited in the period May 19–June 8, 2017.[35] Participants were recruited via the (online) social network of principal investigator (Joy Schouten; 40%), via Facebook ads (34%) and online political discussion, or survey groups (7%); 19 percent did not indicate their method of recruitment. The final sample consisted of 122 people with an average age of 30.77 (SD = 12.51) and 52.5 percent who were female.

Design and Stimuli

Participants in this experiment were *not* randomly allocated to conditions, but could choose themselves which of three television programs they preferred to see. The three possibilities were: (a) *NOS Journaal*, which is the most popular newscast of the Netherlands; (b) *Zondag met Lubach*, which in 2017 was the most prominent satire show in the Netherlands, often with more than a million viewers; (c) *Tegenlicht*, which is a well-known serious documentary program. No further background information about the contents of the videos was given to respondents, just the titles of the programs. *Zondag met Lubach*, recently, gained international fame with its clip "The Netherlands welcomes Trump in his own words: The Netherlands second?" (over 26 million views on YouTube). It is a show comparable to *Last Week Tonight with John Oliver.*

Without the forced exposure component, this study follows an original approach introduced by previous scholars who gave participants agency to choose their own stimuli.[36] Instead of analyzing the further outcome(s) of this exposure, this study is simply interested in the act of choosing stimuli.[37]

Measurements

Education

Highest level of education was measured with a 0 to 5 scale ranging from lower secondary professional education to university education (M = 4.16, SD = 1.16).

Political Ideology

The political preference was measured with a scale that asked to position themselves on an 11-point scale from −5 (*left*) to +5 (*right*). The sample was skewed toward the left (M = −1.21, SD = 2.49).

Political Interest

How interested participants were in politics was tapped on a 7-point scale ($M = 5.21$, $SD = 1.36$).

Affinity for Political Humor

Participants' level of AFPH was measured with eight items in this study. All items were tapped on 7-point disagree-agree Likert scales. The specific items were: I appreciate political humor, when (1) it makes me aware that our political system is dysfunctional, (2) it helps me make better sense of why our political system is dysfunctional [both: *incongruity*], or because (3) it can reveal the weaknesses of our political leaders and institutions, (4) it can make me feel more knowledgeable about politics, (5) it can aid me in reinforcing my political beliefs [all three: *superiority*], (6) it can help me effectively criticize politics and politicians [*anxiety reduction*], (7) it can help me express my political opinions, and (8) it allows me to form stronger bonds with people who hold similar political views as my own [both: *social connectedness*].

All items loaded on one component in an exploratory factor analysis (Eigenvalue = 4.86; explained variance = 60.78%) and formed a reliable scale ($\alpha = .91$). The AFPH scale was created by computing the mean of the eight items ($M = 3.71$, $SD = 1.17$).

Satire Consumption

Instead of measuring the self-reported exposure to political satire shows as in Study 1, this study operationalized satire consumption by the choice participants made when asked which program they wanted to watch. Of all participants, 56.6 percent chose *Zondag met Lubach* (the satire program), 31.1 percent the newscast, and 12.3 percent the documentary.

RESULTS

The following sections present findings of analyses that examined (1) citizens' characteristics predicting AFPH scores, (2) AFPH's role in the consumption of political satire, and (3) the moderating role of AFPH when people are exposed to satire.

Who Has an Affinity for Political Humor?

Following up on the work of Hmielowski et al.,[38] the first study provided data to analyze which citizens have a stronger or weaker AFPH. An ordinary least squares (OLS) regression analysis with the AFPH scale as dependent variable

Table 11.1   OLS Regression Model Predicting Affinity for Political Humor

Model 1: AFPH (d.v.)	b	S.E.	b*	p
Intercept	1.80	(0.22)		.000
Age	0.00	(0.00)	.05	.235
Gender (0 = male; 1 = female)	−0.13	(0.07)	−.07	.076
Education	0.00	(0.02)	.01	.860
Political ideology (left-right)	−0.02	(0.02)	−.05	.180
Political interest	0.05	(0.03)	.12	.079
Political knowledge	−0.03	(0.02)	−.09	.066
Internal political efficacy	0.14	(0.03)	.30	.000
News consumption	0.01	(0.01)	.04	.347
R^2	0.17			
N	665			

Note: Cells contain unstandardized regression coefficients (b) with standard errors (S.E.) in parentheses, standardized effect coefficients (b*) and probabilities (p: two-tailed).

tested which demographics and predispositions were significantly related to AFPH. Model 1 in Table 11.1 provides the results.

The findings are very much in line with those of Hmielowski et al.[39] AFPH only relates to few of the basic characteristics on which people normally are identified. Neither age, education, political ideology, nor news consumption are significantly related to AFPH. Only marginally significant are the relationships with gender, political interest (positively), and political knowledge (negatively). The only factor that really seems to matter is internal political efficacy: citizens who believe they have a relatively good understanding of political affairs tend to have a higher AFPH. The standardized effect coefficient indicates a rather strong effect ($b^* = .30$).

Affinity for Political Humor and the Consumption of Political Satire

AFPH's relationship with the consumption of political satire programs was first examined in Study 1 by predicting the self-reported exposure to several satire shows. Model 2 in Table 11.2 shows the findings. It found that—except for the positive effect of news consumption (those who consume more news, also watch more satire)—a range of demographic and political variables did not significantly predict satire consumption: Neither age, gender, education, ideology, interest, knowledge, or internal efficacy were significantly related to how often people watched satire shows. AFPH, however, positively predicted satire consumption. With every 1-point increase on its 7-point scale, the frequency of watching satire shows increased by 0.32 points. Compared to a model without AFPH ($R^2 = .11$), the AFPH adds 2 percent to the explained variance in self-reported satire consumption.

Table 11.2   Regression Models (Respectively, OLS and Logistic) Predicting Exposure to Political Satire

	Model 2: Self-reported Satire Consumption (d.v.)				Model 3: Self-selected Satire Exposure (d.v.)			
	b	S.E.	b*	p	b	S.E.	O.R.	p
Intercept	0.50	(0.57)		.377	0.27	(0.20)	1.31	.182
Age	−0.01	(0.01)	−.04	.380	−0.58	(0.23)	0.56	.013
Gender (0 = male; 1 = female)	−0.28	(0.18)	−.06	.135	−0.29	(0.23)	0.75	.216
Education	0.00	(0.05)	.00	.950	−0.14	(0.22)	0.87	.543
Political ideology (left-right)	−0.05	(0.04)	−.05	.177	−0.38	(0.23)	0.68	.099
Political interest	−0.10	(0.07)	−.10	.148	0.39	(0.21)	1.47	.070
Political knowledge	0.06	(0.04)	.07	.155				
Internal political efficacy	0.14	(0.08)	.12	.099				
News consumption	0.15	(0.03)	.23	.000				
Affinity for political humor	0.32	(0.10)	.13	.001	0.65	(0.23)	1.91	.005
R^2	0.13							
n	665				120			

Note: Model 2: Cells contain unstandardized regression coefficients (*b*) with standard errors (*S.E.*) in parentheses, standardized effect coefficients (*b**) and probabilities (*p*: two-tailed). Model 3: All independent variables were z-standardized. Cells contain unstandardized coefficients (b) with standard errors (*S.E.*) in parentheses, odds ratios (O.R.) and probabilities (p).

Adding to the cross-sectional nature and the potential bias in self-reports of media exposure in Study 1,[40] Study 2 tested the effect of AFPH under controlled conditions on the preference for a satire show when participants had multiple media options they could choose from. Model 3 in Table 11.2 shows the power of AFPH to predict people's exposure to political satire. All independent variables were z-standardized, so the odds ratios (O.R.) can be compared in terms of effect strength.

A logistic regression predicted whether people selected the satire program (1) or not (0). The results are fairly similar to Study 1. Again, most demographic and political variables were unrelated to satire consumption: gender, education, ideology, and political interest had no significant effect on the choice for political satire. Age, in this case, was a significant predictor: younger people were more likely to choose the satire option (*Zondag met Lubach*). AFPH had the strongest effect on self-selected exposure to political satire. With every standard deviation increase on the AFPH scale, people were 1.91 times more likely to select the satire show instead of the newscast or documentary. Altogether, Study 1 as well as Study 2 thus found evidence in line with Hypothesis 1: AFPH positively affects the likelihood to expose oneself to political satire shows. Only Study 2 replicated the significant, negative relationship with age that Hmielowski et al. found.[41]

Affinity for Political Humor and the Consequences of Political Satire Consumption

AFPH may not only determine the selection of satirical content, it could also affect its appreciation. The following analyses shows whether AFPH influences (a) how much people enjoyed the (random) exposure to political satire and (b) how influential they perceived the satire to be. Accordingly, the analyses only include participants that actually were exposed to a satire clip; in total, eight conditions with 442 participants.

Results are presented in Table 11.3. Regarding the enjoyment of the satire clips, results of Model 4 show that on average male participants enjoyed these more than female participants. Age, education, ideology, interest, knowledge, efficacy, and news consumption did not determine how much people liked the satire videos. Of the manipulated factors, only the nature of attack had a significant effect. People enjoyed the gentle satire videos more than the harsh ones. The provision of background information nor the topic had an effect. AFPH did indeed predict how much people enjoyed the political satire: With every 1-point increase on the AFPH scale, people enjoyed the satire 0.26-points more. This is in line with Hypothesis 2. Compared to a regression model without AFPH, an additional 1 percent of variance is explained by this construct.

Table 11.3 OLS Regression Models Predicting Enjoyment of the Satire Clip That Participants Were Exposed To

	Model 4: Enjoyment (d.v.)				Model 5: Enjoyment (d.v.)			
	B	S.E.	b'	P	b	S.E.	b'	P
Intercept	4.75	(0.79)	-.08	.000	4.06	(0.84)	-.08	.000
Age	-0.01	(0.01)	-.12	.149	-0.02	(0.01)	-.12	.132
Gender (0 = male; 1 = female)	-0.59	(0.25)	-.04	.017	-0.58	(0.24)	-.05	.017
Education	-0.06	(0.07)	-.03	.425	-0.06	(0.07)	-.04	.373
Political ideology (left-right)	-0.04	(0.05)	.02	.489	-0.04	(0.05)	.02	.405
Political interest	0.02	(0.09)	-.05	.815	0.02	(0.09)	-.04	.819
Political knowledge	-0.05	(0.06)	.10	.390	-0.04	(0.06)	.10	.504
Internal political efficacy	0.13	(0.12)	.00	.278	0.12	(0.12)	.00	.281
News consumption	0.00	(0.04)	-.10	.998	0.00	(0.04)	.22	.985
Nature of attack: gentle vs. harsh	-0.50	(0.24)	-.03	.036	1.11	(0.70)	-.03	.111
Background information: no vs. yes	-0.14	(0.24)	-.01	.567	-0.16	(0.24)	-.01	.508
Topic: policy vs. personal	-0.06	(0.24)	.10	.809	-0.06	(0.24)	.21	.815
Affinity for political humor	0.26	(0.13)		.044	0.52	(0.17)	-.36	.002
AFPH × nature of attack					-0.58	(0.24)		.014
R^2	0.06				0.07			

Note: Cells contain unstandardized regression coefficients (b) with standard errors (S.E.) in parentheses, standardized effect coefficients (b') and probabilities (p: two-tailed).

Model 5 examined whether the effect of AFPH on enjoyment was conditional on the type of satire that was presented. The interaction effect between AFPH and nature of attack yielded a significant negative effect. To ease interpretation, Figure 11.1 visualized this interaction effect. It shows that people with a stronger AFPH tended to enjoy the satire more, but *only* in case they saw the gentle satire clip. Enjoyment of the harsh satire item was independent of people's level of AFPH.

Model 6 in Table 11.4 shows the results of the OLS regression predicting how strongly people perceived the influence of exposure to the political satire videos. Of the demographics and political variables, only political interest (positively) and political knowledge (negatively) had an effect on the perceived influence. Neither the nature of attack nor the background information that was provided (or not) influenced how strongly people believed that satire could have an effect. The topic of the video, by contrast, had a significant impact: people perceived the satire clip about policy (budget cuts on public broadcaster) as being more influential than the personal satire about Prime Minister Rutte.

In line with Hypothesis 3, people who scored higher on AFPH perceived a stronger influence of the satire clips. With each 1-point increase on AFPH, the perceived influence of the satire video that a participant saw increased with 0.37 points. AFPH, thereby, added 3 percent of additional explained

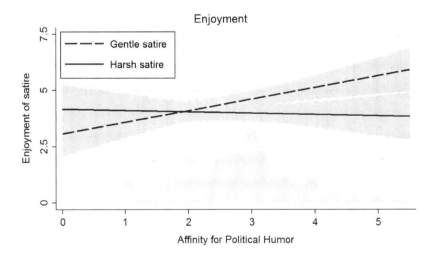

Figure 11.1 Affinity for Political Humor by Enjoyment of Satire. *Note*: The predicted enjoyment for increasing levels of AFPH while being exposed to either the gentle or the harsh satire clip with their 95 percent confidence interval (at the mean values of other independent and control variables). Bars on bottom show distribution of participants on the independent variable AFPH.

Table 11.4 OLS Regression Models Predicting Perceived Influence of the Satire Clips

	Model 6: Perceived Influence (d.v.)				Model 7: Perceived Influence (d.v.)			
	b	S.E.	b´	p	b	S.E.	b´	p
Intercept	3.08	(0.60)		.000	2.94	(0.64)		.000
Age	−0.01	(0.01)	−.04	.492	−0.01	(0.01)	−.04	.483
Gender (0 = male; 1 = female)	−0.04	(0.19)	−.01	.811	−0.04	(0.19)	−.01	.814
Education	−0.09	(0.05)	−.08	.102	−0.09	(0.05)	−.08	.098
Political ideology (left-right)	−0.03	(0.04)	−.03	.482	−0.03	(0.04)	−.04	.460
Political interest	0.18	(0.07)	.22	.013	0.18	(0.07)	.22	.013
Political knowledge	−0.13	(0.04)	−.18	.003	−0.13	(0.04)	−.17	.003
Internal political efficacy	0.00	(0.09)	.00	.965	0.00	(0.09)	.00	.962
News consumption	0.02	(0.03)	.04	.466	0.02	(0.03)	.04	.463
Nature of attack: gentle *vs.* harsh	−0.16	(0.18)	−.04	.382	0.18	(0.53)	.05	.740
Background information: no *vs.* yes	0.01	(0.18)	.00	.943	0.01	(0.18)	.00	.962
Topic: policy *vs.* personal	−0.61	(0.18)	−.16	.001	−0.61	(0.18)	−.16	.001
Affinity for political humor	0.37	(0.10)	.19	.000	0.42	(0.13)	.21	.001
AFPH × nature of attack					−0.12	(0.18)	−.09	.506
R^2	0.12				0.12			

Note: Cells contain unstandardized regression coefficients (b) with standard errors (S.E.) in parentheses, standardized effect coefficients (b´) and probabilities (p: two-tailed).

variance compared to a model without AFPH. Model 7 shows that this effect was not conditional on people's level of AFPH.

DISCUSSION

This chapter has investigated the use of the AFPH for research on political satire. First being introduced by Hmielowski et al. (2011) and Holbert et al. (2013), the scale has still rarely been applied in empirical studies on this topic. That is unfortunate, because the current study shows that AFPH is a strong predictor both for the consumption of political satire but also for how the effects of satire may eventually play out. In statistical models that control for a range of different demographic and political variables, AFPH was the only consistent factor predicting the consumption of satire, its enjoyment, and perceived influence. Altogether, Figure 11.2 illustrates the different functions AFPH could take up in research on political satire: it should both (a) positively predict the consumption of political satire and (b) moderate potential effects of satire consumption.

The first study showed that AFPH is a construct rather unrelated to most variables that are normally employed in political communication research. This means that people's AFPH is an independent factor that could be taken into consideration by scholars interested in the consumption of political satire, besides the traditional variables used in such research. Only internal political efficacy predicts AFPH, but not strongly enough to function as a proxy for this factor. Any model that lacks AFPH as an independent variable could suffer from omitted variable bias and, consequently, be unnecessarily imprecise.

The second study confirmed cross-sectional results of Study 1 that AFPH functions as a significant predictor of satire consumption. Besides

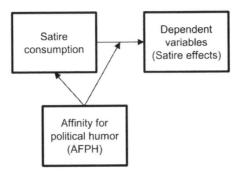

Figure 11.2   The Dual Role AFPH Could Play in Research on Political Satire.

age (i.e., younger people tended to prefer satire), AFPH was a driving force behind the selection of satire shows vis-à-vis a newscast or documentary. This finding not only confirms the validity of the AFPH scale, it also shows the added value of including AFPH in studies on the exposure to political satire. Having studied AFPH in general, future research is needed to disentangle which specific dimensions of AFPH are decisive in causing a preference for political satire. As suggested by Holbert et al. (2013), this could be done by tapping all the eleven items of the AFPH scale and including the different dimensions as separate factors in one's analysis. Employing condensed scales of, respectively, six or eight of the original items, the current work was unable to do so.

Finally, this chapter has shown that the effects of exposure to political satire are conditional on people's AFPH. People who were exposed to political satire perceived the satire clips as having a stronger perceived influence when they had a higher level of AFPH. This may be explained by the nature of this construct as it taps into individuals' appreciation of satire to reveal weaknesses, point out incongruities, reducing anxiety, or ease social interactions. Additionally, the study showed that people enjoyed the satire more when they had a stronger AFPH. Previous research has shown that this may have consequences for the effects satire has on, for example, its persuasiveness.[42] Adding nuance to this finding, the experiment showed that this boost in enjoyment was only the case for gentle forms of political satire. When the satire was harsh—including references to violence or a sex scandal—the enjoyment was unrelated to viewers' level of AFPH. High AFPH people, thus, seem to particularly enjoy more gentle and benign forms of satire.

Altogether, this chapter demonstrates the usefulness of AFPH as a construct for research on political satire. Much more than only using it as a control variable,[43] AFPH could help scholars to better understand the motivations to watch political satire and the effects it has on different groups in the society.

NOTES

I thank you Joy Schouten for sharing the data of her Master thesis, which is Study 2 in this chapter. Also, I thank Sander van de Pavert (*LuckyTV*) for creating the stimuli of Study 1.

1. Jay D. Hmielowski, R. L. Holbert, and Jayeon Lee (2011), "Predicting the Consumption of Political TV Satire: Affinity for Political Humor, The Daily show, and The Colbert Report," *Communication Monographs* 78 (1): 96–114; Dannagal G. Young and Russell M. Tisinger (2006), "Dispelling Late-Night Myths: News Consumption among Late-Night Comedy Viewers and the Predictors of Exposure to

Various Late-Night Shows," *The Harvard International Journal of Press/Politics* 11 (3): 113–34; Dannagal Goldthwaite Young (2013), "Laughter, Learning, or Enlightenment? Viewing and Avoidance Motivations behind the Daily show and the Colbert Report," *Journal of Broadcasting & Electronic Media* 57 (2): 153–69.

2. Julia R. Fox, Glory Koloen, and Volkan M. S. Sahin (2007), "No Joke: A Comparison of Substance in The Daily show with Jon Stewart and Broadcast Network Television Coverage of the 2004 Presidential Election Campaign," *Journal of Broadcasting & Electronic Media* 51 (2): 213–27; Michel M. Haigh and Aaron Heresco (2010), "Late-Night Iraq: Monologue Joke Content and Tone from 2003 to 2007," *Mass Communication and Society* 13 (2): 157–73; Jonathan S. Morris (2009), "The Daily Show with Jon Stewart and Audience Attitude Change during the 2004 Party Conventions," *Political Behavior* 31 (1): 79–102.

3. Jody Baumgartner and Jonathan S. Morris (2006), "The Daily Show Effect: Candidate Evaluations, Efficacy, and American Youth," *American Politics Research* 34 (3): 341–67; Amy B. Becker and Don J. Waisanen (2013), "From Funny Features to Entertaining Effects: Connecting Approaches to Communication Research on Political Comedy," *Review of Communication* 13 (3): 161–83; Mark Boukes, Hajo G. Boomgaarden, Marjolein Moorman, and Claes H. de Vreese (2015), "At Odds: Laughing and Thinking? The Appreciation, Processing, and Persuasiveness of Political Satire," *Journal of Communication* 65 (5): 721–44.

4. Hmielowski et al., "Predicting the Consumption of Political TV Satire," 96–114; R. Lance Holbert, Jayeon Lee, Sarah Esralew, Whitney O. Walther, Jay D. Hmielowski, and Kristen D. Landreville (2013a), "Affinity for Political Humor: An Assessment of Internal Factor Structure, Reliability, and Validity," *Humor* 26 (4): 551–72.

5. Amy B. Becker (2014), "Playing with Politics: Online Political Parody, Affinity for Political Humor, Anxiety Reduction, and Implications for Political Efficacy," *Mass Communication and Society* 17 (3): 424–45.

6. Geoffrey Baym and Jeffrey P. Jones (2012), "News Parody in Global Perspective: Politics, Power, and Resistance," *Popular Communication* 10 (1–2): 2–13.

7. Holbert et al., "Affinity for Political Humor."

8. Hmielowski et al., "Predicting the Consumption of Political TV Satire."

9. Dannagal Goldthwaite Young (2008), "The Daily Show as New Journalism: In Their Own Words," in *Laughing Matters: Humor and American Politics in the Media Age*, eds. Jody C Baumgartner and Jonathan S. Morris, 241–262 (New York: Routledge).

10. John C. Meyer (2000), "Humor as a Double-Edged Sword: Four Functions of Humor in Communication," *Communication Theory* 10 (3): 310–31.

11. Melanie Booth-Butterfield, Steven Booth-Butterfield, and Melissa Wanzer (2007), "Funny Students Cope Better: Patterns of Humor Enactment and Coping Effectiveness," *Communication Quarterly* 55 (3): 299–315; Nicolas A. Kuiper, Rod A. Martin, and L. Joan Olinger (1993), "Coping Humour, Stress, and Cognitive Appraisals," *Canadian Journal of Behavioural Science/Revue Canadienne Des Sciences Du Comportement* 25 (1): 81–96.

12. Markus Prior (2013), "Media and Political Polarization," *Annual Review of Political Science* 16 (1): 101–27; Natalie Jomini Stroud (2010), "Polarization and Partisan Selective Exposure," *Journal of Communication* 60 (3): 556–76.

13. Melissa Bekelja Wanzer, Melanie Booth-Butterfield, and Steve Booth-Butterfield (1996), "Are Funny People Popular? An Examination of Humor Orientation, Loneliness, and Social Attraction," *Communication Quarterly* 44 (1): 42–52.

14. John T. Cacioppo, Richard E. Petty, Chuan Feng Kao, and Regina Rodriguez (1986), "Central and Peripheral Routes to Persuasion: An Individual Difference Perspective," *Journal of Personality and Social Psychology* 51 (5): 1032–43.

15. Young and Tisinger, "Dispelling Late-Night Myths."

16. Hmielowski et al., "Predicting the Consumption of Political TV Satire."

17. Hmielowski et al., "Predicting the Consumption of Political TV Satire"; Holbert et al., "Affinity for Political Humor."

18. Hmielowski et al., "Predicting the Consumption of Political TV Satire," 110.

19. Becker, "Playing with Politics."

20. OSOR, see Hazel Markus and Robert B. Zajonc (1985), "The Cognitive Perspective in Social Psychology," in *Handbook of Social Psychology*, eds. Gardner Lindzey and Elliot Aronson, 3rd ed., Vol. 1, 137–230 (New York: Random House); D. M. McLeod, G. M. Kosicki, and J. M. McLeod (2009), "Political Communication Effects," in *Media Effects: Advances in Theory and Research*, eds. Jennings Bryant and Mary Beth Oliver, 3rd ed., 228–51 (New York: Routledge).

21. Patti M. Valkenburg and Jochen Peter (2013), "The Differential Susceptibility to Media Effects Model," *Journal of Communication* 63 (2): 221–43.

22. Hoon Lee and Nojin Kwak (2014), "The Affect Effect of Political Satire: Sarcastic Humor, Negative Emotions, and Political Participation," *Mass Communication and Society* 17 (3): 307–28.

23. R. Lance Holbert, Jay Hmielowski, Parul Jain, Julie Lather, and Alyssa Morey (2011), "Adding Nuance to the Study of Political Humor Effects: Experimental Research on Juvenalian Satire versus Horatian Satire," *American Behavioral Scientist* 55 (3): 187–211.

24. R. Lance Holbert, John M. Tchernev, Whitney O. Walther, Sarah E. Esralew, and Kathryn Benski (2013b), "Young Voter Perceptions of Political Satire as Persuasion: A Focus on Perceived Influence, Persuasive Intent, and Message Strength," *Journal of Broadcasting & Electronic Media* 57 (2): 170–86; Heather L. LaMarre, Kristen D. Landreville, Dannagal Young, and Nathan Gilkerson (2014), "Humor Works in Funny Ways: Examining Satirical Tone as a Key Determinant in Political Humor Message Processing," *Mass Communication and Society* 17 (3): 400–23.

25. R. Lance Holbert (2016), "Entertainment Television and Political Campaigns: The Political Satire Appropriateness (PSA) Model," in *Praeger Handbook of Political Campaigning in the United States*, ed. W. L. Benoit. Volume I: Foundations and Campaign Media Edition, 171–90 (Santa Barbara, CA: Praeger).

26. R. Lance Holbert (2013), "Developing a Normative Approach to Political Satire: An Empirical Perspective," *International Journal of Communication* 7 (Breaking Boundaries): 305–23.

27. Boukes et al., "At Odds: Laughing and Thinking?"

28. Hmielowski et al., "Predicting the Consumption of Political TV Satire."

29. Holbert et al., "Young Voter Perceptions."

30. Holbert et al., "Affinity for Political Humor."

31. Daniel M. Oppenheimer, Tom Meyvis, and Nicolas Davidenko (2009), "Instructional Manipulation Checks: Detecting Satisficing to Increase Statistical Power," *Journal of Experimental Social Psychology* 45 (4): 867–72.

32. For a detailed description, see Boukes et al., "At Odds: Laughing and Thinking?"

33. Boukes et al., "At Odds: Laughing and Thinking?"

34. Stephen Coleman, Anke Kuik, and Liesbet van Zoonen (2009), "Laughter and Liability: The Politics of British and Dutch Television Satire," *The British Journal of Politics and International Relations* 11 (4): 652–65.

35. For details, see Joy Schouten (2017), "The News of the Future: Satire. The Effects of Satire Compared to Traditional Forms of News on Comprehension and Political Engagement," MA thesis, University of Amsterdam.

36. Kevin Arceneaux, Martin Johnson, and John Cryderman (2013), "Communication, Persuasion, and the Conditioning Value of Selective Exposure: Like Minds May Unite and Divide but They Mostly Tune Out," *Political Communication* 30 (2): 213–31; Shanto Iyengar and Kyu S. Hahn (2009), "Red Media, Blue Media: Evidence of Ideological Selectivity in Media Use," *Journal of Communication* 59 (1): 19–39; Silvia Knobloch-Westerwick and Simon M. Lavis (2017), "Selecting Serious Or Satirical, Supporting Or Stirring News? Selective Exposure to Partisan versus Mockery News Online Videos," *Journal of Communication* 67 (1): 54–81.

37. Similar to Alyssa C. Morey, Steven B. Kleinman, and Mark Boukes (2018), "Political Talk Preferences: Selection of Similar and Different Discussion Partners and Groups," *International Journal of Communication* 12: 359–79.

38. Hmielowski et al., "Predicting the Consumption of Political TV Satire."

39. Hmielowski et al., "Predicting the Consumption of Political TV Satire."

40. See Markus Prior (2009), "The Immensely Inflated News Audience: Assessing Bias in Self-Reported News Exposure," *Public Opinion Quarterly* 73 (1): 130–43.

41. Hmielowski et al., "Predicting the Consumption of Political TV Satire."

42. Boukes et al., "At Odds: Laughing and Thinking?"; Heather L. LaMarre and Whitney Walther (2013), "Ability Matters: Testing the Differential Effects of Political News and Late-Night Political Comedy on Cognitive Responses and the Role of Ability in Micro-Level Opinion Formation," *International Journal of Public Opinion Research* 25 (3): 303–22; Nabi et al., "All Joking Aside."

43. For example Hsuan-Ting Chen, Chen Gan, and Ping Sun (2017), "How Does Political Satire Influence Political Participation? Examining the Role of Counter-and Pro-Attitudinal Exposure, Anger, and Personal Issue Importance," *International Journal of Communication* 11: 3011–29.

REFERENCES

Arceneaux, Kevin, Martin Johnson, and John Cryderman. 2013. "Communication, Persuasion, and the Conditioning Value of Selective Exposure: Like Minds May Unite and Divide but They Mostly Tune Out." *Political Communication* 30 (2): 213–31.

Baumgartner, Jody, and Jonathan S. Morris. 2006. "The Daily Show Effect: Candidate Evaluations, Efficacy, and American Youth." *American Politics Research* 34 (3): 341–367.

Baym, Geoffrey, and Jeffrey P. Jones. 2012. "News Parody in Global Perspective: Politics, Power, and Resistance." *Popular Communication* 10 (1–2): 2–13.

Becker, Amy B. 2014. "Playing with Politics: Online Political Parody, Affinity for Political Humor, Anxiety Reduction, and Implications for Political Efficacy." *Mass Communication and Society* 17 (3): 424–45.

Becker, Amy B., and Don J. Waisanen. 2013. "From Funny Features to Entertaining Effects: Connecting Approaches to Communication Research on Political Comedy." *Review of Communication* 13 (3): 161–83.

Booth-Butterfield, Melanie, Steven Booth-Butterfield, and Melissa Wanzer. 2007. "Funny Students Cope Better: Patterns of Humor Enactment and Coping Effectiveness." *Communication Quarterly* 55 (3): 299–315.

Boukes, Mark, Hajo G. Boomgaarden, Marjolein Moorman, and Claes H. de Vreese. 2015. "At Odds: Laughing and Thinking? The Appreciation, Processing, and Persuasiveness of Political Satire." *Journal of Communication* 65 (5): 721–44.

Cacioppo, John T., Richard E. Petty, Chuan Feng Kao, and Regina Rodriguez. 1986. "Central and Peripheral Routes to Persuasion: An Individual Difference Perspective." *Journal of Personality and Social Psychology* 51 (5): 1032–43.

Chen, Hsuan-Ting, Chen Gan, and Ping Sun. 2017. "How Does Political Satire Influence Political Participation? Examining the Role of Counter-and Pro-Attitudinal Exposure, Anger, and Personal Issue Importance." *International Journal of Communication* 11: 3011–29.

Coleman, Stephen, Anke Kuik, and Liesbet van Zoonen. 2009. "Laughter and Liability: The Politics of British and Dutch Television Satire." *The British Journal of Politics and International Relations* 11 (4): 652–65.

Fox, Julia R., Glory Koloen, and Volkan M. S. Sahin. 2007. "No Joke: A Comparison of Substance in the Daily Show with Jon Stewart and Broadcast Network Television Coverage of the 2004 Presidential Election Campaign." *Journal of Broadcasting & Electronic Media* 51 (2): 213–27.

Haigh, Michel M., and Aaron Heresco. 2010. "Late-Night Iraq: Monologue Joke Content and Tone from 2003 to 2007." *Mass Communication and Society* 13 (2): 157–73.

Hmielowski, Jay D., R. L. Holbert, and Jayeon Lee. 2011. "Predicting the Consumption of Political TV Satire: Affinity for Political Humor, The Daily Show, and The Colbert Report." *Communication Monographs* 78 (1): 96–114.

Holbert, R. Lance. 2013. "Developing a Normative Approach to Political Satire: An Empirical Perspective." *International Journal of Communication* 7 (Breaking Boundaries): 305–23.

———. 2016. "Entertainment Television and Political Campaigns: The Political Satire Appropriateness (PSA) Model." In *Praeger Handbook of Political Campaigning in the United States*, edited by W. L. Benoit. Volume I: Foundations and Campaign Media Edition, 171–90. Santa Barbara, CA: Praeger.

Holbert, R. Lance, Jay Hmielowski, Parul Jain, Julie Lather, and Alyssa Morey. 2011. "Adding Nuance to the Study of Political Humor Effects: Experimental Research on Juvenalian Satire versus Horatian Satire." *American Behavioral Scientist* 55 (3): 187–211.

Holbert, R. Lance, Jayeon Lee, Sarah Esralew, Whitney O. Walther, Jay D. Hmielowski, and Kristen D. Landreville. 2013a. "Affinity for Political Humor: An Assessment of Internal Factor Structure, Reliability, and Validity." *Humor* 26 (4): 551–72.

Holbert, R. Lance, John M. Tchernev, Whitney O. Walther, Sarah E. Esralew, and Kathryn Benski. 2013b. "Young Voter Perceptions of Political Satire as Persuasion: A Focus on Perceived Influence, Persuasive Intent, and Message Strength." *Journal of Broadcasting & Electronic Media* 57 (2): 170–86.

Iyengar, Shanto, and Kyu S. Hahn. 2009. "Red Media, Blue Media: Evidence of Ideological Selectivity in Media Use." *Journal of Communication* 59 (1): 19–39.

Knobloch-Westerwick, Silvia, and Simon M. Lavis. 2017. "Selecting Serious or Satirical, Supporting or Stirring News? Selective Exposure to Partisan versus Mockery News Online Videos." *Journal of Communication* 67 (1): 54–81.

Kuiper, Nicolas A., Rod A. Martin, and L. Joan Olinger. 1993. "Coping Humour, Stress, and Cognitive Appraisals." *Canadian Journal of Behavioural Science/ Revue Canadienne Des Sciences Du Comportement* 25 (1): 81–96.

LaMarre, Heather L., Kristen D. Landreville, Dannagal Young, and Nathan Gilkerson. 2014. "Humor Works in Funny Ways: Examining Satirical Tone as a Key Determinant in Political Humor Message Processing." *Mass Communication and Society* 17 (3): 400–23.

LaMarre, Heather L., and Whitney Walther. 2013. "Ability Matters: Testing the Differential Effects of Political News and Late-Night Political Comedy on Cognitive Responses and the Role of Ability in Micro-Level Opinion Formation." *International Journal of Public Opinion Research* 25 (3): 303–22.

Lee, Hoon, and Nojin Kwak. 2014. "The Affect Effect of Political Satire: Sarcastic Humor, Negative Emotions, and Political Participation." *Mass Communication and Society* 17 (3): 307–28.

Markus, Hazel, and Robert B. Zajonc. 1985. "The Cognitive Perspective in Social Psychology." In *Handbook of Social Psychology*, edited by Gardner Lindzey and Elliot Aronson. 3rd edition. Volume 1, 137–230. New York: Random House.

McLeod, D. M., G. M. Kosicki, and J. M. McLeod. 2009. "Political Communication Effects." In *Media Effects: Advances in Theory and Research*, edited by Jennings Bryant and Mary Beth Oliver. 3rd edition, 228–51. New York: Routledge.

Meyer, John C. 2000. "Humor as a Double-Edged Sword: Four Functions of Humor in Communication." *Communication Theory* 10 (3): 310–31.

Morey, Alyssa C., Steven B. Kleinman, and Mark Boukes. 2018. "Political Talk Preferences: Selection of Similar and Different Discussion Partners and Groups." *International Journal of Communication* 12: 359–79.

Morris, Jonathan S. 2009. "The Daily Show with Jon Stewart and Audience Attitude Change during the 2004 Party Conventions." *Political Behavior* 31 (1): 79–102.

Nabi, Robin L., Emily Moyer-Gusé, and Sahara Byrne. 2007. "All Joking Aside: A Serious Investigation into the Persuasive Effect of Funny Social Issue Messages." *Communication Monographs* 74 (1): 29–54.

Oppenheimer, Daniel M., Tom Meyvis, and Nicolas Davidenko. 2009. "Instructional Manipulation Checks: Detecting Satisficing to Increase Statistical Power." *Journal of Experimental Social Psychology* 45 (4): 867–72.

Prior, Markus. 2009. "The Immensely Inflated News Audience: Assessing Bias in Self-Reported News Exposure." *Public Opinion Quarterly* 73 (1): 130–43.

———. 2013. "Media and Political Polarization." *Annual Review of Political Science* 16 (1): 101–27.

Schouten, Joy. 2017. "The News of the Future: Satire. The Effects of Satire Compared to Traditional Forms of News on Comprehension and Political Engagement." MA thesis, University of Amsterdam.

Stroud, Natalie Jomini. 2010. "Polarization and Partisan Selective Exposure." *Journal of Communication* 60 (3): 556–76.

Valkenburg, Patti M., and Jochen Peter. 2013. "The Differential Susceptibility to Media Effects Model." *Journal of Communication* 63 (2): 221–43.

Wanzer, Melissa Bekelja, Melanie Booth-Butterfield, and Steve Booth-Butterfield. 1996. "Are Funny People Popular? An Examination of Humor Orientation, Loneliness, and Social Attraction." *Communication Quarterly* 44 (1): 42–52.

Young, Dannagal Goldthwaite. 2008. "The Daily Show as New Journalism: In Their Own Words." In *Laughing Matters: Humor and American Politics in the Media Age*, edited by Jody C Baumgartner and Jonathan S. Morris, 241–62. New York: Routledge.

Young, Dannagal Goldthwaite. 2013. "Laughter, Learning, or Enlightenment? Viewing and Avoidance Motivations behind The Daily show and The Colbert Report." *Journal of Broadcasting & Electronic Media* 57 (2): 153–69.

Young, Dannagal G., and Russell M. Tisinger. 2006. "Dispelling Late-Night Myths: News Consumption among Late-Night Comedy Viewers and the Predictors of Exposure to Various Late-Night Shows." *The Harvard International Journal of Press/Politics* 11 (3): 113–34.

Chapter 12

Freedom of the Press in Israeli and American Satire

Edo Steinberg

A wave of populism and nationalism across the world now threatens the core values of many democratic nations. In various democracies, from the United States and Western Europe to Eastern Europe and the Middle East, nationalist candidates like Donald Trump, parties like Alternative for Germany, and referenda like Brexit have gained substantial popular support. Contempt for established elites, including what is perceived as the media elite, is one of the most potent fuels fanning the flames of this movement. Of particular concern is government hostility toward journalists, attempts to influence the media, and declining support for democratic institutions.

This chapter focuses on satirical coverage of threats to the core democratic value of freedom of speech and freedom of the press in the United States and Israel. Core values are cultural, political, and moral principles that are widely shared by a society as a result of its historical development. While some core values are unique to specific countries, others are shared. For example, liberal democracies tend to have some core values in common due to a shared philosophical evolution going back all the way to ancient Greece. In a stable society, challenging these values is seen as challenging society itself, and those who do so are often ostracized.[1]

Freedom of the press is one such core value shared by democratic nations. It is a pillar of liberal democracy. A strong Fourth Estate is a prerequisite for an informed citizenry. Without journalists fulfilling the surveillance function of the press, citizens cannot remain informed about the actions of their leaders and cannot keep them accountable. A country with unaccountable leaders is, arguably, no longer truly democratic.

The United States and Israel were selected for comparison as exemplars of the populist wave in democracies. In particular, both are experiencing populist attacks on their core values by their heads of government, President Donald

Trump and Prime Minister Benjamin Netanyahu. These take the form, among other things, of attacks on those tasked with scrutinizing the government's actions in the media and law enforcement agencies. These attacks represent two of the three elements of constitutional retrogression, the gradual erosion of liberal democratic norms of free and fair elections, the right to free speech and association, and the rule of law, which ultimately lead to constitutional crises.[2] While the attacks are not identical in both countries, they have much in common, including a disdain for criticism of people in power. Additionally, Israeli politicians adopted some of the rhetoric from President Trump's vocabulary, such as the increasing use of the term, "fake news." Furthermore, despite these attacks, both countries have vibrant media systems, including critical investigative journalism and political satire.

One case study for each country was selected: for the United States, Donald Trump's October 2017 comments regarding network licenses; and for Israel, the week in March 2017 during which Prime Minister Benjamin Netanyahu attempted to change the structure of public broadcasting and had his libel suit against a journalist argued in court. In both cases, these actions caused a stir in the media regarding possible chilling effects on the free press, if not immediate threats to most journalists. By threatening such measures, even if the president and prime minister are not capable of carrying them out on their own due to a lack of legal authority, they signal that they can curb press freedoms in other ways, such as limiting access to government officials and information.

THE ROLE OF SATIRE IN THE REINFORCEMENT OF DEMOCRATIC CORE VALUES

There is debate about whether satire emerges when there is a strong normative framework in society or when such a shared framework is lacking, with the middle ground being that it emerges when it exists but is being seriously challenged.[3] In this chapter, the core values are a widely shared political, cultural, and moral framework under threat. While moral norms are not synonymous with political and cultural norms, they are greatly intertwined, the former being informed by the latter two. At a time when long-standing principles of democratic governance are questioned, satire should be especially prominent in holding up a mirror to society and reminding the audience of the importance of those principles. Here, satire, as an important form of mass communication, fulfills the cultural transmission function of media, conveying the most basic shared values to viewers.[4]

Modern satire is rooted in the Enlightenment movement.[5] The Enlightenment, freedom of the press, and satire all share critical thinking as a central characteristic. Satire was used to criticize conservatives who thought uncritically about the existing order. It was also directed inward, at rival factions within the Enlightenment movement, as well as at the Enlightenment itself, since self-criticism is an important aspect of the movement.

Satire has several other important functions in society, all related to conveying and upholding norms. It exposes hypocrisy and governmental and societal injustices, promotes a critical public discourse, and allows as many citizens as possible to join the conversation. Other forms of political criticism also share these functions, but satire's uniqueness is the fact that it is an artful blend of humor, wit, and playfulness.[6] It also adds biting criticism and aggression to the blend.[7]

Jones argues that the comedians of the twenty-first century have a new role, which is a development of the traditional role of satirists. They fill a role that political pundits cannot, as they are criticizing not only politics, but traditional political commentary.[8] Likewise, Baym also suggests that satire, focusing on *The Daily Show with Jon Stewart*, is more critical of politics than the news media is and, as such, is an alternative form of journalism and a role model for traditional journalists.[9]

This double role is particularly heightened in a time when trust in the media has been declining, though it has somewhat rebounded in 2017.[10] Comedic news programs in the United States now may serve as both media critics and a form of alternative journalism, even more so than when Jones and Baym first proposed the existence of this role.

CRITICISM OF THE MEDIA IN POLITICAL SATIRE

Although news parody shows have been on television for decades, studies of their critiques of the news media have focused mainly on *The Daily Show* and, to a lesser extent, on its spin-off, *The Colbert Report*. *The Daily Show with Jon Stewart* was the first to use the format to focus on criticizing both politics and the news media itself rather than to focus on generating punchlines.[11]

Some studies have examined the show's critiques of the media. A content analysis found that *The Daily Show* dedicated as much as 15 percent of its stories to the media in 2005, much of it critical.[12] Another study found that the number of episodes containing critiques of the media grew steadily over the years from 2000 to 2012, with the focus shifting from personal foibles to professional standards.[13]

While Jon Stewart is no longer hosting *The Daily Show* and Stephen Colbert is no longer hosting *The Colbert Report*, there is reason to believe that many late-night comedy shows will follow in their footsteps rather than the largely non-satirical tradition of shows like *The Tonight Show*. Colbert himself is now the host of *The Late Show* and many *Daily Show* alumni now host their own programs. *Late Night with Seth Meyers* has also come into its own as a political satire show.[14]

Had it not been for the election of Donald Trump and his frequent attacks on the media, it would have been easy to predict that American satirical shows would continue to be very critical of news organizations. However, now news parodies may also find themselves defending the First Amendment rights of the news media.

Israeli satire is less focused on critiquing the media, and there has not been much research on the subject. However, the country's leading satirical show, *Eretz Nehederet*, is structured as a fake news program, and used to have regular appearances by journalist characters.

FREEDOM OF THE PRESS

Freedom of expression and of the press are cornerstones of democracy. Thomas Jefferson, who believed that an informed public was the only way to make sure the government would remain answerable to the people, famously pronounced that "were it left to me to decide whether we should have a government without newspapers, or newspapers without a government, I should not hesitate a moment to prefer the latter."[15] The United States enshrined this right in the First Amendment to the Constitution, and though the American version is the most extreme (i.e., closest to absolute freedom),[16] all other liberal democracies have a free press and grant free speech to their citizens. Arguably, without these freedoms, a country cannot be called a liberal democracy. A free press is such a strong symbol of democracy that even countries like Russia include it in their constitutions and laws in order to be able to claim they are a free society, even if in practice censorship is rampant.[17]

THREATS TO FREEDOM OF THE PRESS IN THE UNITED STATES

During the presidential election, then-candidate Donald Trump often claimed the media was not treating him fairly. This continued, and even escalated, after the election and once he entered office. He has taken to calling the media "fake news," and has gone as far as calling broadcast and print outlets "the enemies of the American People."[18] Pro-Trump media outlets that have often promoted hoaxes, such as Gateway Pundit, have been included in

White House press briefings in what looks like an attempt to replace tough questions with friendly ones[19] while in at least one incident, mainstream outlets were excluded from off-camera briefings with then-Press Secretary Sean Spicer.[20]

President Trump continues to regularly tweet accusations of "fake news" at the media and to call out CNN reporters at press conferences. He even retweeted a video of himself from one of his World Wrestling Entertainment (WWE) appearances in which he beats up an opponent, whose face is replaced by the CNN logo. In the midst of the controversy over his ambiguous condemnation of the neo-Nazi rally in Charlottesville, Virginia, he also retweeted and quickly deleted a cartoon of a train, with the word "Trump" on its front and side, running over a person with the CNN logo superimposed on his face.[21] At his own rally in Phoenix, he accused the media of distorting his reaction to the Charlottesville rally.[22]

On October 11, 2017, President Trump published two posts on Twitter that raised the possibility of revoking the broadcast licenses of NBC and other networks due to perceived bias. This followed unflattering reports by NBC News that the president sought to increase the American nuclear arsenal tenfold, reportedly leading to Secretary of State Rex Tillerson calling him a moron behind his back. Despite the fact that the president lacks the authority to revoke licenses, and that individual stations have licenses rather than the networks as a whole, such pronouncements can be seen as attempts to create a chilling effect among journalists and news outlets. He also repeated sentiments to that effect in person at the White House that same day.[23]

American Case Study: "Licenses Must Be Challenged"

As mentioned above, on October 11, 2017, following an unflattering report on NBC regarding the background for Secretary of State Rex Tillerson's private comments calling President Trump a moron, the president tweeted a series of attacks on the media. Two of those tweets raised the question of revoking broadcast licenses. "With all of the Fake News coming out of NBC and the Networks, at what point is it appropriate to challenge their License? Bad for country!,"[24] read one tweet in the morning, followed in the evening by a tweet saying, "Network news has become so partisan, distorted and fake that licenses must be challenged and, if appropriate, revoked. Not fair to public!"[25] The same day, he told the press at the White House that it was "frankly disgusting the way the press is able to write whatever they want to write and people should look into it."[26]

Stephen Colbert responded that night on *The Late Show* by saying, "Sir, for the record, people did look into it. In fact, *We* the people looked into it and thought, 'yeah, they should write whatever they want.' You should read it sometime. It's a very short read." By harkening back to the Founding Fathers and the phrase "we the people," Colbert is not simply pointing out dry constitutional law. He is emphasizing the shared values of "we the people," one of the most important of which is the freedom of the press.

Next, Colbert showed Trump's tweet challenging NBC's license because of what the president calls "fake news" on the network. Colbert then asked two questions: "When is it appropriate for Twitter to deactivate the account of a president who doesn't believe in the First Amendment? And can that be yesterday?"

Colbert again emphasized the founding principles inherent in the First Amendment. However, there is an undeniable paradox here when Colbert essentially asks Twitter to punish Trump's assault on freedom of speech by curtailing the president's own freedom of speech, though as the most powerful person in the country, he could easily get his message across through other methods and media platforms.

Colbert did not frame all his critiques in terms of freedom of the press or the First Amendment. For instances, Colbert discussed a tweet in which Trump accuses the media for falsely reporting that White House Chief of Staff John Kelly is about to be fired, but says that no media outlet actually reported such a story about Kelly. "Oh my God, the Fake News is coming from inside his head! Get out of there!"

The same night, Seth Meyers on *The Late Show*, started out with a silly, non-substantive joke, saying that if NBC didn't lose its license for a monkey hospital show, it won't lose it for Trump, either. However, he then continued into a criticism that, like Colbert, referenced the First Amendment, but went even further. He asked whether President Trump was having trouble reading it. He then suggested putting it in red to make it more visible, then "how about in peach, yeah, in peach." Here he is suggesting that Trump's attacks on the media are worthy of impeachment. This implies that Meyers sees Trump as someone who does not share the value of freedom of the press and, in fact, is an active threat to it. After all, one does not call for a president's impeachment lightly.

In his "A Closer Look" segment, Meyers presents Trump as a threat to the media outlets he does not like. If Trump had his way, he says, the channel guide would be limited to two channels, Fox News and the Golf Channel. Meyers also links Trump's attitude toward the media to his threats to sue the women who accused him of sexual assault and harassment. Meyers sees both as manifestations of Trump's attempts to silence his critics. Here the show does not specifically tie this to freedom of speech as a core value but to Trump's own personal inability to hear dissenting voices.

Surprisingly, even the less-satirical *Tonight Show Starring Jimmy Fallon* discussed Trump as a threat to democracy. In response to Trump's comments about NBC's license, Fallon, whose show airs on NBC before Seth Meyers, joked, "America is like, hey, you can threaten our democracy but you do not mess with *This Is Us*," in reference to the network's popular drama. He also joked that when the president talked about the First Amendment, he confused it with the rule about not discussing what happens at Fight Club. His references to democracy and the Constitution were much briefer and lighthearted than Colbert and Meyers, but were no less critical of the president's comments.

Jimmy Kimmel, who is more political than Fallon but much less than Colbert and Meyers, did not discuss Trump's comments about the media on his show on October 11. Equally non-political James Corden on *The Late Late Show* decided to focus on the fact that Donald Trump capitalized the word "license" in his tweet, saying it was "bad for grammar." He also joked about Fox News getting its license from a man who sells fake IDs behind a liquor store. Corden does not criticize Trump's statements, focusing on jokes instead.

The Daily Show with Trevor Noah (TDS) and *The Opposition with Jordan Klepper*, both on Comedy Central, were on break on October 11. The next episode of *TDS* was the first in a special week of shows in Chicago, focusing on Chicago issues, which may explain why the show did not address Trump's comments. Klepper's show did not address the comments on his next episode, either. Klepper discussed the Values Voters Summit, which he could have used to contrast the conservative convention with the value of freedom of the press, but he did not do so.

On *Saturday Night Live*, which aired on October 14, the show barely mentioned the president's comments about the press, except for saying that had the press been able to write whatever they wanted to write, they would have written that Hillary Clinton is the next president. Of all the major news of the week, including the first revelations of the Harvey Weinstein's sexual abuse scandal, as well as other news related to Trump, the show decided not to focus on freedom of the press, not even in the news parody segment's "Weekend Update" or during the cold open, which featured Trump (Alec Baldwin) addressing truck drivers. The only sketch that focused on the Trump administration's relationship with the press was one where advisor Kellyanne Conway is likened to the killer clown Pennywise from the movie *It*. However, the focus is on Conway's wish to get on the news rather than Trump's attacks on the media.

Three other weekly shows were also examined. However, they did not include references to Trump's comments. These shows were *Last Week Tonight with John Oliver*, *Full Frontal with Samantha Bee*, and *The Rundown with Robin Thede*.

THREATS TO FREEDOM OF THE PRESS IN ISRAEL

In Israel, Prime Minister Netanyahu has stepped up his attacks on the press as well. He has often claimed journalists who aired exposés critical of him were leftist partisans. He has sent long rebuttals to journalists, demanding that they read them in full. American rhetoric has even seeped into Israeli political discourse. Netanyahu's public security minister accused liberal newspaper Haaretz of being "fake news," using the English phrase in a Hebrew sentence.[27] Netanyahu used the term himself at a rally in front of his cheering supporters.[28]

Additionally, much like Donald Trump has given multiple interviews to friendly hosts on Fox News while ignoring other outlets, Netanyahu has done the same with Channel 20, a small religious heritage channel with a right-wing bent. Because the channel's license requires it to focus on Jewish heritage and limits its news coverage to one hour a day, the Netanyahu interviews were possibly violations of the license, leading to possible fines or even closure.[29] The operators of Channel 20 also won a tender to broadcast from the Knesset, on a channel equivalent to C-SPAN, but the tender was canceled by the Supreme Court due to irregularities.[30]

Prime Minister Netanyahu also served simultaneously as communication minister from November 2014 to February 2017. In this capacity, he spearheaded several changes to the television market and media regulations. Following an independent commission's recommendation to merge two independent regulatory bodies into one, he attempted to merge them into the Communication Ministry under his control.[31]

In 2014, the Knesset passed legislation to dismantle the Israel Broadcasting Authority (IBA), the public television and radio broadcaster, and replace it with the new Israel Broadcasting Corporation (IBC). The IBA had existed since 1965, and though originally envisioned as an independent broadcaster like the BBC, it was often politicized, was structurally and economically inefficient, and its television arm, once Israel's only channel, suffered from very low ratings in the last two decades. There was wide consensus about the need to reform it, if not scrap it altogether and begin anew. The new IBC, also known as Kan (Here), was meant to be independent, especially its news division.[32]

In March 2017, Netanyahu opened negotiations with his coalition partner, Treasury Minister Moshe Kahlon, over the future of the IBC. Two months before it was set to replace the Israeli Broadcasting Authority, Netanyahu suddenly demanded that he appoint the IBC's heads, that its news division be a separate entity and demanded that the IBC would not start broadcasting until this separation was completed. A compromise was reached and new legislation was passed that allowed the IBC to take over from the IBA on

May 15, with its news division set to be split from it in the near future.[33] However, the Supreme Court has delayed the creation of a separate news corporation.[34]

Netanyahu has also had a tumultuous relationship with the commercial channels. He at times intervened on behalf of Channel 10, which had aired investigative reports about him, trying to convince regulators to forgive some of the channel's debts to the government, and at other times attempted to shut down the channel, citing those debts.[35] Netanyahu himself admitted that he attempted to shut the channel down when he defended himself against police recommendations to indict him, including on the charge that his intervention on behalf of Channel 10 was a quid pro quo for bribes from channel co-owner Arnon Milchan.[36]

In the name of the diversification of the media market, Netanyahu forced two companies that had shared one channel, Channel 2, to split it into two channels, but failed to force them to split their news division immediately, which could have potentially weakened another news outlet that had aired exposés about him. The companies had opposed the move because they did not believe the Israeli advertising market was large enough to sustain three commercial channels.[37]

Prime Minister Netanyahu and his wife Sara have also filed several libel suits against journalists. Some were successful, including a lawsuit against journalist Igal Sarna, who claimed in 2016 in a Facebook post that Sara Netanyahu kicked her husband out of a car in the middle of a busy highway, stopping the whole motorcade of security vehicles. The judge ruled that Sarna must pay the Netanyahus 100,000 shekels (about $28,300) in damages plus 15,000 shekels for court expenses.[38]

Israeli Case Study: IBC and Netanyahu's Libel Suit

In March 2017, two important events took place that are relevant to the issue of freedom of the Israeli press. Benjamin and Sara Netanyahu's libel suit against Igal Sarna was argued in court; and at the same time, negotiations between Prime Minister Netanyahu and Treasury Minister Kahlon regarding the fate of the IBC's news division were underway.

Israel, as a smaller country and smaller media market, has fewer satirical shows than the United States. The two longest running and highest rated satire shows currently on television are *Eretz Nehederet (Wonderful Country)* and *Gav Ha'Uma (Back of the Nation)*, both of which air weekly. *Eretz Nehederet* could be described as an expanded version of *Saturday Night Live*'s Weekend Update segment. The host (or anchor), Eyal Kitzis, interviews cast members in character in the studio and presents "field pieces," which unlike *Daily Show* field pieces, do not usually include correspondents interviewing real people but are pre-taped sketches. *Gav Ha'Uma*, on the other hand, is a panel show. Host Lior Schleien and panelists comment on the week's news. The show also often features interviews with politicians. It usually ends with a monologue by Schleien.

On an episode that aired on March 20, *Eretz Nehederet* started with a studio discussion about the second anniversary of the current government. Netanyahu says he just returned from China, where he learned "how they control the media in a civilized democracy." While most of the first part of the sketch is about other issues, it is full of jokes about Netanyahu trying to control the IBC and other outlets. Then it turns to the "public broadcasting piñata game," where one coalition leader invites other politicians to hit a piñata representing the IBC, but Kahlon tries to protect it.

Kitzis accuses Netanyahu of trying to control another media outlet, on top of pro-Netanyahu billionaire Sheldon Adelson's Yisrael Hayom. Netanyahu says he is just trying to include "as many of my views" as possible, in a riff on his claim that he is trying to allow a whole spectrum of political views to be included in the media. Kitzis worriedly comments that the media is about to become subservient, at which point Igal Sarna enters the conversation and vows not to allow it to happen. Kitzis asks him whether he stands by the Facebook post that prompted the Netanyahus' libel suit against him. He says that he does but the show presents him as an unreliable journalist who posted gossip that his newspaper deemed unworthy of printing.

Kitzis then asks Netanyahu whether the fact that he sued Sarna but not the other journalists who published or aired exposés about him means that the other journalists' stories are true. Netanyahu says that will be determined by a court the day he will be stupid enough to sue reporters for factual stories. This sketch criticizes both an unscrupulous journalist and politicians who try to curb the free press. However, by contrasting Sarna with other journalists and saying their stories are true, it emphasizes that the criticism is not aimed at the media as a whole but toward one bad apple. In fact, it defends the integrity of other journalists and of the profession as a whole when it points out that Sarna's newspaper did not publish his unfounded claims.

Another sketch was a fake promo for BBTV (a play on Bibi, Benjamin Netanyahu's nickname). It is a new cable box (known in Hebrew as a con-verter), "the perfect channel package that will convert even the last of the leftists." One of the channels is Channel 20, the right-leaning religious heri-tage channel, where host Shimon Riklin (impersonated by a cast member) is shown adoringly interviewing Sara Netanyahu with softball questions. Another "channel" features Sandra Ringler, a television personality who is also Sara Netanyahu's personal stylist, and the Netanyahu family dog. Ringler puts positive spin on negative stories such as overcrowded hospitals. She also says that investigative journalist Raviv Drucker will soon come out to discuss one of the criminal investigations involving Netanyahu, and that she will give him a hotdog-coated blazer, which the dog immediately starts biting. This is followed by *MasterChef* and *Amazing Race* parodies depicting the Netanyahus as corrupt and decadent, and Riklin and Ringler as the couple's unquestioning followers. This, like the Meyers joke about Fox News and the Golf Channel, shows leaders who are uninterested in a critical news media. Freedom of the press is not explicitly expressed as a value but is heavily implied. It includes a depiction of the Netanyahu family and their followers avoiding hard questions and attacking those, like Drucker, who investigate them.

On *Gav Ha'Uma,* in an episode that aired on March 25, Lior Schleien jokes that Netanyahu learned in China that you can eat democracy's watchdog. Then, in a callback to a classic Israeli sketch from the late 1990s, during Netanyahu's first term, Schleien says in a sexually suggestive manner that Netanyahu should open the IBC and control it. He also calls the communication bill the government was trying to pass "dictatorial," saying it is meant to threaten the private media outlets.

Members of the press are worried that freedom of speech is in danger, Schleien says, adding that they complain of attempts to silence them. He jokes that "we are not saying this, because complaining is for leftists" and that the show's panel isn't afraid of the government, because they can tell the truth about politicians without media outlets. He then asks the panel how to do this, and they offer different methods for pointing out criticisms. For instance, one panelist recommends using Ben Gurion Airport's public address system, voiced by famous chef Gil Hovav, to point out that just like Hovav makes security announcements without having a military background, Defense Minister Avigdor Lieberman doesn't have such a background either.

A few days before the episode aired, when asked by Minister Kahlon why he decided to demand changes to the IBC's structure, Netanyahu controversially replied that "my Mizrahi gene popped up," referring to the word for Jews of Middle Eastern and North African descent, a group to which he does not belong. He later apologized for the comment. Panelist Tom Aharon, who is Mizrahi, says this is a new Mizrahi stereotype he never heard of, asking since when they are known for trying to shutter public broadcasting corporations. He says that now people will point at him on the street and say, "look at that thug, violating the independence of journalists and media organizations in order to preserve his power and position."

In the next segment, about ultra-Orthodox Jews rioting in protest of military conscription, Schleien inserts a critique of Culture Minister Miri Regev asking what good the IBC will bring if the government does not control it. He says she can get the ultra-Orthodox to pray for the IBC to close.

Both shows are highly critical of the attacks on the media and protective of the journalistic profession. They both include references to democracy, even contrasting Israel with China, which Netanyahu had just visited.

CONCLUSION: AN INTERNATIONAL COMPARISON

Comparing any two countries is tricky. Israel and the United States, for example, have very different political and media systems. Israel does not have a constitution or anything akin to the First Amendment, but as a democratic country, it does share freedom of speech as a core value with the United States and other democracies. Israel also doesn't have as many satirical shows, especially long running ones. For this reason, any comparison should be done carefully. However, most importantly, both countries share strong, independent media outlets, both in terms of journalism and satire.

Since the various American shows did not treat Trump's threat against NBC in the same way, running the gamut from dedicating whole segments to it to ignoring it completely, a more systematic examination with a large sample is required in order to reach more sweeping conclusions about the differences between the countries.

However, even with the present case studies, the American shows that did dedicate time to freedom of the press were similar to the two Israeli shows in emphasizing its importance and defending journalists. Satire shows in both countries present journalists as crucial elements of democratic governance. They defend their rights and, instead of the institutional critiques of the journalistic profession common to Jon Stewart's *Daily Show*,[39] they do not present the media as being in crisis due to its own failings. On the Israeli shows, critiques of individual journalists are framed in terms of those individuals' misconduct rather than an indictment of the profession as a whole.

In both countries, critiques of attacks on the press served to convey the value of a free press to democracy. As such, they fulfilled the important function of cultural transmission.[40] They did not usually do this in the same man-.ner, however. Two of the American television shows, *The Late Show with Stephen Colbert* and *Late Night with Seth Meyers*, pointed toward the First Amendment and the principles on which the Founding Fathers established the country. The Israeli shows did not do anything that could be considered the Israeli equivalent. Since Israel does not have a constitution nor were personal liberties important motivators behind Israel's founding, Israeli satirists could not be expected to use the same appeals. However, they could have implied that attacks on the press were un-Israeli or did not represent Israeli values. Neither did they contrast Netanyahu's attitude toward freedom of the press with the attitude of "the people," as Colbert did with Trump when he references the preamble to the Constitution. However, by no means did they let Netanyahu off the hook. Their criticisms of his attacks on the media were consistent, clear, and framed as threats to democracy itself.

Interestingly, shows from both countries sometimes used similar tactics to portray attacks on the media. Both Seth Meyers and *Eretz Nehederet* present Trump and Netanyahu as creating their own channel package. This is reminiscent of an earlier *Eretz Nehederet* sketch from the 2009 election night broadcast. In that sketch, nationalist politician Avigdor Lieberman's character declares that all remote controls will be replaced with one that has one button, "a variety of channel [sic]," his own. In these three sketches, the senior politician is depicted as a threat to all media outlets that are not in his good graces.

Despite systemic differences, American and Israeli satire conveyed similar values about the importance of freedom of the press to democracy, sometimes even portraying their subjects in similar manners. Future research should explore how satire in other democratic countries facing similar pressures deals with this issue, as well as various other core democratic values.

NOTES

1. Jerzy Smolicz, "Core Values and Cultural Identity." *Ethnic and Racial Studies* 4, no. 1 (1981): 75.

2. Nadiv Mordechay and Yaniv Roznai, "A Jewish and (Declining) Democratic State? Constitutional Retrogression in Israel." *Maryland Law Review* 77 (2017): 252–53, doi:10.3366/ajicl.2011.0005.

3. Dustin H Griffin, *Satire: A Critical Reintroduction* (Lexington: University Press of Kentucky, 1994), 134.

4. Charles R. Wright, "Functional Analysis and Mass Communication." *The Public Opinion Quarterly* 24, no. 4 (1960): 608–09, doi:http://www.jstor.org/stable/2746529.

5. Gidi Nevo, *Moshav Letzim: Ha'rhetorica Shel Ha'satira Ha'ivrit [The Rhetoric of Hebrew Satire]* (Or Yehuda, Israel: Dvir, 2010), 12.

6. Rachel Paine Caufield, "The Influence of 'Infoenterpropagainment': Exploring the Power of Political Satire as a Distinct Form of Political Humor." in *Laughing Matters: Humor and American Politics in the Media Age*, eds. Jody C Baumgartner and Jonathan S. Morris (New York: Routledge, 2008), 6–8.

7. George A. Test, *Satire: Spirit and Art* (Tampa: University of South Florida Press, 1991), 15–31; David Alexander, *Leitzan Ha'hatzer ve'hashalit: Satira Politit Be'Yisrael [The Court Jester and the Ruler: Political Satire in Israel]* (Tel-Aviv: Sifriyat Poalim, 1985), 17.

8. Jeffrey P. Jones, *Entertaining Politics: New Political Television and Civic Culture* (Lanham, MD: Rowman & Littlefield, 2005), 100.

9. Geoffrey Baym, "The Daily Show: Discursive Integration and the Reinvention of Political Journalism." *Political Communication* 22, no. 3 (July 2005): 268, doi:10.1080/10584600591006492.

10. Art Swift, "Democrats' Confidence in Mass Media Rises Sharply from 2016," last modified September 21, 2017, http://news.gallup.com/poll/219824/democrats-confidence-mass-media-rises-sharply-2016.aspx.

11. Baym, "The Daily Show: Discursive Integration," 263–64, 268.

12. Paul R. Brewer and Emily Marquardt, "Mock News and Democracy: Analyzing The Daily Show." *Atlantic Journal of Communication* 15, no. 4 (2007): 261.

13. Edo Steinberg and Julia R. Fox, "News You Can't Use: A Content Analysis of the Daily Show's Media Criticism." Paper presented at the Association for Education in Journalism and Mass Communication Annual Conference, Montreal, Canada (Montreal, QC, Canada, 2014), 14–16.

14. Dave Itzkoff, "Seth Meyers Confronts the Trump Era on 'Late Night.'" *The New York Times*, January 25, 2017, https://www.nytimes.com/2017/01/25/arts/television/seth-meyers-late-night-donald-trump.html.

15. Thomas Jefferson, "From Thomas Jefferson to Edward Carrington, 16 January 1787." *Archives.Gov*, 1787, https://founders.archives.gov/documents/Jefferson/01-11-02-0047. (Accessed October 1, 2017).

16. Stephen Gardbaum, "The Myth and the Reality of American Constitutional Exceptionalism." *Michigan Law Review* 107, no. 3 (2008): 401–02.

17. Doris A. Graber, "Freedom of the Press: Theories and Realities." In *The Oxford Handbook of Political Communication*, eds. Kate Kenski and Kathleen Hall Jamieson (New York: Oxford University Press, 2015), 237, doi:10.1093/oxfordhb/9780199793471.013.80.

18. Matea Gold and Jenna Johnson, "Trump Calls the Media 'the Enemy of the American People.'" *The Washington Post*, February 17, 2017, https://www.washingtonpost.com/news/post-politics/wp/2017/02/17/trump-calls-the-media-the-enemy-of-the-american-people/.

19. Ben Schreckinger, "'Real News' Joins the White House Briefing Room." *Politico*, February 15, 2017, http://www.politico.com/magazine/story/2017/02/fake-news-gateway-pundit-white-house-trump-briefing-room-214781.

20. Callum Borchers, "White House Blocks CNN, New York Times from Press Briefing Hours after Trump Slams Media." *The Washington Post*, February 24, 2017, https://www.washingtonpost.com/news/the-fix/wp/2017/02/24/white-house-blocks-cnn-new-york-times-from-press-briefing-hours-after-trump-slams-media/.

21. Eileen Sullivan and Maggie Haberman, "Trump Shares, Then Deletes, Twitter Post of Train Hitting Cartoon Person Covered by CNN Logo." *The New York Times*, August 15, 2017, https://www.nytimes.com/2017/08/15/us/politics/trump-shares-then-deletes-twitter-post-of-cnn-cartoon-being-hit-by-train.html?mcubz=3&_r=0.

22. Jennifer Epstein, "Trump Hits Media, Angrily Defends Charlottesville Response." *Bloomberg*, August 23, 2017, https://www.bloomberg.com/news/articles/2017-08-22/trump-seeks-rebound-with-rally-focus-on-immigration-in-arizona.

23. Peter Baker and Cecilia Kang, "Trump Threatens NBC over Nuclear Weapons Report." *The New York Times*, October 11, 2017, https://www.nytimes.com/2017/10/11/us/politics/trump-nbc-fcc-broadcast-license.html.

24. Donald Trump (@realDonaldTrump), "With All of the Fake News Coming Out of NBC and the Networks, at What Point is it Appropriate to Challenge their License? Bad for country!" *Twitter post*, October 11, 2017, https://twitter.com/realDonaldTrump/status/918112884630093825.

25. Donald Trump (@realDonaldTrump), "Network News has Become so Partisan, Distorted and Fake that Licenses must be Challenged and, if Appropriate, Revoked. Not Fair to Public!" *Twitter post*, October 11, 2017, https://twitter.com/realDonaldTrump/status/918267396493922304.

26. Baker and Kang, "Trump Threatens NBC over Nuclear Weapons Report."

27. Gilad Erdan, "Haaretz: Gam Fake News v'gam Megabim et Peilei Ha-BDS [Haaretz: Both Fake News and Supporters of BDS Activists]." *Facebook*, March 22, 2017, https://www.facebook.com/gilad.erdan/photos/a.225201850853267.56972.207139259326193/1570811912958914/?type=3&theater.

28. Jonathan Lis and Lee Yaron, "Netanyahu Assails Israel's 'Fake News Industry' to Thousands of Supporters." *Haaretz (English Edition)*, August 30, 2017, http://www.haaretz.com/israel-news/1.809851.

29. Marissa Newman, "Right-Wing Channel 20 Faces Closure over News Offerings." *The Times of Israel*, September 7, 2017, https://www.timesofisrael.com/right-wing-channel-20-faces-closure-over-news-offerings/.

30. Raoul Wootliff and TOI Staff, "Right-Leaning Channel 20 Loses Rights to Broadcast Knesset TV." *The Times of Israel*, December 7, 2017, https://www.timesofisrael.com/right-leaning-channel-20-loses-rights-to-broadcast-knesset-tv/.

31. "Freedom of the Press 2017: Press Freedom's Dark Horizon - Country Report: Israel," Freedom House, accessed September 1, 2017, https://freedomhouse.org/report/freedom-press/2017/israel.

32. Asaf Wiener and Elad Man, "Hamechokek Ke'measder: Migbalot va'ilutzei Chakika Be'asdarat Tikshoret ve'shidurim [Legislator as Regulator: The Limitations of Media Regulation Legislation]." *Hukim [Laws]* (forthcoming): 13, 33, https://papers.ssrn.com/sol3/papers.cfm?abstract_id=3063865.

33. Shai Niv, "Pshara Be'nosse Ha'taagid: Tukam Chevrat Chadashot Nifredet Be'hanhala Chadasha [Compromise Regarding the Corporation: A Separate News Corporation Will Be Established with New Management]." *Globes*, March 30, 2017, http://www.globes.co.il/news/article.aspx?did=1001183329.

34. Aviv Guter, "Bagatz Romez La'medina: Yitachen She'nevatel et Ha'chok Le'hakamat Taagid Ha'chadashot [Supreme Court Hints to Government: We May Overturn the Law to Establish a News Corporation]." *Calcalist*, November 11, 2017, https://www.calcalist.co.il/marketing/articles/0,7340,L-3724469,00.html.

35. Nati Tucker, "Netanyahu Amad Meachorei Sidrat Hakalot Le'Arutz 10 She'be'baalut Mekoravav Milchan ve'Lauder [Netanyahu Was behind a Series of Breaks for Channel 10, Which Is Owned by His Associates Milchan and Lauder]." *The Marker*, January 15, 2017, https://www.themarker.com/advertising/1.3233906.

36. Allison Kaplan Sommer, "Bibi Bombshells Explained: Your Updated Guide to All the Netanyahu Cases." *Haaretz*, February 21, 2018, https://www.haaretz.com/israel-news/bibi-bombshell-explained-your-guide-to-the-netanyahu-cases-1.5810633.

37. Yonatan Kitain, "Likrat Ha'pitzul: Keshet, Reshet, ve'Arutz 10 Be'milchama Mi Yafsid Pachot [Ahead of Split: Keshet, Reshet, and Channel 10 at War over

Who Will Lose Less]." *Globes*, October 19, 2017, https://www.globes.co.il/news/article.aspx?did=1001208305; Li-Or Averbuch, "Ha'tochnit Shel Netanyahu: Lehotzi et Reshet ve'Keshet Mi'Arutz 2 [Netanyahu's Plan: Take Reshet and Keshet out of Channel 2]." *Globes*, June 11, 2015, http://www.globes.co.il/news/article.aspx?did=1001043511.

38. TOI Staff, "Reporter Ordered to Pay NIS 100k for Claim Netanyahu Was Kicked out of Car." *Times of Israel*, June 11, 2017. https://www.timesofisrael.com/reporter-ordered-to-pay-nis-100k-for-claim-netanyahu-was-kicked-out-of-car/.

39. Steinberg and Fox, "News You Can't Use: A Content Analysis of the Daily Show's Media Criticism," 16.

40. Wright, "Functional Analysis and Mass Communication," 608–09.

REFERENCES

Alexander, David. *Leitzan Ha'hatzer Ve'hashalit: Satira Politit Be'Yisrael [The Court Jester and the Ruler: Political Satire in Israel"]*. Tel-Aviv: Sifriyat Poalim, 1985.

Averbuch, Li-Or. "Ha'tochnit Shel Netanyahu: Lehotzi Et Reshet Ve'Keshet mi'Arutz 2 [Netanyahu's Plan: Take Reshet and Keshet out of Channel 2]." *Globes*. June 11, 2015. http://www.globes.co.il/news/article.aspx?did=1001043511.

Baker, Peter, and Cecilia Kang. "Trump Threatens NBC over Nuclear Weapons Report." *The New York Times*. October 11, 2017. https://www.nytimes.com/2017/10/11/us/politics/trump-nbc-fcc-broadcast-license.html.

Baym, Geoffrey. "The Daily Show: Discursive Integration and the Reinvention of Political Journalism." *Political Communication* 22, no. 3 (July 2005): 259–76. doi:10.1080/10584600591006492.

Borchers, Callum. "White House Blocks CNN, New York Times from Press Briefing Hours after Trump Slams Media." *The Washington Post*. February 24, 2017. https://www.washingtonpost.com/news/the-fix/wp/2017/02/24/white-house-blocks-cnn-new-york-times-from-press-briefing-hours-after-trump-slams-media/.

Brewer, Paul R., and Emily Marquardt. "Mock News and Democracy: Analyzing The Daily Show." *Atlantic Journal of Communication* 15, no. 4 (2007): 249–67.

Caufield, Rachel Paine. "The Influence of 'Infoenterpropagainment': Exploring the Power of Political Satire as a Distinct Form of Political Humor." In *Laughing Matters: Humor and American Politics in the Media Age*, edited by Jody C Baumgartner and Jonathan S. Morris, 3–20. New York: Routledge, 2008.

Epstein, Jennifer. "Trump Hits Media, Angrily Defends Charlottesville Response." *Bloomberg*. August 23, 2017. https://www.bloomberg.com/news/articles/2017-08-22/trump-seeks-rebound-with-rally-focus-on-immigration-in-arizona.

Erdan, Gilad. "Haaretz: Gam Fake News V'gam Megabim et Peilei Ha-BDS [Haaretz: Both Fake News and Supporters of BDS Activists]." *Facebook*. March 22, 2017. https://www.facebook.com/gilad.erdan/photos/a.225201850853267.56972.207139259326193/1570811912958914/?type=3&theater.

Freedom House. "Freedom of the Press 2017: Press Freedom's Dark Horizon—Country Report: Israel." Accessed September 1, 2017. https://freedomhouse.org/report/freedom-press/2017/israel.

Gardbaum, Stephen. "The Myth and the Reality of American Constitutional Exceptionalism." *Michigan Law Review* 107, no. 3 (2008): 391–466.

Gold, Matea, and Jenna Johnson. "Trump Calls the Media 'the Enemy of the American People.'" *The Washington Post*. February 17, 2017. https://www.washingtonpost.com/news/post-politics/wp/2017/02/17/trump-calls-the-media-the-enemy-of-the-american-people/.

Graber, Doris A. "Freedom of the Press: Theories and Realities." In *The Oxford Handbook of Political Communication*, edited by Kate Kenski and Kathleen Hall Jamieson, 237–48. New York: Oxford University Press, 2015. doi:10.1093/oxfordhb/9780199793471.013.80.

Griffin, Dustin H. *Satire: A Critical Reintroduction*. Lexington: University Press of Kentucky, 1994.

Guter, Aviv. "Bagatz Romez La'medina: Yitachen She'nevatel et Ha'chok Le'hakamat Taagid Ha'chadashot [Supreme Court Hints to Government: We May Overturn the Law to Establish a News Corporation]." *Calcalist*. November 11, 2017. https://www.calcalist.co.il/marketing/articles/0,7340,L-3724469,00.html.

Itzkoff, Dave. "Seth Meyers Confronts the Trump Era on 'Late Night.'" *The New York Times*. January 25, 2017. https://www.nytimes.com/2017/01/25/arts/television/seth-meyers-late-night-donald-trump.html.

Jefferson, Thomas. "From Thomas Jefferson to Edward Carrington, 16 January 1787." *Archives.gov*. 1787. Accessed October 1, 2017. https://founders.archives.gov/documents/Jefferson/01-11-02-0047.

Jones, Jeffrey P. *Entertaining Politics: New Political Television and Civic Culture*. Lanham, MD: Rowman & Littlefield, 2005.

Kaplan Sommer, Allison. "Bibi Bombshells Explained: Your Updated Guide to All the Netanyahu Cases." *Haaretz*. February 21, 2018. https://www.haaretz.com/israel-news/bibi-bombshell-explained-your-guide-to-the-netanyahu-cases-1.5810633.

Kitain, Yonatan. "Likrat Ha'pitzul: Keshet, Reshet, ve'Arutz 10 Be'milchama Mi Yafsid Pachot [Ahead of Split: Keshet, Reshet, and Channel 10 at War over Who Will Lose Less]." *Globes*. October 19, 2017. https://www.globes.co.il/news/article.aspx?did=1001208305.

Lis, Jonathan, and Lee Yaron. "Netanyahu Assails Israel's 'Fake News Industry' to Thousands of Supporters." *Haaretz (English Edition)*. August 30, 2017. http://www.haaretz.com/israel-news/1.809851.

Mordechay, Nadiv, and Yaniv Roznai. "A Jewish and (Declining) Democratic State? Constitutional Retrogression in Israel." *Maryland Law Review* 77 (2017): 244–70. doi:10.3366/ajicl.2011.0005.

Nevo, Gidi. *Moshav Letzim: Ha'rhetorica Shel Ha'satira Ha'ivrit [The Rhetoric of Hebrew Satire]*. Or Yehuda, Israel: Dvir, 2010.

Newman, Marissa. "Right-Wing Channel 20 Faces Closure over News Offerings." *The Times of Israel*. September 7, 2017. https://www.timesofisrael.com/right-wing-channel-20-faces-closure-over-news-offerings/.

Niv, Shai. "Pshara Be'nosse Ha'taagid: Tukam Chevrat Chadashot Nifredet Be'hanhala Chadasha [Compromise Regarding the Corporation: A Separate News Corporation will be Established with New Management]." *Globes.* March 30, 2017. http://www.globes.co.il/news/article.aspx?did=1001183329.

Schreckinger, Ben. "'Real News' Joins the White House Briefing Room." *Politico.* February 15, 2017. http://www.politico.com/magazine/story/2017/02/fake-news-gateway-pundit-white-house-trump-briefing-room-214781.

Smolicz, Jerzy. "Core Values and Cultural Identity." *Ethnic and Racial Studies* 4, no. 1 (1981): 75–90.

Steinberg, Edo, and Julia R. Fox. "News You Can't Use: A Content Analysis of the Daily Show's Media Criticism." Paper presented at the Association for Education in Journalism and Mass Communication Annual Conference. Montreal, QC, Canada, 2014.

Sullivan, Eileen, and Maggie Haberman. "Trump Shares, Then Deletes, Twitter Post of Train Hitting Cartoon Person Covered by CNN Logo." *The New York Times.* August 15, 2017. https://www.nytimes.com/2017/08/15/us/politics/trump-shares-then-deletes-twitter-post-of-cnn-cartoon-being-hit-by-train.html?mcubz=3&_r=0.

Swift, Art. "Democrats' Confidence in Mass Media Rises Sharply from 2016." Last modified September 21, 2017. http://news.gallup.com/poll/219824/democrats-confidence-mass-media-rises-sharply-2016.aspx.

Test, George A. *Satire: Spirit and Art.* Tampa: University of South Florida Press, 1991.

TOI Staff. "Reporter Ordered to Pay NIS 100k for Claim Netanyahu was Kicked Out of Car." *Times of Israel.* June 11, 2017. https://www.timesofisrael.com/reporter-ordered-to-pay-nis-100k-for-claim-netanyahu-was-kicked-out-of-car/.

Trump, Donald. "With All of the Fake News Coming Out of NBC and the Networks, at What Point is it Appropriate to Challenge Their License? Bad for Country!" *Twitter post.* October 11, 2017. https://twitter.com/realDonaldTrump/status/918112884630093825.

———. "Network News has Become so Partisan, Distorted and Fake that Licenses must be Challenged and, if Appropriate, Revoked. Not Fair to Public!" *Twitter post.* October 11, 2017, https://twitter.com/realDonaldTrump/status/918267396493922304.

Tucker, Nati. "Netanyahu Amad Meachorei Sidrat Hakalot le'Arutz 10 She'be'baalut Mekoravav Milchan ve'Lauder [Netanyahu was behind a Series of Breaks for Channel 10, Which Is Owned by His Associates Milchan and Lauder]." *The Marker.* January 15, 2017. https://www.themarker.com/advertising/1.3233906.

Wiener, Asaf, and Elad Man. "Hamechokek Ke'measder: Migbalot Va'ilutzei Chakika Be'asdarat Tikshoret Ve'shidurim [Legislator as Regulator: The Limitations of Media Regulation Legislation]." *Hukim [Laws]* (forthcoming), https://papers.ssrn.com/sol3/papers.cfm?abstract_id=2964583.

Wootliff, Raoul, and TOI Staff. "Right-Leaning Channel 20 Loses Rights to Broadcast Knesset TV." *The Times of Israel.* December 7, 2017. https://www.timesofisrael.com/right-leaning-channel-20-loses-rights-to-broadcast-knesset-tv/.

Wright, Charles R. "Functional Analysis and Mass Communication." *The Public Opinion Quarterly* 24, no. 4 (1960): 605–20. doi:http://www.jstor.org/stable/2746529.

PROSPECTS FOR A NEW GENERATION OF LAUGHTER

The Evolution of Political Comedy

Chapter 13

A New Generation of Satire Consumers?

A Socialization Approach to Youth Exposure to News Satire

Stephanie A. Edgerly

Satire matters. This alternative form of journalism can enlighten and engage audiences with a unique blend of critique and humor. It can motivate citizens to discuss issues of public policy and empower them to take political action.[1] While research over the past two decades provides a rich understanding of satire exposure and effects among various adult populations,[2] there is still much we don't know about news satire, particularly as it relates to the next generation of satire consumers who are coming of age in the high-choice, multi-device media era.

This chapter extends research on satire to a yet-to-be-studied population: youth ages 12 to 17 years. Are adolescents—at the doorstep of adulthood—developing the habit of consuming news satire? This young cohort has only known a media environment with an array of media sources and devices at its disposal. As such, it is unclear how such an ample and diverse media environment impacts the relationship they are forging with the specific genre of news satire. This chapter uses a national survey of US parents and youth to explore (1) the prevalence of youth exposure to news satire across a range of media devices and compared to other forms of news use and (2) the extent to which socialization factors—parents, school curriculum, peers—predict news satire use among today's youth. Given that today's youth are tomorrow's adults, findings from this chapter shed light on the future generation of news satire consumers.

A SOCIALIZATION APPROACH TO SATIRE

Scholars have long recognized that news use is a learned habit.[3] People are not born with the proclivity to consume news, nor does this habit automatically emerge when reaching adulthood. Instead, there is a long and winding socialization process, in which individuals learn which values, attitudes, and behaviors they should embrace and which to disregard. By most accounts, this process is first set into motion at an early age, with adolescence being an influential time period in the socialization process.[4] Research points to three primary agents of socialization.

The first is the strong role that parents play in socializing their children. Decades of political socialization research shows a strong tendency for children to adopt the political beliefs and participation habits of their parents.[5] Far from a mere coincidence, socialization researchers argue that the specific beliefs and behaviors of parents serve as an endorsement for the beliefs and behaviors that youth should adopt. A similar tendency is observed with news use. Early studies on this topic showed that teenagers who were heavy newspaper readers tended to have parents who were also heavy newspaper readers.[6] More recent research finds that parents' computer news use predicts computer news use among children and the strongest predictor of youth television news use is parent's own television news use.[7] In describing the news habits (or lack thereof) of youth and young adults, Mindich summarizes this socialization process as children reaping what their parents sow.[8]

Of course, parents are not the only source of socialization. A socialization perspective also points to the role of schools in providing youth with the opportunity to develop news habits. News can be integrated into classrooms in a variety of ways: formal news media literacy programs, journalism publications at schools, teacher-driven classroom activities, and industry sponsored programs.[9] These types of news-in-the-classroom activities socialize youth into news habits; it spurs skill development and produces students who are more motivated to consume news.[10] For example, Poindexter found that news-based interventions in middle school classrooms produced a higher level of interest in following the news. When parental influences are weaker, other factors, such as schools, play a stronger role in socializing youth.[11]

A final agent of socialization involves the role of peers. Peer groups are reference groups that establish, and incentivize, certain norms and behavior. This influence can be especially potent in explaining news habits. Parents and teachers can encourage youth to follow the news, but what happens if peers see little value in news and think following the news is uncool?[12] Peer groups that place great value in discussing current events provide additional incentives for youth to develop, and sustain, news habits. Indeed, Mindich found news use was highest when youth and young adults belonged to peer groups where news consumption was the norm.[13] Research specifically on adolescent youth found belonging to a peer group where current events were commonly discussed was related to higher levels of television news exposure, even when considering the role of parents and school curriculum.[14]

Taken together, approaching news satire from a socialization perspective requires looking at a variety of factors. Parents—commonly thought to carry great influence—are only one route to socialization.[15] We must also consider outside-the-home factors of school curriculum and peer groups. While there is nothing new about approaching news use from a socialization perspective, this focus *is* innovative in applying this perspective to a specific genre of news use. News socialization studies tend to focus on news exposure overall, or at the general medium level.[16] In developing a socialization model for news satire among a pre-adult population, it is important to also consider what past research tells us about the type of adults who seek out this specific type of media.

Adults and News Satire

Among adults, news satire is a niche genre of news exposure. According to Pew's 2014 study of media habits, only 12 percent of adults were self-identified as viewers of *The Daily Show* (10% for the *Colbert Report*).[17] This point is mirrored in more recent Nielsen television data—*The Daily Show with Trevor Noah* averages approximately 1.5 million viewers; which pales in comparison to other television news options (over 9 million people watch *NBC Nightly News*; 3.2 million people watch *Hannity*).[18]

Beyond a relatively small size, news satire is distinct in *who* consumes it and *why*. In terms of demographics, research suggests that younger adults, men, those identified as nonwhite, and with higher socioeconomic status are more likely to consume television and online forms of news satire.[19] There is also evidence that exposure to news satire is common among liberals and Democrats, and individuals with a greater distrust of the news media.[20]

A substantial body of research also examines the level of political engagement among those who consume news satire. Bill O'Reilly famously described *Daily Show* viewers as "stoned slackers."[21] While the validity of this exact statement has not been tested, the implication that *The Daily Show* audience is politically disengaged and uninformed has been empirically tested. By most accounts, research supports the idea that news satire appeals to a sophisticated audience, who—in order to understand and appreciate the humor and critique of satire—are informed and engaged.[22] Feldman and Young found that during the 2004 presidential campaign and immediately after, *Daily Show* viewers devoted a steady level of attention to current events.[23] Baumgartner and Morris found college students who consumed news satire were more knowledgeable about politics and more participatory.[24] Another study described *The Daily Show* audience as "political junkie[s]."[25] Taken together, adult consumers of news satire tend to possess high interest in politics and public affairs.

Less clear are the media preferences that motivate this type of genre exposure. Because news satire offers a hybridity of news and entertainment elements, several studies have explored the media preferences that drive satire use. Young found that the top reason for preferring news satire was its entertainment value (80% indicated that news satire is appealing because it is entertaining and humorous).[26] Coming in a distant second—but still with a sizable 41 percent—was the motivation to learn about the news. Baumgartner and Morris provide stronger evidence for news-based motivations, at least among college students. They found news satire was negatively related to the preference for entertainment, but positively related to the preference for information about international affairs, and Washington, DC events.[27] Research from Prior indicates that the preference for entertainment (over news) enables adults to disengage and avoid news altogether, however, there is some murkiness in whether this holds true for the genre of news satire— which straddles the news-entertainment divide.[28]

Ultimately, the challenge for this chapter is to apply these very specific characteristics of adult news satire consumption to the general process of youth socialization. There is likely something very specific about the youth who consume news satire. Similar to adults, this news genre will not appeal to youth universally. If past research of adults is any indication, certain demographic and psychographic factors will be related to youth developing a proclivity for this genre. At the same time, a socialization perspective suggests that certain agents—parents, schools, and peers—should explain which youth develop the habit of satire use.

The Next Generation of Satire Consumers

This chapter explores several aspects of youth satire consumption. First, the prevalence of news satire exposure is examined across a range of media devices and compared to other forms of news. Based on past research among adults, there is reason to expect that youth consumption of news satire will not rival that of other, more mainstream types of news. That being said, exposure to news satire is more common among younger adults.[29] It may be that youth mirror this trend and are seeking out this genre over more conventional sources of news. Additionally, it is unclear the extent to which youth consume news satire across an array of media devices. While television has been the primary medium for news satire over the past decade or so, this may not still be the case. Particularly among youth raised in a digital age in which 92 percent report going online daily, and nearly three-quarters have access to a smart phone.[30]

RQ1a: How common is youth exposure to news satire compared to other forms of news use?
RQ1b: Which media devices (e.g., television, computer, mobile phone, tablet) are youth using to consume news satire?

Next, a model of youth news satire is more deeply explored by first accounting for factors related to the socialization perspective. It is expected that parents should play a strong role in modeling the habit of news use. This influence is accounted for by parents' level of news use. It is unclear, however, whether parents modeling *any* type of news consumption works to spur youth developing the habit of satire, or if parents need to model the specific habit of satire exposure in order to develop that habit in their children. Next, news-based classroom curriculum should also play a positive role in youth developing the habit of news satire. Past studies have found this to be true for general news habits, and the same should also hold for news satire.[31] Similarly, youth who have friends who value news consumption and frequently talk about current events are more likely to consume news satire.[32]

H1: Parents' news exposure will be positively related to youth exposure to news satire.
RQ2: Which is more strongly related to youth news satire exposure—parents' use of any type of news, or their use of news satire?
H2: News-based classroom curriculum will be positively related to youth exposure to news satire.
H3: Peer groups that value and discuss current events will be positively related to youth exposure to news satire.

Youth exposure to news satire is further explored by considering the demographic and psychographic factors that past studies of adults have found to play a significant role. In addition to standard demographic factors, four psychographic variables are considered: partisanship, perceptions of news bias, political interest, and the preference for entertainment over news. It is unclear whether these factors—common in explaining which adults consume news satire—will also carry over to the youth satire audience.

RQ3: To what extent is youth news satire exposure related to the same demographic and psychographic factors found among adults?

METHOD

To explore these areas of interest, data from a national online survey is used. The commercial survey firm IPSOS was contracted to obtain a sample of US youth aged 12–17 and one associated parent. Data were collected between August 12 and September 20, 2014, using stratified quota sampling to mirror the national population in terms of (parent) gender, geographic region, household income, and ethnicity. Participants were pre-recruited by IPSOS to take the occasional survey in return for small incentives. IPSOS identified a sample of 2,235 households with youth ages 12 to 17, and contacted the parent enrolled in the panel. The parent filled out the first part of the survey, and then notified the adolescent with the most recent birthday, who filled out the remainder of the survey ($N = 1,505$ parent-child dyads).

Measures

Youth News Satire Use

Youth were asked specific questions about the extent to which they consumed news satire across a variety of devices. Prior to answering these questions, a filter question asked youth if they ever consumed *any type* of news or information when using a television, computer, mobile phone, and tablet device. For youth that indicated "never," no additional questions related to that device were asked. Only youth that indicated actually using a specific device for any type of news and information purpose were asked more specific questions about that use.

Level of *news satire exposure* was measured by four device-specific questions. Youth separately indicated how many days per week they consumed "news satire/news comedy (e.g., Jon Stewart, *The Onion*)" using a television, computer, mobile phone, and tablet. Descriptive statistics are provided in Table 13.1. In later analyses, the four items are combined into a single overall measure of news satire use ($M = 1.04$, $SD = 1.64$; *Cronbach's Alpha* = .93).

Three additional forms of news use were measured as a basis of comparison to news satire. Youth separately indicated how many days a week they consumed *network news*, *local news*, and *cable news* across the four devices. Descriptive statistics are provided in the appendix.

Parental News Use

Parents' own news use was measured in three ways. First, parents indicated how often they consumed *news satire* on a six-point scale ranging from "never" (0) to "multiple times a day" (5) ($M = 1.54$, $SD = 1.65$). Note that the parental news questions are *not* device-specific. Using the same scale,

Table 13.1   Youth Consumption of News Satire by Media Device

	News Satire Television	News Satire Computer	News Satire Tablet	News Satire Phone
Average weekly exposure[1]	1.33	1.14	1.38	1.20
	(1.98)	(1.88)	(2)	(1.98)
Audience size among device news users[2]	42.2%	36.3%	42.4%	36.6%
Audience size among all youth[3]	36.2%	36.3%	20.4%	21.7%
N	1290	1505	727	893

[1] Mean indicates the number of days in a week news satire is consumed; standard deviation in parentheses.
[2] Includes only the youth who reported using that specific device for any type of news and information. Percentage reflects the proportion of youth who consume at least one day of news satire on the device.
[3] Percentage reflects the proportion of youth in the full sample who consume at least one day of news satire on the device.

parents also reported how often they consumed television network news and local news. Responses to these two items were averaged to create an overall measure of *mainstream television news* use ($M = 3.25$, $SD = 1.42$; $r = .68$). Finally, parents indicated their level of *cable news* exposure ($M = 2.65$, $SD = 1.74$).

School and Peer Factors

A measure of *news-based school curriculum* was measured by five items. Youth indicated how often, from "never" (0) to "very often" (4), they: (1) followed the news as part of a class assignment, (2) learned in school what makes good news reporting, (3) learned the difference between news and opinion, (4) learned about how government works, and (5) learn about political or social issues in class. Responses were averaged to create an overall measure of news-based curriculum ($M = 1.83$, $SD = .99$; *Cronbach's alpha* = .89).

Youth also indicated the extent to which news is an important part of their peer group. A measure of *peer news norms* was obtained by youth recording their level of agreement from "Strongly disagree" (1) to "Strongly agree" (5) with the statement, "Among my friends, it's important to know what's going on in the world" ($M = 3.45$, $SD = 1.02$). Youth also indicated how often they *talk with friends* about current issues and events ($M = 2.4$, $SD = 1.17$), from "never" (1) to "very often" (5).

Demographics and Psychographics

Parents and youth also provided relevant demographic and psychographic information. From parents, information about their age ($M = 44.87$, $SD = 8.3$) and overall household income (mean corresponding to: $60,000 to $64,999) was obtained. From youth, data related to their age ($M = 14.59$, $SD = 1.67$), gender (dichotomized: 49.2% female), and racial identification (dichotomized: 68.1% white) was obtained.

Youth also indicated their *political party identification* on a seven-point scale, ranging from "Strong Democrat" (1) to "Strong Republican" (7), with the midpoint labeled as "Independent" ($M = 3.82$, $SD = 1.35$). A measure of *perceived news bias* was taken from youth indicating their level of agreement with the statement "Most news coverage is biased against my views," on a scale ranging from "Strongly disagree" (1) to "Strongly agree" (5) ($M = 3.02$, $SD = .94$). *Political interest* was similarly measured by agreement with the statement: "I am interested in politics" ($M = 2.66$, $SD = 1.23$). Lastly, youth *preference for entertainment* media was measured by level of agreement with the statement: "I'd rather watch entertainment programing than watch the news" ($M = 4.07$, $SD = 1.01$).

RESULTS

Youth Exposure to News Satire

The first research question addresses how common, and through which media devices, youth consume news satire. As seen in Table 13.1, youth consume news satire an average of one day a week across each of the media devices examined. Interestingly, it is television ($M = 1.33$) and tablet ($M = 1.38$) exposure to news satire that produces the highest means. This suggests that youth are using "newer" media devices to consume news satire at roughly the same rate as the "older" medium of television. In terms of audience size, 42.2 percent of youth who use a television for any type of news and information report consuming news satire at least once a week. This proportion translates to approximately one-third (36.2%) of all youth sampled. Similarly, 42.4 percent of youth who use a tablet for any type of news and information, indicate that they consume news satire at least once a week. However, tablet access and use for news and information purposes is much lower compared to television and the other devices. As such, the overall proportion of youth who consume news satire on a tablet is much smaller (only 20.4% of all youth sampled). A similar proportion is reported for mobile phone use (21.7% of all youth sampled); while computer news satire use is more common among youth (36.3% of all youth sampled).

As a point of comparison, the appendix includes exposure levels and audience size for network news, local news, and cable news. These other forms of news use are used more frequently and are more popular than news satire—particularly true for television viewers of local news which seven in ten youth report watching at least once a week. Moreover, the average level of exposure of local news consumed on a television is 2.8 days a week. This suggests that the youth audience for news satire is narrow and not the dominant forms of news exposure among pre-adults.

Having contextualized the extent to which youth are consuming news satire, the next analysis explains which youth develop this habit.

Modeling Exposure to News Satire

A hierarchical linear regression model was constructed to predict youth consumption of news satire. Given the similar results of satire exposure across the four devices, a single measure of news satire exposure was constructed by averaging exposure across the four device items. The regression model included three blocks of variables: (1) demographics, (2) socialization factors, and (3) psychographics.

As seen in Table 13.2, the regression model explains 42.6 percent of the overall variance in youth news satire use, with all three variable blocks contributing significantly. The majority of variance explained is derived

Table 13.2   Regression Predicting Youth News Satire Consumption

	Model 1 St. beta	Model 2 St. beta	Model 3 St. beta
Block 1: Demographics			
Parent's age	−.156***	−.068**	−.065**
Household income	.157***	.038#	.036#
Youth age	.075**	.053*	.054*
Youth gender (male)	−.04	−.028	−.024
Youth race (white)	−.112***	−.036#	−.022
Block 2: Socialization factors			
Parent's mainstream news use	—	−.013	−.014
Parent's cable news use	—	.014	.005
Parent's news satire use	—	.464***	.442***
News-based school curriculum	—	.074**	.071*
Peer news norms	—	.011	−.025
Peer current events talk	—	.203***	.168***
Block 3: Psychographics			
Political Party ID (Republican)	—	—	−.06**
News bias	—	—	.065**
Political interest	—	—	.116***
Preference for entertainment	—	—	.042#
Incremental change in R^2 (%)	—	35.9***	1.5***
Total Adjusted R^2 (%)	5.2***	41.1***	42.6***
N = 1442			

#$p \leq .1$, *$p \leq .05$, **$p \leq .01$, ***$p \leq .001$.

from the second block of socialization factors (35.9%). Consistent with the expectations of *H1*, parents' own news use plays a significant role in youth news satire use. That being said, the nature of this influence is quite specific. In addressing *RQ2*, we see that it is only parents' consumption of news satire, and not any other type of news exposure, that is related to youth consumption of satire. The size of the standardized regression beta for this relationship, even when accounting for all other variables in the model, is quite impressive (*b* = .442). Results also support the significant role that news-based curriculum plays (*H2*), as well as peer influence (*H3*). Regarding the latter, it is noteworthy that only peer talk about current events, and not peer norms about being informed, corresponds to increased satire exposure.

Next, we turn to *RQ3*, which explores the demographic and psychographic profile of youth satire consumers. The first block of demographic variables explains 5.2 percent of variance. However, much of this influence is channeled through the second block of socialization factors. The addition of the socialization variables renders many demographic factors non-significant (see model 2). The only variables that remain significant in the final model are age (parent and youth), and to a lesser extent, household income. Specifically, youth that are older, have younger parents, and come from households with higher incomes consume higher levels of news satire.

The third block of psychographic variables contributes an additional 1.5 percent of explained variance to the overall model. As such, this group of variables does not reach the magnitude of influence generated by the socialization variables. However, there is evidence that youth consumers of news satire share many of the same profile characteristics as adult satire consumers. Youth consumption of satire is related to identifying as a Democrat, higher levels of perceived news bias, and higher levels of political interest. The preference for entertainment (over news) is moderately related to satire consumption.

DISCUSSION

The past two decades of scholarly work have produced a dense line of research examining the content of news satire, audience exposure to satire, and the potential of news satire to produce democratically positive effects.[33] The goal of this chapter was to add to this line of research by exploring news satire exposure among a pre-adult, adolescent sample. Research consistently points to the popularity of news satire among young adults, and college students in particular, yet we know little about whether this habit is developed in the years pre-dating adulthood.[34]

Findings from this study indicate several similarities between adult consumers of news satire and youth of today. One way this is seen is in audience size. News satire provides individuals with a specific news experience. This genre does not appeal to all adults, nor does it appeal to all youth. In total, 44 percent of youth consume some type of news satire on *either* a television, computer, mobile phone, or tablet. While a sizeable number of youth are integrating news satire into their media diets, it should be noted that levels of exposure are generally low. Youth consume news satire an average of once a week. This is similar to what Baumgartner and Morris found among college students (average of 1.31 days/week), though their focus was on *The Daily Show* specifically.[35] In this study, only 15 percent of youth consume news satire more than three days a week. Other forms of news use—such as local news and network news—are consumed at a higher frequency and by a larger proportion of youth. In other words, news satire is not the dominant form of news exposure among youth. Conventional news forms are the most popular, even among an age group who has only known a high-choice media environment.

That being said, we should not discount news satire on this basis. Small audiences formed around specific types of news have the potential to produce strong effects. This is due to the high degree of loyalty that niche audiences tend to exhibit.[36] It may be that youth consumers of news satire feel a deeper connection to, and identification with, news satire than they do with local and network news. As such, they may be more prone to the effects that past studies have found among an adult audience.[37] Second, exposure to news satire will likely increase as youth enter adulthood. There is evidence that news exposure levels increase with age.[38] The period of adolescence is important because it establishes the unequal starting points from which youth begin adulthood.[39] Forty-four percent of youth are making news satire part of their media diet. This is a strong starting point that more frequent use of news satire can grow from. The finding that older youth consume more news satire speaks to this possibility. While news satire will never appeal to all, there is reason to expect that current youth consumers will rely on it more as they enter adulthood.

There is also evidence that the audience profile for youth news satire is similar to that of adults. News satire is more frequently sought out by older youth (e.g., those approaching young adulthood) from higher income households. It also appeals more to youth identifying as Democrats, those with a higher level of perceived news bias, those interested in politics, and those who prefer entertainment (over news). This suggests that even at an early age, news satire appeals to a certain type of media consumer. However, these findings also raise questions about the reciprocal nature of satire exposure and effects. The current study uses cross-sectional data. Outside of relying on theory to establish the ordering of variables (e.g., socialization literature, uses and gratifications), claims about causality cannot be empirically tested. The current study cannot discern, for example, whether youth with higher levels of perceived news bias are attracted to news satire, or whether consuming news satire results in higher levels of perceived news bias. It is also possible—some would say likely—that both options are at work.[40]

At the heart of this study is the approach of exploring news satire from a socialization perspective. This study highlights the socialization factors related to youth developing the habit of news satire use. And these factors are extremely predictive. The six socialization variables account for nearly 36 percent of the variance in youth satire exposure, compared to a mere 7 percent explained by the nine demographics and psychographic variables. A critique of past research on satire exposure is low explanatory power.[41] Results from this study demonstrate the power of socialization factors in gaining a clearer picture of who is consuming satire. There is reason to believe that this explanatory influence is not confined to the period of adolescence. The influence of satire socialization can extend into adulthood, as the media choices of adults can be predicted by their specific socialization experiences at 15 years of age.[42]

The role that parents, school, and peers play in explaining youth satire exposure both confirms past work on news socialization, while also providing some nuance. This is particularly true for parental influence. Similar to past studies parents continue to play a strong role in modeling the value of news through their own news usage.[43] However, this modeling takes a specific form—the strongest predictor of youth consuming news satire is a parent who also consumes news satire. Parents' consumption of other news (e.g., mainstream news, cable news) has no bearing on youth developing the habit of satire news. This suggests that as the media environment continues to expand and news genres become more specialized, the nature of parental modeling will also become more specific. It may no longer be the case that "newsy" parents raise "newsy" children, but rather that parents with specific news preferences raise children who also embrace those preferences. Presumably these parents see great value in consuming satire and have transferred this value to their child. Of course, the current study only scratches the surface of this strong relationship. It is unknown whether parents and youth are consuming satire together, or the extent to which parents are explicitly encouraging their child to consume satire or even recommending specific sources of satire to their children. It should be noted that this parental modeling influence is significant even when separately examining youth news use on the various devices. This raises the additional question of how the processes of observational modeling occur from a parent to their child, when media consumption takes place on smaller, more individualized media devices.

Findings also point to the significance of outside-the-home factors in socializing youth into news satire. There is a positive relationship between youth exposure to news-based classroom curriculum and increased consumption of news satire. Past research demonstrates the ability of news-in-the-classroom to spur news use among youth.[44] This study's findings suggest that the same is true for the spurring of news satire. These types of classroom activities are thought to increase students' news consumption by sparking their general interest to follow news, developing a greater awareness of specific news sources, and providing youth with a skillset to better understand news content. It is beyond the scope of this study to know which, if any, of these mediating processes are at work for satire exposure. It may be that teachers are bringing satire into the classroom as a way to engage students with media that mixes news and entertainment. Or youth consumption of news satire could be the result of more traditional news-based activities that increase their interest to follow news. There is certainly more work to be done in this area to understand the specific classroom activities and mediating processes that ultimately socialize youth into news satire use.

Peer groups also exert influence. Talking with friends about current events is a powerful factor related to youth consumption of news satire. Above and beyond the influence of parents and schools, youth who belong to peer groups where discussions about current events frequently occur are more likely to consume news satire. This peer influence provides additional incentive for youth to make news satire part of their media diet. It may be that news satire has additional value because it provides youth with current events information and does so in a humorous and accessible way that plays well among friends. Moreover, the expectation of future talk with friends can lead youth to pay closer attention to satire content, resulting in knowledge acquisition.[45]

Ultimately, news satire provides audiences with an alternative style of news. "It encourages critical debate, sheds light upon perceived wrongs within society and government, points out hypocrisy, and makes political criticism accessible to the average citizen."[46] This chapter sheds light on the forces that shape news satire exposure in the high-choice media age by examining satire use across a range of media devices and among a pre-adult age cohort. If the results from this study are any indication, this genre will continue into the future. Not only are today's youth (tomorrow's adults) consuming satire on a variety of media devices, but adult satire consumers are also ensuring the survival of the genre—by socializing their children into the habit of news satire use.

APPENDIX

Table 13.3 **Youth Consumption of Other News Forms across Devices**

	Television	Computer	Tablet	Phone
Local TV news	2.8 (2.25)	1.88 (2.25)	1.72 (2.21)	1.44 (2.08)
	80.9% device news users	*56.7% device news users*	*51.4% device news users*	*43.8% device news users*
	69.3% of all youth	*·56.7% of all youth*	*24.8% of all youth*	*26% of all youth*
Network TV news	2.5 (2.29)	1.76 (2.16)	1.75 (2.21)	1.47 (2.15)
	73.9% device news users	*54.9% device news users*	*52.7% device news users*	*43% device news users*
	63.3% of all youth	*54.9% of all youth*	*25.4% of all youth*	*25.5% of all youth*
Cable news	1.91 (2.21)	1.45 (2.09)	1.64 (2.18)	1.32 (2.05)
	58.5% device news users	*44.3% device news users*	*49.1% device news users*	*40.1% device news users*
	50.1% of all youth	*44.3% of all youth*	*23.7% of all youth*	*23.7% of all youth*
N	1290	1505	727	893

Note: Mean indicates the number of days in a week the specific type of is consumed; standard deviation in parentheses.

NOTES

1. Dannagal G. Young and Sarah E. Esralew, "Jon Stewart a Heretic? Surely You Jest: Political Participation and Discussion Among Viewers of Late-Night Comedy Programing," in *The Stewart/Colbert Effect: Essays on the Real Impacts of Fake News*, ed. Amarnath Amarasingam (Jefferson, NC: McFarland, 2011), 110–12.

2. Jody C Baumgartner and Jonathan S. Morris, "MyFaceTube Politics: Social Networking Websites and Political Engagement of Young Adults," *Social Science Computer Review* 28, no. 1 (2010): 24–44, https://doi.org/10.1177/0894439309334325; Lauren Feldman and Dannagal G. Young, "Late-Night Comedy as a Gateway to Traditional News: An Analysis of Time Trends in News Attention Among Late-Night Comedy Viewers During the 2004 Presidential Primaries," *Political Communication* 25, no. 4 (2008): 401–22, https://doi.org/10.1080/10584600802427013; Jay Hmielowski, R. Lance Holbert, and Jayeon Lee, "Predicting the Consumption of Political TV Satire: Affinity for Political Humor, The Daily Show, and The Colbert Report," *Communication Monographs* 78, no. 1 (2011): 96–114, https://doi.org/10.1080/03637751.2010.542579.

3. Peter Clarke, "Parental Socialization Values and Children's Newspaper Reading," *Journalism Quarterly* 42, no. 4 (1965): 539–46.

4. Judith Torney-Purta and Jo-Ann Amadeo, "Participatory Niches for Emergent Citizenship in Early Adolescence: An International Perspective," *The Annals of the American Academy of Political and Social Science* 633, no. 1 (2011): 180–200, https://doi.org/10.1177/0002716210384220.

5. Richard G. Niemi and M. Kent Jennings, "Issues and Inheritance in the Formation of Party Identification," *American Journal of Political Science* 34, no. 4 (1991): 970–88, http://www.jstor.org/stable/2111502.

6. Clarke, "Parental Socialization Values"; Cathy J. Cobb, "Patterns of Newspaper Readership Among Teenagers," *Communication Research* 13, no. 2 (1986): 299–326.

7. Sarah E. Vaala and Amy Bleakley, "Monitoring, Mediating, and Modeling: Parental Influence on Adolescent Computer and Internet Use in the United States," *Journal of Children and Media* 9, no. 1 (2015): 40–57, https://doi.org/10.1080/174 82798.2015.997103; Stephanie Edgerly and Kjerstin Thorson, "Developing Media Preferences in a Post-Broadcast Democracy," in *Political Socialization in a Media Saturated World*, eds. Esther Thorson, Mitchel S. McKinney, and Dhavan V. Shah (New York: Peter Lang Publishing, 2016), 383.

8. David T. Z. Mindich, *Tuned Out: Why Americans Under 40 Don't Follow the News* (Oxford: Oxford University Press, 2005).

9. Paula M. Poindexter, *Millennials, News, and Social Media* (New York: Peter Lang Publishing, 2012).

10. Adam Maksl, Stephanie Craft, Seth Ashley, and Dean Miller, "The Usefulness of a News Media Literacy Measure in Evaluating a News Literacy Curriculum," *Journalism & Mass Communication Educator* 72, no. 2 (2017), https://doi. org/10.1177/1077695816651970.

11. Kent M. Jennings, Laura Stoker, and Jake Bowers, "Politics across Generations: Family Transmission Reexamined," *The Journal of Politics* 71, no. 3 (2009): 782–99, http://www.jstor.org/stable/10.1017/s0022381609090719.

12. Poindexter, *Millennials, News, and Social Media*, 24.

13. Mindich, *Tuned Out*.

14. Edgerly and Thorson, "Developing Media Preferences."

15. Emily K. Vraga, Leticia Bode, JungHwan Yang, Stephanie Edgerly, Kjerstin Thorson, Chris Wells, and Dhavan V. Shah, "Political Influence Across Candidate Evaluations in the 2008 Election," *Information, Communication & Society* 17, no. 2 (2014): 184–202, https://doi.org/10.1080/1369118X.2013.872162.

16. Edgerly and Thorson, "Developing Media Preferences"; Maksl, Craft, Ashley, and Miller, "The Usefulness of a News Media Literacy"; Vaala and Bleakley, "Monitoring, Mediating, and Modeling."

17. Amy Mitchell, Jeffrey Gottfried, Jocelyn Kiley, and Katerina Eva Matsa, "Political Polarization and Media Habits," *Pew Research Center: Journalism & Media*, October 21, 2014, http://www.journalism.org/2014/10/21/ political-polarization-media-habits/.

18. Lucas Shaw, "'The Daily Show' Host Trevor Noah Lands New Deal after Ratings Success," *Bloomberg*, September 14, 2017, https://www.bloomberg.com/ news/articles/2017–09–14/-daily-show-host-noah-lands-new-deal-as-trump-bits-lift-

ratings; A. J. Katz, "The Top Cable News Programs of January 2018 Were . . . ," *TVNewser*, January 30, 2018, http://www.adweek.com/tvnewser/the-top-cable-news-programs-of-january-2018-were/356297; Chris Ariens, "Evening News Ratings: Week of January 22," *TVNewser*, January 30, 2018, http://www.adweek.com/tvnewser/evening-news-ratings-week-of-january-22/356239.

19. Xiaoxia Cao, "Political Comedy Shows and Knowledge about Primary Campaigns: The Moderating Effect of Age and Education," *Mass Communication and Society* 11, no. 1 (2008): 52, https://doi.org/10.1080/15205430701585028; comScore, "Media Overview. The Onion.com," *comScore*, February 2017; Hmielowski, Holbert, and Lee, "Predicting the Consumption of Political TV Satire," 108; Dannagal G. Young, "Laughter, Learning, or Enlightenment? Viewing and Avoidance Motivations Behind *The Daily Show* and *The Colbert Report*," *Journal of Broadcasting & Electronic Media* 57, no. 2 (2013): 163, https://doi.org/10.1080/08838151.2013.787080.

20. Jody C Baumgartner and Jonathan S. Morris, "The Daily Show Effect: Candidate Evaluations, Efficacy, and American Youth," *American Politics Research* 34, no. 3 (2006): 341–67, https://doi.org/10.1177/1532673X05280074; Mitchell, Gottfried, Kiley, and Matsa, "Political Polarization and Media Habits."

21. The O'Reilly Factor, "The Jon Stewart and Undecided Voter Connection," *Fox News*, September 20, 2004, http://www.foxnews.com/story/2004/09/20/jon-stewart-and-undecided-voter-connection.html.

22. Patricia Moy, Michael A. Xenos, and Verena K. Hess, "Communication and Citizenship: Mapping the Political Effects of Infotainment," *Mass Communication and Society* 8, no. 2 (2015): 111–131, https://doi.org/10.1207/s15327825mcs0802_3.

23. Feldman and Young, "Late-Night Comedy as a Gateway."

24. Baumgartner and Morris, "MyFaceTube," 34–35.

25. Dannagal G. Young and Sarah E. Esralew, "Jon Stewart a Heretic?" 113.

26. Young, "Laughter, Learning, or Enlightenment."

27. Baumgartner and Morris, "MyFaceTube."

28. Markus Prior, *Post-Broadcast Democracy* (New York: Cambridge University Press, 2007).

29. Jody C Baumgartner and Jonathan S. Morris, "Stoned Slackers or Super-Citizens? The Daily Show Viewing and Political Engagement of Young Adults," in *The Stewart/Colbert Effect: Essays on the Real Impacts of Fake News*, ed. Amarnath Amarasingam (Jefferson, NC: McFarland, 2011), 63–78; Mitchell, Gottfried, Kiley, and Matsa, "Political Polarization and Media Habits."

30. Amanda Lenhart, "A Majority of American Teens Report Access to a Computer, Game Console, Smartphone, and a Tablet," *Pew Research Center: Internet & Technology*, April 9, 2015, http://www.pewinternet.org/2015/04/09/a-majority-of-american-teens-report-access-to-a-computer-game-console-smartphone-and-a-tablet/.

31. Maksl, Craft, Ashley, and Miller, "The Usefulness of a News Media Literacy"; Poindexter, *Millennials, News, and Social Media*.

32. Edgerly and Thorson, "Developing Media Preferences"; Mindich, *Tuned Out*.

33. Amarnath Amarasingam, *The Stewart/Colbert Effect: Essays on the Real Impacts of Fake News* (Jefferson, NC: McFarland, 2011).

34. Baumgartner and Morris, "Stoned Slackers or Super-Citizens"; Mitchell, Gottfried, Kiley, and Matsa, "Political Polarization & Media Habits."

35. Baumgartner and Morris, "Stoned Slackers or Super-Citizens," 70.

36. James G. Webster, "Beneath the Veneer of Fragmentation: Television Audience Polarization in a Multichannel World," *Journal of Communication* 55, no. 2 (2005): 366–82, doi:10.1111/j.1460–2466.2005.tb02677.x.

37. Moy, Xenos, and Hess, "Communication and Citizenship"; Young and Esralew, "Jon Stewart a Heretic?"

38. Angela M. Lee and Hsiang Iris Chyi, "Motivational Consumption Model: Exploring the Psychological Structure of News Use," *Journalism & Mass Communication Quarterly* 91, no. 4 (2014): 706–24, https://doi.org/10.1177/1077699014550088.

39. Sidney Verba, Nancy Burns, and Kay Lehman Schlozman, "Unequal at the Starting Line: Creating Participatory Inequalities Across Generations and Among Groups," *The American Sociologist* 34, no. 1 (2003): 45–69, https://doi.org/10.1007/s12108–003–1005-y.

40. Michael D. Slater, "Reinforcing Spirals: The Mutual Influence of Media Selectivity and Media Effects and their Impact on Individuals Behavior and Social Identity," *Communication Theory* 17, no. 3 (2007): 281–303, doi:10.1111/j.1468–2885.2007.00296.x.

41. Hmielowski, Holbert, and Lee, "Predicting the Consumption of Political TV Satire."

42. Paul Hendricks Vettehen, Ruben P. Konig, Henk Westerik, and Hans Beentjes, "Explaining Television Choices: The Influence of Parents and Partners," *Poetics* 40, no. 6 (2012): 565–85.

43. Clarke, "Parental Socialization Values"; Cobb, "Patterns of Newspaper Readership"; Vaala and Bleakley, "Monitoring, Mediating, and Modeling."

44. Poindexter, *Millennials, News, and Social Media.*

45. William P. Eveland Jr., "The Effect of Political Discussion in Producing Informed Citizens: The Roles of Information, Motivation, and Elaboration," *Political Communication 21* (2004): 177–94.

46. Rachel Paine Caufield, "The Influence of 'Infoenterpropagainment': Exploring the Power of Political Satire as a Distinct Form of Political Humor," in *Laughing Matters: Humor and American Politics in the Media Age*, eds. Jody C Baumgartner and Jonathan S. Morris (New York: Routledge, 2008), 4.

REFERENCES

Amarasingam, Amarnath. *The Stewart/Colbert Effect: Essays on the Real Impacts of Fake News.* Jefferson, NC: McFarland, 2011.

Ariens, Chris. "Evening News Ratings: Week of January 22." *TVNewser.* January 30, 2018. http://www.adweek.com/tvnewser/evening-news-ratings-week-of-january-22/356239.

Baumgartner, Jody C, and Jonathan S. Morris. "The Daily Show Effect: Candidate Evaluations, Efficacy, and American Youth." *American Politics Research* 34, no. 3 (2006): 341–367. https://doi.org/10.1177/1532673X05280074.

———. "MyFaceTube Politics: Social Networking Websites and Political Engagement of Young Adults." *Social Science Computer Review* 28, no. 1 (2010): 24–44. https://doi.org/10.1177/0894439309334325.

———. "Stoned Slackers or Super-Citizens? The Daily Show Viewing and Political Engagement of Young Adults." In *The Stewart/Colbert Effect: Essays on the Real Impacts of Fake News*, edited by Amarnath Amarasingam, 63–78. Jefferson, NC: McFarland, 2011.

Cao, Xiaoxia. "Political Comedy Shows and Knowledge about Primary Campaigns: The Moderating Effect of Age and Education." *Mass Communication and Society* 11, no. 1 (2008): 43–61. https://doi.org/10.1080/15205430701585028.

Caufield, Rachel Paine. "The Influence of 'Infoenterpropagainment': Exploring the Power of Political Satire as a Distinct Form of Political Humor." In *Laughing Matters: Humor and American Politics in the Media Age*, edited by Jody C Baumgartner and Jonathan S. Morris, 3–20. New York: Routledge, 2008.

Clarke, Peter. "Parental Socialization Values and Children's Newspaper Reading." *Journalism Quarterly* 42, no. 4 (1965): 539–46.

Cobb, Cathy J. (1986). "Patterns of Newspaper Readership among Teenagers." *Communication Research* 13, no. 2 (1986): 299–326.

comScore. "Media Overview. The Onion.com." *comScore*. February 2017.

Edgerly, Stephanie, and Kjerstin Thorson. "Developing Media Preferences in a Post-Broadcast Democracy." In *Political Socialization in a Media Saturated World*, edited by Esther Thorson, Mitchel S. McKinney, and Dhavan V. Shah, 375–91. New York: Peter Lang Publishing, 2016.

Eveland, William P., Jr. "The Effect of Political Discussion in Producing Informed Citizens: The Roles of Information, Motivation, and Elaboration." *Political Communication* 21, no. 2 (2004): 177–94. https://doi.org/10.1080/10584600490443877.

Feldman, Lauren, and Dannagal G. Young. "Late-Night Comedy as a Gateway to Traditional News: An Analysis of Time Trends in News Attention among Late-Night Comedy Viewers during the 2004 Presidential Primaries." *Political Communication* 25, no. 4 (2008): 401–422. https://doi.org/10.1080/10584600802427013.

Hmielowski, Jay D., R. Lance Holbert, and Jayeon Lee. "Predicting the Consumption of Political TV Satire: Affinity for Political Humor, The Daily Show, and The Colbert Report." *Communication Monographs* 78, no. 1 (2011): 96–114. https://doi.org/10.1080/03637751.2010.542579.

Jennings, Kent M., Laura Stoker, and Jake Bowers. "Politics Across Generations: Family Transmission Reexamined." *The Journal of Politics* 71, no. 3 (2009): 782–799. http://www.jstor.org/stable/10.1017/s0022381609090719.

Katz, A. J. "The Top Cable News Programs of January 2018 Were . . ." *TVNewser*. January 30, 2018. http://www.adweek.com/tvnewser/the-top-cable-news-programs-of-january-2018-were/356297.

Lee, Angela M., and Hsiang Iris Chyi. "Motivational Consumption Model: Exploring the Psychological Structure of News Use." *Journalism & Mass Communication Quarterly* 91, no. 4 (2014): 706–724. https://doi.org/10.1177/1077699014550088.

Lenhart, Amanda. "A Majority of American Teens Report Access to a Computer, Game Console, Smartphone, and a Tablet." *Pew Research Center: Internet &*

Technology. April 9, 2015. http://www.pewinternet.org/2015/04/09/a-majority-of-american-teens-report-access-to-a-computer-game-console-smartphone-and-a-tablet/.

Maksl, Adam, Stephanie Craft, Seth Ashley, and Dean Miller. "The Usefulness of a News Media Literacy Measure in Evaluating a News Literacy Curriculum." *Journalism & Mass Communication Educator* 72, no. 2 (2017): 228–41. https://doi.org/10.1177/1077695816651970.

Mindich, David T. Z. *Tuned Out: Why Americans under 40 Don't Follow the News*. Oxford: Oxford University Press, 2005.

Mitchell, Amy, Jeffrey Gottfried, Jocelyn Kiley, and Katerina Eva Matsa. "Political Polarization and Media Habits." *Pew Research Center: Journalism & Media*. October 21, 2014. http://www.journalism.org/2014/10/21/political-polarization-media-habits/.

Moy, Patricia, Michael A. Xenos, and Verena K. Hess. "Communication and Citizenship: Mapping the Political Effects of Infotainment." *Mass Communication and Society* 8, no. 2 (2015): 111–31. https://doi.org/10.1207/s15327825mcs0802_3.

Niemi, Richard G., and M. Kent Jennings. "Issues and Inheritance in the Formation of Party Identification." *American Journal of Political Science* 34, no. 4 (1991): 970–88. http://www.jstor.org/stable/2111502.

Poindexter, Paula. M. *Millennials, News, and Social Media*. New York: Peter Lang Publishing, 2012.

Prior, Markus. *Post-Broadcast Democracy*. New York: Cambridge University Press, 2007.

Shaw, Lucas. "'The Daily Show' Host Trevor Noah Lands New Deal after Ratings Success." *Bloomberg*. September 14, 2017. https://www.bloomberg.com/news/articles/2017–09–14/-daily-show-host-noah-lands-new-deal-as-trump-bits-lift-ratings.

Slater, Michael D. "Reinforcing Spirals: The Mutual Influence of Media Selectivity and Media Effects and their Impact on Individuals Behavior and Social Identity." *Communication Theory* 17, no. 3 (2007): 281–303. doi:10.1111/j.1468–2885.2007.00296.x.

The O'Reilly Factor. "The Jon Stewart and Undecided Voter Connection." *Fox News*. September 20, 2004. http://www.foxnews.com/story/2004/09/20/jon-stewart-and-undecided-voter-connection.html.

Torney-Purta, Judith, and Jo-Ann Amadeo. "Participatory Niches for Emergent Citizenship in Early Adolescence: An International Perspective." *The Annals of the American Academy of Political and Social Science* 633, no. 1 (2011): 180–200. https://doi.org/10.1177/0002716210384220.

Vaala, Sarah E., and Amy Bleakley. "Monitoring, Mediating, and Modeling: Parental Influence on Adolescent Computer and Internet Use in the United States." *Journal of Children and Media* 9, no. 1 (2015): 40–57. https://doi.org/10.1080/17482798.2015.997103.

Verba, Sidney, Nancy Burns, and Kay Lehman Schlozman. "Unequal at the Starting Line: Creating Participatory Inequalities across Generations and among Groups." *The American Sociologist* 34, no. 1 (2003): 45–69. https://doi.org/10.1007/s12108–003–1005-y.

Vettehen, Paul Hendricks, Ruben P. Konig, Henk Westerik, and Hans Beentjes, "Explaining Television Choices: The Influence of Parents and Partners." *Poetics* 40, no. 6 (2012): 565–85.

Vraga, Emily K., Leticia Bode, JungHwan Yang, Stephanie Edgerly, Kjerstin Thorson, Chris Wells, and Dhavan V. Shah. "Political Influence across Candidate Evaluations in the 2008 Election." *Information, Communication & Society* 17, no. 2 (2014): 184–202. https://doi.org/10.1080/1369118X.2013.872162.

Webster, James G. "Beneath the Veneer of Fragmentation: Television Audience Polarization in a Multichannel World." *Journal of Communication* 55, no. 2 (2005): 366–82. doi:10.1111/j.1460–2466.2005.tb02677.x.

Young, Dannagal G. "Laughter, Learning, or Enlightenment? Viewing and Avoidance Motivations Behind *The Daily Show* and *The Colbert Report*." *Journal of Broadcasting & Electronic Media* 57, no. 2 (2013): 153–69. https://doi.org/10.1080/08838151.2013.787080.

Young, Dannagal G., and Sarah E. Esralew. "Jon Stewart a Heretic? Surely You Jest: Political Participation and Discussion Among Viewers of Late-Night Comedy Programing." In *The Stewart/Colbert Effect: Essays on the Real Impacts of Fake News*, edited by Amarnath Amarasingam, 99–115. Jefferson, NC: McFarland, 2011.

Chapter 14

The Context for Comedy

Presidential Candidates and Comedy Television

Michael Parkin

Most Americans have become accustomed to seeing serious presidential candidates on comedy television. Gone are the days when a late-night talk show interview or sketch comedy cameo would generate widespread curiosity or scorn. We now live in an era where comedic appearances are practically expected and where candidates book time on shows they would have once avoided. The candidate-comedy connection has become an essential part of modern American presidential campaigns; and yet, questions remain about exactly how this relationship started and endured over the past quarter century. How did we get to a place where presidential candidates are expected to demonstrate their good humor by engaging with comedians? How did the connection between presidential candidates and comedy television become so ingrained in the electoral process?

The conventional explanation is that candidates have sought out these venues for the opportunity to appear likeable in front of millions of viewers. Brief cameos on shows like *Saturday Night Live* can showcase the candidate's fun-loving nature, while interviews on late-night talk shows like *The Tonight Show*, *The Late Show*, and *The Daily Show* are thought to provide an ideal setting for promoting the candidate's personality. Researchers have long pointed to this candidate-centered explanation by noting, for example, that "politicians and their media consultants see these programs as forums through which the candidate can address hard-to-reach audiences [and] show their 'human' side (including their ability to be good-humored and self-deprecating)."[1] While image promotion is certainly a critical part of the explanation, it is not the entire story.

In this chapter, I want to steer the discussion in a different direction by arguing that the candidate-comedy connection is at least partly the result of a changing political communications environment that has made it increasingly difficult for candidates to avoid these types of comedic encounters. It is not simply the case that candidates suddenly found these appearances to be in their best strategic interests and thus pursued them with vigor. Key contextual factors have bolstered the connection between candidates and comedy television, making it hard for reticent candidates to stay away and easy for eager candidates to engage. In a sense, this connection is the result of candidate motivations interacting with changes in the political communications environment that have helped to cement the relationship over time. Without these external factors, the relationship would be much more tenuous, or even non-existent.

In the next section, I describe how presidential candidates have engaged with comedy television over the years. I then discuss how, although it seems almost mundane at this point, it is actually rather puzzling that presidential candidates have taken to routinely campaigning on late-night talk shows and sketch comedy programs. Comedy television poses certain risks and candidates have many other ways to reach voters, particularly when discussing serious issues. I then explain how this relationship has been affected by three key external forces: (1) changes in the candidates' need for exposure brought on by crowded primaries; (2) the enhanced opportunities brought on by an increase in comedy shows with an interest in politics, and (3) the growing legitimacy of connecting politics with comedy that has developed over the past few decades. I conclude with a brief summary and discussion.

THE CANDIDATE-COMEDY CONNECTION

Presidential candidates first toyed with comedy television in the 1960s. Both John F. Kennedy and Richard Nixon appeared on *The Tonight Show with Jack Paar* in 1960, with Nixon later returning to the show, along with making a five-second cameo on *Laugh-In*, as he geared up for the 1968 campaign.[2] These early precursors, while interesting and entertaining to some extent, were generally met with disdain from the media and uneasiness from the general public. Some in the press, for example, winced as they watched Nixon's first late-night interview in 1960, later calling it "revolting" and wondering whether it provided "too much show business and not enough political business."[3] These appearances failed to catch on, in large part, because they were out of context for the time. They were new, and most viewers were not accustomed to thinking about presidential candidates in such an informal way.

Presidential candidates generally stayed away from comedy television until 1992 when Bill Clinton made his widely discussed appearance on *The Arsenio Hall Show*.[4] The now-famous saxophone opening and subsequent interview were considered risky and perhaps even desperate at the time,[5] and while some in the press seemed enamored, others expressed reservations, calling it "undignified" and claiming that it was "not how a presidential candidate [was] supposed to act."[6] Clinton's appearance clearly hit a nerve, as it generated far more media attention than the handful of other late-night interviews and cameos in the 1992 campaign.[7] Although press reaction was mixed, the Clinton-Hall encounter nevertheless provided a model of how candidates could communicate with voters who might not otherwise be closely following the race. It also showed that voters were warming up to the idea of candidates reaching out to them in unconventional ways, as many had grown tired of the traditional media and "hungered for an honest level of conversation missing in most encounters between politicians and journalists."[8]

The Clinton-Hall interview is often cited as the start of a solid candidate-comedy connection.[9] However, the relationship almost faded away in 1996 when, with a significant lead in the polls, President Clinton decided to side-step the late-night routine. Meanwhile, his opponent, Bob Dole, used an appearance on *The Late Show with David Letterman* to officially announce his candidacy and demonstrate a connection with popular culture. While the interview was generally well received, Dole refused to do any more late-night interviews, explaining that he found his encounter with Letterman "intimidating" due to its unpredictability.[10] Comedic interviews were still something of a novelty at this time, making it relatively easy for candidates to stay away without drawing a lot of attention.

Expectations began to change rather dramatically during the 2000 campaign, as candidates took to the comedy airwaves like they had never done before. Along with their primary challengers and third-party candidate, Ralph Nader, the two major party nominees, Al Gore and George W. Bush, sought out comedic venues throughout the entire campaign.[11] Bush started with a disastrous satellite appearance on *The Late Show* before rebounding with generally successful stops at *The Tonight Show with Jay Leno* (twice) and a return, face-to-face encounter with Letterman. For his part, Al Gore managed some amiable, if sometimes awkward, exchanges with both Leno (two interviews and a cameo) and Letterman. Then, as the campaign neared an end, Ralph Nader stopped by *Saturday Night Live* while Bush and Gore taped comedic bits for *SNL's Presidential Bash 2000*. The 2000 campaign showed that late-night talk shows and comedy programs were interested in hosting presidential candidates, and while the media's reaction was still occasionally critical, the repeated use of comedy television demonstrated "America's acceptance of the candidates as celebrity entertainers."[12]

The candidate-comedy connection continued to pick up pace in 2004, propelled by a packed field of Democratic primary contenders eager to challenge George W. Bush. Like his predecessor, President Bush steered clear of late-night television while leading candidates on the Democratic side, from Howard Dean and Wesley Clark to John Edwards and John Kerry, accepted invitations to *The Tonight Show* and/or *The Late Show*, where they gave solid but somewhat unremarkable performances.[13] They also joined some of their colleagues, like Dick Gephardt, Joe Lieberman, and Dennis Kucinich on emerging cable shows like *The Daily Show with Jon Stewart* and *Real Time with Bill Maher*, where interviews were often less gentle and more policy-oriented.[14] The 2004 campaign also featured self-deprecating "Top Ten" lists by Gephardt, Kucinich, Edwards, and Dean as well as a *Saturday Night Live* hosting gig by Al Sharpton a full four months before suspending his campaign. Although it was the first presidential election after 9/11 and candidates ran the risk of seeming insensitive, the large field of Democratic contenders flocked to comedy television, including up-and-coming cable shows designed to mix politics with comedy. Despite the somber era, it still seemed reasonable and perhaps even necessary for candidates to connect with voters beyond the confines of the traditional news media.

In 2008, heavily contested primaries on both sides combined with an array of shows eager to host resulted in a veritable explosion of comedic appearances. Primary candidates conducted a barrage of interviews and cameos leading up to the conventions, after which the nominees continued to engage with late-night audiences in ways that reflected their overall campaign styles. Barack Obama's interviews with Jon Stewart, Jimmy Kimmel, Jay Leno, and David Letterman were generally agreeable and self-deprecating, while John McCain's exchanges were more unpredictable, with interviews ranging from successful to nearly disastrous. For example, McCain was booed after making an insensitive joke on *The Daily Show* and later skipped a scheduled interview with Letterman, for which he took considerable heat.[15] The 2008 campaign also featured more than a dozen cameos, including *Saturday Night Live* bits by Obama, Clinton, and McCain. There was little doubt by the end of 2008 that comedy television had become something of a necessity for modern presidential candidates.

The 2012 campaign, like that of 2004, found a large number of primary contenders battling for the right to take on an incumbent president. However, unlike past years, 2012 was the first time that a sitting president took to the late-night airwaves in search of votes. Both the Republican primary candidates and President Obama got off to an early start. Republicans Newt Gingrich, Tim Pawlenty, Ron Paul, and Jon Huntsman crowded the cable late-night shows, while others like Mitt Romney, Michele Bachmann, Rick Perry, and Herman Cain accepted invitations to chat with the likes of Letterman, Leno, and Fallon. Huntsman even appeared on *Saturday Night Live*'s "Weekend Update" and Perry delivered his own "Top Ten" list of excuses for botching his debate performance. President Obama countered with three of his own pre-convention appearances before stopping by *The Late Show* and returning to *The Daily Show* and *The Tonight Show* during the general election. After securing the Republican nomination, Mitt Romney avoided comedy television, despite the fact that he had had two relatively successful interviews with Leno and one with Letterman earlier in the campaign. Speaking candidly, Romney noted in his now-infamous "47 percent video" the possibility that Letterman "hated" him for appearing on *The Tonight Show* more often than *The Late Show*.[16] It was the first time in nearly two decades that a prominent politician publicly expressed reservations with the strategy, putting him in stark contrast with President Obama's embrace of the comedy format.

The 2016 campaign saw the return of a near wholesale commitment to the candidate-comedy connection. Late-night television had changed a great deal since the last presidential race, but Republicans and Democrats nevertheless found their way to multiple cameos and dozens of interviews with established hosts like Bill Maher, Jimmy Kimmel, Jon Stewart, and Jimmy Fallon; new hosts like Seth Meyers, Larry Wilmore, Trevor Noah, and Samantha Bee; and even an old host with a new show, Stephen Colbert. As in 2008, primaries on both sides led to a large number of early interviews. After securing the Republican nomination, Donald Trump returned for a third time to *The Tonight Show with Jimmy Fallon* for an interview that was derided by some as a "genial, hair-mussing" exchange with "mostly uncontroversial questions."[17] Meanwhile, Hillary Clinton followed up her six pre-convention interviews with a *Saturday Night Live* cameo and a general election exchange with Jimmy Kimmel where the two chatted about the campaign and Clinton's health before Kimmel challenged her to read actual Donald Trump quotes without laughing (she never cracked a smile).

Figure 14.1 presents the total number of comedic appearances—that is, late-night talk show interviews and sketch comedy cameos—made by presidential candidates as they campaigned in the candidate-comedy era between 1992 and 2016.[18] The results show that the relationship started slowly with five appearances in 1992 and only a single late-night interview in 1996. By 2000, however, candidates were hitting the late-night stage with greater regularity, conducting eleven interviews and making four cameos over the course of the campaign. The number of appearances more than doubled to twenty-nine during the 2004 contest before exploding to ninety-five in 2008. Candidates then returned to late-night television and sketch comedy shows thirty-six more times in 2012 and an additional seventy-one times in 2016. All told, presidential candidates conducted 214 late-night interviews and made thirty-eight brief comedic appearances between 1992 and 2016.

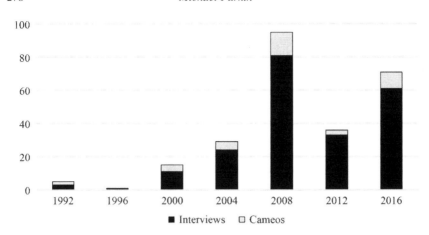

Figure 14.1 Comedic Appearances by Campaign Year.

Table 14.1 Comedic Appearances by Candidates

	Comedic Appearances		Total Estimated Time on Comedy Television
	Interviews	Cameos	(Hours and Minutes)
John McCain (2000 and 2008)	18	4	3:58
Barack Obama (2008 and 2012)	17	3	5:02
Bernie Sanders (2016)	16	2	4:01
Hillary Clinton (2008 and 2016)	11	8	3:02
John Edwards (2004 and 2008)	12	1	2:19
Mike Huckabee (2008)	10	2	1:12
Ron Paul (2008 and 2012)	11	0	1:43

The candidate-comedy connection has become an essential part of campaigning, as nearly every presidential candidate over the past two decades has sat down with a comedic host at least a couple of times, with some of the nation's most prominent politicians committing to dozens of late-night campaign stops. Table 14.1, which lists the number and total length of late-night interviews and cameos by top candidates, shows that some of them have spent hours on comedy television. John McCain, for example, spent nearly four hours making twenty-three appearances in 2000 and 2008, Barack Obama spent five hours making twenty appearances in 2008 and 2012, and Bernie Sanders spent four hours making eighteen appearances in 2016. Added to these are the comedic interviews and cameos of many other candidates, and it becomes obvious that comedy television has come to play a key role in American presidential campaigns.

THE PUZZLING CONNECTION BETWEEN
CANDIDATES AND COMEDY

At this point, the connection between candidates and comedy television may appear somewhat normal. After all, candidates have made hundreds of appearances and most people no longer balk at the sight of a serious presidential candidate joking with a comedian host or playing along with a comedic bit. However, this relationship, as normal as it may now seem, is actually somewhat puzzling upon further reflection. Questions remain about the contours of the candidate-comedy connection and why presidential candidates have pursued it with such vigor and persistence. The desire to promote their personal image to large audiences is no doubt part of the answer, but it does not fully explain the evolution and intensity of the relationship.

To begin with, if image promotion was the sole or even primary reason for appearing on comedy television, candidates would have arguably started much earlier. As noted above, the connection between candidates and comedy television was slow to take off and only really became established in the 2000s. This initial hesitancy is curious given that campaigns have long understood the need to connect with voters on a personal level. As far back as the 1960s, practitioners clearly understood the power of personal image in modern campaigns,[19] and researchers have been confirming the central role that perceptions of candidates' personalities play in voters' evaluations for more than thirty years.[20] Yet, candidates were initially reluctant to embrace comedy television, suggesting that factors other than candidate incentives were shaping their decisions. Perhaps the political and media environment of the time helps to explain why they did not flock to comedy television the moment they recognized its potential.

Image promotion also seems to be an inadequate explanation for the intensity and persistence of this relationship. Nearly every presidential candidate since 2000 has appeared on comedy television despite the potential risks and clear incentives to stop. It is difficult to understand why presidential candidates, who tend to be carefully scripted and controlled, would pursue comedy shows with such determination when they have so many safer options at their disposal (e.g., campaign ads, social media, traditional news shows). Comedic appearances can go wrong and there is always the potential for embarrassment or awkwardness, which is particularly the case with candidates who seem better suited for traditional or more predictable venues. Why, for example, would a well-known candidate like Hillary Clinton feel compelled to spend hours on comedy television when she would have likely been more comfortable playing it straight on a conventional news program? Presumably, candidates like Clinton and many others (e.g., Bernie Sanders, Jeb Bush, and

John Kerry) would have seriously considered skirting the comedy appearance routine had others not set a precedent.

The same logic applies to candidates who have returned to comedy television after disastrous outings. Most appearances work out but a good number of them have failed to deliver large audiences and some have even backfired in terms of projecting likeability.[21] Candidates from George W. Bush and Michele Bachmann to John McCain and John Kerry have all endured awkward or tense exchanges with late-night interviewers, yet this hardly dampened their continued pursuit of these shows. In fact, Bush visited with Leno less than a week after his seriously awkward exchange with Letterman, and McCain was on *Jimmy Kimmel Live* less than a month after a *Daily Show* audience nearly booed him off stage.[22]

Questions also remain about why presidential candidates continued to engage with comedy television when the political situation became particularly dire after 2001. While political issues are always serious, there was seemingly little to joke about after thousands were killed on 9/11 and many more were sent overseas to fight terrorism, or when millions struggled with the possibility of financial ruin in 2008, and yet presidential candidates continued their trips to comedy television. The risk of offense was higher than normal and candidates, who have always had incentives to avoid situations that voters might consider frivolous or demeaning to the electoral process, could have easily curtailed their comedic activities without being criticized. The fact that no candidate publicly shunned these programs out of respect for these serious issues suggests that powerful forces other than simple image promotion were likely at work.

All of this suggests that the candidate-comedy connection was the result of more than just candidate incentives to promote a positive personal image to millions of hard-to-reach voters. It is difficult to reconcile the intensity and persistence of this connection with the mere pursuit of image promotion given that presidential candidates could have stuck to safer venues or taken the opportunity to stop the comedy strategy when their appearances were uncomfortable, embarrassing, or risked offending voters during serious political times. What other factors might have propelled candidates to maintain and even strengthen this practice?

Contextual Factors and the Candidate-Comedy Connection

Candidate behavior has always been affected by context. While the decision to appear on comedy television has certainly been motivated by image considerations, candidates have also been affected by factors outside their control in the political communications environment. Crowded primaries have increased the need for candidate exposure and differentiation, while changes in the comedy television landscape have provided all sorts of candidates with greater opportunities to achieve these objectives. Perceptions of political media and culture have also changed, making it increasingly acceptable or even necessary for serious presidential contenders to engage with comedy television. These factors, when combined and added to candidates' objectives, help to more fully explain why they have pursued this relationship so intensely over time.

Campaign Context

The presidential nominating process was once a relatively closed affair in which candidates sought the support of state and local party leaders. The media did not play a large role in the nomination process because potential nominees were reaching out to party leaders, not average voters watching at home. This changed, however, after the tumultuous 1968 Democratic nomination contest led both parties to adopt a primary system for delegate selection.[23] The new primary system would eventually have an important impact on the relationship between presidential candidates and the media, including comedy television.[24]

Almost immediately, the primary system increased the number of candidates competing for the nomination. No longer beholden to the favor of party leaders, candidates could now campaign directly to the masses regardless of their relative standing in the party, which led to a noticeable increase in the number of long-shot contenders. Figure 14.2 shows that the number of candidates seeking the Democratic and Republican nominations began to increase in the 1970s.[25] Whereas primaries between 1956 and 1968 generally featured two or three candidates in the non-incumbent party, this number was nearly twice that in every election after 1972 with the total combined number of primary candidates consistently reaching double digits starting in 1996.

Heavily contested primaries have had a direct and rather predictable impact on the intensity of the candidate-comedy connection. Comparing Figures 14.1 and 14.2 shows that the number of primary candidates parallels the number of comedic appearances in each campaign cycle. Large primaries (e.g., 2008, 2016) have resulted in more appearances than primaries with fewer contestants (e.g., 2000, 2004) because a larger number of candidates understandably mean that there are more people contributing to the total number of comedic appearances in an election cycle. Growth in the number of candidates is therefore at least partially responsible for the apparent surge in comedy television use after 2000.

Crowded primaries also increase the number of appearances per candidate, meaning that the average candidate tends to appear more frequently when the field is large than when it is small. In 1992, six Democrats made five

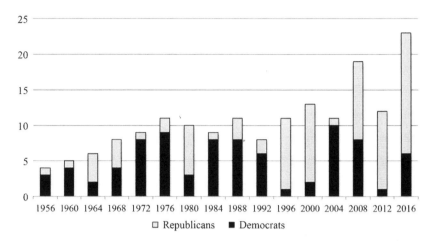

Figure 14.2   Number of Presidential Candidates by Year.

appearances for an average of 0.8 appearances per candidate. In 1996, the average per candidate was only 0.1, but then, as primary fields expanded, the average climbed to 1.2 in 2000, 2.9 in 2004, and 5.0 in 2008 before settling at 2.6 in 2012 and 3.1 in 2016.[26]

Candidates tend to appear more often when the primary field is large because they have a greater need for exposure, particularly if they are not well-known nationally. An intense battle for airtime makes them more willing to accept potentially risky or smaller-audience engagements, such as those on lesser-known cable shows, in the hopes of breaking through with voters or the press. Failure to appear could leave them trailing their opponents, which seems to explain why, for example, long-shot candidates like Wesley Clark, Dennis Kucinich, and Ron Paul accepted multiple invitations to chat with Jon Stewart, Bill Maher, and later Stephen Colbert in 2004 and 2008. Had the competition been less intense, candidates might have skipped potentially risky comedy shows in favor of more traditional venues.

Crowded primaries also create incentives for candidates to distinguish themselves from opponents who likely share their position on most policy matters. When policy distinctions are difficult to make—as they typically are in primaries—candidates have to set themselves apart with other considerations, such as their personality and character. There is a premium on being perceived as more likeable than your competitors when there is considerable agreement on the issues.[27] As such, large primaries intensify the motivation to promote image whenever possible, as doing so may allow candidates to pull ahead of their opponents and gain momentum in the race. The fact that Mike Huckabee, for example, briefly surpassed his 2008 opponents with a "Colbert

Bump" supports the idea that image matters more when choosing between like-minded candidates.[28]

The campaign context, particularly the number of contenders in the race, can affect how candidates approach comedy television. Large fields naturally increase the total number of comedic appearances, but they also encourage candidates to seek out comedy venues to gain exposure and set themselves apart from their competitors. Less-crowded primaries, on the other hand, result in fewer comedic appearances, not just because there are fewer candidates who can make appearances, but also because there is less need to promote image. It is difficult to imagine the candidate-comedy connection growing as it did after 2000 had there not been so many candidates clamoring for airtime.

The Comedy Television Environment

Changes in the comedy television environment have also had a demonstrable impact on the intensity with which candidates have pursued this relationship.[29] As the comedy landscape grew and changed in character throughout the 2000s, candidates had new opportunities and incentives to appear. Candidates, especially those in search of exposure and differentiation, intensified the candidate-comedy connection with appearances across a range of new shows that combined politics with comedy in new and exciting ways.

Candidates were once fairly constrained in the opportunities they had to appear on comedy television. Although *Saturday Night Live* and major network shows like *The Tonight Show* have historically had relationships with some major presidential aspirants, it was not until the 1990s that they became interested in a broader and more sustained partnership. It was around this time, as viewers were growing accustomed to seeing candidates across the cable news airwaves and beyond, that major comedy programs started to contemplate the potential ratings that could be gained by getting more heavily involved in presidential campaigns.[30] During the 2000 race, *The Late Show with David Letterman* and *The Tonight Show with Jay Leno* took the plunge, combining for a total of ten interviews with presidential contenders.

An even more significant change occurred in the early 2000s when cable shows emerged with an intense focus on politics. While early cable programs like *Dennis Miller Live* and Bill Maher's *Politically Incorrect* featured political content, they rarely landed presidential candidates as their guests. This began to change when *The Daily Show with Jon Stewart* burst onto the scene with its perceptive and penetrating analysis of American politics, quickly becoming a trusted source of political news and information for many.[31] Seizing on this, the ten contenders for the 2004 Democratic nomination flocked to *The Daily Show*, along with *Real Time with Bill Maher*, for eighteen interviews. *The Daily Show*'s rise provided candidates like Joe Lieberman, Howard Dean, and Wesley Clark valuable exposure in a crowded field—exposure they likely would not have received without these shows.

The number of network late-night and cable comedy shows willing to host candidates continued to grow after 2004. On the network side, hosts such as Conan O'Brien, Jimmy Kimmel, Jimmy Fallon, and later Seth Meyers got into the mix while cable shows hosted by Stephen Colbert and later Trevor Noah, Larry Wilmore, and Samantha Bee also provided opportunities. The increase in available venues allowed candidates to sustain and grow their relationship with comedy television. Without it, candidates, particularly long-shot candidates, would have found it difficult, if not impossible, to engage with comedy television and the number of comedic appearances would have never reached the height it has in recent years.

Comedy television also grew more attractive to candidates with time. As more network hosts conducted interviews over the years, candidates could better predict what they were going to get when they appeared—they no longer needed to be "intimated" by the unpredictability. Although there was still the potential to be surprised (e.g., Michele Bachmann's tense encounter with Jay Leno), network interviews began to take on a fairly routine feel that allowed candidates to be more at ease with the situation. Interviews on cable comedy shows also had the advantage of mixing personality with serious policy discussion, as it was routine for hosts like Stewart, Maher, and Colbert to drill down on the issues when politicians arrived.[32] Although these hosts could be tough, candidates trusted that their exchanges would not be frivolous and thus avoided the risk of offending viewers. The fact that candidates could maintain an air of professionalism while still playing along with the humor is particularly important for understanding how the candidate-comedy relationship survived and even excelled after 2001. These cable shows gave candidates the opportunity to address serious issues so that any light-hearted moments would not be offensive to the millions watching at home.

Changes in the comedy television environment help to explain how the candidate-comedy relationship flourished over the years. Candidates, particularly those most in need of exposure, found new opportunities as the number of shows willing to host them expanded. They also benefited from an improved sense of what to expect and the routine opportunity to mix humor with policy. Without these changes, the relationship would have likely plateaued or even faded. At most, leading presidential candidates might have made the occasional appearance on a major network talk show. Instead, the abundance of new shows and the opportunities they provided allowed the candidate-comedy connection to develop by enabling scores of candidates to continue their relentless pursuit of late-night talk shows and sketch comedy programs.

Accepting the Candidate-Comedy Connection

Changes in press and public perceptions have also played a role in maintaining the candidate-comedy connection. Although there will always be some critics ready to grumble and some viewers who are still uncomfortable with candidates on comedy television, both the press and the public have generally come to accept the comedy routine.[33] Had they continued to express their early disdain (1960s–1990s), candidate usage of comedy television would have likely faltered, as the risks of continuing would have outweighed the benefits. Instead, a culture of candidate comedy has developed in which the press write fewer scathing reviews and viewers have generally come to accept and even expect candidate appearances on comedy television.[34]

This gradual acceptance grew out of the fact that, as mentioned above, comedic appearances are almost invariably grounded in political discussion. There are always the requisite light-hearted moments and some appearances border on inane, but the vast majority feature political content that viewers can use as they contemplate their vote choice—they are more than "cozy gab sessions."[35] In one exchange, for example, David Letterman peppered Al Gore with so many policy questions that the vice president eventually turned to his host with "a baffled look, as if he were thinking, 'hey, this is supposed to be a comedy show.'"[36] In fact, research shows that late-night talk show interviews, particularly those on cable, tend to average at least 40 percent political content and can, at times, "feature as much substantive discussion as those on some of the most highly regarded political news shows."[37] Viewers are not simply being sold on image but are getting solid political information and a sense of the candidate's position on the issues, often explained in plain language.

Acceptance of the candidate-comedy connection has also been aided by the growing respect that the press and public have of these shows and their hosts. The perception of these shows started to change when hosts long known for their goofiness (Letterman) or agreeableness (Leno) began providing an important window into presidential campaigns. Meanwhile, Jon Stewart and later Stephen Colbert gained respect for their willingness to challenge candidates and hold their feet to the fire. By 2008, millions of Americans were getting their political news from comedy television and Jon Stewart was named as one of the most admired and trusted people in the news industry.[38] For many Americans, candidate appearances on these shows had become as legitimate and useful as the interviews conducted by the esteemed hosts of long running Sunday political news shows like *Meet the Press*.[39] This respectability and popularity made it easy, and perhaps even necessary, for candidates to appear.

Press and public acceptance have also been motivated by the fact that nearly every presidential candidate has been willing to engage with comedy at some point. The political class has clearly endorsed the relationship, as some of the country's most revered and dignified politicians have found their way to the late-night stage. The respectability of this practice was perhaps aided most by Barack Obama's full embrace of comedy venues. Obama, both as an incumbent in search of votes and as a president promoting policy initiatives, showed that comedy programming could be used to connect with ordinary Americans—his late-night talk show interviews, sketch comedy cameos, and even online videos (e.g., *Between Two Ferns*) brought politics to the people.[40] Obama's appearances, along with those of nearly every other serious politician, showed that engaging with comedy television did not have to be demeaning to the process or the office.

It took some time, but the culture surrounding the candidate-comedy connection eventually softened. The press and the public became more accepting as appearances grew more frequent and routine, and with greater acceptance came the expectation that candidates would appear on these shows as they pursued the White House. Whereas candidates like Bob Dole once enjoyed the freedom to avoid comedy encounters, the campaign culture shifted to a place where "would-be presidents have no choice but to get with the program."[41] The press and the public, once disdainful of the practice, now raise questions when candidates like John McCain ditch an interview or Mitt Romney decides to avoid comedy television.[42] The expectation to appear helps to explain why nearly every presidential candidate, even those who seem uncomfortable on these shows, have nevertheless engaged with comedy television so intensely over the years.

CONCLUSION

Presidential candidates have been appearing on comedy television for the better part of the past twenty-five years. Considerable research has explored the impact that this has had on viewers and the political system, yet relatively little attention has been paid to the role that contextual factors have played in developing and sustaining this connection. Most commentators and researchers believe that candidates use late-night talk shows and sketch comedy programs to promote their image to millions of hard-to-reach voters. While that is part of the explanation, external forces have also been at work helping to sustain the candidate-comedy relationship.

The connection between candidates and comedy television has at least as much to do with the changing political communications environment as it does with the individual decisions that candidates and their teams make about appealing to voters. This relationship persisted and grew in spite of the risks and incentives to stop, in large part, because the primary system generated crowded primaries filled with candidates in need of exposure and differentiation, just as the comedy television market expanded into cable, giving candidates more opportunities to appear. This led to hundreds of comedic encounters and the normalization of the candidate-comedy connection, which the press and the public eventually came to accept and even expect. It is hard to imagine this connection surviving and flourishing without the need for exposure, the opportunity to appear on so many shows, or the press and public's acceptance. Uncomfortable and awkward candidates, for example, could have stuck to formal news programs had there not been a precedent to appear; long-shot contenders could have been shut out if not for the emerging shows on cable; and all candidates may have ended the connection after 9/11 had these shows not mixed comedy with policy. These external forces, beyond the control of individual candidates, help to explain the contours of this relationship—how it started, how it progressed, and how it grew into such a critical part of modern presidential campaigns.

The context for comedy continues to evolve. As candidates gear up for the 2020 race, they face an increasingly partisan political communications environment in which comedy programs are deciding between maintaining their impartiality or offering a satirical critique that emulates wider partisan divisions.[43] Democratic and Republican candidates may come to believe that certain shows are "friendlier" than others, and if interviews become increasingly partisan, viewers may see them as less legitimate in terms of their ability to offer a fresh perspective rather than just another venue for partisan acrimony. All of this could ultimately weaken the candidate-comedy connection, but whatever the case, the *context* will play an important role in determining the relationship between candidates and comedy television in the years to come.

NOTES

1. Jeffrey P. Jones, *Entertaining Politics: Satiric Television and Political Engagement, Second Edition* (Lanham, MD: Rowman & Littlefield, 2010), 11; see also, for example, Matthew A. Baum, "Talking the Vote: Why Presidential Candidates Hit the Talk Show Circuit," *American Journal of Political Science* 49, no. 2 (2005); Michael Parkin, *Talk Show Campaigns: Presidential Candidates on Daytime and Late Night Television* (New York: Routledge, 2014); S. Robert Lichter, Jody C Baumgartner, and Jonathan S. Morris, *Politics Is a Joke! How TV Comedians Are Remaking Political Life* (Boulder, CO: Westview Press, 2015), 188–203.

2. For details on these and other historical appearances, see Parkin, *Talk Show Campaigns*, 22–57; Lichter, Baumgartner, and Morris, *Politics Is a Joke*, 188–203.

3. Ed Koterba, "Assignment Washington," *Reading Eagle*, August 27, 1960, 4; Richard Shepard, "Nominees and TV Face a Problem," *New York Times*, August 27, 1960, 39.

4. The only appearances in the 1970s and 1980s that might be considered relevant were Ronald Reagan's spot on *The Sonny and Cher Show* in 1972, Gerald Ford's brief campaign appearance on *Saturday Night Live* in 1976, and Jesse Jackson's hosting of *Saturday Night Live* in 1984.

5. Joseph R. Hayden, *Covering Clinton: The President and The Press in the 1990s* (Westport, CT: Greenwood Press, 2001), 8–9.

6. Hayden, *Covering Clinton*, 19; see also David Gergen on "92-Gergen and Shields," *MacNeil/Lehrer News Hour* (New York: Public Broadcasting Service, June 5, 1992).

7. Parkin, *Talk Show Campaigns*, 4.

8. Hayden, *Covering Clinton*, 20; see also S. Robert Lichter and Richard E. Noyes, *Good Intentions Make Bad News: Why Americans Hate Campaign Journalism* (Boston: Rowman & Littlefield, 1995), 232.

9. See, for example, Baum, "Talking the Vote," 213; Patricia Moy, Michael A. Xenos, and Verena K. Hess, "Priming Effects of Late-Night Comedy," *International Journal of Public Opinion Research* 18, no. 2 (2005): 199.

10. Jerry Berger, "Dole's Out of the Race—to the Talk Shows," *St. Louis Dispatch*, February 9, 1995, 1G.

11. Gary Levin, "Bush, Gore Work Late Shift for Laughs; Humor May Help Sway Young Voters," *USA Today*, October 23, 2000, 4D.

12. Paul Farhi, "Al and Dubya's Saturday Night Date; Candidates Follow Laugh Track to Voters," *Washington Post*, November 4, 2000, A01; see also Sharyn Vane, "Late Night Al and Dubya," *American Journalism Review*, November 2000, 10–11.

13. See, for example, Michael Parkin, "Taking Late Night Comedy Seriously: How Candidate Appearances on Late Night Television Can Engage Viewers," *Political Research Quarterly* 63, no. 1 (March 2010): 3–15.

14. Parkin, *Talk Show Campaigns*, 96–128.

15. Bill Carter, "Letterman, Spurned," *New York Times*, September 25, 2008, A24.

16. Lisa de Moraes, "Romney and the Sharp Tongues? Bring it On!" *Washington Post*, September 20, 2012, C06; see also Martha T. Moore, "Romney Skips Entertainment TV; Medium Offers Risky Foray on Trail," *USA Today*, October 25, 2012, 5A.

17. Dave Itskoff, "From One Comedic Host to Another: Criticism Over Trump," *New York Times*, September 21, 2016, C1.

18. Late-night interviews are extended campaign discussions (i.e., interviews on the campaign trail) between Democratic, Republican, or independent presidential candidates and these late-night talk hosts: Arsenio Hall, David Letterman, Dennis Miller, Bill Maher, Jay Leno, Jon Stewart, Stephen Colbert, Conan O'Brien, Jimmy Fallon, Seth Meyers, Jimmy Kimmel, Larry Wilmore, Trevor Noah, and Samantha Bee. Non-campaign interviews have been excluded. Cameos are brief appearances on late-night talk shows (e.g., Top Ten lists, video messages) and comedic bits on sketch comedy shows like *Saturday Night Live*.

19. Joe McGinnis, *The Selling of the President 1968* (New York: Trident Publishing, 1969).

20. Donald R. Kinder, et al., "Presidential Prototypes," *Political Behavior* 2, no. 4 (1980): 315–37; David P. Glass, "Evaluating Presidential Candidates: Who Focuses

on Personal Attributes?" *The Public Opinion Quarterly* 49, no. 4 (1985): 517–34; Kenneth L. Hacker, *Candidate Images in Presidential Elections* (Lanham, MD: Rowman & Littlefield, 2004).

21. On ratings, see Parkin, *Talk Show Campaigns*, 58–95. On the mixed results of how late-night interviews impact viewers, see Moy, Xenos, and Hess, "Priming Effects of Late Night Comedy"; Parkin, "Taking Late Night Comedy Seriously."

22. For more on these and other awkward encounters, see Parkin, *Talk Show Campaigns*, 22–57.

23. Nelson W. Polsby, *Consequences of Party Reform* (New York: Oxford University Press, 1983).

24. Shanto Iyengar, *Media Politics: A Citizen's Guide, Third Edition* (New York: W. W. Norton, 2016), 23.

25. Data for 1956 to 2008 come from Alan Silverlieb and William G. Mayer, "By the Numbers: A Statistical Guide to the Presidential Nomination Process," in *The Making of the Presidential Candidates: 2012*, eds. William G. Mayer and Jonathan Bernstein (Lanham, MD: Rowman & Littlefield, 2012), 203–25. Data for 2012 and 2016 come from *The New York Times* website.

26. The 2016 average is deflated by including Lawrence Lessig, Jim Webb, and Lincoln Chafee, all of whom polled under 5 percent nationally and never appeared on comedy television. Excluding them increases the average to 3.6 in 2016. While other factors, such as the increase in comedy venues after 2000, may have kept this relationship from being perfectly linear, the fact remains that the average candidate tends to appear more often when the primary field is crowded.

27. Alan I. Abramowitz, "Viability, Electability, and Candidate Choice in a Presidential Primary Election: A Test of Competing Models," *The Journal of Politics* 51, no. 4 (1989): 977–92.

28. On the "Colbert Bump," see James H. Fowler, "The Colbert Bump in Campaign Donations: More Truthful than Truthy," *PS: Political Science and Politics* 41, no. 3 (2008): 533–39.

29. See Richard Davis and Diana Owen, *New Media and American Politics* (New York: Oxford University Press, 1998).

30. Lichter and Noyes, *Good Intentions Make Bad News*, 232; Fahri, "Al and Dubya's Saturday Night Date," A01; Elizabeth Kolbert, "The 1992 Campaign: Media, Talk Show Wrangling to Book the Candidates," *New York Times*, July 6, 1992, A10. On ratings, see Parkin, *Talk Show Campaigns*, 58–95.

31. Michiko Kakutani, "The Most Trusted Man in America?" *New York Times*, August 15, 2008, AR1.

32. For more on the content of these appearances, see Parkin, *Talk Show Campaigns*, 96–128.

33. See, for example, Travis M. Andrews, "From Kennedy to Trump, the Much-Deplored History of Presidential Candidates on Late-Night TV," *The Washington Post*, September 22, 2016.

34. See Parkin, *Talk Show Campaigns*, 166–95.

35. Julie Mason, "Kerry Makes TV Rounds to Aid Image: More Candidates Seeking Advantages of Popular Shows," *Houston Chronicle*, September 22, 2004, A14; Parkin, "Taking Late Night Comedy Seriously," 8.

36. Caryn James, "Blurring Distinctions while Chasing Laughs," *New York Times*, September 22, 2000, A19.

37. Parkin, *Talk Show Campaigns*, 107.

38. See, for example, Pew Research Center, "Cable and Internet Loom Large in Fragmented Political News Universe," January 11, 2004; Kakutani, "The Most Trusted Man in America?" AR1.

39. On the relative utility of talk show interviews, see Matthew A. Baum and Angela S. Jamison, "The Oprah Effect: How Soft News Helps Inattentive Citizens Vote Consistently," *American Journal of Political Science* 68, no. 4 (2006): 946–59.

40. Tom Huddleston, "How Barack Obama Became the Late Night Comedy President," *Fortune*, November 4, 2016.

41. Frank Rich, "Paar to Leno, J.F.K to J.F.K.," *New York Times*, February 8, 2004, AR1.

42. Carter, "Letterman, Spurned," A24; Adam Clark Estes, "Why Won't Mitt Romney Go on Any Late Night Shows?" *The Atlantic*, October 28, 2012; Moore, "Romney Skips Entertainment TV," 5A.

43. Gretel Kauffman, "Stephen Colbert vs. Jimmy Fallon: What's the Role of Satire in the Trump Era?" *Christian Science Monitor*, February 15, 2017. For a longer-term perspective on partisanship and political comedy, see Alison Dagnes, *A Conservative Walks into a Bar: The Politics of Political Humor* (New York: Palgrave Macmillan, 2012).

REFERENCES

Abramowitz, Alan I. "Viability, Electability, and Candidate Choice in a Presidential Primary Election: A Test of Competing Models." *The Journal of Politics* 51, no. 4 (1989): 977–92.

Andrews, Travis M. "From Kennedy to Trump, the Much-Deplored History of Presidential Candidates on Late-Night TV." *The Washington Post*, September 22, 2016.

Baum, Matthew A. "Talking the Vote: Why Presidential Candidates Hit the Talk Show Circuit." *American Journal of Political Science* 49, no. 2 (2005): 213–34.

Baum, Matthew A., and Angela S. Jamison, "The Oprah Effect: How Soft News Helps Inattentive Citizens Vote Consistently." *American Journal of Political Science* 68, no. 4 (2006): 946–59.

Berger, Jerry. "Dole's Out of the Race—to the Talk Shows." *St. Louis Dispatch*, February 9, 1995.

Carter, Bill. "Letterman, Spurned." *New York Times*, September 25, 2008.

Dagnes, Alison. *A Conservative Walks into a Bar: The Politics of Political Humor.* New York: Palgrave Macmillan, 2012.

Davis, Richard, and Diana Owen. *New Media and American Politics.* New York: Oxford University Press, 1998.

De Moraes, Lisa. "Romney and the Sharp Tongues? Bring it On!" *Washington Post*, September 20, 2012.

Estes, Adam Clark. "Why Won't Mitt Romney Go on Any Late Night Shows?" *The Atlantic*, October 28, 2012.

Farhi, Paul. "Al and Dubya's Saturday Night Date; Candidates Follow Laugh Track to Voters." *Washington Post*, November 4, 2000.

Fowler, James H. "The Colbert Bump in Campaign Donations: More Truthful than Truthy." *PS: Political Science and Politics* 41, no. 3 (2008): 533–39.

Gergen, David. "92-Gergen and Shields." *MacNeil/Lehrer News Hour*. New York: Public Broadcasting Service, June 5, 1992.

Glass, David P. "Evaluating Presidential Candidates: Who Focuses on Personal Attributes?" *The Public Opinion Quarterly*, 49, no. 4 (1985): 517–34.

Hacker, Kenneth L. *Candidate Images in Presidential Elections*. Lanham, MD: Rowman & Littlefield, 2004.

Hayden, Joseph R. *Covering Clinton: The President and The Press in the 1990s*. Westport, CT: Greenwood Press, 2001.

Huddleston, Tom. "How Barack Obama Became the Late Night Comedy President." *Fortune*, November 4, 2016.

Itskoff, Dave. "From One Comedic Host to Another: Criticism Over Trump." *New York Times*, September 21, 2016.

Iyengar, Shanto. *Media Politics: A Citizen's Guide, Third Edition*. New York: W. W. Norton, 2016.

James, Caryn. "Blurring Distinctions while Chasing Laughs." *New York Times*, September 22, 2000, A19.

Jones, Jeffrey P. *Entertaining Politics: Satiric Television and Political Engagement, Second Edition*. Lanham, MD: Rowman & Littlefield, 2010.

Kakutani, Michiko. "The Most Trusted Man in America?" *New York Times*, August 15, 2008, AR1.

Kauffman, Gretel, "Stephen Colbert vs. Jimmy Fallon: What's the Role of Satire in the Trump Era?" *Christian Science Monitor*, February 15, 2017.

Kinder, Donald R., Mark D. Peters, Robert P. Abelson, and Susan T. Fiske. "Presidential Prototypes." *Political Behavior* 2, no. 4 (1980): 315–37.

Kolbert, Elizabeth. "The 1992 Campaign: Media, Talk Show Wrangling to Book Candidates." *New York Times*, July 6, 1992, A10.

Koterba, Ed. "Assignment Washington." *Reading Eagle*, August 27, 1960.

Levin, Gary. "Bush, Gore Work Late Shift for Laughs; Humor May Help Sway Young Voters." *USA Today*, October 23, 2000.

Lichter, S. Robert, Jody C Baumgartner, and Jonathan S. Morris. *Politics Is a joke! How TV Comedians Are Remaking Political Life*. Boulder, CO: Westview Press, 2015.

Lichter, S. Robert, and Richard E. Noyes. *Good Intentions Make Bad News Why Americans Hate Campaign Journalism*. Boston: Rowman & Littlefield, 1995.

Mason, Julie. "Kerry Makes TV Rounds to Aid Image: More Candidates Seeking Advantages of Popular Shows." *Houston Chronicle*, September 22, 2004, A14.

McGinnis, Joe. *The Selling of the President 1968*. New York: Trident Publishing, 1969.

Moore, Martha T. "Romney Skips Entertainment TV; Medium Offers Risky Foray on Trail." *USA Today*, October 25, 2012.

Moy, Patricia, Michael A. Xenos, and Verena K. Hess. "Priming Effects of Late-Night Comedy." *International Journal of Public Opinion Research* 18, no. 2 (2005): 198–210.

Parkin, Michael. *Talk Show Campaigns: Presidential Candidates on Daytime and Late Night Television*. New York: Routledge, 2014.

————. "Taking Late Night Comedy Seriously: How Candidate Appearances on Late Night Television Can Engage Viewers." *Political Research Quarterly* 63, no. 1 (March 2010): 3–15.

Pew Research Center. "Cable and Internet Loom Large in Fragmented Political News Universe." January 11, 2004.

Polsby, Nelson W. *Consequences of Party Reform*. New York: Oxford University Press, 1983.

Rich, Frank. "Paar to Leno, J.F.K to J.F.K." *New York Times*, February 8, 2004, AR1.

Shepard, Richard. "Nominees and TV Face a Problem." *New York Times*, August 27, 1960.

Silverlieb, Alan, and William G. Mayer. "By the Numbers: A Statistical Guide to the Presidential Nomination Process." In *The Making of the Presidential Candidates: 2012*, edited by William G. Mayer and Jonathan Bernstein, 203–25. Lanham, MD: Rowman & Littlefield, 2012.

Vane, Sharyn. "Late Night Al and Dubya." *American Journalism Review*, November 2000.

Chapter 15

The Ides of September

Jimmy Fallon, Donald Trump, and the Changing Politics of Late Night Television

Jonathan S. Morris

The reshuffling of the late-night television comedy landscape set the stage for a very different slate of hosts and venues as the 2016 election season approached. For example, Jon Stewart had transitioned out of the scene, and Stephen Colbert had abandoned his alter ego on Comedy Central's *The Colbert Report* to play himself on the broadcast network stage. Jay Leno and David Letterman had left the airwaves, and the undisputed king of late-night talk was Jimmy Fallon. As Josef Adalian noted, "[Fallon] built his considerable lead by carving out a clear identity as Mr. Nice Guy, the unthreatening 'host next door' who just wants to kibitz and chill with any celebrity, newsmaker, or politician who stops by his Rockefeller Center studio."[1]

Fallon, who was a fixture on late-night comedy's *Saturday Night Live* for fifteen years, took over for Jay Leno as host of NBC's *The Tonight Show* in 2014, and quickly outpaced his competitors in the ratings game by the time the presidential primary season was beginning in 2015. Ratings data from Nielsen in December 2015 (age 18–49) had Fallon far above his network competitors, registering a 1.1 average compared to .77 for Stephen Colbert on CBS and .60 for Jimmy Kimmel on ABC.[2]

Indeed a poll conducted of 1,000 late-night comedy viewers in November 2015 found that people liked Jimmy Fallon more than his competitors, and he was more likely to be labeled "authentic," "cool," and a "party animal" when compared to the others. Also, he was viewed as significantly less "opinionated" than his counterpart, Stephen Colbert. Jon Penn, the head pollster for the study summed up the findings, by stating, "[Fallon's] the unpredictable, cool dude you want to be friends with, and his silly, witting and non-offensive humor is connecting with Leno fans and young, married, moderate women."[3] The polling results also found that men would be more likely to want to have a beer with Fallon over Colbert or Jimmy Kimmel, and women would prefer to date Fallon to the other hosts.[4] Jimmy Fallon was the *King of Late Night*.

As 2017 came to a close, however, Fallon's domination of the late-night landscape had ended. He was consistently losing to Colbert in the ratings, and was closely competing with Jimmy Kimmel for the second place spot.[5] How did Jimmy Fallon's lead in the ratings dwindle in such a short time period? For most observers and media critics the answer is simple: Donald Trump.

Donald Trump has a long history of publicly feuding with political and entertainment figures and inflicting varying levels of damage to their reputation. Consider the examples—Rosie O'Donnell, Megyn Kelly, Marco Rubio, Jeb Bush, his former wife, some Kardashians, Kristen Stewart, and even President Obama. While Trump did not win all of these feuds outright, he certainly had the ability to make public news when he pointed his ire in the direction of another public figure. Of course, his most infamous feud was against Hillary Clinton, and the winner is now self-evident as we see who occupies 1600 Pennsylvania Avenue.

The effect that Donald Trump had on ending Jimmy Fallon's reign as the king of late night was unique in that the two men did not feud. On the contrary, they had a pleasant conversation in mid-September of 2016. It is the purpose of this chapter to examine Trump and Fallon's conversation, which took place on *The Tonight Show*, and try to shed light on how such a seemingly innocuous interview became a public relations fiasco for Mr. Fallon.

THE INTERVIEW AND THE FALLOUT

Presidential candidate Donald Trump appeared as the featured guest on *The Tonight Show* on September 15, 2016. That particular news day had been one in several poor cycles for Mr. Trump. His prominent role in the anti-Obama "Birther" movement, in which he claimed the president was not born in the United States, had come back to light when Trump was still refusing to acknowledge that Obama was a natural born citizen.[6] Mr. Trump's son was also the focus of attention that day by invoking the Holocaust when discussing what he perceived to be media bias in favor of Hillary Clinton. Specifically, Trump Jr. claimed:

> The media has been her number-one surrogate in this. Without the media, this wouldn't even be a contest. But the media has built her up. They've let her slide

on every indiscrepancy [*sic*], on every lie, on every DNC game trying to get Bernie Sanders out of this thing.

He went on to say, "If Republicans were doing that, they'd be warming up the gas chamber right now."[7]

When Trump sat down to be interviewed on September 15, none of these issues were discussed, nor were any of the major issues or policy discussions that had set Mr. Trump apart from his primary and general election competitors. In true Jimmy Fallon fashion, the interview was lighthearted and apolitical, a style that closely mirrored that of his apolitical predecessor, Jay Leno. They discussed Trump's eating habits, favorite board game (Monopoly), and the rigors of campaigning. Toward the end of the interview, Mr. Fallon scored what he considered a victory when Trump allowed the host to reach across the desk and mess up the candidate's famously unique hair.

A day after the interview, the backlash on social media was immediate. While Fallon was not the first late-night program to bring Trump onto his show during the primaries and general election campaign, the playful manner in which he interacted with the candidate brought heavy criticism. Consider a small sample of tweets regarding the interview:[8]

> Was Jimmy Fallon supposed to do a hard-hitting interview? Of course not. Was he supposed to shower a racist with love? No. Not that, either.

> I can't make any jokes about Jimmy Fallon. The way he showcased Trump like a lovable old grandpa was sickening.

> I don't fault Jimmy Fallon for not being a journalist. I do fault him for his willingness to serve as hell's court jester.

> It must've been nice for Jimmy Fallon's all-black band to watch their boss pal around with a white supremacist.

Some critics on Twitter speculated as to how Fallon might have interviewed historical monsters from past generations.

Jimmy Fallon: "So Mr. Manson, how difficult is it juggling family and work?"
Fallon interviewing Hitler: "Let's talk about your book!"
Jimmy Fallon: "Mind if I touch your moustache?" Adolf Hitler: "*chuckles* Nein."
Next up: Fallon and Trump slow jam to MEIN KAMPF. Hilarious

As the shaming of Jimmy Fallon took-off on social media, reporters and critics were also discussing the host's perceived misstep. Maxwell Strachan, senior reporter for the Huffington Post observed that people were "justifiably infuriated" with the tone of the interview, and also declared that Fallon "humanized a dangerous man."[9] Josef Adalian, writer for Vulture.com, made the case that Fallon's soft treatment of the Republican nominee could possibly swing the election:[10]

What may have made a difference last night was timing: The election is now less than two months away. Sensitivities are heightened all around. Those who oppose Trump, on both the left and the right, are nervous about polls showing a closer race. And Fallon didn't just joke around with Trump or put him in a lame sketch. He literally laid hands on the man, petting his hair like he was your adorable crazy uncle you see once a year. If you're a suburban Republican woman who'd been worried supporting Trump would mean endorsing all those -isms in Hillary Clinton's basket of deplorables, Nice Guy Jimmy gave you permission to feel okay about voting for the man who says not-nice things.

James Fallows, award-winning writer for *The Atlantic*, posted his concerns about the possible effects of the interview the night it aired. Less than an hour after the episode had ended, Fallows wrote:[11]

Effective 53 days from now, [Fallon] may have a lot to answer for. Performances like the one he put on this evening with Donald Trump, including a "charming" mussing of the candidate's famous hair, are a crucial part of the "normalizing" process of a candidate who is outside all historical norms for this office. . . . Fallon's humoring of Trump was a bad move, a destructive and self-indulgent mistake, which I hope Fallon becomes embarrassed about but the rest of us don't have long-term reason to rue.

Joseph Adalian also put the interview in a historic context, making reference to the original patriarch of *The Tonight Show*, Jack Paar, when he argued:

You almost have to go back to 1959, when Jack Paar flew to Cuba to interview Fidel Castro for *The Tonight Show* just weeks after he came to power, to come up with another example of so many Americans being riled by a late-night host coddling a dictator in the making.[12]

Sonia Saraiya of *Variety* said of the interview:

If Trump becomes President, that image of Fallon ruffling Trump's hair will be the moment when the tide turned. The gesture was so affectionate and grandfatherly that Fallon provided Trump with a seal of mainstream approval that he does not deserve.[13]

Following the Trump interview and the subsequent negative reaction from journalists and social media, Fallon said little about the incident, except to answer a question from *TMZ* the following week. When asked what he thought about the negative reactions to the interview, Fallon answered, "I mean, have you seen my show? . . . I'm never too hard on anyone."[14] It would be a while before he would speak publicly about the incident again.

In the weeks following Trump's visit to *The Tonight Show*, the outrage seemed to dissipate, as the presidential election was closing in, and Hillary Clinton was the strong favorite to win. Trump himself was convinced he would lose, and was planning a concession speech on election night.[15] Then, Trump did not lose. While very few Hillary Clinton supporters publicly blamed the Trump victory on Jimmy Fallon's shoulders, the subsequent drop in *The Tonight Show*'s share of the late-night audience indicated that there may have been hard feelings.

PRESIDENTIAL CANDIDATES AS LATE-NIGHT GUESTS

Ever since presidential candidates started appearing on late-night comedy programs, the nature of the interviews typically mirrored the tenor of Fallon and Trump's discussion in September 2016. Researchers in political science and communication have discussed the allure of broadcast late-night talk shows for presidential candidates. The venue (a) reaches a segment of the potential electorate that tends to follow politics less closely, and more importantly (b) gives the candidates an ability to show the audience a more personable—and potentially and more likeable—side of themselves.[16] This practice is almost as old as television itself, starting with John Kennedy meeting with Jack Paar, Richard Nixon playing the piano on *The Tonight Show* (as well as the infamous "sock it to me" introduction on Rowan and Martin's *Laugh-In*), and Bill Clinton's saxophone moments with Johnny Carson and (later) Arsenio Hall.[17] By 2004, most candidates in the primary and general election had made appearances on late-night comedy, a basic element of their campaign strategy—sit down with the host and display the lighter side of their personality by fielding mostly non-political softball questions. And, when possible, make use of some self-deprecating humor, which has been shown to increase a candidate's likeability.[18] By 2008, when both parties had large fields of presidential hopefuls, there were over 100 visits to the late-night circuit by the candidates.[19]

The 2016 election cycle was not much different, except for fewer candidates on the Democratic side, but the list of Republican contenders exceeded fifteen in the early stages. Most of these candidates hit the talk shows, with varying levels of success. During the primary season, Trump himself was a host on *Saturday Night Live*, and appeared as a guest twice on *The Late Show with Stephen Colbert* (once by phone) and *Jimmy Kimmel Live*. Those interviews were certainly not anything that could be characterized as "hard-hitting." Yet, it was Jimmy Fallon who took the criticism for "humanizing" candidate Donald Trump. Why? The remainder of this book chapter considers some possible explanations and ends with a case that the expectations for the role of television comics in the political sphere have been set ridiculously high. The effects of these expectations may have a significant impact on the future of political comedy in America.

TIMING

As mentioned before, *The Tonight Show* was not Donald Trump's first stop on the late-night circuit. Many of his other appearances occurred significantly earlier, when the possibility of "President Trump" had not yet materialized in the minds of voters and the rest of the mass public. But by the middle of September, Trump had been steadily gaining ground on Hillary Clinton in the national polls. On August 9th, the realclearpolitics.com polling average had Clinton leading nationally by 7.9 points. By September 15, the day of his visit to *The Tonight Show*, Clinton's lead had shrunk to 1.9 points. Trump had also closed the gap in several swing states assumed to vote blue on election day, and other states Democrats were hoping to steal from long-time Republican dominance were clearly no longer within reach. These trends may have highlighted that a Trump victory was possible, if not probable. The timing of Jimmy Fallon's interview may have been unlucky, and inconveniently coincided with a growing sense of anxiety among the anti-Trump portion of the public. Additionally, the days leading up to September 15 had been especially problematic for Trump in the news. As discussed earlier in this chapter, Trump had failed to acknowledge in *The Washington Post* interview that President Obama had been born in the United States,[20] and his son had publicly made reference to the Holocaust by suggesting that the media would be "warming up the gas chamber" if his father lied as much as Hillary Clinton.[21] Some Americans were probably not thrilled to see a talk show host sit down with the candidate and not ask any tough questions about the events of that same day.

DIVERGING TONE

There was a time when late-night comics were equally critical of both sides of the aisle. Personal foibles and physical attributes were the primary targets. In the 2000 election, the frames were oriented around Al Gore as one who tended to stretch the truth, such as allegedly claiming to have invented the Internet, and George W. Bush as one who was intellectually challenged.[22]

The preceding presidential contest was equally simple in nature, with Bill Clinton cast as a serial philanderer,[23] and Bob Dole as old.[24] By 2004, in the midst of the second Gulf War, the amount of jokes targeted at Republicans compared to Democrats began to increase, especially on cable talk shows. For example, Jon Stewart was publicly criticized by journalist Tucker Carlson for favoring one side over the other. On CNN's *Crossfire*, Carlson asked Stewart:

> You had a chance to interview the Democratic nominee [John Kerry], and you asked him questions such as, "How are you holding up? Is it hard not to take the attacks personally? Have you ever flip-flopped, etc." Didn't you feel like, you got the chance to interview the guy, why not ask him a real question, instead of just suck up to him?[25]

In 2008, the bias against Republican candidates had increased dramatically, with the large majority of jokes targeting Republican nominee John McCain over Barack Obama.[26] This overall favoritism did not keep McCain from visiting most of the late-night outlets during the primaries and the general election. But in the months preceding the election there was evidence that the candidates were being treated differently by some hosts. David Letterman was especially critical of McCain after the Republican nominee cancelled his appearance on *The Late Show* the day he suspended his campaign to focus on the financial crisis in September 2008. Letterman's outrage was apparent, stating, "This doesn't smell right. This is not the way a tested hero behaves." Later in the broadcast, a still indignant Letterman declared, "the road to the White House runs right through me."[27] Apparently, Letterman's criticism was enough to prompt a visit later in the campaign from McCain, in which he apologized for cancelling, stating, "I screwed up. What can I say?" Letterman suggested that he was willing to put the cancellation "behind them," to which McCain replied, "Thank you, thank you, thank you, thank you."[28]

The ire directed toward Trump on late-night television in the 2016 was unprecedented, and it didn't go unnoticed. Conservative writer David Marcus, "While it is probably true that the Trump campaign has led to an increase in over-the-top partisanship on our TV screens in the wee hours, this phenomenon has been building."[29] Perhaps the starkest reflection of this trend came from Seth Meyers on NBC's *The Late Show*, who publicly banned Trump from appearing on his show. Meyers explained the reasoning behind the decision:

> Trump is stoking fear and spreading hate, and this is important because we can't become immune to it. . . . We cannot allow it to become normalized, which is why we need robust, independent press like the newspapers Trump banned from his campaign to challenge the fear mongering, and provide us with sober, clear-eyed reporting.[30]

Ironically, the same day Trump appeared on *The Tonight Show* on September 15, 2016, *Time* magazine published a cover story on "The New Politics of Late Night."[31] In the article, Richard Zoglin painted a clear picture of how 2016 was an entirely new game for the televised comedy world:

Political Comedy on TV used to be a polite, easy-listening affair. Longtime Tonight Show host Johnny Carson—along with his chief heirs in late-night, Jay Leno and David Letterman—poked plenty of fun at political figures, but mainly for their personal foibles, both real and comically exaggerated: Gerald Ford's clumsiness, Ronald Reagan's age, Bill Clinton's appetites. No obvious political agenda, nothing to offend either side—just a gentle brew to help you process the day's news and drift to sleep with a smile. . . . But the game has changed, thanks largely to the man at the top of the GOP ticket. With his orange skin tone, animal-pelt hairdo and overweening ego, Trump may be the greatest gift to comedians since the invention of the mother-in-law joke. Hillary Clinton gets her share of jabs (most recently for her "basket of deplorables" remark and her campaign's slowness to reveal her health problems), but Trump has galvanized the late-night crowd, prompting a new sense of urgency, outrage, even panic.[32]

Zoglin also notes in his article that, "Jimmy Fallon, host of the top-rated *Tonight Show*, still carries on the Carson tradition of evenhanded, softball one-liners, along with a Trump impression that even the Donald can laugh along with." Put differently, Jimmy Fallon didn't get the memo that the televised late-night world was shifting dramatically. At the same time that viewers were taking note the comics were lining-up to slam the Republican nominee for president, Fallon brought the man onto his show and treated the man as his predecessors would. That decision, and the subsequent reaction was a pivotal moment in the history of late-night comedy. The Republican nominee for president of the United States was not just the political opposition: he was evil, and Jimmy Fallon "humanized" this repulsive creature, and thus possibly helped pave the way to a Trump presidency.

The year following Trump's election has confirmed the sense of "us" versus "them" in the tone of late-night television. Jimmy Kimmel, who had been largely apolitical, became a forceful critic of the president and Republicans on healthcare policy as Congress considered measures to repeal The Affordable Care Act. Kimmel's son was born with a serious heart defect, which led the host to focus several of his monologues on the importance of providing health insurance to those with preexisting conditions—like his son. Laura Bradley of *Vanity Fair* labeled Kimmel as "a reluctant progressive hero," as his perspectives on the efforts to repeal The Affordable Care Act (Obamacare) became commonplace in his monologues.[33] His focus on healthcare policy intensified throughout 2017, leading one of the Obamacare repeal architects, Senator Bill Cassidy, to appear on Kimmel's program to promise reform that would pass "The Jimmy Kimmel Test."[34] While the nature of that test was never quite defined by Cassidy, it displayed the powerful role Kimmel had assumed in critiquing healthcare policy reform in an era of Republican control of the White House and Congress.

NEW EXPECTATION FOR LATE-NIGHT TV COMICS

If the drops in Jimmy Fallon's ratings are any indication, the late-night audience is no longer satisfied with cheap laughs at the expense of political figures. More than ever, viewers are looking for insightful (and funny) critiques of the political opposition. The 2016 election according to Richard Zoglin "triggered an extreme makeover for political satire, which is now more ubiquitous, more pointed, more passionate, and more partisan than ever before."[35] For more than a decade, most of the partisan political humor was reserved for Jon Stewart and Stephen Colbert on *Comedy Central*, but now it is the rule, rather than the exception, and it translates into higher ratings. *Forbes* magazine recently published an article titled, "Dumping on Trump Pays off for Late-Night TV Shows" showing that those most critical of Republicans have seen their ratings increase in 2017.[36] Jimmy Fallon's refusal to fall in line has cost him his crown as the king of late-night comedy.

The job of late-night comedy host has transformed from clown to political analyst. Whether or not these hosts have purposely sought this new role is debatable. Kimmel has expressed trepidation, while at the same time taking some credit for the demise of the Graham-Cassidy Bill to repeal and replace Obamacare.[37] Some, such as Jimmy Fallon, clearly wish to avoid this role. Many seemed to have embraced it. Some observers, however, are not happy with this transition. Rich Lowry of the *New York Post* wrote, "If this trend is inevitable, it's not a good thing. It removes yet another neutral zone, free of social and political contention, from American life."[38] The president himself voiced concern as well, and posted two messages online. The first read, "Late-Night host are dealing with the Democrats for their very 'unfunny' & repetitive material, always anti-Trump! Should we get Equal Time?" The second post, four minutes later, argued, "More and more people are suggesting the Republicans (and me) should be given Equal Time on T.V. when you look at the one-sided coverage?"[39]

There is, perhaps, a larger concern, and it relates to who is most qualified to provide political information to the mass public. For the majority of this republic's history, it was the party organizations, which are politically accountable institutions, which held the responsibility of providing contrasting ideas for what was best for America. As the party's infrastructure eroded in the 1960s and 1970s, the responsibility for providing information to voters and the public at large fell to the mass media, an institution that was not designed—nor equipped—to handle the role of educating the public on differing policy perspectives.[40] Political scientist Thomas Patterson argues that the media have failed in their new role, particularly in the context of presidential elections:

> Even if the media did not want the responsibility for organizing the campaign, it is theirs by virtue of an election system built upon entrepreneurial candidacies, floating voters, freewheeling interest groups, and weak political parties. It is an unworkable arrangement: the press is not equipped to give order and direction to a presidential campaign. And we expect it to do so. . . . Yet news and truth are not the same thing. The news is a highly refracted version of reality. The press magnifies certain aspects of politics and downplays others, which are often more central to issues of governing.[41]

So complete is the failure of the media in their new role, many Americans are looking elsewhere for information and perspective. In 2009, a poll from *Time* magazine asked readers, "Now that Walter Cronkite has passed on, who is American's most trusted newscaster." Jon Stewart came out on top with 44 percent, followed by Brian Williams (29%), Charlie Gibson (19%), and Katie Couric (7%).

As this chapter has argued, Jon Stewart was just the beginning, and many Americans are leaning on late-night comics to give information and perspective on the state of the world—provided that perspective is critical of the president and congressional Republicans. The problem is that the expectations exceed the abilities of many of these entertainers. Like the traditional media, late-night comics are not equipped to provide the information necessary to serve in the place of institutions designed to provide choice to Americans, such as political parties. Jon Stewart himself noted so much himself when journalist Tucker Carlson question Stewart's bias toward John Kerry in the 2004 election. Stewart replied:

> I didn't realize, and maybe this explains quite a bit, is that the news organizations look to *Comedy Central* for their cues on integrity. . . . You're on *CNN.* The show that leads into me [on *Comedy Central*] is puppets making crank phone calls.[42]

While the role of late-night comics had been in flux for years, we should look back to September 15, 2016, and Jimmy Fallon's tussle of the Republican nominee's hair as the pivotal moment—the moment when Fallon failed in his new political role—one he did not even know he had.

NOTES

1. Josef Adalian, "How Does Jimmy Fallon's Interview Fit into Late Night's History with Politics?" *Vulture*, September 16, 2016, http://www.vulture.com/2016/09/jimmy-fallon-donald-trump-in-historical-context.html.

2. Bill Carter, "How Jimmy Fallon Crushed Stephen Colbert (and Everyone Else) in Late Night," *The Hollywood Reporter*, December 25, 2015, https://www.hollywoodreporter.com/news/bill-carter-how-jimmy-fallon-848851.

3. Matthew Belloni, "The Great Late-Night Poll: Where the Hosts Stand Now," *The Hollywood Reporter*, November 27, 2015, https://www.hollywoodreporter.com/news/great-late-night-poll-hosts-840910.

4. Ibid.

5. Josef Adalian, "Post-Trump, Jimmy Fallon Continues to Lose Ground in the Late-Night Wars," *Vulture*, October 10, 2017, http://www.vulture.com/2017/10/jimmy-fallon-continues-to-lose-ground-in-the-late-night-wars.html.

6. Dave Itzkoff, "Jimmy Fallon Was on Top of the World. Then Came Donald Trump," *New York Times*, May 17, 2017. https://www.nytimes.com/2017/05/17/arts/television/jimmy-fallon-tonight-show-interview-trump.html.

7. Aaron Blake, "Donald Trump Jr. says Media would be 'Warming up the Gas Chamber' if Trump Lied Like Clinton," *Washington Post*, September 15, 2016, https://www.washingtonpost.com/news/the-fix/wp/2016/09/15/donald-trump-jr-says-media-would-be-warming-up-the-gas-chamber-if-trump-lied-like-clinton/?utm_term=.7ed54abcbc7a.

8. Brittany King, "Jimmy Fallon Under Fire for Lighthearted Interview with Donald Trump," *People*, September 16, 2016, http://people.com/tv/jimmy-fallon-receives-backlash-after-donald-trump-interview/; Jethro Nededog, "Jimmy Fallon is Under Fire for Going Easy on Donald Trump in 'sickening' Interview," *Business Insider*, September 16, 2016, http://www.businessinsider.com/jimmy-fallon-donald-trump-interview-critics-2016–9.

9. Maxwell Strachan, "People are Justifiably Infuriated with How Jimmy Fallon Handled Trump," *Huffington Post*, September 16, 2016, https://www.huffingtonpost.com/entry/jimmy-fallon-donald-trump_us_57dbecd4e4b0071a6e06801e.

10. Adalian, September 16, 2016.

11. James Fallows, "The Daily Trump: Filling a Time Capsule," *The Atlantic*, September 16, 2016, https://www.theatlantic.com/notes/2016/09/trump-time-capsule-104-jimmy-fallon/500312/.

12. Adalian, September 16, 2016.

13. Sonia Saraiya, "Jimmy Fallon Gets Trumped by Donald Trump," *Variety*, September 16, 2016, http://variety.com/2016/tv/opinion/jimmy-fallon-donald-trump-tonight-show-no-credibility-1201862755/.

14. Laura Bradley, "Jimmy Fallon Answers Critics of His Trump Interview: 'Have you Seen my Show?'" *Vanity Fair*, September 19, 2016, https://www.vanityfair.com/hollywood/2016/09/jimmy-fallon-donald-trump-interview-response.

15. Jennifer Jacobs and Billy House, "Trump Says He Expected to Lose Election Because of Poll Results," *Bloomberg*, December 13, 2016, https://

www.bloomberg.com/news/articles/2016–12–14/trump-says-he-expected-to
-lose-election-because-of-poll-results.

16. Matthew A. Baum, "Talking the Vote: Why Presidential Candidates Hit the
Talk Show Circuit," *American Journal of Political Science* 49, no. 2 (April 2005):
213.

17. S. Robert Lichter, Jody C Baumgartner, and Jonathan S. Morris, *Politics Is a
Joke!* (Boulder, CO: Westview Press, 2015).

18. Jody C Baumgartner, Jonathan S. Morris, and Jeffrey M. Coleman. "Did the
'Road to the White House Run Through' Letterman? Christ Christie, Letterman, and
Other-Disparaging Versus Self-Deprecating Humor," *Journal of Political Marketing*,
forthcoming, http://www.tandfonline.com/doi/full/10.1080/15377857.2015.1074137.

19. Lichter, Baumgartner, and Morris, *Politics Is a Joke!*

20. Robert Costa, "Trump Tells Post He Is Unwilling to Say Obama was
Born in the U.S." *Washington Post*, September 15, 2016, https://www.wash-
ingtonpost.com/politics/trump-defiant-as-polls-rise-wont-say-obama-was-born-
in-united-states/2016/09/15/48913162–7b61–11e6-ac8e-cf8e0dd91dc7_story.
html?utm_term=.34eaa518b500.

21. Eric Bradner, "Donald Trump Jr. Makes 'Gas Chamber' Reference in Criticizing Media," *CNN*, September 15, 2016, https://www.cnn.com/2016/09/15/politics/
donald-trump-jr-gas-chamber/index.html.

22. Dannagal E. Goldthwaite, "Pinocchio v Dumbo: Priming Candidate Caricature
Attributes in Late-Night Comedy Programs in Election 2000 and the Moderating
Effects of Political Knowledge." Presented at the Annual Meeting of the American
Political Science Association (2002).

23. David Niven, S. Robert Lichter, and Daniel Amundson, "Our First Cartoon
President: Bill Clinton and the Politics of Late Night Comedy," in *Laughing Mat-
ters: Humor and American Politics in the Media Age*, eds. Jody C Baumgartner and
Jonathan S. Morris (New York: Routledge, 2008), 151.

24. Lichter, Baumgartner, and Morris, *Politics Is a Joke!*

25. https://www.youtube.com/watch?v=aFQFB5YpDZE.

26. Lichter, Baumgartner, and Morris, *Politics Is a Joke!*

27. Tim Grierson, "Letterman, Seriously: Dave's Most Profound Moments,"
Rolling Stone, May 14, 2015, https://www.rollingstone.com/tv/lists/letterman-
seriously-daves-10-most-profound-moments-20150514/letterman-goes-off-on-
john-mccain-september-24–2008–20150513.

28. https://www.youtube.com/watch?v=m_HSOSOTc50.

29. David Marcus, "Trump Is No Excuse for Turning Late-Night Comedy into Propaganda." *The Federalist*, September 19, 2016, http://thefederalist.com/2016/09/19/
trump-no-excuse-turning-late-night-comedy-propaganda/.

30. Adam Howard, "Donald Trump is no Laughing Matter to Some Late Night
Comics," *NBC News*, August 3, 2016, https://www.nbcnews.com/pop-culture/tv/
donald-trump-no-laughing-matter-some-late-night-comics-n622151.

31. Richard Zoglin, "The New Politics of Late Night," *Time*, September 15, 2016,
http://time.com/4494764/the-new-politics-of-late-night/.

32. Ibid.

33. Laura Bradley, "Jimmy Kimmel is a Reluctant Progressive Hero," *Vanity Fair*, October 30, 2017, https://www.vanityfair.com/hollywood/2017/10/jimmy-kimmel-politics-ratings-trump-late-night.

34. Sarah Kliff, "Jimmy Kimmel Defines the 'Jimmy Kimmel Test' on Health Care," *Vox*, May 9, 2017, https://www.vox.com/health-care/2017/5/9/15591764/jimmy-kimmel-test-ahca.

35. Zoglin, September 15, 2016.

36. Madeline Berg, "Dumping on Trump Pays off for Late Night TV Show," *Forbes*, February 3, 2017, https://www.forbes.com/sites/maddieberg/2017/02/03/john-oliver-stephen-colbert-jimmy-fallon-daily-show-in-late-night-tv-it-pays-off-to-dump-on-trump/#57d2ed5135d7.

37. Ian Schwartz, "Kimmel Celebrates Collins Opposition to Graham-Cassidy: I May Have Stopped it," *RealClearPolitics*, September 26, 2017, https://www.realclearpolitics.com/video/2017/09/26/jimmy_kimmel_celebrates_collins_opposition_to_graham-cassidy_i_may_have_stopped_it.html.

38. Rich Lowry, "From Carson to Kimmel: The Collapse of the Late-Night Empire," *New York Post*, October 16, 2017, https://nypost.com/2017/10/16/from-carson-to-kimmel-the-collapse-of-the-late-night-empire/.

39. Aric Jenkins, "Donald Trump: 'Unfunny' Late-Night Hosts Should Give Republicans 'Equal Time,'" *Time*, October 7, 2017, http://time.com/4973432/donald-trump-late-night-television-hosts/.

40. Thomas Patterson, *Out of Order* (New York: Vintage Books, 1994).

41. Ibid, 28–29.

42. Alex Felker, "Jon Stewart on Crossfire," online video clip. *YouTube*, January 16, 2006, https://www.youtube.com/watch?v=aFQFB5YpDZE.

REFERENCES

Adalian, Josef. "How Does Jimmy Fallon's Donald Trump Interview Fit into Late Night's History with Politics?" *Vulture*, September 16, 2016. http://www.vulture.com/2016/09/jimmy-fallon-donald-trump-in-historical-context.html.

———. "Post-Trump, Jimmy Fallon Continues to Lose Ground in the Late-Night Wars." *Vulture*, October 10, 2017. http://www.vulture.com/2017/10/jimmy-fallon-continues-to-lose-ground-in-the-late-night-wars.html.

Baum, Matthew A. "Talking the Vote: Why Presidential Candidates Hit the Talk Show Circuit." *American Journal of Political Science* 49, no. 2 (April 2005): 213.

Baumgartner, Jody C, Jonathan S. Morris, and Jeffrey M. Coleman. "Did the 'Road to the White House Run Through' Letterman? Christ Christie, Letterman, and Other-Disparaging Versus Self-Deprecating Humor." *Journal of Political Marketing*, forthcoming. http://www.tandfonline.com/doi/full/10.1080/15377857.2015.1074137.

Belloni, Matthew. "The Great Late-Night Poll: Where the Hosts Stand Now." *Hollywood Reporter*, November 27, 2015. https://www.hollywoodreporter.com/news/great-late-night-poll-hosts-840910.

Berg, Madeline. "Dumping on Trump Pays off for Late Night TV Show." *Forbes*, February 3, 2017. https://www.forbes.com/sites/maddieberg/2017/02/03/john-oliver-stephen-colbert-jimmy-fallon-daily-show-in-late-night-tv-it-pays-off-to-dump-on-trump/#57d2ed5135d7.

Blake, Aaron. "Donald Trump Jr. says Media would be 'Warming Up the Gas Chamber' if Trump Lied Like Clinton." *Washington Post*, September 15, 2016. https://www.washingtonpost.com/news/the-fix/wp/2016/09/15/donald-trump-jr-says-media-would-be-warming-up-the-gas-chamber-if-trump-lied-like-clinton/?utm_term=.7ed54abcbc7a.

Bradley, Laura. "Jimmy Kimmel is a Reluctant Progressive Hero." *Vanityfair*, October 30, 2017. https://www.vanityfair.com/hollywood/2017/10/jimmy-kimmel-politics-ratings-trump-late-night.

Bradley, Laura. "Jimmy Fallon Answers Critics of His Trump Interview: 'Have You Seen My Show?'"*Vanityfair*, September 19, 2016. https://www.vanityfair.com/hollywood/2016/09/jimmy-fallon-donald-trump-interview-response.

Bradner, Eric. "Donald Trump Jr. Makes 'Gas Chamber' Reference in Criticizing Media." *CNN*, September 15, 2016. https://www.cnn.com/2016/09/15/politics/donald-trump-jr-gas-chamber/index.html.

Carter, Bill. "How Jimmy Fallon Crushed Stephen Colbert (and Everyone Else) in Late Night." *The Hollywood Reporter*, December 25, 2015. https://www.hollywoodreporter.com/news/bill-carter-how-jimmy-fallon-848851.

Costa, Robert. "Trump Tells Post He Is Unwilling to Say Obama was Born in the U.S." *Washingtonpost*, September 15, 2016. https://www.washingtonpost.com/politics/trump-defiant-as-polls-rise-wont-say-obama-was-born-in-united-states/2016/09/15/48913162–7b61–11e6-ac8e-cf8e0dd91dc7_story.html?utm_term=.34eaa518b500.

Fallows, James. "The Daily Trump: Filling a Time Capsule." *The Atlantic*, September 16, 2016. https://www.theatlantic.com/notes/2016/09/trump-time-capsule-104-jimmy-fallon/500312/.

Goldthwaite, Dannagal E. "Pinocchio v Dumbo: Priming Candidate Caricature Attributes in Late-Night Comedy Programs in Election 2000 and the Moderating Effects of Political Knowledge." Paper presented at the annual meeting of the American Political Science Association, Boston Marriott Copley Place, Sheraton Boston and Hynes Convention Center, Boston, Massachusetts, August 28, 2002.

Grierson, Tim. "Letterman, Seriously: Dave's Most Profound Moments." *Rolling Stone*, May 14, 2015. https://www.rollingstone.com/tv/lists/letterman-seriously-daves-10-most-profound-moments-20150514/letterman-goes-off-on-john-mccain-september-24–2008–20150513.

Howard, Adam. "Donald Trump is no Laughing Matter to Some Late Night Comics." *NBC News*, August 3, 2016. https://www.nbcnews.com/pop-culture/tv/donald-trump-no-laughing-matter-some-late-night-comics-n622151.

Itzkoff, Dave. "Jimmy Fallon was on Top of the World. Then Came Donald Trump." *New York Times*, May 17, 2017.

Jacobs, Jennifer, and Billy House. "Trump Says He Expected to Lose Election Because of Poll Results." *Bloomberg*, December 13, 2016. https://www.bloomberg.com/news/articles/2016–12–14/trump-says-he-expected-to-lose-election-because-of-poll-results.

Jenkins, Aric. "Donald Trump: 'Unfunny' Late-Night Hosts Should Give Republicans 'Equal Time'." *Time*, October 7, 2017. http://time.com/4973432/donald-trump-late-night-television-hosts/.

King, Brittany. "Jimmy Fallon under Fire for Lighthearted Interview with Donald Trump." *People*, September 16, 2016. http://people.com/tv/jimmy-fallon-receives-backlash-after-donald-trump-interview/.

Kliff, Sarah. "Jimmy Kimmel Defines the 'Jimmy Kimmel Test' on Health Care." *Vox*, May 9, 2017. https://www.vox.com/health-care/2017/5/9/15591764/jimmy-kimmel-test-ahca.

Lichter, S. Robert, Jody C Baumgartner, and Jonathan S. Morris. *Politics Is a Joke!: How TV Comedians Are Remaking Political Life*. Boulder, CO: Westview Press, 2014.

Lowry, Rich. "From Carson to Kimmel: The Collapse of the Late-Night Empire." *New York Post*, October 16, 2017. https://nypost.com/2017/10/16/from-carson-to-kimmel-the-collapse-of-the-late-night-empire/.

Marcus, David. "Trump Is No Excuse For Turning Late-Night Comedy Into Propaganda." *Thefederalist.com*, September 19, 2016. http://thefederalist.com/2016/09/19/trump-no-excuse-turning-late-night-comedy-propaganda/.

Niven, David, S., Robert Lichter, and Daniel Amundson. "Our First Cartoon President: Bill Clinton and the Politics of Late Night Comedy." In *Laughing Matters: Humor and American Politics in the Media Age*, edited by Jody C Baumgartner and Jonathan S. Morris. New York: Routledge, 2008.

Patterson, Thomas. *Out of Order*. New York: Vintage Books, 1994.

Saraiya, Sonia. "Jimmy Fallon Gets Trumped by Donald Trump." *Variety*, September 16, 2016. http://variety.com/2016/tv/opinion/jimmy-fallon-donald-trump-tonight-show-no-credibility-1201862755/.

Schwartz, Ian. "Kimmel Celebrates Collins Opposition to Graham-Cassidy: I May Have Stopped it." *Realclearpolitics.com*, September 26, 2017. https://www.realclearpolitics.com/video/2017/09/26/jimmy_kimmel_celebrates_collins_opposition_to_graham-cassidy_i_may_have_stopped_it.html.

Strachan, Maxwell. "People are Justifiably Infuriated with How Jimmy Fallon Handled Trump." *Huffingtonpost.com*, September 16, 2016. https://www.huffingtonpost.com/entry/jimmy-fallon-donald-trump_us_57dbecd4e4b0071a6e06801e.

Zoglin, Richard. "The New Politics of Late Night." *Time*, September 15, 2016. http://time.com/4494764/the-new-politics-of-late-night/.

Conclusion

Looking Ahead to the Future: Why Laughing and Political Humor Will Matter Even More in the Decade to Come

Amy B. Becker and Jody C Baumgartner

In the spring of 2016, Amy sat down with her political science colleague, Celia Paris, to brainstorm about co-teaching a new course at Loyola University Maryland that would mix perspectives from the disciplines of communication and political science. The new course would be somewhat generically titled, *Entertainment, Media, and Politics*, and would be offered for the first time during the Spring 2018 semester.

The objective for the *Entertainment, Media, and Politics* course and for so many similarly-themed courses across American college campuses: engage undergraduates in the study of the exciting, often curious intersection of entertainment and politics by critically examining a whole range of media content: late-night comedy, political satire, sitcoms, national security melodramas, film, dystopian fiction, and in our case, even the wonderful world of Harry Potter.

Over the course of a fifteen-week semester, we'd work with students so they would walk away with an understanding of the effects of consuming this politically entertaining media content on knowledge and learning, civic and political engagement, and the health of our American democracy more broadly. We'd also take a closer look at how entertainment influences our perceptions of the political process and our resulting attitudes toward politicians.

As a scholar of political humor, Amy was tasked with preparing the funny half of the course, guiding the study of satire, parody, intertextuality, and the effects of consuming this nontraditional media content on attitudes and behavior.

When Amy last taught a course like this way back in 2012, *Laughing Matters: Humor and American Politics in the Media Age*, served as the main text as it offered a clear roadmap for navigating the contemporary world of political humor and comedy. The problem was that by 2016, *Laughing Matters* seemed pretty out-of-date. Even Jody - a co-editor of the book - agreed.

After reviewing the syllabi for similar courses taught by esteemed colleagues, many of whom have authored chapters in this current volume, it became clear that we were all piecing various materials together. We were in desperate need of a new roadmap or a singular text to follow when preparing or updating courses that dealt with the intersection of entertainment, media, and politics.

One of the prime motivations for putting together *Political Humor in a Changing Media Landscape* was indeed to update *Laughing Matters* for a new generation of political comedy teachers and scholars. A secondary, but perhaps equally important goal was to provide a new text for undergraduate courses across the country (and even outside the United States) that were trying to carefully tackle the fast-paced, changing world of political entertainment and comedy.

Moving forward, we hope that Political Humor in a Changing Media Landscape: A New Generation of Research can serve as an important instructional tool for a whole new generation of students and teachers.

TEACHING ABOUT POLITICAL
HUMOR IN THE TRUMP ERA

Now back to that *Entertainment, Media, and Politics* class. A funny thing happened in between the Spring 2016 proposal for the joint course and the Spring 2018 semester when Amy and Celia were first slated to teach it. That funny thing was a little something called the 2016 general election and the first year of the Trump presidency (academia does really move at a snail's pace sometimes relative to the "real world").

We weren't necessarily expecting to be teaching in such an ultimately uncivil media environment—one driven by presidential attacks on Twitter, a seemingly endless discussion of alternative facts versus fake news, and hyper partisan cable news and late-night political comedy content. As journalist Brian Stelter so aptly noted in his *CNN Special Report: Late Night in the Age of Trump*, the Trump presidency quickly turned the world of late-night comedy upside down and made teaching about entertainment, media, and politics in this new era an interesting, evolving, and dynamic challenge.[1]

There were a few significant and striking takeaways from this Spring 2018 semester experience that can be useful for those thinking about the ways that comedy and entertainment can spur engagement and activism. And in many ways, they complement the themes present in *Political Humor in a Changing Media Landscape.*

First, students enjoy political comedy because it can make them laugh and teach them a little bit about what's going on in the world. Much like research by Danna Young has suggested, they see comedy as entertainment, first and foremost, not news.[2] Comedy is color commentary, not fact. For some, the proliferation of anti-Trump comedy is promising because they see it as a tool that helps keep the administration in check. For others, it's just too much of a constant attack on the president and his authority. Not surprisingly, these students tended to be in the minority in our class and seemed to have a harder time speaking up. But it's important that we really continue to hear their voices and take their perspectives into account.

Just because students see comedy as comedy, doesn't mean that they are happy with what they classify as traditional news content. In class, we asked students to list the news sources they trust and rely upon and those that they don't trust and try to avoid. The size of the two lists, separated by a thin line on the chalkboard, was about the same. Interestingly, we have some students who actively avoid networks like Fox News, MSNBC, and CNN given their perceived partisanship and the hyperreality that's emphasized in their coverage of political events.[3] Other students make a conscious effort to consume this cable news content as a way to be exposed to varying, often personally contrary points of view. Students who have spent a semester or more studying abroad are more likely to select BBC News and other international outposts as their top news outlets.

While most students are okay with the fact that late-night comedy has gotten more political in the Trump era, it is not always okay when events that are traditionally entertainment-oriented get political. While one student shared Hillary Clinton's cameo at the Grammy Awards with the class and there was a lot of discussion of Oprah's speech at the Golden Globes, there's a general consensus that some areas of everyday entertainment life—like professional sports—have just gotten too political.

While we read a relatively new text called *Political TV* by Chuck Tryon (turns out it's a decent primer given the dated nature of *Laughing Matters*), students have recognized that classifying what counts as "political TV" is a tricky business.[4] These days dramas like *Grey's Anatomy* tackle the political with recent episodes (January 2018) focusing on policing and guns and domestic violence. The political themes in cartoons like *Family Guy*, *South Park*, and *The Simpsons* continue unabated. While a lot of what our students watch doesn't fall into the explicit category of "political TV," almost everyone in the class noted that it's increasingly difficult to find entertainment programming that doesn't at least touch on or occasionally address political issues and themes.

Underlying all of our discussions was the reality and presence of social media. So much of the content these students are consuming comes to them in the form of short clips that their friends share on Facebook and other social media platforms. In a class of about thirty, everyone had a Netflix account. While there is cable in the dorms, they are effectively cord cutters at heart. In truth, what they consume is often as important as how they consume it. While many are certainly up during the late-night comedy live window, they are not tuning into Stephen Colbert or Seth Meyers in real-time, except perhaps when it's assigned for that week's out-of-class watching.

THE LESSONS OF *POLITICAL HUMOR IN A CHANGING MEDIA LANDSCAPE*

Political Humor in a Changing Media Landscape directly addresses so many of these key takeaways or themes from the Spring 2018 *Entertainment, Media, and Politics* course, making it both a key research and teaching text. In Section I we considered the idea that comedy is not just comedy, but perhaps something more. Maybe it is advocacy satire as Don Waisanen notes, or satiric journalism as Julia Fox notes in her analysis of *Last Week Tonight*. At the very least, it was clear across all of the political comedy content that we looked at in class, whether newer, more investigative offerings from John Oliver and Samantha Bee, traditional satire like *The Daily Show with Trevor Noah*, or network late-night comedy offerings from Stephen Colbert, Jimmy Kimmel, Jimmy Fallon, and Seth Meyers, that the jokes being presented had become more partisan and one-sided in nature as Bob Lichter and Stephen Farnsworth so aptly document in chapter 3. Very astutely, both the undergraduate students and the scholars writing in the first section of *Political Humor in a Changing Media Landscape* noted that comedy is trying to do more in the post-Trump era, and sometimes that means it's asking more of its audience members with calls to direct action.[5]

We've known for a long time that political comedy has an effect on viewers, even if these effects are limited in duration and small in scope. In Section II of this volume, we consider how critical comedy content impacts (or doesn't impact) attitudes toward Trump and Clinton with Jody's contribution, and consider the connections that viewers make between comedy interviews with politicians and what they already know from other news content or learning with Amy's chapter. Josh Compton's focus on inoculation theory suggests we should use this theoretical frame to consider whether political humor can prevent us from being persuaded by other competing messages and narratives and whether politicians ultimately benefit from engaging with comedy to thwart or foil critical attacks. Many times throughout the semester, we paused to consider what true or real effects comedy was having on viewers, politicians, and our larger political culture. Section II of this volume adds quite nicely to that discussion.

As evidenced in the classroom when you bring together a group of students with diverse political perspectives and viewpoints, not all comedy is created or appreciated equally. While some students—particularly those who despised Trump the most—appreciated the partisan turn being embraced by network late-night comedy hosts, other students saw this highly politicized content as offensive and a sign of disrespect for the office of the presidency. In Section III of *Political Humor in a Changing Media Landscape*, the focus on humor appreciation recognizes that audience members engage with and have a differential appreciation of political humor. While Stewart and colleagues measure this differential appreciation through audience responses of laughter, applause, and booing during the 2016 presidential debates, Sophia McClennen goes to great lengths to consider what happens when satire goes too far and encourages blowback or works to undermine our social fabric. Christiane Grill rounds out this section with a theoretical focus on the construct of humor appreciation and how both ego involvement and information appreciation drive the reception of humorous content. As a prelude to Section IV, Grill's investigation turns toward an international case (comparing content from political comedy programs in Austria) to empirically examine variation in humor appreciation.

At first it was surprising to see so many students who had studied abroad list the BBC as a preferred news source. Given the globalized nature of our media environment and the international spread and reach of political entertainment and comedy, perhaps the preference for the BBC shouldn't be all that surprising. As Xenos, Moy, Mazzoleni, and Meuller-Herbst note in their chapter, the time is ripe to apply key theoretical concepts from the first generation of political comedy scholarship—like the gateway effect—to international contexts like Germany, Italy, and the United Kingdom that have comparatively diverse media systems and satire programming, when juxtaposed against the default context of the United States. Mark Boukes further adds to the international perspective of this volume by testing the application of the affinity for political humor (AFPH) scale first developed by Holbert and colleagues in the context of the Netherlands with a two-study experimental design.[6] Finally, Edo Steinberg compares and contrasts the effect of satirical coverage in the United States and Israel on issues of free speech and a free press. We've known for years that political comedy research needs to become more international in its approach. We are pleased to have devoted a whole section of this volume to engaging in just that.

Undergraduate students today represent a whole new generation of media consumers. Not only are they digital natives, but they literally grew up and came of age during the era of Jon Stewart's *The Daily Show* and Stephen Colbert's *The Colbert Report*. For them, political satire isn't something new or different; it's simply part of their existing media environment. Section V of this volume looks to the future, beginning with Stephanie Edgerly's study of youth news consumption and culture. It seems that we should anticipate a new generation of savvy media consumers, who may mimic their parents in their preference for satirical, entertaining news. Michael Parkin considers the future of candidate engagement with political comedy and why politicians continue to flock to comedy rather than stay away. Finally, Jonathan Morris considers the evolution of network late-night comedians, and the growing expectations for these entertainers in the Trump era and beyond.

Collectively, *Political Humor in a Changing Media Landscape* certainly offers a blueprint or roadmap for classrooms focusing on the study of political comedy and humor. It also promotes what we see as a second generation of political humor scholarship and research. At the same time, we recognize that there are still some questions for future research and discussion worth exploring in the decade ahead, as the prevalence and importance of political comedy in our congested media environment will only continue to grow.

QUESTIONS FOR FUTURE RESEARCH AND FOR THE CLASSROOM

As we noted at the outset of this volume, the political comedy landscape has certainly changed since *Laughing Matters* was first published in 2008. Today's political comedy offerings have certainly brought new voices and faces to the forefront (e.g., Trevor Noah, Samantha Bee, John Oliver, Seth Meyers) and seen others fade out of the spotlight (e.g., Jon Stewart, David Letterman, Jay Leno). Some comedians have reinvented themselves like Stephen Colbert, while others have taken heat for not addressing the current political moment, like Jimmy Fallon. Still others like Jimmy Kimmel have dabbled in politics when it seems salient. Programs like *Saturday Night Live* have experienced a resurgence in popularity and impact, and viral video continues to expand in importance and reach. As we approach the 2018 midterm elections here in the United States, it's pretty clear that we are dealing with both a very rich and full and very different political comedy landscape. These new voices, faces, and platforms bring us a wider range of content and new questions and areas for future research.

Moving forward, and extending beyond *Political Humor in a Changing Media Landscape,* we see three critical questions for future research on political comedy—both in terms of examining content and ultimately better understanding the effects of comedy exposure.

First, it is no secret that we live in an increasingly fragmented, high choice media environment. We also exist within a truly divided and polarized political climate, both here in the United States and increasingly in many places around the globe. Understanding how and why certain segments of the population flock to political comedy content, while others try their hardest to avoid it, will be an increasingly important area for future research. We will need to understand the effects of this fractured, dichotomous media experience on both individuals and society as a whole.

As recent research has pointed out, we can no longer consider the effects of exposure to political comedy content in a vacuum.[7] In today's media environment, it is not just the effects of exposure to critical content that matter, but also the circulating media response and competing narratives that play a role. Today, political comedy's impact is as much about the response to that initial comedy sketch via social media and other platforms as it is the preliminary response to that first round of jokes. Future research will need to take a more ecological approach toward the study of political comedy exposure effects, ultimately accounting for the YouTube effect and other changing media dynamics.

Finally, as the students so often asked in the *Entertainment, Media, and Politics* class, what happens after the Trump era? Does network late-night political comedy return to normalcy and focus more on entertaining us rather than bombarding us with satirical political critique? Do the interview conversations on comedy programs return to a state where it's all about light-hearted conversation and warming the attitudes of voters from the other party?[8] Will comedy return to some semblance of what it was before the 2016 election or is that era lost and gone forever? Are we really just experiencing a new paradigm that will turn out to be the new normal for political comedy and entertainment? Clearly this is a question for future research and the next generation of political humor scholarship. Think of it as a topic for a potential *Laughing Matters 3.0* or *Political Humor in a Changing Media Landscape 2.0*.

Over the next few years, we expect both the amount of political humor and comedy content and research on this new content to increase. We anticipate that classes like *Entertainment, Media, and Politics* will be a real thing across even more US college campuses and in a wide range of locations abroad. We are grateful for the support we received in putting together *Political Humor in a Changing Media Landscape* which serves as a compilation of what we see as the second generation of political comedy scholarship. We are eager to be a part of future conversations, research, and teaching that move us ahead toward a third generation of political humor scholarship and extend beyond this volume.

NOTES

1. Brian Stelter, "Late Night in the Age of Trump," *CNN Special Reports*, 2017.

2. Dannagal G. Young, "Laughter, Learning, or Enlightenment? Viewing and Avoidance Motivations behind The Daily Show and The Colbert Report," *Journal of Broadcasting and Electronic Media* 57, no. 2 (2013): 153–69.

3. Michael X. Delli Carpini and Bruce A. Williams, "Let Us Infotain You: Politics in the New Media Environment," in *Mediated Politics: Communication in the Future of Democracy*, ed. W. Lance Bennett and Robert M. Entman (New York: Cambridge University Press, 2001), 160–81.

4. Chuck Tryon, *Political TV* (New York: Routledge, 2016).

5. Amy B. Becker and Leticia Bode, "Satire as a Source for Learning? The Differential Impact of News versus Satire Exposure on Net Neutrality Knowledge Gain," *Information, Communication & Society* 21, no. 4 (Apr. 3, 2018): 612–25. doi: 10.1080/1369118X.2017.1301517.

6. R. Lance Holbert, Jay Hmielowski, Parul Jain, Julie Lather, and Alyssa Morey, "Adding Nuance to the Study of Political Humor Effects: Experimental Research on Juvenalian Satire versus Horatian Satire." *American Behavioral Scientist* 55, no. 3 (2011): 187–211. doi: 10.1177/0002764210392156; Jay D. Hmielowski, R. Lance Holbert, and Jayeon Lee, "Predicting the Consumption of Political TV Satire: Affinity for Political Humor, *The Daily Show*, and *The Colbert Report*," *Communication Monographs* 78, no. 1 (2011): 96–114. doi: 10.1080/03637751.2010.542579.

7. Amy B. Becker, "Trump Trumps Baldwin? How Trump's Tweets Transform SNL into Trump's Strategic Advantage," *Journal of Political Marketing* (2017): 1–19. doi:10.1080/15377857.2017.1411860; Becker, "Live from New York, It's Trump on Twitter! The Effect of Engaging with *Saturday Night Live* on Perceptions of Authenticity and the Saliency of Trait Ratings," *International Journal of Communication* 12 (2018): 1736–57.

8. Matthew A. Baum, "Talking the Vote: Why Presidential Candidates Hit the Talk Show Circuit," *American Journal of Political Science* 49, no. 2 (Apr. 2005): 213–34. doi: 10.1111/j.0092–5853.2005.t01–1-00119.x.

REFERENCES

Baum, Matthew A. "Talking the Vote: Why Presidential Candidates Hit the Talk Show Circuit." *American Journal of Political Science* 49, no. 2 (April 2005): 213–34. doi: 10.1111/j.0092–5853.2005.t01–1-00119.x.

Becker, Amy B. "Trump Trumps Baldwin? How Trump's Tweets Transform SNL into Trump's Strategic Advantage." *Journal of Political Marketing* (2017): 1–19. doi: 10.1080/15377857.2017.1411860.

———. "Live from New York, It's Trump on Twitter! The Effect of Engaging with *Saturday Night Live* on Perceptions of Authenticity and the Saliency of Trait Ratings." *International Journal of Communication* 12 (2018): 1736–57.

Becker, Amy B., and Leticia Bode. "Satire as a Source for Learning? The Differential Impact of News versus Satire Exposure on Net Neutrality Knowledge Gain." *Information, Communication & Society* 21, no. 4 (April 3, 2018): 612–25. doi:10.1080 /1369118X.2017.1301517.

Delli Carpini, Michael X., and Bruce A. Williams. "Let Us Infotain You: Politics in the New Media Environment." In *Mediated Politics: Communication in the Future of Democracy*, edited by W. Lance Bennett and Robert M. Entman, 160–81. New York: Cambridge University Press, 2001.

Hmielowski, Jay D., R. Lance Holbert, and Jayeon Lee. "Predicting the Consumption of Political TV Satire: Affinity for Political Humor, *The Daily Show*, and *The Colbert Report*." *Communication Monographs* 78, no. 1 (2011): 96–114. doi:10.1080 /03637751.2010.542579.

Holbert, R. Lance, Jay Hmielowski, Parul Jain, Julie Lather, and Alyssa Morey. "Adding Nuance to the Study of Political Humor Effects: Experimental Research on Juvenalian Satire Versus Horatian Satire." *American Behavioral Scientist* 55, no. 3 (2011): 187–211. doi:10.1177/0002764210392156.

Stelter, Brian. "Late Night in the Age of Trump." *CNN Special Reports*, 2017.

Tryon, Chuck. *Political TV*. New York: Routledge, 2016.

Young, Dannagal G. "Laughter, Learning, or Enlightenment? Viewing and Avoidance Motivations behind The Daily Show and The Colbert Report." *Journal of Broadcasting and Electronic Media* 57, no. 2 (2013): 153–69. doi:10.1080/08838151.2 013.787080.

Index

activism, of political comedians, 11. *See also* advocacy satire

Adalian, Josef, 296

adults: news satire exposure of, 255–56, 258, 263. *See also* parents

advocacy, 12–13. *See also* political advocacy

advocacy satire: comic precursors to, 12, 13–15; future of, 20–21; international political humor and, 12, 16–17, 20; neoliberal accelerations and, 12, 18–19; new media advocacy and, 12–13; overview, 4, 11–12, 19–21, 21n3; rise of, 11–21. *See also* satiric journalism

affinity for entertaining news: elaborative processing and, 81–82, 86–87; as measurement, 83; in study of impact of political satire interviews, 81–87, *85, 86*

affinity for political humor (AFPH), 87; anxiety reduction dimension, 208–9; citizens with, 209; consequences of political satire consumption and, 210–11; four dimensions, 208; incongruity dimension, 208; latent construct of, 208; overview, 5, 207;

political satire consumption and, 209–10; roles AFPH could play in political satire studies, 224, *224*; social connectedness dimension, 209; superiority dimension, 208. *See also specific AFPH topics*

AFPH causes and consequences, studies of: citizens with AFPH, *217,* 217–18; consequences of political satire consumption and AFPH, 220, *221,* 222, *222, 223,* 224; enjoyment of satire in, 220, *221,* 222; hypotheses, 210, 211; method, 212; nature of attack in, 211; Netherlands in, 207; overview, 207–8, 210–11, 224–25; political satire consumption and AFPH, 217, *218,* 220; research questions, 209, 211; results, 217–24

AFPH causes and consequences, Study 1: AFPH measurement, 214–15; design and stimuli, 212–13; discussion, *224,* 224–25; education measurement, 213; enjoyment measurement, 215; internal political efficacy measurement, 214; measurements, 213–15; news consumption

319

About the Contributors

Jody C Baumgartner is Thomas Harriot College of Arts and Sciences Distinguished Professor of Political Science at East Carolina University. He received his PhD in political science from Miami University in 1998, specializing in the study of campaigns and elections. He has authored or edited eight books and over four dozen journal articles and book chapters, individually or in collaboration with others, on political humor, the vice presidency, and other subjects.

Amy B. Becker (PhD, University of Wisconsin–Madison) is associate professor in the Department of Communication at Loyola University Maryland. Her research focuses on public opinion and citizen participation on controversial political issues, the political effects of exposure and attention to hybrid media, especially political comedy and entertainment, new media and computational research methods, and elections and political engagement. Becker has published more than two dozen articles in leading peer-reviewed journals on public opinion, political communication, and media effects. She teaches courses on political entertainment, communication theory, the internet and new media, and media and culture. She is a former political pollster and marketing research consultant.

Mark Boukes (PhD, 2015) is a postdoctoral researcher at the Amsterdam School of Communication Research at the University of Amsterdam. His research focuses on media effects of journalistic versus entertainment formats. In particular, he investigates the content and effects of infotainment genres, such as soft news and political satire. His research combines different theoretical frameworks (e.g., framing, disposition theory, exemplification theory, uses, and gratifications) and mainly relies on experimental methods, although more recently he investigates the content and consequences of economic news coverage using a combination of content analysis and panel surveys. Mark's work has been published in some of the flagship journals of the field, including *Journal of Communication, Communication Research, Communication Theory, Journalism and Mass Communication Quarterly, Mass Communication and Society,* and *International Journal of Communication.*

Josh Compton is associate professor in the Institute for Writing and Rhetoric at Dartmouth College. His research explores the theory and application of inoculation theory, with special attention to the contexts of health, sport, and education. He has been named Distinguished Lecturer by Dartmouth College and has won the Outstanding Professor Award from the National Speakers Association and has twice won the L. E. Norton Award for Outstanding Scholarship.

Reagan G. Dye is a master's student in the Department of Political Science at the University of Arkansas. Her research interests include political communication, political psychology, and voting behavior.

Stephanie A. Edgerly (PhD, University of Wisconsin–Madison) is an associate professor in the Medill School of Journalism, Media, Integrated Marketing Communications at Northwestern University, with a specialization in audience insight. Her research explores how features of new media alter the way audiences consume news and impact political engagement. She is particularly interested in the mixing of news and entertainment content, how individuals share news over social network websites, and how audiences selectively consume media. Recent projects have explored the process of news socialization among youth, how young adults makes sense of the high-choice news media environment, and the role of millennial-focused news in fostering political learning during the 2016 presidential election.

Austin D. Eubanks is an experimental psychology PhD student in the Department of Psychological Science at the University of Arkansas under the mentorship of Scott Eidelman, PhD. His research focuses on political psychology (broadly) and he is most interested in the formations and understandings of political ideology and political value systems.

Stephen J. Farnsworth, PhD, is professor of political science and international affairs at the University of Mary Washington in Fredericksburg, Virginia, where he directs the university's Center for Leadership and Media Studies. Dr. Farnsworth is the author or co-author of six books, most recently *Presidential Communication and Communication: White House News*

Management from Clinton and Cable to Twitter and Trump (2018), as well as dozens of research articles on the mass media, the presidency, and US and Virginia politics. Dr. Farnsworth was a 2017 recipient of the State Council of Higher Education for Virginia's Outstanding Faculty Award and previously served as a Canada-US Fulbright Research Scholar at McGill University in Montreal.

Julia R. Fox is associate professor in The Media School at Indiana University. She was lead author on a content analysis published in the *Journal of Broadcasting and Electronic Media* that found presidential election campaign coverage in *The Daily Show with Jon Stewart* and the broadcast networks' nightly newscasts to be equally substantive. She also contributed a chapter in a previous compilation, *The Stewart/Colbert Effect: Essays on the Real Impacts of Fake News* (2011), comparing Stewart and Stephen Colbert to court jesters. She has contributed articles about Stewart and Colbert to *The Conversation*, an independent, online news source written by academic researchers. She and fellow contributor Edo Steinberg have also authored an annotated bibliography on comedic news for Oxford Bibliographies.

Christiane Grill is a postdoctoral researcher for the project "The Conversations of Democracy: Citizens' Everyday Communication in the Deliberative System" at the Mannheim Center for European Social Research at the University of Mannheim. She obtained her PhD in communication science at the University of Vienna. Her primary research focuses on political offline and online communication. In addition, she is interested in political satire and its effects on public opinion.

S. Robert Lichter is professor of communication at George Mason University, where he also directs the Center for Media and Public Affairs, which conducts scientific studies of the news and entertainment media. Dr. Lichter previously taught at Princeton, Georgetown, and George Washington Universities. He has also served as a postdoctoral fellow in politics and psychology at Yale University, senior research fellow at Columbia University, and National Endowment for the Humanities Fellow at Smith College. He received his PhD in government from Harvard University. Dr. Lichter has authored or co-authored fourteen books and numerous scholarly articles and monographs. His op-ed articles have appeared in *The Washington Post, Wall Street Journal, Los Angeles Times*, and other newspapers. His most recent book (with Jody Baumgartner and Jonathan Morris) is *Politics Is a Joke!: How Late Night Comedians Are Remaking Politics* (2015).

Gianpietro Mazzoleni is professor of political communication at the University of Milan in Italy. Fields of his research include popular culture, sociology of communication, journalism and politics, and media and populism. He co-founded and served as editor of the peer-reviewed Italian journal, *Comunicazione Politica* (2000–2013), and is general editor of *The International Encyclopedia of Political Communication* (2016).

Sophia A. McClennen is professor of international affairs and comparative literature, founding director of the Center for Global Studies, and associate director of the School of International Affairs, all at Penn State University. She studies human rights, satire, and politics, with two recent books on related topics, *Is Satire Saving Our Nation?: Mockery and American Politics* (2014), coauthored with Remy Maisel, and *The Routledge Companion to Literature and Human Rights* (2016), co-edited with Alexandra Schultheis Moore. She also has a weekly column with *Salon* where she regularly covers politics and culture.

Jonathan S. Morris (PhD, Purdue University) is professor of political science at East Carolina University. His research focuses on the media and politics, including political humor, cable news, and political communication on social media. He is co-author of *Politics Is a Joke! How TV Comedians Are Remaking Political Life* (2015), and has published in several journals, including *Political Research Quarterly*, *Public Opinion Quarterly*, *Legislative Studies Quarterly*, *Political Behavior*, *Social Science Quarterly*, *Political Communication*, and *Sociological Forum*.

Patricia Moy is associate vice provost for Academic and Student Affairs at the University of Washington, where she is the Christy Cressey Professor of Communication and adjunct professor of political science. Her research focuses on the political and social effects of communication, particularly as they relate to public opinion and citizenship. She is the editor of *Public Opinion Quarterly*, president-elect-select of the International Communication Association, and past president of the World Association for Public Opinion Research.

Julian Mueller-Herbst is a graduate student in communication science in the Department of Communication Arts at the University of Wisconsin–Madison. He is interested in how news and social media influence political processes, and how they shape public perception, opinion, and awareness. He is specifically focused on global and cross-national contexts, such as comparative work between the United States and Germany.

Michael Parkin is professor of politics at Oberlin College and director of the Oberlin Initiative in Electoral Politics. His research and teaching interests focus on mass political behavior and campaign strategies. His work includes the book, *Talk Show Campaigns: Presidential Candidates on Daytime and Late Night Television* (2014), and articles in journals such as the *American Political Science Review*, *The Journal of Politics*, *Political Communication*, *Political Research Quarterly*, and the *Journal of Political Marketing*.

Edo Steinberg is a PhD candidate in The Media School at Indiana University. He has master's degrees in Middle Eastern studies and creative writing, both from Ben-Gurion University of the Negev in Be'er-Sheva, Israel. His research focuses on satirical shows in Israel and the United States and their portrayal of politicians, the news media, and political issues such as the Israeli show *Eretz Nehederet*'s portrayal of war and peace. Of particular interest is satire's reinforcement and criticism of national core values. He also researches how satire affects political efficacy and trust in the news media.

Patrick A. Stewart is associate professor in the Department of Political Science at the University of Arkansas. He does research on non-verbal communication and the use of humor in political interactions. His books include *Debatable Humor: Laughing Matters on the 2008 Presidential Primary Campaign* (2012) and *The Invisible Hands of Political Parties in Presidential Elections* (2013).

Don J. Waisanen is associate professor in the Marxe School of Public and International Affairs at Baruch College, CUNY, where he teaches courses and workshops in public communication—including executive speech training, communication strategy, media analysis, and seminars on leadership, improvisation, and humor. All his research projects seek to understand how communication works to promote or hinder the force of citizens' voices. Previously, Don was a Coro Fellow and worked in broadcast journalism as a speechwriter and on political campaigns. He is the founder of Communication Upward, and received a PhD in communication from the University of Southern California's Annenberg School for Communication and Journalism.

Michael A. Xenos is department chair and Communication Arts Partners professor in the Department of Communication Arts at the University of Wisconsin–Madison, where he is also an affiliate faculty member in the Department of Life Sciences Communication and the School of Journalism and Mass Communication. He also serves as editor-in-chief of *Journal of Information Technology & Politics*. His research focuses on how individuals, political candidates, journalists, and other political actors adapt to changes in information and communication technologies, and how these adaptations affect broader dynamics of political communication and public deliberation.